PARIS

ILE-DE-FRANCE

&

THE LOIRE VALLEY

with the best of

GUIDE GAULT·MILLAU

published in French by SPES (Paris)

English-Language Staff

Editor-in-Chief
André Gayot

Editor
Sheila Mooney

Contributing Editors
Françoise Boisard, Heidi Ellison,
Odile Granier, Brigitte du Tanney

Coordination
Sophie C

Publis
Alain Ga

Paris ■ Los Angeles ■ New York ■ San Francisco ■ London ■ Munich ■ Turin

GAYOT PUBLICATIONS

The Best of Chicago
The Best of Florida
The Best of France
The Best of Germany
The Best of Hawaii
The Best of Hong Kong
The Best of Italy
The Best of London
The Best of Los Angeles

The Best of New England
The Best of New Orleans
The Best of New York
The Best of Paris
The Best of San Francisco
The Best of Thailand
The Best of Toronto
The Best of Washington, D.C.
The Best Wineries of North America

LA Restaurants, NYC Restaurants, SF Restaurants
The Food Paper, Tastes Newsletter
http://www.gayot.com

Copyright © 1997 by GaultMillau, Inc.

Published by Gault Millau, Inc.
5900 Wilshire Blvd.
Los Angeles, CA 90036

Please address all comments regarding
Paris, Ile-de-France & the Loire Valley to:
GaultMillau, Inc.
P.O. Box 361144
Los Angeles, CA 90036

E-mail: gayots@aol.com

Advertising Sales:
P.M.C.
10 bis rue Jeanne d'Arc
94160 Saint-Mandé, France
Tel (01) 43 28 20 20 Fax (01) 43 28 27 27

Library of Congress Cataloging-in-Publication Data

Paris, Ile-de-France & the Loire Valley / editor-in-chief, André
Gayot, editor, Sheila Mooney.
      p. cm.
   "A. Gayot Publications"--T.p.
   Includes index.
   Cover title: Gayot's Paris, Ile-de-France & the Loire Valley.
   ISBN 1-881066-32-0
   1. Paris (France)--Guidebooks. 2. Ile-de-France (France)-
-Guidebooks. 3. Loire River Valley (France)
I. Gayot, André. II. Mooney, Sheila. III. Title: Paris, Ile-de
-France and the Loire Valley. IV. Title: Gayot's Paris, Ile-de
-France & the Loire Valley.
DC708.P3213   1997
914.4'3604839--DC21   97-4451
                                                           CIP

Printed in the United States of America

CONTENTS

■ INTRODUCTIONS 4

After Paris, we've scoured score upon score of cities, towns, villages, and remote hamlets in the Ile-de-France and the Loire Valley, to uncover all the best restaurants and hotels. Whether you're looking for a world-famous restaurant, a romantic resort, or a charming village inn, you'll find it among these hundreds of in-the-know reviews. And at the end of each chapter, you'll find sources for regional foods and wines. If you are lost, check in the alphabetical index to find the city, or village where a restaurant, inn, or shop you are looking for is located.

■ SYMBOL SYSTEMS 7

Read this short chapter before you go any further. How to decipher the rankings, prices, symbols, and abbreviations.

■ TOQUE TALLY 9

A listing of the very best restaurants.

■ PARIS & ILE-DE-FRANCE 11

■ THE LOIRE VALLEY 119

■ INDEX 151

Looking for a town or restaurant? A winery? A gastronomic specialty or a celebrated chef? Consult the alphabetical index to locate them quickly and easily.

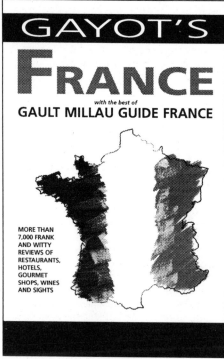

La douce France

Paris belongs to the world. It's every man's city, rich in history, art, science, architecture, philosophy, and, of course, gastronomy, an essential part of French culture. But *Paris* is also enmeshed in a fabric called *Ile-de-France*, the province which surrounds it. Should you lack the time to journey across France, a trip around Paris and Ile-de-France will provide you with a taste of the diversity that exists throughout the country. Only a few miles outside of Paris, the architecture and the habits begin to vary. The western part of Ile-de-France belongs in spirit to Normandy, the eastern part to Champagne. You will find Brie cheese in the Brie/Champagne area and Camembert near Normandy. The local beverages change as you move around the points of the compass, from the Champagne that makes the east sparkle, to beer in the north and wine in the sunny south.

The *Loire Valley*, where fruits, flowers, vegetables, and grapes grow aplenty, is known as the "garden of France". It is also the womb of modern France, the area in which monarchy revived itself and indulged in the pleasures of the Renaissance. So close to the metropolis of Paris, yet so pastoral, the Loire Valley indeed creates the perfect image of *la douce France* with its scenes of rolling hills, quiet rivers and elegant castles.

We have tailored this book to help you appreciate the differences among these three areas, and to discover some of the many charms of France. Our **Paris, Ile-de-France & the Loire Valley** guide, gives you the real lowdown on hundreds of French restaurants and hotels, with inside information that will make you a "traveler in the know," always one step (at least!) ahead of the crowd.

For 32 years, we, at GaultMillau, have scoured the French countryside, visiting urban centers and tiny hamlets, in search of worthwhile places to eat and stay. Contributors from every region of France participate in our national survey of restaurants and hotels. They work to strict standards, ensuring fairness and continuity of the grading system. When, for example, a reviewer spots what appears to be a terrific new place, he or she invariably seeks a second opinion to confirm that the establishment is truly a winner. These thorough, unvarnished appraisals of grand restaurants, bistros, brasseries, auberges and hotels, are presented in a witty, entertaining style that has earned GaultMillau its international reputation. (And thanks to our ever-expanding family of guidebooks, travelers can now rely on GaultMillau for accurate, up-to-date information on destinations all over the globe. See page 6.)

The purpose of this guidebook is to help you steer an informed course through the many restaurants, hotels, and gourmet and wine shops in Paris, Ile-de-France and the Loire Valley. Naturally, the top establishments tend to be quite expensive, but we also take you into cozy bistros and family-style inns where you can indulge your gourmandise without breaking the bank. So whether you are a first-time visitor or a frequent traveler to France, let GaultMillau help you discover the myriad gastronomic pleasures that France has to offer!

André Gayot

GAYOT Gault Millau
ON THE INTERNET

Welcome to Gayot's/GaultMillau Travel Guides...

Where you will find knowledgeable information
on the world of dining

RESTAURANTS

THE FOOD PAPER

TASTES

BOOKS

THE GRAPEVINE

CHEF'S STORE

BIG BOOK

LA TIMES

Special Offers!

TO ORDER

Guest Book!

GAULTMILLAU IS PROUD TO FEATURE RESTAURANT, HOTEL AND TRAVEL INFORMATION FROM OUR
BOOKS AND UPDATES ON MANY INTERNET WEB SITES.

WE SUGGEST YOU START SURFING AT:
http://www.gayot.com

WE WELCOME YOUR QUESTIONS AND COMMENTS AT OUR E-MAIL ADDRESS:
gayots@aol.com

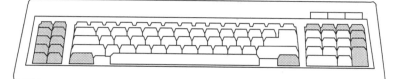

SYMBOL SYSTEMS

RESTAURANTS

Gault Millau/Gayot's ranks restaurants in the same manner that French students are graded: on a scale of zero to twenty, twenty being unattainable perfection. The rankings reflect *only* the quality of the cooking; décor, service, reception, and atmosphere do not influence the rating. They are explicitly commented on within the reviews. Restaurants ranked thirteen and above are distinguished with toques (chef's hats), according to the following table:

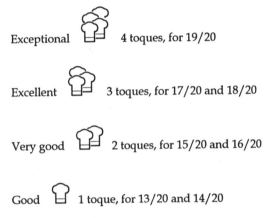

Exceptional   4 toques, for 19/20

Excellent   3 toques, for 17/20 and 18/20

Very good   2 toques, for 15/20 and 16/20

Good   1 toque, for 13/20 and 14/20

Keep in mind that these ranks are *relative*. One toque for 13/20 is not a very good ranking for a highly reputed (and very expensive) temple of fine dining, but it is quite complimentary for a small place without much pretension.

• In addition to the standard **carte**, or à la carte menu, you will frequently be offered a choice of all-inclusive fixed-price meals called **menus**, which are generally a very good value. Also common in finer restaurants is the many-course sampling menu, or **menu dégustation**, a good (though not always economical) way to get an overview of a restaurant's specialties. Daily specials, or **plats du jour**, are usually reliable, inexpensive, and prepared with fresh ingredients that the chef found at the market that morning.

• At the end of each restaurant review, prices are given—either *A la carte* (**C**) or *Menu* (**M**) (fixed-price meal) or both. A la carte prices are those of an average meal (a starter, a main course, dessert, and coffee) for one person, including service and a half-bottle of relatively modest wine. Lovers of the great Bordeaux, Burgundies, and Champagnes will, of course, face stiffer tabs. The menu prices quoted are for a complete multicourse meal for one person, including service but excluding wine, unless otherwise noted. These fixed-price menus often give diners on a budget a chance to sample the cuisine of an otherwise expensive restaurant.

• When you go to a top restaurant, let the **headwaiter** suggest some possibilities from the menu (you'll find that many maître d's quite often speak English, though they always appreciate an attempt on the diner's part to speak French). Likewise, the **sommelier**'s job is to give diners expert advice on the choice of a suitable wine—regardless of price. Don't be afraid to seek his or her opinion, or to state your budget.

- French law mandates that the **service charge**, usually 15 percent, always be included in the menu prices. You are not obliged to leave an additional tip, but it is good form to leave a little more if the service was satisfactory.
- The **opening** and **closing times** we've quoted are always subject to change, particularly holiday closings, so be sure to call ahead.
- Many chefs have the bad habit of **changing restaurants frequently,** which means a restaurant can turn mediocre or even bad in just a few days. Chef-owned restaurants tend to be more stable, but even they can decline. A successful owner may be tempted to accept too many diners, which can result in a drop in quality. Should this be your experience, please don't hold us responsible!

HOTELS

Our opinion of the comfort level and appeal of each hotel is expressed in a ranking system, as follows:

Very luxurious

Luxurious

Very comfortable

Comfortable

Very quiet

The prices indicated for rooms and half-board range from the cheapest for one person to the most expensive for two.

Sadly, prices continue to creep up, so some places may have become more expensive than our estimates by the time you visit. If you expect to pay a little more—you may end up being pleasantly surprised!

OTHER INFORMATION & ABBREVIATIONS

✿ A laurel wreath indicates restaurants serving outstanding traditional or regional recipes.

Rms: Rooms
Seas: Season
Priv rm: Private room
Pkg: Parking
Half-board: Rate per person for room, breakfast, and one other meal (lunch or dinner)

Stes: Suites
Conf: Conference facilities
Air cond: Air conditioning

How to read the locations:

ABBEVILLE	80100	THE CITY	THE ZIP CODE
TGV Paris 160 - Amiens 45 - Dieppe 63	Somme	Kilometers to Paris and nearby major cities	The regional department

TGV : city served by the TGV

TOQUE TALLY

I-d-F: Ile-de-France; LV: Loire Valley

Four Toques
19/20

Arpège, *Paris 7th*

Three Toques
18/20

L'Ambroisie, *Paris 4th*
Apicius, *Paris 17th*
Jean Bardet, *Tours,* (LV)
Carré des Feuillants, *Paris*
Le Grand Véfour, *Paris 1st*
Ledoyen, *Paris 8th*
Lucas Carton, *Paris 8th*
Montparnasse 25, *Paris 14th*
Bernard Robin, *Bracieux,* (LV)
Guy Savoy, *Paris 17th*
Taillevent, *Paris 8th*
Les Trois Marches, *Versailles,* (I-d-F)

Three Toques
17/20

Les Ambassadeurs, *Paris 8th*
Amphyclès, *Paris 17th*
Le Bourdonnais, *Paris 7th*
Les Élysées du Vernet, *Paris 8th*

Faugeron, *Paris 16th*
Goumard Prunier, *Paris 1st*
Grand Hôtel du Lion d'Or,
    Romorantin-Lanthenay, (LV)
Le Jardin du Royal Monceau, *Paris 8th*
Laurent, *Paris 8th*
Paul Minchelli, *Paris 7th*
Le Pré Catelan, *Paris 16th*
La Table d'Anvers, *Paris 9th*
Vivarois, *Paris 16th*

Two Toques
16/20

Les Antiquaires, *Orléans,* (LV)
Auberge des Templiers, *Les Bézards* (LV)
La Belle Époque, *Châteaufort,* (I-d-F)
Le Bistro de Paris, *Laval,* (LV)
Jacques Cagna, *Paris 6th*
La Chancelière, *Montbazon,* (LV)
Château d'Artigny, *Montbazon,* (LV)
Château de Noirieux, *Briollay,* (LV)
Clos Longchamp, *Paris 17th*
Le Clos Morillons, *Paris 15th*
Conti, *Paris 16th*
La Dinée, *Paris 15th*
Le Dôme, *Paris 14th*
Domaine des Hauts de Loire, *Onzain,* (LV)
Le Duc, *Paris 14th*
L'Étoile d'Or, *Paris 17th*
Faucher, *Paris 17th*
La Grande Cascade, *Paris 16th*
Le Grenadin, *Paris 8th*
Le Manoir de Paris, *Paris 17th*
La Marée, *Paris 8th*
Maxim's, *Paris 8th*
Le Meurice, *Paris 1st*
Le Paris, *Paris 6th*
Pavillon Paul Le Quéré, *Angers,* (LV)
La Promenade, *Le Petit Pressigny,* (LV)
Au Plaisir Gourmand, *Chinon,* (LV)
Petrus, *Paris 17th*
Prunier Traktir, *Paris 16th*
Le Régence, *Paris 8th*
Le Relais d'Auteuil, *Paris 16th*
Michel Rostang, *Paris 17th*
Sormani, *Paris 17th*
Taïra, *Paris 17th*
La Timonerie, *Paris 5th*

ALLIANCE AUTOS

Rents chauffeur-driven limousines

RELIABILITY — PRESTIGE

Business – Touring – Events

All types of vehicles
Air conditioning – Telephone
Multilingual chauffeurs

01 43 28 20 20

24-hour reservation and service

10bis, rue Jeanne d'Arc – 94160 Saint-Mandé
Fax: (1) 43 28 27 27
Licence de Grande Remise n°10

PARIS & ILE-DE-FRANCE

A CAPITAL DESTINATION

Despite its name, Ile-de-France is not an island. No spot could be less insular than this province at the heart of Europe, since archaic times a strategic crossroads for culture and commerce between Britain and the Mediterranean, Germany and Spain. Home to some twenty percent of France's inhabitants—that comes to about fifteen million souls—Ile-de-France is the nation's richest, most populous and productive region.

What New York, Chicago, Los Angeles, and Washington are to the United States, **Paris** alone is to France. This single city dominates the nation's government and politics, its industry, business, and finance, its media and communications, its artistic and intellectual life. Paris is the biggest consumer market for everything from vacuum cleaners to theater tickets, and the biggest producer of goods. In recent years, the French government has sought to correct the imbalance between the ever-burgeoning capital and the provinces. "Decentralization" is the order of the day: industries and institutions are offered hefty subsidies to set up their headquarters away from the Paris region. Still, the capital remains a dreamed-of destination for many. Nowhere else in France are jobs more plentiful. To this day, ambitious young provincials still "go up" to Paris hoping to make their name and fortune. Foreigners too, especially from France's former colonies in Africa and Asia, pour into Paris dreaming of a better life. They have put their stamp on the capital, establishing ethnic neighborhoods like the North African quarter of the Goutte d'Or east of Montmartre, the Southeast Asian "Chinatown" around Place d'Italie, and the Black African enclaves of Belleville. Who could recognize the city of the 1950s—the mythical city of An American in Paris—in this multicolored metropolis that is hurtling headlong into the twenty-first century?

Some might be tempted to view Paris, with its sumptuous monuments and historic sites, as a shrine to the glories of past kingdoms and empires. But that is not the whole story. Paris is also a high-energy metropolis, a creative world capital. New urban districts have sprung up. La Défense, on the city's western edge, hosts a major modern landmark, the Arche de La Défense. To the east, the Bercy district is home to the pharaonic national library, the recently inaugurated Bibliothèque de France, as well as the mammoth Palais Omnisports. The city's center has been enriched with the Musée d'Orsay and the expanded Grand Louvre, which now houses an ever greater complement of masterpieces.

A new cathedral for a new town

Cars and trucks from all over Europe rumble into the Paris region via a sophisticated network of high-speed autoroutes. The revamped Métro and regional rapid transit system (RER) cross Paris in just minutes and also serve far-flung suburbs. Bullet trains—the TGV—link the capital to the rest of France and Europe. And a third major airport will soon be built to accommodate the millions of air passengers whose numbers are straining the present kubs of Orly and Roissy Charles-de-Gaulle. Central planners in their Cartesian wisdom have created five *villes nouvelles*, "new towns" complete with schools, parks, and shopping centers, all erected *ex nihilo* in the middle of grain fields. One of them, Évry, built on former farmland south of Paris in 1969, even boasts a brand-new (and highly controversial) cathedral designed by Mario Botta.

Since Hugues Capet, count of Paris, was elected King of France in 987 the destiny of Ile-de-France has been shaped by that of the city on the Seine. Royal residences are scattered throughout Ile-de-France, for Hugues Capet and his successors kept their courts on the move: to oversee their lands and subjects; to keep one step ahead of their enemies; and to indulge their passion for the hunt. Even in their present ruined state, the thick-walled fortresses of **Senlis** and **Dourdan**, and the donjon at **Vincennes** (under reconstruction) evoke a feudal age when kings required protection from rivals nearly as powerful as themselves. The Renaissance graces of **Fontainebleau** and **Saint-Germain-en-Laye** mirror a less brutal era, while **Versailles** embodies the brilliance of absolute monarchy at its zenith. With the curious exception of Versailles, most royal châteaux gave onto huge forests teeming with game, where the king could ride to hounds. Even now woodlands covers an astonishing twenty percent of Ile-de-France. The forests of **Fontainebleau** and **Rambouillet**, two of the most splendid in France, count among the region's greatest beauties.

The ire
of the Sun King

Not all of the 3,000 châteaux in Ile-de-France belonged to the Crown. The princely Montmorency and Condé clans, for example, owned vast domains at **Ecouen** and **Chantilly**. Their sumptuous dwellings (now home to the Musée de la Renaissance and the splendid Musée Condé, respectively) are set amid gardens and woodlands that impress visitors even today. The seventeenth century was a high-water mark for château construction. The patrician châteaux of **Courances** and **Guermantes** combine brick and stone in a style made popular under Louis XIII; the opulence and classic proportions of **Maisons-Laffitte**, designed by François Mansart in mid-century.

That age dawned in 1661 when Louis XIV attended a *fête* given in his honor by finance minister Nicolas Fouquet, at the latter's new and indescribably luxurious château, **Vaux-le-Vicomte**. Put out by Fouquet's showy splendor (and suspicious of how he had obtained his fortune), Louis had the minister thrown into prison. He then proceeded to hire the same architect, decorator, and garden designer to work on his own royal showplace at **Versailles**. From its completion in 1682 until 1789, Versailles supplanted Paris as the political and artistic capital of the realm. On the eve of the Revolution the château and town counted some 50,000 inhabitants. The Age of Elegance, endures in the eighteenth-century château of **Champs-sur-Marne**, with its Rococo interior (featuring the first dining room ever built for that express purpose) and ravishing *jardin à la française*. The owners of the Renaissance château of **Thoiry** turned the grounds into a wild animal reserve. Visitors drive through the estate (with their windows rolled up...) and watch lions, elephants, monkeys, and rhinos roam free.

The rulers of France, "eldest daughter of the Church," endowed Ile-de-France with a fabulous legacy of religious architecture such as the abbey of **Saint-Denis** where sovereigns are interred, the abbey of **Royaumont**, and the sublime Sainte Chapelle.

Gothic architecture was born in Ile-de-France in the twelfth century. Every nuance of Gothic is represented in the region, from the earliest ogives in the abbey church of **Morienval**, to the vertiginous spires and lacy stonework of the late Flamboyant phase, that grace the church of Saint-Jean Baptiste in **Nemours**. Nowhere else but in Ile-de-France is there such a collection of Gothic cathedrals as those at **Saint-Denis**, **Paris**, **Chartres**, **Pontoise**, **Senlis**, **Meaux**...

Just beyond the rose-tinted turrets of Sleeping Beauty's Castle in Disneyland Paris lies the rural **Brie**. A rich agricultural land graced with ancient fortified farms and fine churches, it arcs southward from the town of **Meaux** (famed for Brie cheese and coarse-grain mustard as well as for its splendid architecture) to **Provins**, a well preserved medieval merchant center, once the third largest city in France. And in the wheat-bearing plains of the **Beauce** and of the **Brie** region—still, as always, the breadbasket of France—**Chartres** retains its Gothic serenity despite the throngs of tourists who come to admire the cathedral each year.

While the suburbs of **Asnières** and **Argenteuil**, both close to the capital, are unrecognizable as the arcadian sites painted by Seurat and Monet, **Moret-sur-Loing**, a sleepy town on the edge of the Fontainebleau forest, still bathes in the tender light that Sisley and Renoir captured on canvas. And (in the off-season at least) certain spots of **Auvers-sur-Oise** look much as they did when Cézanne, Pissarro, and Van Gogh planted their easels there.

There are restaurants, *auberges*, and modest eateries aplenty near all the major sites. A few notable exceptions aside (watercress from the Essonne Valley, rabbits and honey from the Gâtinais, cheeses from Meaux, Coulommiers, and Dreux), homegrown foods do not feature prominently in local cuisine. Most ingredients come straight from **Rungis**, the mega-market complex that replaced Paris's Halles in 1969 as the region's supplier of comestibles from France and abroad. There's nothing "provincial" about dishes like the escargots de Bourgogne aux épices tandouri served at the Hostellerie de la Dague in Barbizon, or the beignets de sardines à la ricotta sauce indienne from La Vieille Fontaine in Maisons-Laffitte. Sophistication and virtuosity are key. Paris, of course, is a magnet for ambitious chefs from all over France. From Normandy's legendary Taillevent, who cooked for King Charles V in the 1300s, to Poitou native Joël Robuchon, contemporary culinary genius, Paris is the place where chefs prove their mettle and make their name.

Fine food, ancient monuments, thrilling history: the litany is not exhaustive. Still, it should incite you to venture, as Henry James put it, beyond "the wondrous capital, and the wondrous capital alone" to explore the châteaux and cathedrals, the forests and rivers, the urban and rural treasures of Ile-de-France.

(For an in-depth, insider's guide to the City of Light, its restaurants and hotels, shops, nightlife, monuments, and more, consult GaultMillau's *Best of Paris*.)

PARIS: RESTAURANTS

1ST ARRONDISSEMENT

10/20 Joe Allen

30, rue Pierre-Lescot
01 42 36 70 13, fax 01 40 28 06 94
Open daily until 1am. Bar: until 2am (Sun 1am). Terrace dining. Air cond.
Relaxed and casual: American, in short. Come to Joe's when you feel the urge to sink a few beers or dig into a chef's salad, chili burger, barbecued spare ribs, or apple pie. C 170-250.

Armand

6, rue du Beaujolais
01 42 60 05 11, fax 01 42 96 16 24
Closed Sat lunch, Sun, Aug. Open until 11:30pm. Pkg.
A plush, intimate restaurant near the gardens of Palais Royal. Delicious corn crêpe served with warm foie gras and a cream sauce sparked with Sherry vinegar. M 180 (lunch), 250 (dinner).

Gérard Besson

5, rue du Coq-Héron
01 42 33 14 74, fax 01 42 33 85 71
Closed Sat lunch, Sun. Open until 10:30pm. Air cond. Pkg.
A chic conservatory of cuisine bourgeoise. Polished classicism, not innovation, is Besson's signature; his only failing is a tendency to over-complicate (chicken fricassée with sweetbreads and quenelles). Splendid cellar, but too few half-bottles. Delectable desserts. C 550. M 280 (lunch).

11/20 Brasserie Munichoise

5, rue Danièle Casanova - 01 42 61 47 16
Closed Sat lunch, Sun. Open until 12:30am. Priv rm: 20.
A cozy little brasserie that serves good grilled veal sausages and one of the best choucroutes in Paris. Excellent Hacker-Pschorr beer on tap. C 185.

11/20 Café Bennett

40, pl du Marché-Saint-Honoré - 01 42 86 04 24
Closed Sat pm, Sun. Open daily until 7pm. Terrace dining.
The American-style menu features T-bone steak, burgers, and cheesecake, served by two charming *restauratrices*. Ask for a table upstairs, with a view of the arresting new building by Catalan architect Ricardo Bofill. C 180-220. M 69 (lunch), 98 (dinner), 130.

11/20 Café Marly

93, rue de Rivoli - 01 49 26 06 60
Open daily until 1am. Terrace dining.
Here in the Louvre, you may order the most expensive club sandwich in Paris, tuna sashimi, or a well-made *plat du jour*, served in magnificent surroundings. A very dressy crowd of fashion and literary notables has staked out its turf here—you may find yourself sitting next to Karl Lagerfeld! C 200.

Carré des Feuillants ✪

Alain Dutournier
14, rue de Castiglione
01 42 86 82 82, fax 01 42 86 07 71
Closed Sat lunch, Sun, Aug. Open until 10:30pm. Priv rm: 14. Air cond.
Authentic ingredients from first-rate producers form the basis of Alain Dutournier's Basco-Béarnaise cuisine. Pheasant consommé dotted with chestnuts; foie gras spread on warm cornbread; savory Pauillac lamb in a tight, sapid jus; a robust garbure (cabbage soup) with duck confit; slow-simmered veal shank that is lacquered on the outside and meltingly tender within—all these dishes brim over with vigorous, exhilarating flavors. The exciting cellar harbors a mother lode of (mostly affordable) Southwestern wines. C 650. M 330 (weekday lunch), 600.

Les Cartes Postales

7, rue Gomboust - 01 42 61 23 40, fax 01 42 61 02 93
Closed Sat lunch, Sun. Open until 10:30pm.
Scores of postcards adorn the beige-and-white walls of this small, pretty, flower-filled restaurant. Yoshimasa Watanabe's dual culinary heritage yields a menu that lists tuna carpaccio or barely cooked brill alongside a sauté of duck and foie gras or a fricassée of langoustines in a chicken jus. Nicely balanced cellar. C 250. M 135.

10/20 Le Caveau du Palais

17, pl. Dauphine - 01 43 26 04 28, fax 01 43 26 81 84
Closed Sun (Nov-Apr). Open until 10:30pm. Terrace dining.
Grilled meats and satisfying bourgeois fare served in a charming Place Dauphine cellar. Good wines sold by the pitcher. C 230-360. M 184 (wine incl).

12/20 Il Cortile

Hôtel Castille, 37, rue Cambon
01 44 58 45 67, fax 01 44 58 44 00
Closed Sun. Terrace dining. Air cond. Pkg. Open until 10:30pm. Priv rm: 45.
A lovely Italian restaurant, surely one of the prettiest in town. The rather pricey menu offers clam risotto, gnocchi in Gorgonzola sauce, and beef shanks stewed in Chianti. The flavors need more definition, though, and the cooking can be uneven. C 250. M 195.

L'Espadon

Hôtel Ritz, 15, pl. Vendôme
01 43 16 30 80, fax 01 43 16 33 75
Open daily until 11pm. Air cond. No pets. Valet pkg.
Lackluster cuisine at dizzying prices (250 F for a beef tournedos escorted by a spoonful of macaroni!). Better bets are the pan-roasted langoustines or a "mosaic" of sea bass spiced with mustard seeds. Sumptuous cellar, and the service is sheer perfection. C 800. M 380 (lunch), 600 (dinner).

 Fellini

47, rue de l'Arbre-Sec - 01 42 60 90 66
Open daily until 11:30pm. Priv rm: 30. Air cond.
Mellow stone walls contribute to Fellini's warmly elegant atmosphere. Appetizing Italian *plats du jour*: fresh pasta with scallops, shrimp and artichoke sauté, calf's liver with a bright lemon sauce. C 230. M 110 (lunch).

 Gaya

17, rue Duphot
01 42 60 43 03, fax 01 42 60 04 54
Closed Sun. Open until 10:30pm. Priv rm: 50. Air cond. Valet pkg.
Each day the tide pulls sparkling fresh seafood into this bright and elegant annex of Goumard-Prunier (see below). The catch of the day sometimes features marinated fresh anchovies, pan-roasted red mullet, or tuna with chilis. Be warned, though, that the tab is heftier than you might expect. C 300.

 Goumard Prunier

9, rue Duphot
01 42 60 36 07, fax 01 42 60 04 54
Closed Mon. Open until 10:30pm. Priv rm: 40. Air cond. Pkg.
Jean-Claude Goumard procures the fattest sole and turbot, the sweetest lobsters and prawns, the briniest sea bass and red mullet from his fishermen friends in Brittany and Roussillon. Nothing interferes with the fresh taste of the sea in dishes like scallop carpaccio with oysters, crab with Sherry aspic, or such seasonal delights as sea urchins or baby eels. The cellar spotlights fine white Burgundies. Little remains, alas, of the restaurant's original décor, designed by Majorelle—the only vestiges, it happens, are in the restrooms! C 500-700. M 295 (lunch exc Sun), 750 (dinner exc Sun).

11/20 Le Grand Louvre

Museum entrance, under the pyramid
01 40 20 53 41, fax 01 42 86 04 63
Closed Tue. Open until 10pm. Priv rm: 80. Air cond.
Something is cooking under I.M. Pei's glass pyramid. In contrast with the modern décor, the Louvre's restaurant serves classic cuisine, but not every dish is a masterpiece: good pike quenelles, bland scallop ravioli, cloying fruit gratin. Non-stop service. C 250. M 180.

 Le Grand Véfour

17, rue de Beaujolais
01 42 96 56 27, fax 01 42 86 80 71
Closed Sat, Sun, Aug. Open until 10:15pm. Air cond. No pets. Priv rm: 25. Valet pkg.
Guy Martin's menu grows more inventive by the day, with such exceptional creations as almond-milk flan in sorrel bouillon, lightly cooked salmon terrine with eggplant aspic, and basil shortbread topped with candied fennel. Hearty Alpine offerings have their place as well (Martin is a native of Savoie): how about a double chop of farm-bred pork swaddled in smoky bacon? As always, the Grand Véfour provides sublime surroundings: carved boiserie ceilings, painted allegories under glass, snowy napery, and fragile Directoire chairs. The service is as elegant as the cosmopolitan clientele. C 800. M 325 (weekday lunch), 750.

A la Grille Saint-Honoré

15, pl. du Marché-St-Honoré
01 42 61 00 93, fax 01 47 03 31 64
Closed Sun, Mon, Aug 1-19. Open until 10:30pm. Priv rm: 30. Terrace dining. Air cond.
The Place du Marché Saint-Honoré redesigned by Riccardo Bofill reminds us of Place Beaubourg' Pompidou Museum. But don't let that discourage you from visiting Jean Speyer's Grille, for tasty, imaginative "market cuisine": fragrant crab soup, guinea hen with blackcurrants, smoked haddock with cabbage and chives... Good set meal; affordable wines. C 300-350. M 180.

12/20 Juvenile's

47, rue de Richelieu
01 42 97 46 49, fax 01 47 03 36 93
Closed Sun. Open until 11pm.
We've always felt perfectly at ease in Tim Johnston's hybrid wine-and-tapas bar, where the Queen's English is spoken, and American understood. The premium Sherries that headline the wine list are ideal companions to the Spanish-style bar snacks (chicken wings, marinated fish, grilled squid, and such) that are the house specialty. But the vineyards of southern Burgundy, the Rhône, and Bordeaux are not neglected; and the menu even sounds a British note with a yummy roast-beef sandwich and nursery desserts. C 145. M 98-128.

 Kinugawa

9, rue du Mont-Thabor
01 42 60 65 07, fax 01 42 60 45 21
Closed Sun, May 1, Dec 23-Jan 5. Open until 10pm. Priv rm: 100. No pets. Air cond.
Perfect sushi, sashimi, and shabu-shabu, charmingly served in an intimate setting. But the prices cut like a samurai's sword. C 300-500. M 245 (lunch), 510-700.

*Looking for a restaurant? Refer to the **index**.*

11/20 **Lescure**

7, rue de Mondovi - 01 42 60 18 91
Closed Sat dinner, Sun, Aug. Open until 10:15pm. Terrace dining. Air cond.
Tried-and-trusted French fare served in a feverish bistro atmosphere. Sample the hearty veal sauté or duck confit. Game dishes are highlighted in hunting season. C 150. M 100 (wine incl).

Mercure Galant

15, rue des Petits-Champs
01 42 97 53 85, fax 01 42 96 08 89
Closed Sat lunch, Sun, hols. Open until 10:30pm. Priv rm: 40.
Careful, classic cooking, fairly priced. The 220 F menu offers very good value, as long as you're fond of pastry: feuilleté of snails and mushrooms, chicken fricasséed in Sherry-like vin jaune, and a "mille et une feuilles" for dessert. Interesting cellar with a wide range of half-bottles. C 390-420. M 220-290.

Le Meurice

Hôtel Meurice, 228, rue de Rivoli
01 44 58 10 50, fax 01 44 58 10 15
Open daily until 11pm. Air cond. Priv rm: 180. No pets. Valet pkg.
Rosy nymphs cavort across a ceiling further adorned with gilt and crystal chandeliers, in what is surely one of the city's most sumptuous restaurants. Le Meurice is not all show, however: the food is superb. Marc Marchand eschews pompous cuisine for full-bodied dishes with plenty of rustic flavor: grilled sea bream with fennel chutney, dandelion greens with lamb's brains and a coddled egg, lobster cannelloni in a suave, winy sauce. Faultless service, and a cellar administered by Antoine Zocchetto, an expert sommelier. C 400. M 330 (lunch), 395 (dinner), 150 (children).

Chez Pauline

5, rue Villedo - 01 42 96 20 70, fax 01 49 27 99 89
Closed Sat (exc dinner May-Sep), Sun. Open until 10:30pm. Air cond. Priv rm: 15. Pkg.
A traditional bistro that perfectly represents a certain ideal of French cuisine. Robust and full of frank flavors, the neo-bourgeois dishes are based on uniformly fine ingredients prepared by a veteran chef. Subtlety is not the strong suit here: braises, sautés, and long-simmered stews are André Genin's stock in trade. The cellar holds memorable (and expensive!) Burgundies. We only wish that the dining room were more comfy, and the staff less chilly. C 300-500. M 220.

11/20 **Au Petit Ramoneur**

74, rue Saint-Denis - 01 42 36 39 24
Closed Sat, Sun. Open until 9:30pm. Terrace dining.
Cheap and cheerful homestyle cooking. M 70.

12/20 **Au Pied de Cochon**

6, rue Coquillière - 01 40 13 77 00, fax 01 40 13 77 09
Open daily 24 hours. Terrace dining. Air cond. Priv rm: 40.
The atmosphere is effervescent at this Les Halles landmark, renowned for serving thundering herds of pigs' trotters (85,000 annually) and a ton of shellfish every day of the year. C 180-340. M 123 (dinner, wine incl), 178.

12/20 **Le Pluvinel**

Hôtel Régina, 2, pl. des Pyramides
01 42 60 31 10, fax 01 40 15 95 16
Closed Sat, Sun, hols, Aug. Open until 10pm. No pets. Priv rm: 45. Air cond. Terrace dining.
A promising chef is at work in this hotel kitchen. Sample his sea bass with red-wine butter and roasted shallots or baby lamb in a snappy peppermint jus. An elegant setting, too, just across from the Tuileries Gardens. C 270. M 160 (lunch), 250 (wine incl), 290 (dinner).

Le Poquelin

17, rue Molière - 01 42 96 22 19, fax 01 42 96 05 72
Closed Sat lunch, Sun, Aug 1-20. Open until 10:30pm. Air cond. Priv rm: 8. Pkg.
In the red-and-gold dining room where portraits of Molière look down from the walls, chef Michel Guillaumin wins applause from his regular patrons (many from the Comédie-Française across the street) for his renditions of such popular favorites as warm foie gras with prunes and nuts or sweetbreads and scallops with young turnips. Good notices too for his warm apple tart, and a standing ovation for Maggy Guillaumin's cheery welcome. C 280-320.

11/20 **Le Relais du Sud-Ouest**

154, rue Saint-Honoré - 01 42 60 62 01
Closed Sun, Aug. Open until 11pm. Pkg.
The Southwest, in all its gluttonous glory: house-made cassoulet, duck stewed with prunes, confit de canard. All at unbeatable prices. C 160. M 65 (lunch, wine incl), 85 (dinner).

11/20 **Au Rendez-Vous des Camionneurs**

72, quai des Orfèvres - 01 43 54 88 74
Open daily until 11:30pm.
More cops than truck drivers to be seen here (the criminal division is right nearby), tucking into chicken liver terrine, calf's liver with cranberries, and bitter-chocolate fondant. C 170. M 78 (weekday lunch), 98 (weekdays), 68 (children).

12/20 **Restaurant Costes**

1st arr. - Hôtel Costes, 239, rue Saint-Honoré
01 42 44 50 25, fax 01 42 44 50 01
Open daily until 12:30am. Terrace dining.
The only reason to come to this restaurant is the extraordinary setting and décor—certainly not the steep prices or the food. Choose to sit in the little armchairs or on the delightful terrace (in summer) of this Italianate luxury hotel, in a nineteenth-century town house just steps from

Place Vendôme. You will dine in trendy dishes surrounded by a trendy clientele, and be served by young waiters who don't really look like waiters. C 300-350.

 Chez Rosine

12, rue du Mont-Thabor - 01 49 27 09 23
Closed Sun, Mon lunch, Aug. Open until 11pm (11:30pm Sat). Terrace dining.
Khmer cooking served in a discreetly Asian setting, just behind the Hôtel Meurice. Featured are blue Mekong shrimp, fragrant Cambodian soups, fried ducks' tongues, and grilled catfish with tamarind sauce. Exotic and delicious. C 200-250. M 78-108 (weekday lunch, wine incl), 148 (wine incl), 78 (children).

11/20 **Toupary**

2, quai du Louvre - 01 40 41 29 29, fax 01 42 33 96 79
Closed Sun. Open until 11:30pm. Priv rm: 15. Air cond. Terrace dining. Valet pkg.
Hilton McConnico designed this colorful dining room on the fifth floor of the Samaritaine department store. Along with a splendid view of the Seine, you'll taste essentially classic cooking: cold chayote soup with almonds, lamb with pickled lemons, salmon à la niçoise. C 160-260. M 95 (lunch), 180 (dinner), 45 (children).

11/20 **La Tour de Montlhéry**

5, rue des Prouvaires - 01 42 36 21 82
Closed Sat, Sun, Jul 14-Aug 15. Open 24 hours.
Here, until the wee hours, you can order up a satisfying plate of stuffed cabbage or warming mutton stew. C 230-260.

 Chez Vong

"Aux Halles," 10, rue de la Grande-Truanderie
01 40 39 99 89
Closed Sun. Open until 12:30am. Terrace dining. Priv rm: 60. Valet pkg. Air cond.
Excellent dim-sum, steamed scallops, and shrimp with lotus leaves. The gingered lobster lacks spirit, though, and prices are high. C 250-300. M 150 (lunch).

 Willi's Wine Bar

13, rue des Petits-Champs
01 42 61 05 09, fax 01 47 03 36 93
Closed Sun. Open until 11pm.
Mark Williamson and Tim Johnston are a witty, wise pair of wine experts, whose cellar holds treasures from all over France and the world. Enjoy them (by the glass, or better, the bottle) along with a good quail salad, tarragon-scented rabbit, or a nice bit of Stilton. If you can't nab a table in the smallish dining room, join the customers sitting elbow-to-elbow at the polished wood bar. C 300-450. M 150 (weekday lunch), 180 (weekday dinner).

12/20 **Yvan sur Seine**

26, quai du Louvre - 01 42 36 49 52
Open until 4am. Air cond. Terrace dining.

Yvan's quayside annex specializes in good seafood, served well into the wee hours. The 138 F prix-fixe meal, which includes wine, is just like the one offered at Le Petit Yvan (see *8th arrondissement*). A cheerful mood prevails in the ship-shape dining room; indeed, the ambience gets downright gay as the night wears on! C 240. M 138.

2ND ARRONDISSEMENT

 Café Runtz

16, rue Favart - 01 42 96 69 86
Closed Sat, Sun, hols, Aug. Open until 11:30pm. Priv rm: 44. Air cond.
This is an 1880s Alsatian *winstub* serving rich foie gras, excellent choucroute garnie, and warm potato salad with pork knuckle. Good French Rhine wines; cheeky service. C 180. M 129 (weekdays).

12/20 **Canard'Avril**

5, rue Paul-Lelong - 01 42 36 26 08
Closed Sun, Sun, hols. Open until 10pm. Priv rm: 30.
The menu's just ducky: gizzard salad, confit, and magret de canard feature prominently, alongside a handful of similarly hearty South-western dishes. The bargain-priced set meals are sure to quack you up. C 220. M 89-128.

 Le Céladon

Hôtel Westminster, 13, rue de la Paix
01 47 03 40 42, fax 01 42 61 33 78
Closed Sat, Sun, Aug. Open until 10:30pm. Priv rm: 50. Air cond. Valet pkg.
Three tastefully lit, flower-filled, and impeccably elegant dining rooms form a lovely setting for a romantic dinner. Emmanuel Hodencq, Le Céladon's ever-improving chef, never ceases to delight us with his resolutely refined dishes: taste his subtle terrine of leeks and foie gras, langoustines with tiny Noirmoutier potatoes in a spiced jus, and Mediterranean-inspired lamb pastilla perfumed with pistou. Desserts are divine, especially the brioche pain perdu served with morello-cherry compote. Interesting, eclectic cellar. C 400-450. M 250, 370.

 La Corbeille

154, rue Montmartre
01 40 26 30 87, fax 01 40 26 08 20
Closed Sat lunch, Sun, Aug. Open until 10pm. Priv rm: 30. Air cond. Valet pkg.
An attractive single-price menu is served in the kitsch surroundings of La Corbeille's upstairs dining room. We recently feasted on a tasty celery root salad with gingerbread-coated foie gras, braised ox jowls and calf's foot, a flawlessly matured Cabécou cheese, and a yummy walnut chaud-froid. Not bad for 195 F! C 220. M 125-195, 395 (dinner, wine incl), 100 (children).

The prices in this guide reflect what establishments were charging at press time.

17

Delmonico

Hôtel Édouard VII, 39, av. de l'Opéra
01 42 61 44 26, fax 01 42 61 47 73
Closed Sat, Sun, Aug. Open until 10pm. Priv rm: 20. Air cond. Valet pkg.
With a lightened décor and a brighter atmosphere, this old standby has stepped briskly into the age of the business lunch. The classic *carte* lacks originality, but the dishes are deftly turned out: chicken liver terrine, monkfish in sauce corail, tiramisù... Pricey cellar; professional service. C 175. M 135.

Drouant

18, rue Gaillon - 01 42 65 15 16, fax 01 49 24 02 15
Open daily until 10:30pm (midnight at Le Café). Priv rm: 50. Air cond. Valet pkg.
The cream of the city's biz and show-biz sets meet and greet in the Drouant's grand Art Deco dining room. A master technician, Louis Grondard prepares a menu that lacks only a dash of personality: red mullet with bone marrow, Pauillac lamb in an herbal crust, scallop salad with a lively orange dressing, millefeuille of foie gras and artichokes. The Café Drouant draws business lunchers (at noon) and theater-goers (at night) with reasonably priced bourgeois cooking. C 630. M 290 (lunch), 650 (dinner).

11/20 Gallopin ✿

40, rue Notre-Dame-des-Victoires
01 42 36 45 38, fax 01 42 36 10 32
Closed Sun. Open until midnight. Terrace dining. Priv rm: 15.
The brassy Victorian décor is a feast for the eyes. The food at Gallopin isn't bad either. Try the house specialties: rib steak Gallopin and floating island. Jolly service. C 250. M 150 (dinner).

12/20 Le Grand Colbert

2, rue Vivienne - 01 42 86 87 88, fax 01 42 86 82 65
Closed Aug 10-20. Open until 1am. Air cond.
Classic brasserie cuisine (oysters and shellfish, andouillette ficelle, bœuf gros sel, and poached chicken) served in a sprucely restored historic monument complete with frescoes and ornate plasterwork, brass railings and painted glass panels. Expect a warm welcome and swift, smiling service. C 160-250. M 160.

 Le Moï

5, rue Daunou - 01 47 03 92 05
Open daily until midnight. Air cond. No cards.
At a new address (next door to Harry's Bar), Huguette and her son regale their patrons with fragrant Vietnamese soups, delicate dumplings, and delicious grilled lemongrass chicken. Comfortably exotic surroundings. C 150-250. M 80 (weekday lunch, wine incl).

The ratings are based solely on the restaurants' cuisine. We do not take into account the atmosphere, décor, service, and so on; these are commented upon within the review.

Pile ou Face ✿

52 bis, rue Notre-Dame-des-Victoires
01 42 33 64 33, fax 01 42 36 61 09
Closed Dec 23-Jan 1, Aug. Open until 10:30pm. Priv rm: 16. Pkg. Air cond.
Why fiddle with a winning formula? That's the philosophy of the young couple who runs Pile ou Face. The menu continues to showcase fresh farm produce, served in a red-and-gold setting with *fin de siècle* touches. Wide-ranging cellar. C 350-450. M 245 (weekday lunch), 280-320 (weekday dinner).

12/20 Rôtisserie Monsigny

"Jacques Cagna", 1, rue Monsigny
01 42 96 16 61, fax 01 42 97 40 97
Closed Sat lunch, Aug 10-20. Open until midnight (11pm Sun, Mon). Priv rm: 40. Air cond.
Jacques Cagna is the driving force behind this busy restaurant, where juicy roast lamb and spit-roasted chicken are served forth by an energetic staff under the soft music of a piano. C 200. M 160 (coffe incl), 100 (after 10pm).

12/20 Le Saint-Amour

8, rue de Port-Mahon - 01 47 42 63 82
Open daily until 10:15pm. Air cond. Pkg.
Impeccable service and fresh, generous cuisine. The chef offers a 165 F set meal and a *carte* that delivers (for example) house-made foie gras terrine, eels en persillade, and a millefeuille with blackcurrant coulis. Concise but interesting wine list. C 280. M 165.

 La Taverne du Nil

9, rue du Nil
01 42 33 51 82, fax 01 42 33 01 35
Closed Sat lunch, Sun, Aug. Open until 11pm. Air cond.
Lusty Lebanese specialties based on first-rate ingredients: lamb with bulghur, marinated grilled chicken, an array of tasty mezes and shish kebabs. The dining room is more attractive than the exterior leads one to expect. C 180-220. M 52-70 (weekday lunch), 90 (weekday lunch, wine incl), 135-182 (wine incl), 65 (children).

12/20 Le Vaudeville

29, rue Vivienne
01 40 20 04 62, fax 01 49 27 08 78
Open daily until 2am. Air cond. Terrace dining. Pkg.
This glittering outpost of the Flo empire is decked out in 1930's-style brass, glass, and wood. Waiters swoop and swirl amid the good-natured clamor (the crowd is often studded with stars and celebrities), delivering platters of glossy shellfish, prime meats, the popular house foie gras, and attractively priced little wines. A very Parisian choice for a late bite after the theater. C 250-300. M 119 (weekday lunch & Sat, wine incl), 180 (dinner, wine incl), 121 (dinner, after 10pm, wine incl).

3RD ARRONDISSEMENT

 L'Alisier

26, rue de Montmorency
01 42 72 31 04, fax 01 42 72 74 83
Closed Sat, Sun, Aug. Open until 10pm. Priv rm: 35. Air cond. No pets. Pkg.
An inviting, old-fashioned bistro (ask for a table upstairs) where you can enjoy Jean-Luc Dodeman's deft and clever cooking: cod baked with honey and cumin, lamb's brains in a delicate mussel jus, millefeuille layered with spiced custard and caramel sauce. Another point. C 250. M 150 (weekday lunch), 185.

 Ambassade d'Auvergne 🗘

22, rue du Grenier-Saint-Lazare
01 42 72 31 22, fax 01 42 78 85 47
Open daily until 10:30pm. Air cond. Priv rm: 35.
Come here for an authentic taste of Auvergne: aged country ham, cabbage and Roquefort soup, and the legendary house aligot (satiny mashed potatoes with cheese). Good desserts—try the mousseline glacée à la verveine du Velay. The cellar holds some little-known Auvergnat wines (Chanturgue, Saint-Pourçain) in a wide range of prices. C 260. M 160, 300 (wine incl).

11/20 Le Bar à Huîtres

33, bd Beaumarchais - 01 48 87 98 92
Open daily until 2am. Priv rm: 25. Terrace dining. Air cond.
See *14th arrondissement.* C 250-350. M 98-198.

 Au Bascou 🗘

38, rue Réaumur - 01 42 72 69 25
Closed Sat lunch, Sun, 3 wks in Aug. Open until 11pm. Terrace dining.
Basque-country native Jean-Guy Loustau (formerly the sommelier of Le Carré des Feuillants) runs this smart address. Menu highlights include scallops with fiery Espelette chilis, tiny squid stewed in their ink and presented with a toothsome risotto, and tender tripe en daube with sweet peppers. Top-notch wines. C 220. M 90 (lunch).

 Chez Nénesse

17, rue de Saintonge - 01 42 78 46 49,
Closed Sat, Sun, 1 wk at Feb school hols, Aug. Open until 10pm. No pets.
Nénesse puts on the dog for dinner: he covers the Formica tables of his venerable bistro with tablecloths and flowers! Fresh, flavorful *plats du jour* based on fine ingredients, carefully prepared. Worth a toque. C 180-250. M 85 (weekday lunch).

 Opium Café

5, rue Elzévir - 01 40 29 93 40, fax 01 40 29 93 46
Open daily until midnight. Air cond.
Opposite the Musée Cognacq-Jay (home to an exquisite collection of eighteenth-century art

and antiques), this spacious, elaborately decorated dining room—lovely armchairs and banquettes, gleaming chandeliers, gilded details everywhere—is a great favorite with the city's gay crowd. Highlights from the clever and appealing menu include fresh vegetables in a blood-orange sabayon and fragrant braised pork with spices. We like the friendly atmosphere, but the desserts could stand improvement. Brunch is served on weekends. C 200-300. M 110 (weekday lunch), 100-150 (lunch Sat, Sun).

4TH ARRONDISSEMENT

 L'Ambroisie

9, pl. des Vosges
01 42 78 51 45
Closed Sun, Mon, Feb school hols, 1st 3 wks of Aug. Open until 10:15pm. No pets. Priv rm: 12. Valet pkg.
With its inlaid stone and parquet floors, book-lined shelves, and sumptuous Aubusson tapestry adorning honey-hued walls, L'-Ambroisie has the feel of a beautiful private home, of which Danièle Pacaud is the attentive hostess. Don't expect to see much of Bernard Pacaud, though. He prefers the sizzling sounds of the kitchen to the applause of an appreciative public. His concise *carte* is supplemented by a few *surprises du jour*: marjolaine de foie gras (layered goose liver, truffles, and celery—divine!); flash-cooked sea bass with rosemary-scented artichokes; a majestic poularde en demi-deuil. Each dish is flawlessly finished. Faultless cellar, too, run by Pierre Le Moullac, an exemplary maître d'hôtel–sommelier. C 580-780.

 Baracane

38, rue des Tournelles - 01 42 71 43 33
Closed Sat lunch, Sun. Open until midnight.
Tables fill quickly in this tiny Southwestern enclave, because the cooking is full-flavored and generous to boot. Lentil salad with dried goose breast or cassoulet with duck confit precede delectable desserts. Low-priced regional wines wash it all down. Affable service. C 200-320. M 49-78, 125-220 (wine incl).

 Benoit

20, rue Saint-Martin
01 42 72 25 76, fax 01 42 72 45 68
Closed Sat, Sun, Aug. Open until 10pm. No pets. No cards.
Benoit is the archetypal Parisian bistro (and surely one of the priciest): velvet banquettes, brass fixtures, lace curtains, and a polished zinc bar compose a seductive décor. Owner Michel Petit (who is anything but!) continues the lusty tradition begun before the Great War by his grandfather: delicious bœuf à la parisienne, good cassoulet, creditable codfish with potatoes and cream. The cellar is stocked with good bottles from Mâcon, Sancerre, Beaujolais, and Saumur. C 450-550. M 200 (lunch).

11/20 Bistrot du Dôme

2, rue de la Bastille
01 48 04 88 44, fax 01 40 04 00 59
Open daily until 11:30pm. Air cond. Terrace dining.
See *14th arrondissement.* C 210-260.

 Bofinger

3-7, rue de la Bastille
01 42 72 87 82, fax 01 42 72 97 68
Open daily until 1am. Air cond. Priv rm: 80. Terrace dining. Air cond.
Bofinger's stained-glass ceiling, ceramics, marquetry, mirrors, and tulip-shaped sconces compose a magnificent Belle-Époque décor that has long been a landmark in the Bastille quarter. Parisians, provincials, tourists, and celebrities throng in for generous assortments of extra-fresh shellfish and hearty choucroute garnie. The Flo group, which recently took over this thriving enterprise (the restaurant serves 300,000 meals each year!), plans to put the kitchen on a more even keel. Among the *plats du jour* the roasted lobster, magret de canard, and seasonal game are worth noting. C 200-350. M 169 (wine incl).

11/20 L'Excuse

14, rue Charles-V - 01 42 77 98 97, fax 01 42 77 88 55
Closed Sun, Aug 5-20. Open until 11pm. Priv rm: 18. Air cond.
A dainty little candybox of a restaurant, decorated with mirrors, engravings, and posters. Our most recent meal left us perplexed—is the chef slipping, or does he have an excuse? Let's give him another chance... C 280. M 120 (weekday lunch), 165.

11/20 Le Fond de Cour

3, rue Sainte-Croix-Bretonnerie
01 42 74 71 52, fax 01 42 74 02 04
Open daily until 11:30pm (midnight Sat, Sun). Terrace dining. Air cond.
At the back of the courtyard, as the name suggests, you'll find this cleverly decorated restaurant. Olivier Le Cam proposes such options as langoustines with angel-hair pasta, rabbit wrapped in an herbal crust, and chocolate soufflé studded with candied orange peel. C 250.

 Les Fous d'en Face

3, rue du Bourg-Tibourg
01 48 87 03 75
Open daily until midnight. Terrace dining. Air cond. Pkg.
Generous bistro cooking made even more appealing by expertly chosen wines. Enjoy star anise–spiced salmon, scallops en papillote, and pear tart, in a convivial atmosphere. C 220-290. M 88 (weekday lunch) 175-200 (wine incl).

10/20 Jo Goldenberg

7, rue des Rosiers - 01 48 87 20 16
Open daily until 11pm. Priv rm: 60. Terrace dining. Air cond.
The most picturesque of the Goldenberg restaurants in Paris (see *seventeenth arrondissement*).

The Central European Yiddish cuisine is served in the heart of the Marais's Jewish district. Prepared foods are sold in the take-out shop. C 150-200.

11/20 Au Gourmet de l'Isle

42, rue Saint-Louis-en-l'Ile - 01 43 26 79 27
Closed Mon, Tue. Air cond. Open until 10:30pm.
The reception is charming, the crowd young and cheerful, the stone-and-beams décor convincingly rustic. More than 40 years of deserved success for one of the city's surest-value set menus priced at 130 F. Lots of à la carte choices too: artichoke "Saint Louis", beef stewed in Marcillac wine, andouillette with kidney beans. C 170. M 130.

 Le Grizzli ❂

7, rue Saint-Martin - 01 48 87 77 56
Closed Sun. Open until 11pm. No pets. Priv rm: 30. Terrace dining.
At age 95-plus this Grizzli is still going strong, serving lusty specialties rooted in the Southwest: white-bean salad with duck confit, roast baby lamb, and veal stewed with cèpes. To drink, try the delicious Pécharmant. C 220. M 120 (lunch), 155.

11/20 Chez Léon

11-13, bd Beaumarchais - 01 42 78 42 55
Open daily until 11:30pm. Terrace dining. Air cond.
A favorite with neighborhood hipsters, this Tunisian spot provides solid sustenance—good beef couscous, grilled scampi, crisp brik pastries—at moderate prices. C 150.

 Miravile

72, quai de l'Hôtel-de-Ville
01 42 74 72 22, fax 01 42 74 67 55
Closed Sat lunch, Sun, 3 wks in Aug. Open until 10:30pm. Priv rm: 35. Air cond. Pkg.
Alain Lamaison's has slimed down his tempting single-price menu, and now offers a complete menu—somewhat expensive. We can vouch for the calf's head terrine with roasted tomatoes, juicy pikeperch cooked in its skin, and flaky prune tart showered with lemon zest. Each month brings a fresh selection of recommended wines. C 380. M 240.

 Le Monde des Chimères

69, rue Saint-Louis-en-l'Ile
01 43 54 45 27, fax 01 43 29 84 88
Closed Sun, Mon. Open until 10:30pm.
A delightful old "island bistro" run by former TV personality Cécile Ibane. The cuisine is reminiscent of Sunday dinner *en famille*—if, that is, your family included a French granny who was also a marvelous cook! Try the oxtail terrine garnished with sweet-and-sour quince and cherries, or chicken sautéed with 40 cloves of garlic. Yummy homemade desserts. C 280-380. M 89 (lunch), 160.

L'Orangerie

28, rue Saint-Louis-en-l'Ile - 01 46 33 93 98
Open daily until 12:30am. Air cond.
This elegant dining room adorned with tall mirrors and huge paintings is the "secret garden" of French actor Jean-Claude Brialy, who has owned L'Orangerie for some 30 years. The restaurant reflects Brialy's own urbane refinement, and it is a distinguished choice for after-theater suppers. The actor/waiters recite the selections from the single-price menu, a compendium of full-flavored French classics, which may be escorted by a fine Bordeaux. Only the stiffish tab keeps us from booking here more often... M 400 (wine incl).

12/20 L'Ostéria

10, rue de Sévigné - 01 42 71 37 08
Closed Sat, Sun, Jul 26-Sep 2. Open until 11pm.
Hidden away behind a non-descript façade in the heart of the Marais, this little Italian restaurant plays host to fashion, film, and show-biz luminaries. They delight in the arugula salad showered with Parmesan shavings, spaghetti in a lusty seafood sauce, and potato gnocchi lavished with sage-infused butter, all clemently priced. C 150-200.

 Le Vieux Bistro

14, rue du Cloître-Notre-Dame
01 43 54 18 95, fax 01 44 07 35 63
Open daily until 10:45pm. Priv rm: 30. Terrace dining. Pkg.
Right next to Notre-Dame, an honest-to-god bistro that the tourist crowds have somehow overlooked. Owner Fernand Fleury cultivates a warm, inviting atmosphere; chef Beaudouin Verlaten's prepares a robust menu of vigorous, homestyle favorites. The cellar is a shade too expensive. C 250.

5TH ARRONDISSEMENT

 L'Atlas

12, bd Saint-Germain
01 44 07 23 66, fax 01 40 46 06 56
Open daily until 11pm. Priv rm: 86. Air cond. Pkg.
Surprising, slightly cerebral, determinedly modern Moroccan cuisine. The range of options extends beyond couscous and tagines (though a dozen excellent varieties are offered) to such delicacies as lamb with mallow, monkfish with thyme blossoms, and kidneys with sea-urchin butter. Decorated with mosaics and ornamental plasterwork, the dining room is perfectly lovely; so is the service. C 150-350. M 75 (children).

11/20 Le Bar à Huîtres

33, rue St-Jacques - 01 44 07 27 37, fax 01 43 26 71 62
Open daily until 2am. Pkg.
See *14th arrondissement*. C 98-198. M 89 (children).

 Le Bistrot d'à Côté

16, bd Saint-Germain
01 43 54 59 10, fax 01 43 29 02 08
Closed Sat lunch, Sun. Open until 11pm. Air cond. Terrace dining.
Michel Rostang's popular bistro annex serves up lively specialties that include lentil soup with garlic sausage, codfish fricassée à la lyonnaise, and veal kidney in red-wine sauce. The well-chosen wines are a half-tone too dear—we usually opt for a pitcher of the house red instead. M 119 (lunch), 148, 189.

 Les Bouchons de François Clerc

12, rue de l'Hôtel-Colbert
01 43 54 15 34, fax 01 46 34 68 07
Closed Sat lunch, Sun. Open until 11pm. Priv rm: 20. Air cond.
Sure, the food is good (snails and gnocchi au pistou, rabbit with foie gras...) but what lures us back again and again is the wine list! Pichon-Longueville '87 for 121 F, Ducru-Beaucaillou '90 for 130 F, or Châteauneuf-du-Pape Domaine de Beaucastel '86 for just 92 F: an irresistible deal for wine buffs. Another point this year. M 117 (weekday lunch, wine incl), 219.

 La Bûcherie

41, rue de la Bûcherie
01 43 54 78 06, fax 01 46 34 54 02
Open daily until midnight. No pets. Priv rm: 40. Air cond. Terrace dining. Pkg.
Bernard Bosque is built like a Breton buccaneer and has been running his Bûcherie for three decades with great success. Handsome woodwork and modern prints adorn the walls, and there are views of Notre-Dame beyond the covered terrace. The cuisine, classic and understated, reflects the seasons. There's game in autumn; baby eels from January to March; asparagus and morels in spring. Prices are not of the giveaway variety, but the lunch menu is quite attractive. The wine list favors pricey Bordeaux. C 360-680. M 230 (wine incl).

12/20 Campagne et Provence

25, quai de la Tournelle
01 43 54 05 17, fax 01 43 29 74 93
Closed Sun, lunch Sat & Mon, Aug. Open until 11pm (1am Sat, Sun). Air cond.
Sunny, unhackneyed Southern cuisine. Sample Patrick Jeffroy's cuisine: tasty basil ravioli, sea bream with roasted fennel, and dried cod à la niçoise are so skimpy. All wines are priced under 100 F, and there's a short but sweet 110 F lunch menu. C 270. M 110 (lunch).

11/20 Chieng Mai

12, rue Frédéric-Sauton - 01 43 25 45 45
Closed Aug 1-15, Dec 16-31. Open until 11:30pm. Priv rm: 60. Air cond.
Its cool, stylized atmosphere and spicy Thai menu have won Chieng Mai quite a following. Lately, though, we've noted a lack of subtlety in

the shrimp soup with lemongrass, baked crab claws with angel-hair pasta, steamed seafood served in a crab shell, and coconut-milk flan. Service is courteous and competent, but the tables are set too close together. C 240. M 122, 173.

 ### Au Coco de Mer

34, bd Saint-Marcel
01 47 07 06 64, fax 01 47 07 41 88
Closed Sun, Mon, Aug 10-20. Open until 11pm. No pets.
No, your eyes are not playing tricks: that sandy beach you see is part of the Coco de Mer's exotic décor. The Seychelle Islands inspire the chef's gingery tuna tartare, octopus stewed in coconut milk, grilled pork and duck with tropical fruit. Friendly prices. C 200-250. M 135, 170 (exc Sat lunch).

 ### Dodin Bouffant

25, rue Frédéric-Sauton
01 43 25 25 14, fax 01 43 29 52 61
Closed Sat lunch, Sun. Open until 11pm. Air cond. Terrace dining.
Not a spark of imagination lights the menu, yet patrons continue to crowd into this popular spot for oysters in Champagne sauce, daube provençale, and hot raspberry soufflé. Mostly good-natured service. C 250. M 180, 245 (wine incl).

12/20 Les Fontaines

9, rue Soufflot - 01 43 26 42 80
Closed Sun, Mon, Aug. Open until 10:45pm. Terrace dining.
A charmless corner café that draws a smart Rive Gauche crowd with meat dishes (the boss used to be a butcher), game in season, and even a few fish offerings (lobster salad, salmon crêpes). Excellent wine list; relaxed atmosphere. C 110-220.

12/20 Aux Iles Philippines

9, rue de Pontoise - 01 43 29 39 00, fax 01 44 07 17 44
Closed Sat lunch, Sun. Open until 11pm. No pets. Air cond. Terrace dining.
Nicely crafted Philippine dishes: scrambled eggs with crab on a bed of crispy noodles, glazed pork, and delectable banana cake. C 130-215. M 78 (weekday lunch), 120, 150, 250 (wine incl).

12/20 Inagiku

14, rue de Pontoise
01 43 54 70 07, fax 01 40 51 74 44
Closed Sun, Aug 1-15. Open until 10:45pm. Air cond.
Since we often leave Japanese restaurants as hungry as we came, we ordered a side of sashimi with our Matsu, or big menu. Well, after putting away the assorted fresh raw fish, sushi with avocado, crisp fried hors d'œuvres, pile of fat shrimp, tender beef fillet, and duo of ginger and chestnut sorbets, we waddled out happy and absolutely stuffed! C 200-300. M 88 (lunch), 148-248.

 ### Mavrommatis

42, rue Daubenton
01 43 31 17 17, fax 01 43 36 13 08
Closed Mon. Open until 11pm. No pets. Priv rm: 25. Terrace dining. Pkg.
The Mavrommatis brothers have raised the level of Greek cuisine served in Paris by several notches! There are 30 delicious starters (octopus salad, tuna carpaccio, stuffed eggplant, lamb meatballs, etc.), and worthwhile main dishes, too: red mullet grilled in vine leaves, smothered leg of lamb with herbs, or veal with oaten pasta. Good Greek wines. C 160-240. M 120 (weekday lunch, Sat, wine incl), 140.

 ### Moissonnier   ✦

28, rue des Fossés-St-Bernard - 01 43 29 87 65
Closed Sun dinner, Mon, Aug. Open until 10pm.
Despite a page of history that turns because of the departure of Louis Moissonnier, nothing has changed, in this landmark Paris bistro. Ex-Troisgros and Senderens chef Philippe Mayet turns out the same robust Lyonnais specialties. Tasty Beaujolais wines are on hand to slake your thirst. C 280. M 150 (weekdays).

11/20 Chez Pento

9, rue Cujas - 01 43 26 81 54
Closed Sat lunch, Sun. Open until 11pm.
This neighborhood favorite serves generous portions of salt-cured duck with lentils, sausage with butter-braised cabbage, homey chocolate cake and the like, along with astutely chosen wines (offered by the glass or bottle). C 170-240. M 83 (weekday lunch), 104 (dinner).

11/20 Perraudin

157, rue Saint-Jacques - 01 46 33 15 75
Closed lunch Sat & Mon, Sun, last 2 wks of Aug. Open until 10:15pm. Garden dining. Pkg.
Known to every publisher and professor in the Latin Quarter, this modest eatery provides solid sustenance—roast leg of lamb with scalloped potatoes, bœuf bourguignon, tarte Tatin—in a lively setting. C 125. M 63 (lunch).

12/20 Le Petit Navire

14, rue des Fossés-St-Bernard - 01 43 54 22 52
Closed Sun, Mon. Open until 10:15pm. Priv rm: 25. Terrace dining.
Anchored not far from the Seine for the past twenty-odd years, Le Petit Navire regales its many regular customers with tapenade, garlicky shellfish soup, grilled sardines, and delightful growers' wines. C 250. M 150.

12/20 Chez René

14, bd Saint-Germain - 01 43 54 30 23
Closed Sat, Sun, Aug. Open until 11pm. Terrace dining. Pkg.
Boiled beef, chard gratin, and coq au vin are served forth by speedy yet attentive waiters at this popular bistro. The tipple of choice here is Beaujolais *au compteur* (you pay for what you drink). C 250. M 153 (lunch, wine incl).

12/20 Rôtisserie du Beaujolais

19, quai de la Tournelle
01 43 54 17 47, fax 01 44 07 12 04
Closed Mon. Open until 11:15pm. Air cond. Terrace dining.
Claude Terrail of the Tour d'Argent (across the road) owns this Lyonnais-style bistro, a nice little place to spend a lively evening with friends over spit-roasted Challans duck, saucisson pistaché, or a salad of boiled beef and lentils. Splendid cheeses and exemplary Beaujolais from Dubœuf. **C** 230.

12/20 La Timbale Saint-Bernard

18, rue des Fossés-St-Bernard
01 46 34 28 28 fax 01 46 34 66 26
Closed Sat lunch, Sun, July 26-Aug 27. Open until 10pm. Priv rm: 20. Terrace dining.
We don't think the chef is living up to his potential, but this vivacious bistro still has plenty of appeal. An adorable staff delivers simmered scallops, pork with aïoli, a flaky turnover stuffed with potato and foie gras... Goodly number of wines available by the half-bottle. **C** 135-255. **M** 88-132 (weekday lunch), 162-230.

La Timonerie

35, quai de la Tournelle - 01 43 25 44 42
Closed Sun, Mon lunch, Aug. Open until 10:30pm. Air cond.
Philippe de Givenchy continues to surprise us with his streamlined cuisine, based on simple, unpretentious ingredients: mackerel, pollack, inexpensive cuts of meat, offal, and pork. Another chef would make bistro chow out of foods like these, but Givenchy turns them into great modern dishes. What he does with hogs' jowls and a little red wine, or with a mackerel fillet and a handful of herbs, is pure magic. Desserts follow the same vein: a homey repertoire glorified by virtuoso technique. The cellar is not vast, but it is perfectly à propos, with a fine range of growers' wines. **C** 350-450. **M** 240 (lunch).

La Tour d'Argent

15-17, quai de la Tournelle
01 43 54 23 31, fax 01 44 07 12 04
Closed Mon. Open until 10:30pm. Priv rm: 60. Air cond. Valet pkg.
Claude Terrail is as savvy as he is charming. He knows that a reputation—no matter how exalted—is not sufficient to survive in the highly competitive world of world-class restaurants. He recently appointed Bernard Guilhaudin (formerly of the *luxe* La Mamounia resort in Marrakech) to succeed veteran chef Manuel Martinez and infuse some new blood into the Tour d'Argent. It remains to be seen how this venerable institution (and its legendary specialties, canard à l'orange and the rest) will respond to efforts to modernize... For the moment, the repertoire is still classic and is executed with impeccable technique. Fabled cellar, with thousands of pricey bottles and a few affordable ones, too. A la carte prices are stuck in the stratosphere, but there is a more accessibly priced set lunch. **C** 950. **M** 395 (lunch).

12/20 Toutoune

5, rue de Pontoise - 01 43 26 56 81
Closed Mon lunch, Sun. Open until 10:45pm.
The arrival of a chef with a Provençal repertoire infused fresh life into this popular spot. The 158 F single-price menu features fragrant soups, tasty terrines, snails in a garlicky tomato sauce, sea bream with zucchini, and grapefruit gratin with sabayon sauce. Lively atmosphere. **M** 108 (weekday lunch), 158.

11/20 La Truffière

4, rue Blainville - 01 46 33 29 82, fax 01 46 33 64 74
Closed Mon, 2 wks in Aug. Open until 10:30pm. Priv rm: 40. Air cond.
Candlelight flickers amid the dining room's ancient beams, a Chopin sonata plays softly in the background: the romantic mood is set, and perhaps that's just as well, for it will help you ignore the misfires that mar the kitchen's classic cuisine, and the annoying supplemental charges on the so-called single-price menu (130 F for less than half an ounce of truffles). **C** 350-450. **M** 98 (lunch, exc Sun), 140 (dinner, exc Sun), 198, 78 (children).

6TH ARRONDISSEMENT

12/20 Chez Albert

43, rue Mazarine - 01 46 33 22 57
Closed Sun, Mon lunch, Aug. Open until 11pm.
Many patrons don't realize that this is a Portuguese restaurant. The menu is mostly French, but the coriander clams, rabbit à la Ranhado, and half-dozen dishes starring salt cod (we like the one with eggs and onions) point clearly to the owner's Lusitanian origins. So does the wine list, with its Douros and Dãos. **C** 180-200. **M** 80 (lunch), 135.

Allard

41, rue St-André-des-Arts
01 43 26 48 23, fax 01 46 33 04 02
Closed Sun, 1 wk in Aug. Open until 10:30pm. Air cond.
Little has changed at Allard, from the mellow décor to the classic menu (sole meunière, duck with olives, tarte Tatin). This nostalgic ambience continues to charm the cosmopolitan patrons, but we still find the prices too high. Another point. **C** 250. **M** 150 (weekday lunch), 200.

11/20 Arbuci

25, rue de Buci - 01 44 41 14 14, fax 01 44 41 14 10
Open daily until dawn. Priv rm: 80. Air cond. Terrace dining.
Those in the know dine downstairs at the Blanc Brothers' Arbuci: the food and prices are the same as upstairs, with live jazz to boot, at no extra charge. **C** 210-280. **M** 72-98 (lunch), 79-135.

La Bastide Odéon

7, rue Corneille · 01 43 26 03 65, fax 01 44 07 28 93
Closed Sun, Mon, Aug. Open until 11pm. Priv rm: 8. No pets.
Gilles Ajuelos impressed us from the start with his sunny Southern cooking. But now his menu is in danger of becoming a cliché. Provençal cuisine is more than just heaps of herbs and fresh vegetables! Gilles needs to hone his technique, balance his seasonings, learn to choose only prime ingredients... Still, the atmosphere is friendly, prices are moderate, and the wine list offers wonderful Provençal wines. C 230. M 139-180.

 ## Le Bistrot d'Alex ✿

"La Foux", 2, rue Clément · 01 43 54 09 53
Closed Sat lunch, Sun, Dec 24-Jan 2. Open until 10pm. Priv rm: 12.
Lyon and Provence (with a penchant for the latter) inspire Stéphane Guini's zestful menu. You're sure to like the pistachio-studded saucisson, fragrant daube de bœuf, and tasty orange flan. Delightful welcome. C 220-250. M 140, 170.

 ## Les Bookinistes

53, quai des Grands-Augustins
01 43 25 45 94, fax 01 43 25 23 07
Open daily until midnight. Priv rm: 25. Air cond. Terrace dining. Pkg.
This addition to Guy Savoy's string of bistros sports an avant-garde look that obviously suits the mostly young, mostly Left Bank crowd. Crowded is how you might feel in this elbow-to-elbow eatery, but don't let that diminish your enjoyment of the gnocchi with mussels and spinach, sweetbread fricassée, and gingerbread millefeuille. Snappy service. C 240-260. M 160 (weekday lunch), 180 (dinner Sun).

 ## Bouillon Racine

3, rue Racine · 01 44 07 34 07
Closed Sun. Open until 1am.
Olivier Simon, a talented young Belgian chef, presides in the kitchen of this freshly (and beautifully) refurbished Belle Époque jewel. Not only are the surroundings a feast for the eye, the *carte* promises a corresponding treat for the palate: tomatoes stuffed with tiny shrimp, mousse of smoky Ardennes ham with juniper aspic, beef braised in beer à la flamande, pheasant à la brabançonne, and buttery Belgian brioche given the French-toast treatment. Tempting list of Belgian beers; brunch served on Saturdays. C 150-200. M 78, 108.

12/20 Brasserie Lutétia

Hôtel Lutétia, 23, rue de Sèvres
01 49 54 46 76, fax 01 49 54 46 00
Open daily until midnight. Priv rm: 100. Air cond. Valet pkg.
The no-nonsense cooking is prepared with considerable finesse in the same kitchens as Le Paris (see below). The seafood is attractively priced, and the satisfying bourgeois dishes (veal chop with macaroni gratin, poulet au thym) always hit the spot. Brunch served on Sundays. C 200-250. M 180, 295 (wine incl), 60 (children).

 ## Jacques Cagna

14, rue des Grands-Augustins
01 43 26 49 39, fax 01 43 54 54 48
Closed Sat lunch, Sun, 3 wks in Aug, 1 wk at Christmas. Open until 10:30pm. Priv rm: 12. Air cond.
Near the Seine, in the refined setting of his wood-panneled sixteenth-century mansion decorated with Flemish paintings, Jacques Cagna keeps turning out the classic dishes that built his success over the years. Not only are the products he uses are superb (sea-bass from Brittany, fatted chicken from Normandy, lamb from the Pyrénées) but we have known a more audacious Cagna. That's why we give him kudos when he dares adding to his classics, dishes like tiny escargots hidden under ground tomato in a Charentes potato. The wine cellar is superb and has a fine collection of old Ports. C 350. M 280 (lunch), 490.

11/20 Le Caméléon

6, rue de Chevreuse · 01 43 20 63 43
Closed Sat lunch, Sun, 1 wk in Jan, 3 wks in Aug, 1 wk in Apr or May. Open until 10:30pm. Pkg. .
A pretty and authentic bistro with a different *plat du jour* every day of the week: house-made sausage, stuffed tomatoes, codfish with aïoli. Boring desserts. C 200-250.

12/20 Casa Bini

36, rue Grégoire-de-Tours
01 46 34 05 60, fax 01 46 34 07 32
Closed Aug 10-20, 1 wk at Christmas. Open until 11pm. Priv rm: 18. Terrace dining.
Anna Bini travels all the way to Tuscany to seek out the best ingredients for her little restaurant. The concise menu of carpaccio, crostoni, pasta, and good daily specials suits her trendy Saint-Germain patrons to a T. Reasonably priced Italian wines. C 220. M 150, 170.

 ## Le Chat Grippé

87, rue d'Assas · 01 43 54 70 00, fax 01 43 26 42 05
Closed Sat lunch, Mon, Aug. Open until 10:30pm. Air cond.
Well-spaced tables in an intimate setting, where diners tuck into a fine 240 F menu that includes marinated tuna with anchovies, sea bream with tomatoes and ginger, roast rabbit with peppers, and licorice custard with prune coulis. Heartwarming welcome. M 160 (weekday lunch), 200, 240, 325.

12/20 Le Clocher Saint-Germain

22, rue Guillaume Apollinaire
01 42 86 00 88, fax 01 42 60 37 75
Open daily until midnight. Air cond. Terrace dining.

Tourists and locals alike fetch up at this pleasant bistro for such hearty regional classics as warm saucisson lyonnais, salmon with green lentils, and silky blancmange embellished with caramel jam. The frisky wines, offered by the bottle or glass, are ideally suited to the bill of fare. For the neighborhood, a pretty darn good deal. C 180. M 72 (lunch, exc Sun), 148.

 Dominique

19, rue Bréa - 01 43 27 08 80, fax 01 43 26 88 35
Closed Sun, Mon lunch, Jul 20-Aug 20. Open until 11:30pm. Terrace dining.
This famed Montparnasse Russian troika-take-out shop/bar/restaurant—steadfastly refuses perestroika when it comes to cuisine and décor. Rostropovitch and Solzhenitsyn have been spotted here, sampling the delicious smoked salmon, borscht, and blinis. And there's vodka, of course, both Russian and Polish. C 250-300. M 98 (weekday lunch, wine incl), 170.

 L'Écaille de PCB

"Pierre et Colette Bardèche," 5, rue Mabillon
01 43 26 73 70, fax 01 46 33 07 98
Closed Sat lunch, Sun. Open until 11pm. No pets. Priv rm: 10. Terrace dining.
Marinated sardines with fennel or a salad of finnan haddie and bacon segue into osso buco de lotte à l'orientale, John Dory with coarse-grain mustard, or scallops in a creamy garlic sauce. The cellar is of only middling interest, save for a fine, bone-dry Jurançon from Charles Hours. C 280-350. M 195.

 L'Épi Dupin

11, rue Dupin - 01 42 22 64 56, fax 01 42 22 30 42
Closed Sat, Sun. Open until 11pm. Terrace dining.
Well-deserved praise has been heaped on young François Pasteau's lively, clever cooking. A worthy pupil of some of the city's finer chefs, he proposes a vivid menu that includes briefly seared tuna set atop a zesty onion pizza, scallops paired with celery in a fragrant Provençal-style broth, breaded calf's head with saffron potatoes (try it, it's delicious!), and a bouquet of light, inventive desserts. And surprise! A meal here will set you back only 153 F (plus wine, of course). Remember to book your table in advance. M 97 (weekday lunch, wine incl), 153.

12/20 Chez Henri

16, rue Princesse - 01 46 33 51 12
Open daily until 11:30pm. No pets. No cards.
There's no sign outside, since the trendy denizens of the Rue Princesse know just where to find Henri's bistro specialties. The cooking can be uneven, but calf's liver with creamed onions, farm chicken in vinegar, roast lamb, and apple clafoutis are usually good bets. Nervous service; bare-bones cellar. C 220-250.

12/20 Joséphine

"Chez Dumonet", 117, rue du Cherche-Midi
01 45 48 52 40, fax 01 42 84 06 83
Closed Aug. Open until 10:30pm. Terrace dining.
Joséphine draws a crowd of prominent jurists, journalists, and theater folk who appreciate the good cuisine bourgeoise and the fabulous (though pricey) wine list. Chummy atmosphere, animated by owner Jean Dumonet, a former yachting champ. C 300.

Lipp

151, bd Saint-Germain
01 45 48 53 91, fax 01 45 44 33 20
Closed 3 wks Aug. Open until 1am. Air cond.
Despite often disappointing food (choucroute, bœuf gros sel) and the cruel whims of fashion, this glossy brasserie still manages to serve some 400 to 500 customers a day. And one often catches sight of a powerful politician or a beauty queen ensconced at a ground-floor table, admiring the gorgeous décor. C 280. M 200 (wine incl).

11/20 La Lozère

4, rue Hautefeuille - 01 43 54 26 64
Closed Sun, Mon, Jul 12-Aug 12, 1 wk at Christmas. Open until 10pm. Air cond. Pkg.
You can smell the bracing air of the rural Lozère region in the warming winter soups, herbed sausages, pâtés, and cheese-laced mashed potatoes (aligot) served at this crafts shop-cum-restaurant. C 180-220. M 93 (lunch, wine inc).

 La Marlotte

55, rue du Cherche-Midi
01 45 48 86 79, fax 01 44 44 34 80
Closed Sat, Sun, Aug. Open until 11pm. No pets. Priv rm: 9. Air cond. Terrace dining. Pkg.
A rustic, timbered setting softened by madras upholstery and candlelight in the evening. Patrick Duclos crafts a classic repertoire: veal kidney perfumed with rosemary, duck breast with apples, nougat with raspberry jus. Crowded both at lunch and dinner, often with the smart set. C 200.

11/20 La Méditerranée

Pl. de l'Odéon - 01 43 26 02 30, fax 01 43 26 18 44
Open daily until 11pm. Priv rm: 25. Terrace dining.
A trim seafood restaurant moored on the Place de l'Odéon, offering shipshape fish tartare, grilled sea bass, and bouillabaisse. C 200-250.

 Le Muniche

7, rue St-Benoît - 01 42 61 12 70, fax 01 42 60 37 75
Open daily until 2am. Priv rm: 35. Air cond. Terrace dining.
See *Le Clocher Saint-Germain*, page 23. C 250-300. M 99 (lunch), 149.

 Le Paris

Hôtel Lutétia, 45, bd Raspail
01 49 54 46 90, fax 01 49 54 46 00
Closed Sat, Sun, Jul 26-Aug 24. Open until 10pm. Air cond. Priv rm: 16. Valet pkg.
Philippe Renard reigns in the kitchens of Le Paris, one of the best tables on the Left Bank.

Rich, well-defined flavors distinguish his terrine of boiled beef and foie gras, turbot cooked in seaweed and sea salt, and rack of pork braised for 36 hours with truffles and leeks. Note the luscious chocolate desserts, and the excellent 260 F prix-fixe lunch. C 480. M 260 (lunch), 350, 565, 60 (children).

10/20 Le Petit Saint-Benoît

4, rue Saint-Benoît - 01 42 60 27 92
Closed Sun, hols. Open until 10:30pm. Terrace dining. No pets.
The crowded sidewalk terrace is a refuge for fashionable fast-food haters in search of cheap eats: hachis parmentier, bacon with lentils, bœuf bourguignon, roast lamb. C 110.

12/20 Le Petit Zinc

11, rue Saint-Benoît
01 42 61 20 60, fax 01 42 60 37 75
Open daily until 2am. Priv rm: 8. Air cond.
See *Le Clocher Saint-Germain*, page 23. C 260-310. M 168 (wine inc).

12/20 La Petite Cour

8, rue Mabillon - 01 43 26 52 26, fax 01 44 07 11 53
Closed Jan. Open until 11pm (11:30pm in summer). Priv rm: 45. Terrace dining.
Chef Patrick Guyander generally plays it safe, but he sometimes produces a dish with extra dash (duck breast with honey and soy sauce). C 320-370.

11/20 Polidor

41, rue Monsieur-le-Prince - 01 43 26 95 34
Open daily until 12:30am (Sun 11pm). No cards.
Familiar and soothing blanquettes, bourguignons, and rabbit in mustard sauce are served in a dining room that time has barely touched in more than a century. C 140. M 55 (weekday lunch), 100.

10/20 Le Procope

13, rue de l'Ancienne-Comédie
01 43 26 99 20, fax 01 43 54 16 86
Open daily until 1am. Priv rm: 80. Air cond. Terrace dining.
The capital's oldest café, founded in 1686, restored to its original seventeenth-century splendor, may not be your best bet for a full meal. Tables of tourists feed on unexceptional brasserie fare (shellfish, coq au vin). C 240. M 106 (lunch), 123 (dinner, wine incl), 169, 185.

 Relais Louis XIII

8, rue des Grands-Augustins
01 43 26 75 96, fax 01 44 07 07 80
Open daily until 10:15pm. No card.
Louis XIII was proclaimed King of France in this luxurious tavern with its beams and polished paneling... And today chef Manuel Martinez from La Tour d'Argent arrives to redefine a most often heavy cuisine. At the best part is that the prices have been halved and the service rejuvenated. On the other hand dishes vary from mediocre to a most acceptable mil-

lefeuille of rouget and game hen with wild mushrooms, and a stupendous, shockingly expensive cellar. C 600-700. M 200, 250 (lunch), 260, 360 (dinner).

12/20 Le Rond de Serviette

97, rue du Cherche-Midi
01 45 44 01 02, fax 01 42 22 50 10
Closed Sat lunch, Sun, Aug 1-24. Open until 10:45pm. Priv rm: 35. Air cond. Terrace dining.
The owners cosset their clients in a fresh, pretty setting with lively cuisine: red-mullet tart with basil, creamy asparagus soup. The chef sometimes falters (bland saddle of lamb), but on balance he does pretty well. Fair prices. C 220-250. M 132-250 (lunch), 168, 250.

 La Rôtisserie d'en Face

2, rue Christine - 01 43 26 40 98 fax 01 43 54 54 48
Closed Sat lunch, Sun. Open until 11pm (11:30pm Sat, Sun). Air cond.
Jacques Cagna's smart rotisserie continues to attract Parisians hungry for rousing bistro food at reasonable prices. For 198 F you could sit down to (say) duck pâté, Moroccan-style guinea hen with eggplant, and an iced caramel-walnut vacherin. M 135-159 (weekday lunch), 198 (dinner).

12/20 Santal des Prés

6, rue du Dragon - 01 45 44 26 35
Closed Sun. Open until 11:30pm. Pkg.
A former Saigonese lawyer defends the cause of authentic Vietnamese cuisine with her delicious "grandmother's" shrimp, duck breast with chilis and glacéed fruit, peppery salmon, and plum duck. C 150. M 59 (lunch), 87-290, 50 (children).

 Yugaraj

14, rue Dauphine
01 43 26 44 91, fax 01 46 33 50 77
Closed Mon lunch. Open until 11pm. Priv rm: 26. Air cond.
The best Indian restaurant in the city, hands down. We love the refined surroundings, the smiles of the formally suited waiters, and—especially—the rare delicacies culled from every province of the subcontinent. Savor the cumin-spiced crab balls, tender lamb that is first roasted in a tandoori oven then sautéed with herbs, or cod suavely spiced with turmeric and fenugreek; the subtly harmonized flavors bloom on the palate. C 270. M 130 (lunch), 180, 220.

7TH ARRONDISSEMENT

12/20 Apollon

24, rue Jean-Nicot
01 45 55 68 47, fax 01 47 05 13 60
Closed Sun. Open until 11pm. Terrace dining. Pkg.
First-rate mezes (chopped olives with saffron, meatballs, brochettes) make this one of the city's top Greek eateries. Chummy service. C 100. M 79 (lunch), 128 (dinner).

Arpège

Alain Passard,
84, rue de Varenne
01 45 51 47 33, fax 01 44 18 98 39
Closed Sat, Sun lunch. Open until 10:30pm. Air cond. Priv rm: 12.
Although he sits now at the top of the Mount Olympus of gastronomy, Alain Passard has not changed his down-to-earth manner. While some others invest time and money in marble floors and gold faucets, he devotes all his efforts to his twelve tables set in an almost spartan décor of wood and etched glass, overseen by a portrait of his ancestor. Some call the restaurant cold and stark, but Passard believes in no gimmicks, no tricks, no show off—in the dining room or his cuisine. Subtle hamornies mark his splendid and delicate compositions, each the result of a reflection about the complementary flavors and textures of the ingredients. If "art cuisine" exists, this is it. Arpège (Arpeggio), a rapid succession of harmonious tones, best describes Passard's virtuosity: spicy fresh ginger melts in the sweeteness of minced apple and sublimates the oceanic scent of sole; crispy suckling pig in a sweet horse-radish mousse is glorified by melon sautéed in salt-edged butter. Perhaps one reason Passard's cuisine is so far above the majority of others, is because each dish reflects his considerable thought as well as his respect for the eater. C 700-1,000. M 320 (weekday lunch), 690.

 Le Bamboche

15, rue de Babylone
01 45 49 14 40, fax 01 45 49 14 44
Closed Sat, Sun, Aug. Priv rm: 14.
Wee but wildly charming, David Van Laer's new restaurant (tucked away behind the Bon Marché department store) harbors a solid toque for herb-strewn snail and lentil soup, lamb simmered in spices, and a deeply delectable chocolate-passion fruit millefeuille. The cellar, understandably, is still young. C 250. M 180-240.

12/20 Le Basilic

2, rue Casimir Périer - 01 44 18 94 64
Open daily until 10:30pm. Terrace dining.
Here's a pretty brasserie across from the stately church of Sainte-Clotilde, where you can count on a warm welcome and a good meal. We can vouch for the saddle of hare en compote, grilled steak with Roquefort, and the fruit gratins offered for dessert. Interesting cellar. C 200.

 Beato

8, rue Malar - 01 47 05 94 27
Closed Sun, Mon, Aug, end Dec. Open until 11:30pm.
Sure, the setting and service are still starchy, but Beato's menu has visibly loosened up. Alongside the incomparable scampi fritti, lobster risotto, and noble chop of milk-fed veal, you'll find zuppa di fagioli, bollito misto, and tasty gnocchi with hare. C 300-350. M 145 (weekday lunch).

 Au Bon Accueil

14, rue de Monttessuy - 01 47 05 46 11
Closed Sat lunch, Sun, Aug, 1 wk at Christams. Open until 10pm. Terrace dining. No pets.
Unbeatable value. Jacques Lacipière's 120 F market-fresh menu might propose a hearty terrine of calf's foot and kidney, skate with Sherry butter or bœuf bourguignon, and creamy cherry chiboust. A la carte, look for beef fillet à la bordelaise or turbot in an herbal vinaigrette. Just as the sign says, you'll find a friendly welcome. C 250. M 120.

 Le Bourdonnais

113, av. de La Bourdonnais
01 47 05 47 96, fax 01 45 51 09 29
Closed Jan 1, May 1, Dec 24-25. Open until 11pm. Priv rm: 30. Air cond. Garage pkg.
Owner Micheline Coat, a peach of a hostess, greets newcomers as warmly as the politicos and financiers who number among her faithful customers (on the rare occasions when Micheline is absent, however, the ambience is not quite so chic). At lunchtime the 240 F menu (it even includes wine) is a paragon of generosity. The more expensive set meals also give you quality for your dining dollar, with lobster in brik pastry, spiced langoustines, rosemary-scented Lozère lamb, and a vanilla-berry feuillantine. C 450. M 240 (lunch, wine incl), 320 (dinner), 420.

11/20 Café de Mars

11, rue Augereau - 01 47 05 05 91
Closed Mon. Open daily until 11:30pm (4:30pm Sun). Bar until 2am.
A menu that provides an engaging mix of American (spareribs, salads) and Mediterranean (breaded mozzarella with arugula, grilled scampi), a jovial atmosphere, and a cosmopolitan crowd account for the Café's continuing success. The staff goes all out to produce a traditional American brunch on Sunday. C 150. M 70 (weekday lunch).

12/20 Clémentine

62, av. Bosquet - 01 45 51 41 16
Closed Sat lunch, Sun, Aug 15-30. Open until 10:30pm. Terrace dining. Air cond. Pkg. .
Here's a friendly little bistro with a summer terrace, where the chef produces tasty, unpretentious fare: grilled ham with shallots, corned duck with vegetables, creamy fresh cheese swirled with acacia honey. C 180. M 139.

 Écaille et Plume

25, rue Duvivier - 01 45 55 06 72
Closed Sat lunch, Sun, 1 wk in Feb, Aug. Open until 11pm. Priv rm: 10. Air cond.
Seasonal game specialties and seafood are Marie Naël's strong points: try the briny salade océane, shark roasted with lemongrass, hare à la royale or, in its short season, Scottish grouse flambéed with single-malt whisky. The dining room is cozy, the Loire wines well chosen. C 260-340. M 180, 195.

12/20 La Fontaine de Mars

129, rue Saint-Dominique - 01 47 05 46 44
Closed Sun. Open until 11pm. Air cond. Terrace dining.
A smiling staff and tasty family-style cooking make this a popular spot. You'll surely relish the warm cèpe pâté, andouillette sausage laced with Chardonnay, or duck breast with cranberries. To drink, look no further than the good Cahors priced at 40 F. C 220. M 85 (lunch).

 Chez Françoise

Aérogare des Invalides
01 47 05 49 03, fax 01 45 51 96 20
Open daily until midnight. Terrace dining. Valet pkg.
Chez Françoise is an immense subterranean restaurant, a perennial favorite with hungry parliamentarians from the neighboring Assemblée Nationale. They blithely ignore the prix-fixe specials and opt instead for the pricier à la carte offerings, like duck terrine, roast rack of lamb, poule au pot, and crêpes Suzette. We, on the other hand, usually choose one of the set meals, which are really a good deal (although the cooking can be a mite uneven at times). C 250. M 120 (dinner), 168, 60 (children).

 Gaya Rive Gauche

44, rue du Bac - 01 45 44 73 73, fax 01 42 60 04 54
Closed Sun lunch, Aug. Open until 11pm. Terrace dining. Air cond. Pkg.
The smart literary set of the Faubourg Saint-Germain quickly staked out their turf at this annex of the Goumard-Prunier seafood empire. They come here to savor ultrafresh fish in such unfussy preparations as a bracing tartare of tuna and John Dory, tiny deep-fried red mullet, and line-caught sea bass grilled with roasted tomatoes. C 260-360.

 Les Glénan

54, rue de Bourgogne - 01 45 51 61 09
Closed Sat, Sun, 1 wk in Feb, Aug. Open until 10pm. Air cond. Priv rm: 20.
Christine Guillard manages Les Glénan with energy and charm, while the kitchen is in the capable hands of Thierry Bourbonnais. His sensitive touch brings out all the delicate nuances of seafood and other seasonal ingredients. The 195 F set meal, which includes a half-bottle of Loire Valley wine, features creamy cumin-spiced tomato soup, grilled sea bream with smothered artichokes, and chocolate-swirled pear shortbread. C 350. M 195 (wine incl).

 Jules Verne

Tour Eiffel, second floor
01 45 55 61 44, fax 01 47 05 29 41
Open daily until 10:30pm. Air cond. No pets. Valet pkg.
Dining in this sophisticated room high atop the Eiffel Tower is a treat in itself. Chef Alain Reix's menu majors in seafood: Chinese-style steamed oysters with roasted tomatoes, scallop carpaccio with asparagus and Parmesan, and fricasséed cuttlefish paired with pan-roasted foie gras are all fine, modern dishes. Superior, surely, to the poached sole immobilized in a sabayon studded with sea snails. Certain offerings have a pleasing Alsatian accent, and the desserts are delicious. Perfect service. C 750-800. M 300 (weekday lunch), 420 & 460 (weekday lunch, Sat), 680 (exc weekday lunch), 720 & 770 (wine incl).

 Kamal

20, rue Rousselet - 01 47 34 66 29
Open daily until 11pm. Priv rm: 40. Air cond.
Kamal means lotus, a symbol of purity. Pure pleasure is what we derive from this moderately spicy North Indian fare; you too will savor the tender tandooris, shrimp and lamb curries, red hacked chicken, saffron rice, and naans. M 69 (weekday lunch, wine incl), 85 (lunch), 129.

 Le Divellec

107, rue de l'Université
01 45 51 91 96, fax 01 45 51 31 75
Closed Sun, Mon, Dec 24-Jan 1. Open until 10pm. Air cond. No pets. Valet pkg.
We are still disapointed by Le Divellec which was one of the great seafood restaurant of Paris. The crew will have to steer a simpler and (if possible) less costly course to regain its past grandeur. Classic cellar; well-bred welcome and service. C 700-900. M 290-390 (lunch).

 Le Luz

4, rue Pierre-Leroux - 01 43 06 99 39
Closed Sat lunch, Sun, Aug 11-18. Open until 10pm. No pets. Air cond.
Behind its fresh and tidy façade, this cozy little restaurant offers clever but uncomplicated seafood, prepared with quality ingredients. Try the tasty fresh cod with roasted vegetables or scallops sparked with orange vinegar, followed by one of the alluring desserts. Varied wine list; professional welcome. C 235. M 155.

12/20 Maison de l'Amérique Latine

217, bd Saint-Germain
01 45 49 33 23, fax 01 40 49 03 94
Closed Sat, Sun, hols, Aug 4-25. Open until 10:30pm. No pets. Priv rm: 150. Terrace dining.
Don't come here looking for churrasco or feijoada—the chef is Japanese and his repertoire is resolutely French (with a barely discernible Eastern touch). Among the menu's highlights are a squab raviolo with shiitake aspic, pan-roasted salmon with sesame seeds and bok choy, and beef tournedos sparked with preserved lemon. The garden is a delightful place to dine, weather permitting. C 320-375. M 195-225 (weekday lunch).

12/20 Le Maupertu

94, bd de Latour-Maubourg - 01 45 51 37 96
Closed Sat lunch, Sun, 1 wk in Feb, 2 wks in Aug. Open until 10pm. Terrace dining. No pets.

Seasonal, market-fresh cooking figures on Le Maupertu's unbeatable 135 F prix-fixe meal. Try the lush millefeuille layered with shrimp and crabmeat, the satisfying daube provençale, and bright-flavored orange and almond terrine. Among the attractive selection of half-bottles in the cellar, you'll find a tasty '93 Chinon from Couly-Dutheuil. C 250. M 135.

 Paul Minchelli

54, bd Latour-Maubourg
01 47 05 89 86, fax 01 45 56 03 84
Closed Sun, Mon, hols, Aug, 1 wk at Christmas-New Year's. Open until 10:30pm. Air cond. Priv rm: 10.
Remember Paul Minchelli? He's the man who "reinvented seafood," stripping away meretricious sauces to reveal pure, virginal flavors. He shipped out of Le Duc, the restaurant he ran with his late brother, and fetched up here, in Art Deco-style premises featuring Norwegian birch, frosted glass, and a huge black bar with a few stools for casual dining. Minchelli's minimalism requires fish of optimal quality. He chooses sea bass that is delectable even in its raw state, just sliced and drizzled with olive oil, or briefly steamed to reveal its briny essence. Depending on what the tide brings in, he might offer lobster (for example) in several different guises. In one winning version, the crustacean is flavored with a touch of honey and chili. Each dish is prepared to order, so service can be painfully slow. C 500.

12/20 **L'Œillade**

10, rue Saint-Simon - 01 42 22 01 60
Closed Sat lunch, Sun, last 2 wks of Aug. Open until 11pm. Air cond. Pkg.
The single-price menus looks reasonable enough, and the eggplant caviar, duck ballottine, and berry gratin with Champagne sabayon are perfectly decent, but beware of the expensive wine list which could send your bill right through the roof! C 220. M 158.

 Le Petit Laurent

38, rue de Varenne
01 45 48 79 64, fax 01 42 66 68 59
Closed Sat lunch, Sun, Aug. Open until 10:15pm.
Sylvain Pommier turns out an impeccable warm scallop salad enriched with chive butter, terrine of sweetbreads and mushrooms dressed with herbed oil, sea bream roasted with mango and lime, guinea hen intriguingly perfumed with lemongrass, and a luscious apple and chocolate confection laced with Banyuls wine. Diligent service in a comfortable, Louis XVI-style setting. And the 185 F menu is one of the better deals on the Left Bank. C 300-400. M 185, 250.

 Le Récamier

4, rue Récamier - 01 45 48 86 58, fax 01 42 22 84 76
Closed Sun. Open until 10:30pm. Terrace dining. Air cond. Priv rm: 12.
Martin Cantegrit, owner of this elegant establishment, oversees the service of Burgundian classics (jambon persillé, prime rib bourgui-

gnon, pike mousse with sauce Nantua) and a few lighter options (John Dory with an herbal emulsion). The clientele—politicians, publishers, media moguls—visibly enjoy tapping the magnificent 100,000-bottle cellar. In summer the terrace spills across a pedestrian zone for fume-free outdoor dining. Expect a hefty tab. C 400. M 230 (lunch Sat, coffee incl).

12/20 **Chez Ribe**

15, av. de Suffren - 01 45 66 53 79
Closed Sat lunch, Sun, Aug, Christmas-New Year's. Open until 10:30pm. Terrace dining. Pkg.
Granted, a 168 F prix-fixe meal is not—yet—hard to find, even in Paris, but this frequently changing menu is reliably delicious and well prepared. Possibilities include eggplant gâteau with tomato coulis, rack of lamb with mild garlic, and tiramisù, all graciously served in Belle Époque surroundings. C 220. M 118, 168.

 Tan Dinh

60, rue de Verneuil
01 45 44 04 84, fax 01 45 44 36 93
Closed Sun, Aug. Open until 11pm. Priv rm: 30. No cards.
Tan Dinh's huge wine list has few equals, even among the city's top restaurants—some say it outclasses the food. But the Vifians are justly proud of their innovative Vietnamese menu, which spotlights light, refined dishes like smoked-goose dumplings, lobster toast, chicken with Asian herbs, and veal with betel nuts. If you resist the cellar's pricier temptations, a dinner here amid the stylish Left-Bank crowd needn't lead to financial disaster. C 350.

Le Télégraphe

41, rue de Lille - 01 40 15 06 65, fax 01 42 60 36 03
Open daily until 12:30am. Terrace dining. No cards.
A furiously fashionable restaurant, Le Télégraphe is more society scene than gastronomic mecca. The Art Nouveau setting is lovely indeed, the waiters' attire is ever so chic...and the food? The current chef acquits himself pretty well, but by the time you read this a new face may be at the stoves—the kitchen seems to be equipped with a revolving door! C 280-400. M 125 (lunch), 195.

11/20 **Thoumieux**

79, rue Saint-Dominique - 01 47 05 49 75
Open daily until midnight. Air cond. Priv rm: 25-120.
Regional favorites from the rugged Corrèze region are Thoumieux's stock in trade: chestnut-studded boudin, milk-fed veal, and the rustic fruit flan known as flognarde. Lively atmosphere. C 230. M 72, 150 (wine incl).

> *The C(A la carte) restaurant prices given are for a complete three-course meal for one, including a half-bottle of modest wine and service. M (Menu) prices are for a complete fixed-price meal for one, excluding wine (unless otherwise noted).*

Vin sur Vin

20, rue de Montteessuy - 01 47 05 14 20
Closed Sun, lunch Sat & Mon, Aug 1-20, Dec 23-Jan 2. Open until 10pm. Air cond.
Former sommelier Patrice Vidal has assembled a first-rate cellar made up exclusively of growers' wines, from which he selects a few each week to sell by the glass. They accompany such sturdy bistro standbys as sardine gâteau, salmon trout with Banyuls-wine butter, and apple clafoutis with caramelized cider sauce. Prices are high, however, with no prix-fixe relief in sight. **C** 300-350.

8TH ARRONDISSEMENT

12/20 Al Ajami

58, rue François-Ier
01 42 25 38 44, fax 01 42 56 60 08
Open daily until midnight. Priv rm: 25. Air cond.
Fortunately the menu's perfunctory French offerings are outnumbered by authentic dishes from the Lebanese highlands—assorted mezes, chawarma, keftedes, and sticky pastries. The wines lend a dash of local color to the refined, yellow-and-blue dining room. **C** 180-200. **M** 79 (weekday lunch exc Sun), 99-140.

12/20 L'Alsace

3, av. des Champs-Élysées
01 53 93 97 00, fax 01 53 93 97 09
Open daily 24 hours. Priv rm: 80. Terrace dining. Air cond.
Since this lively brasserie never closes, any time's a good time for perfect oysters, delicious sauerkraut, and fresh Alsatian wines. Expect a hospitable welcome, whatever the hour. **C** 200-400. **M** 123 (weekday dinner, wine incl), 178.

 Les Ambassadeurs

Hôtel de Crillon,
10, pl. de la Concorde
01 44 71 16 16, fax 01 44 71 15 02
Open daily until 10:30pm. Priv rm: 140. Terrace dining. Air cond. No pets. Valet pkg.
The magnificent and intimidating dining room, rich with gilt and marble, seems more fitting for an ambassadors' banquet than a convivial feast. Diners keep their voices low and their elbows off the table. Happily, Christian Constant's vivid cuisine goes far to warm up the formal setting. His millefeuille of tongue and foie gras, curry-marinated tuna, and aromatic braise of baby hog jowls share an earthy directness that excites the appetite. The excellent wine list can make an already stiff bill harder to swallow, but the sommelier can usually recommend some more affordable selections. **C** 850. **M** 340 (weekday lunch), 610 (exc weekday lunch).

11/20 Aux Amis du Beaujolais

28, rue d'Artois - 01 45 63 92 21
Closed Sat dinner (& lunch Easter-Oct), Sun, hols. Open until 9pm. Air cond. Pkg.
Vigorous French bistro cooking (the menu changes daily) and tasty Beaujolais. Full plates, friendly prices. **C** 150-200.

 Androuet

41, rue d'Amsterdam
01 48 74 26 90, fax 01 49 95 02 54
Closed Sun. Open until 10:30pm. Priv rm: 20. Air cond. Valet pkg.
Androuet, long noted as a purveyor of first-class *fromages* (they may be purchased in the shop downstairs from the restaurant), regales tyrophiles with all manner of cheese-based dishes. Try the ravioli stuffed with fresh chèvre, or pikeperch and sauerkraut with a pungent Munster sauce, or a sampler that supplies several varieties served with appropriate breads. **C** 350. **M** 96 (lunch), 230, 250.

12/20 L'Appart'

9, rue du Colisée - 01 53 75 16 34, fax 01 53 76 15 39
Open daily until midnight. Air cond.
Decked out to look like a private home—living room, dining room, library—L'Appart' is not just an amusing scene, it's also a pretty good restaurant. You'll enjoy the cheese ravioli, pan-roasted cod with meat juices, and French toast with caramel sauce. Brunch is served on Sundays. **C** 190-245. **M** 175 (wine incl) 110, 160, 85 (children).

Astor Madeleine

11, rue Astorg - 01 53 05 05 20, fax 01 53 05 05 30
Closed Sat, Sun. Open until 10pm. No pets. Priv rm: 20. Air cond. Valet pkg.
The restaurant of the freshly rehabbed Astor Madeleine hotel is under the supervision of Joël Robuchon. He's put one of his star pupils, Éric Lecerf (a two-toque winner in his previous post), in charge of the kitchen, and we're expecting great things. We'll let you know how he's doing as soon as we've had the chance to sample his wares—watch this space! **C** 400-500. **M** 290 (lunch, wine & coffee incl).

 L'Avenue

41, av. Montaigne - 01 40 70 14 91, fax 01 49 52 13 00
Open daily until midnight. Priv rm: 180. Air cond.
If you book a table in the elegant upstairs dining room, you can mingle with the chic couture and media crowd that flocks into L'Avenue for such stylish specialties as risotto d'escargots au pistou, spiced scampi fricassée, and lemony veal piccata. Shellfish assortments and a good club sandwich are also on hand. Worthy cellar. Considering the classy location in the heart of the Golden Triangle, prices are downright reasonable. **C** 260-460. **M** 175 (weekday dinner).

11/20 Barfly

49-51, av. George V - 01 53 67 84 60
Closed Sat lunch. Open until 1am. Air cond. Terrace dining.
Here's a stylish eatery on the Champs, with a menu that offers sushi, pasta dishes, burgers, spiced chicken breast, and other trendy edibles.

A DJ is on hand in the evening to liven things up. Reasonable prices, but the welcome is not exactly warm. C 150-200.

 ## Le Bistrot du Sommelier

97, bd Haussmann - 01 42 65 24 85, fax 01 53 75 23 23
Closed Sat, Sun, Dec 25, Jan 1. Open until 11pm. Air cond. Priv rm: 24.
Crowned "World's Best Sommelier" in 1992, Philippe Faure-Brac naturally encourages his new chef to cook with wine. Thus, the menu features chicken au vin du Jura and rabbit with tiny onions in Chablis. But it's the cellar that captures the wine buff's interest, with bottles from all over France—and the world. A special prix-fixe dinner brings six courses paired with compatible wines. C 300. M 390 (dinner, wine incl).

12/20 Le Bœuf sur le Toit

34, rue du Colisée
01 43 59 83 80, fax 01 45 63 45 40
Open daily until 2am. Air cond. Priv rm: 24. Valet pkg.
From a seat on the mezzanine watch the dazzling swirl of diners and waiters reflected a hundredfold in this mirrored, Art Deco dining room. But don't get so distracted that you can't enjoy the plentiful shellfish platters, juicy steaks, or choucroutes de poissons. C 150-230. M 123 (lunch, wine incl), 169 (dinner, wine incl), 128 (dinner, after 10pm, wine incl).

12/20 Boucoléon

10, rue de Constantinople - 01 42 93 73 33
Closed Sat lunch, Sun, 3 wks in Aug, Christmas-New Year's. Open until 10:30pm. Terrace dining. No pets.
An address where value goes hand-in-hand with lively, inventive cooking. Here in a quiet district near Place de l'Europe you'll dine happily on ravigote de joue de bœuf (ox jowls in a tangy sauce), lamb sauté showered with juniper-spiced breadcrumbs, and crème brûlée brightened with mango and passion fruit. C 180-250. M 90 (weekdays), 150 (weekdays & Sat dinner).

Le Bristol

Hôtel Le Bristol, 112, rue du Fg-St-Honoré
01 53 43 43 00, fax 01 53 43 43 01
Open daily until 10:30pm. Air cond. No pets. Priv rm: 60. Terrace dining. Valet pkg.
Think that hotel dining rooms are boring? The Bristol is out to prove the opposite. The management has put its efforts where its mouth is, by hiring culinary troubadour Michel del Burgo, fresh from Carcassonne, to cook up a lyrical new menu. It features cream-glazed langoustines with caviar flanked by a chive-showered blend of crushed cauliflower and fresh sheep cheese, and rabbit served three ways (the saddle stuffed with chard and herbs, the roasted rack, and the shoulder braised with black olives). Trained by megachef Alain Ducasse, del Burgo earned three toques and 17/20 at La Barbacane, his previous

post. We have little doubt that he will soon vault to the same exalted level here at the Bristol. C 710. M 350-630.

12/20 Café Terminus

Hôtel Concorde Saint-Lazare, 108, rue St-Lazare
01 40 08 43 30, fax 01 42 93 01 20
Open daily until 10:30pm. Priv rm: 250. Air cond. Valet pkg.
A bar/bistro/restaurant in the huge and luxurious Concorde Saint-Lazare hotel. The 198 F menu includes a glass of Champagne and a half-bottle of wine, along with pistachio-studded duck terrine, salmon gratinéed with walnuts, and saffron-spiced banana crumble. Effective, very attentive service. C 300. M 148, 198 (wine incl).

 ## Cap Vernet

82, av. Marceau - 01 47 20 20 40, fax 01 47 20 95 36
Open daily until midnight. Priv rm: 140. Terrace dining.
A kitchen crew trained by Guy Savoy runs this show, producing a fresh, flavorful menu that features a zingy dish of sole with lemon and capers, and rack of lamb en petite marmite escorted by Noirmoutier potatoes and tender carrots. Don't overlook the oyster and raw shellfish bar. C 220-240.

 ## Le Carpaccio

Hôtel Royal Monceau, 35-39, av. Hoche
01 42 99 98 90, fax 01 42 99 89 94
Closed Aug. Open until 10:30pm. No pets. Valet pkg.
Executives in expensive suits are the backbone of Le Carpaccio's sleek clientele. Here, in a spectacular winter-garden setting, they feed on warm octopus salad brightened with preserved lemon, veal garnished with either porcini mushrooms or white truffles, shellfish and assorted fresh vegetables encased in sheer tempura batter, dusky cuttlefish tagliatelle topped with spears of crisp asparagus, and an improbably good raspberry-vinegar gelato. Outrageously priced, these fine dishes (and excellent wines) are served by a rather haughty staff. C 450-550.

 ## Cercle Ledoyen

Carré des Champs-Élysées
01 53 05 10 01, fax 01 47 42 55 01
Closed Sun. Open until 11:30pm. Air cond. No pets. Terrace dining. Valet pkg.
Jacques Grange is the man behind the elegantly spare interior of this spacious restaurant, a favorite haunt of the city's chic and famous. Jean-Paul Arabian oversees the impeccable service, while Ghislaine Arabian does the same for the menu, which changes practically every day. Zesty starters like a gently poached egg in a sea-urchin shell or finnan-haddie terrine with lentils segue into rabbit en pot-au-feu, sea bass with celery root, or old-fashioned blanquette de veau. Irrigated by modest but tasty little wines, they add up to perfectly modern meals at a perfectly moderate price. C 250-300.

Chiberta

3, rue Arsène Houssaye
01 45 63 77 90, fax 01 45 62 85 08
*Closed Sat, Sun, Aug. Open until 11pm. Priv rm:
45. Air cond. Pkg.*
Louis-Noël Richard, the soul of this elegant
restaurant, recently passed away. But as he himself would have been the first to say, "The show
must go on." Éric Coisel, late of the Hôtel de la
Mirande in Avignon, has been chosen to take
over Chiberta's kitchens. He arrived too close to
press time for us to rate his efforts, but as soon
as we do, we'll be back with our report. We're
betting that Chiberta's two toques will come
back. C 450. M 290.

 Le Clovis

Hôtel Sofitel Arc de Triomphe, 4, av. Bertie-Albrecht
01 53 89 50 53, fax 01 53 89 50 51
*Closed Sat, Sun, hols, Aug, Dec 23-Jan 2. Open until
10:30pm. Air cond. Priv rm: 70. Valet pkg.*
The understated setting of Le Clovis is conducive to doing business, a fact that has not
escaped the city's executives. The kitchen
produces well-wrought dishes with an occasional bold touch: we're thinking of a salad
that combines tiny artichokes and firm pears
with bits of chorizo sausage. Or even better, the
rosemary-roasted kid with braised fennel. Delicate desserts (try the iced verbena délice). Extensive cellar; attentive service. C 380. M 195
(dinner), 235, 320.

 Le Copenhague

142, av. des Champs-Élysées
01 44 13 86 26, fax 01 42 25 83 10
*Closed Sun, hols, 1st wk of Jan, Aug. Open until
10:30pm. No pets. Priv rm: 80. Air cond. Terrace
dining.*
This Danish enclave is perhaps the last high-
class restaurant on the Champs-Élysées, the last
to survive the onslaught of hamburger chains,
pizzerias, and other fast-food eateries. In the
muted atmosphere of the upstairs dining room,
salmon is featured in myriad guises, of course,
but there is also smoked eel paired with creamy
scrambled eggs, duck à la danoise, and spiced
reindeer fillet. And there's plenty of Danish
aquavit to wash it all down. Elegant but impersonal service. C 400. M 250 (weekdays, wine
incl), 550 (2 per), 80 (children).

 La Couronne

Hôtel Warwick, 5, rue de Berri
01 45 63 78 49, fax 01 45 59 00 98
*Closed Sat lunch, Sun, Aug. Open until
10:30pm. Priv rm: 6. Air cond. Valet pkg.*
Posh and conservative: that about sums up
both the food and the setting of this well-
regarded hotel restaurant. No flaws to be found
in the warm salad of lotte and foie gras dressed
with Sherry vinegar, rosemary-scented red mullet fillets, or lamb pot-au-feu spiced with star
anise (though from the latter we expected more
layers of flavor). Courteous reception; stylish
service. C 450-510. M 250, 270.

11/20 Drugstore des Champs-Élysées

133, av. des Champs-Élysées - 01 44 43 79 00
*Open daily until 2am. Terrace dining. Air cond. No
pets.*
Believe it or not, the food at this landmark of
1960s chic is not bad at all. The main-course
salads, grills, and crisp pommes frites go very
well with the noisy, bustling atmosphere. C 150-
300. M 59, 85 (weekday, wine incl), 38 (children).

Chez Edgard

4, rue Marbeuf - 01 47 20 51 15, fax 01 47 23 94 29
*Closed Sun. Open until 11:30am. Priv rm: 35. Valet
pkg.*
Just because the *gratin* of French politics eats
here, don't expect to see Jacques Chirac or Alain
Juppé seated across from you. "Monsieur Paul"
serves up to 500 meals here each day, and in any
case the Parisian powers-that-be are always
whisked off to the quiet private rooms upstairs.
Downstairs, amid the typically Gallic brouhaha,
the rest of us can choose from a wide range of
good grilled meats and hearty cuisine bourgeoise, prepared with care and skill. C 220-350.
M 195, 250-355 (wine incl).

 Les Élysées du Vernet

Hôtel Vernet, 25, rue Vernet
01 44 31 98 98, fax 01 44 31 85 69
*Closed Sat, Sun, hols, Jul 28-Aug 22, Dec 22-26.
Open until 10pm. Priv rm: 16. Air cond. No pets.
Valet pkg.*
Which way to the Riviera, please? We'd suggest this elegant address just off the Champs-
Élysées. Although you won't have a view of the
Mediterranean, chef Alain Solivérès brings the
perfumes and savors of Provence into the
Vernet's glass-roofed dining room. His salt cod
with roasted tomatoes, mesclun, and anchoïade
beneath a paper-thin chickpea galette is an elo-
quent dialogue of Southern flavors. Lately the
menu has also made incursions into the Southwest, paying homage to that region's fabulous
duck, Chalosse beef, and Pyrenees lamb. Desserts? They're exciting indeed: consider the
lemon-bergamot soufflé flanked by quince marmalade, ewe's-milk ice cream, and Szechuan
pepper—a clever and delicious conceit. Competent, attentive service; exemplary cellar. C 550-
650. M 340 (lunch), 390 & 530 (dinner).

 L'Étage Baumann

"Baumann Marbeuf," 15, rue Marbeuf
01 47 20 11 11, fax 01 47 23 69 65
*Closed Sat lunch, wk of Aug 15. Open until mid-
night. Priv rm: 30. Air cond.*
The name is new and so is the refurbished
décor, but the menu still features glossy fresh
shellfish, colossal choucroutes (topped with fish,
or ham shanks, or confit de canard...), and expertly aged meats. We like the chocolate cake,
too, and the thirst-quenching Alsatian wines. C
180-200. M 128, 170 (wine incl), 55 (children).

Fakhr el Dine

3, rue Quentin-Bauchart
01 47 23 44 42, fax 01 47 27 11 39
Open daily until 12:30am. Air cond. No pets. Valet pkg.
Delicious Lebanese mezes dazzle the eye as they delight the palate: bone-marrow salad, brains in lemon sauce, spinach fritters, fried lamb's sweetbreads, etc. These tidbits are offered in batches of 8, 10, 15, or 20, depending on the size of the company and your appetite. C 250. M 120 (lunch), 150-300, 85 (children).

12/20 **Finzi**

182, bd Haussmann - 01 45 62 88 68
Closed Sun lunch. Open until 11:30pm.
The white-collar crowd that spills out of neighboring offices gladly risks spotting their ties with Finzi's good pasta sauces. Look for lusty Italian hams and salamis, too, and apricot ravioli with custard sauce for dessert. C 230.

 Flora Danica

142, av. des Champs-Élysées
01 44 13 86 26, fax 01 42 25 83 10
Closed May 1, Dec 24 dinner. Open until 11pm. Terrace dining. Air cond.
Salmon—smoked, pickled, marinated, or grilled—and delicious tender herring prepared in every imaginable way are the stars of this limited menu. Upstairs, more elaborate (and costly) dishes are served (there's an interesting terrine of foie gras and reindeer). If the weather is fine, ask to be seated on the patio behind the Flora Danica. C 300. M 150 (lunch, exc Sat, beer incl), 525 (2 per), 80 (children).

11/20 **Fouquet's**

99, av. des Champs-Élysées
01 47 23 70 60, fax 01 47 20 08 69
Open daily until 1am. Priv rm: 200. Terrace dining. Valet pkg.
After a bout of bad publicity, Fouquet's is poised for a fresh departure. This listed landmark on the Champs-Élysées has acquired the services of Gérard Salé from the Plaza, and Bernard Leprince of La Tour d'Argent. Snapers en escabèche, and osso buco à l'orange bring back good memories. Impeccable service, something that has disappeared on the the Champs. Here's wishing them luck... C 350-500. M 265.

Pierre Gagnaire

Hôtel Balzac, 6, rue Balzac
01 44 35 18 25, fax 01 44 35 18 37
Closed Sat, Sun dinner. Open until 10:30pm. Air cond.
After the demise of his fabulous restaurant in Saint-Étienne, where he earned the highest awards from GaultMillau, talented Pierre Gagnaire has resurfaced on the Champs-Élysées. The former premises of Bice, in the hotel Balzac, have been redesigned in sober blue and gray tones. Like an artist, Gagnaire improvises original conjunctions of flavors and textures, and often takes risks to reach new heights. He is also

a perfectionist, and like a painter, adds subtle touches until the last minute before sending his dishes to your table. Try his incredeable cigale de mer in a cider sabayon with crushed walnuts, his light roasted turbot in gray shallot juice, his delicate soupe soufflée with honey and mirabelle marmelade, or exciting grapefruit aspic with a crunchy cumin caramel. At the bar, for lunch, no reservation is required for the *plat du jour* option for at 130-180 F. C 700. M 450 (lunch), 480 (dinner).

 Le Grenadin

44-46, rue de Naples
01 45 63 28 92, fax 01 45 61 24 76
Closed Sat lunch, Sun, 1 wk in Jul, 1 wk in Aug. Open until 10:30pm. Priv rm: 14. Terrace dining. Air cond.
Pungent herbs and bold harmonies are the hallmarks of Patrick Cirotte's repertoire. His affinity for keen, acidulous flavors shows up in the delicious oysters with alfalfa sprouts and lemony cream sauce, and in a pork tenderloin served with quince compote. But he can also strike a suave note, as in the saddle of rabbit cloaked in a mild, creamy garlic sauce. Desserts don't get short shrift either: the ethereal vanilla millefeuille-minute, wine granita, or spiced fruit croûte tempt even flagging appetites. Mireille Cirotte offers reliable advice on wine (note that Sancerres are the pride of her cellar). C 400-450. M 200-330.

 Hédiard

21, pl. de la Madeleine
01 43 12 88 99, fax 01 43 12 88 98
Closed Sun. Open until 10:30pm. Priv rm: 12. Air cond. Valet pkg.
Upstairs over their celebrated fine-foods emporium, Hédiard has inaugurated a French colonial-style restaurant where modern dishes (game aspic, herb salad with Parmesan and porcini) vie with bistro cooking (vegetable soup, steak au poivre) for your attention. All starters are priced at 65 F, meats at 120 F. Noble cellar; amateur service. C 260-400.

 Le Jardin des Cygnes

Hôtel Prince de Galles, 33, av. George-V
01 47 23 55 11, fax 01 47 20 61 05
Open daily until 11pm. Garden dining. Air cond. No pets. Valet pkg.
A jewelbox of a dining room that opens onto a charming patio is an alluring stage for Dominique Cécillon's sun-struck cuisine. All the items on the menu—house foie gras au torchon, pigeon pastilla, red mullet with Provençal vegetables—are very nearly as delicious as they are expensive, and are delivered to your table by a high-class staff. If economy is your aim, head over instead to the hotel's Regency Bar, for a good, light little meal. C 350-600. M 290 (wine incl).

Looking for a celebrated chef? Refer to the **index.**

Le Jardin
du Royal Monceau

Hôtel Royal Monceau, 35, av. Hoche
01 42 99 98 70, fax 01 42 99 89 94
Closed Sat, Sun. Open until 10:30pm. Priv rm: 500. Garden dining. Air cond. No pets. Valet pkg.
You step into another world when you enter the candy-pink dining room, its french windows opening onto manicured lawns and flower beds: a garden that seems to have been brought to Paris by the wave of a magic wand. The same spell holds in the kitchen, where Bruno Cirino conjures up a modern, exquisitely delicate menu with a gracious Provençal lilt. Why not order his spider crab in pistou broth—a marvel of subtlety; follow it with sautéed sole escorted by a superb chard gratin, then indulge in the richness of a banana roasted in its skin, laced with amber rum, and flanked by lush Malaga raisin ice cream. Service is impeccable, and a youthful sommelier provides sound advice on a wine list studded with rarities. C 550-700. M 280, 340 (weekday lunch), 430 (weekday dinner).

 ### Lasserre

17, av. Franklin-Roosevelt
01 43 59 53 43, fax 01 45 63 72 23
Closed Sun, Mon lunch, Aug. Open until 10:30pm. No pets. Valet pkg.
One of the few surviving examples of *le grand restaurant à la française*, Lasserre merits our attention for the ethnological interest it presents. Nowhere else is the service so minutely choreographed, the atmosphere so well-bred (piano music, soft lights, glowing silver...). After a disapointing era, Lasserre has retrieved its standards of quality and food—on the classic side—has greatly improved. Don't forget to look up as Lasserre's retractable roof brings you (weather and visibility permitting) the stars. C 700-1,000.

 ### Laurent

41, av. Gabriel
01 42 25 00 39, fax 01 45 62 45 21
Closed Sat lunch, Sun, hols. Open until 11pm. Priv rm: 70. Terrace dining. No pets. Valet pkg.
The economic climate must be warming up! At Laurent this welcome change in the weather has brought smiles back to the waiters' faces, and the *carte*, too, reflects the sunnier trend, with lighter dishes and sprightlier sauces. Philippe Braun executes a menu designed by his mentor, Joël Robuchon, which includes fresh anchovies on a bed of fresh-tasting vegetable brunoise, duck liver set atop black beans fired up with hot chilis, and a superb veal chop set off by tender hearts of lettuce in a savory jus. Now, you may have to sell off a few T-bones to pay the bill—or else you can do as many of the other high-powered patrons do, and order the excellent prix-fixe menu. Whatever course you choose, sommelier Patrick Lair will advise you on the appropriate wine. C 800-1,000. M 390.

 ### Ledoyen

Carré des Champs-Élysées
01 53 05 10 01, fax 01 47 42 55 01
Closed Sat, Sun, Aug. Open until 10:30pm. Priv rm: 250. Air cond. No pets. Valet pkg.
Lille's Ghislaine Arabian has made her mark at the luxurious and oh-so-Parisian Ledoyen. After teaching locals to love Flemish flavors—sauces laced with beer and gin, smoked mussels, gingerbread, and pungent Northern cheeses—she is working wonders outside of her regional register. Thus, while signature dishes like Zeeland oysters with smoked ham and buttermilk, smoked sprats on a potato galette, turbot roasted in beer, or potjevleish (a meaty Flemish terrine) with rhubarb chutney hold their own on the menu, she balances them with, for example, lightly salt-cured salmon poached in milk and served with sorrel hollandaise or roasted sweetbreads marinated with smoked garlic and flanked by melting endives. Such marvels have their price, of course, but we say they're worth it! C 550-850. M 290 (lunch), 520 & 590 (dinner).

11/20 Lloyd's Bar

23, rue Treilhard - 01 45 63 21 23, fax 01 45 63 36 83
Closed Sat, Sun lunch, Dec 24-Jan 2. Open until 10:30pm. Terrace dining.
Lloyd's is a little bit of London in Paris. The clubby dining room, with its dark paneling adorned by horse and hunting prints, is the scene of decent if not exciting meals. Be sure to give our regards to Daniel, a veteran waiter with a rather unpredictable character! C 320. M 185 (dinner).

 ### Lucas Carton

9, pl. de la Madeleine
01 42 65 22 90, fax 01 42 65 06 23
Closed Sat lunch, Aug 2-24. Open until 10:30pm. Priv rm: 14. Air cond. No pets. Valet pkg.
In a magnificent Belle Époque dining room warmed by mellow woodwork, Alain Senderens and his chef, Bernard Gueneron, propose a clever blend of Senderens's most celebrated creations—canard Apicius, foie gras de canard steamed in a cabbage leaf, red-mullet fillets with olives, lemon, and capers—and a (very) few recent inventions. Outstanding among the latter are the pan-roast of frogs' legs and asparagus paired with hot gingered crab and cooling hollandaise sauce; sea bream with thyme-scented potatoes and cuttlefish ravioli; and crisp-crusted veal sweetbreads with crayfish and popcorn. Every recipe is intelligently composed and the execution is invariably faultless. Inspired desserts; legendary cellar. C 1,000. M 395 (weekday lunch).

 ### La Luna

69, rue du Rocher - 01 42 93 77 61, fax 01 40 08 02 44
Closed Sun. Open until 11pm. Air cond.
The tides deposit first-quality fish at La Luna's door, and the kitchen's modern approach to seafood (brief cooking times, light sauces) enhances its natural flavors. The menu changes from day to day, but you could start out with an

ultrafresh carpaccio of sea bream and red mullet, then go on to pan-roasted baby lotte sparked with lemon, or skate with a lively sauce gribiche. Summary wine list, though the choices are good. C 350.

 ## Maison Blanche

15, av. Montaigne
01 47 23 55 99, fax 01 47 20 09 56
Closed Sat lunch, Sun, Aug. Open until 11pm. Priv rm: 50. Air cond. Terrace dining. Valet pkg.
Here atop the Théâtre des Champs-Élysées, diners look out on the glittering dome of the Invalides, the shimmering Seine, and the handsome buildings that line the quais. In contrast, the dining room sports a spare, vaguely Californian look. The service, though chilly, is efficient and the cellar ranges wide. So far so good, you say, but how about the food? It's very good indeed: José Martinez's talent shines brightest in dishes that blend simplicity and sophistication: sweet peppers stuffed with lamb's trotters, for example, or duck pie with a snappy herb salad. C 400.

 ## La Maison Porte Bonheur

12, av. de Wagram - 01 42 27 69 82, fax 01 44 09 90 70
Open daily until 11:30pm. Air cond.
A blessed change from the surrounding fast-food outlets, this "Lucky House" offers delicate steamed dumplings, fragrant Thai soups and salads, seafood and vegetables grilled on a hot stone, and warming stews served in individual pots. C 200-250. M 65, 85.

 ## Le Marcande 🌜

52, rue de Miromesnil
01 42 65 19 14, fax 01 40 76 03 27
Closed Sat, Sun, Aug. Open until 10pm. Terrace dining.
The well-spaced tables in an elegant setting punctuated by paintings are not always crowded. Still, Le Marcande's team is betting on its good 240 F menu and revamped *carte* to attract discriminating diners. Best bets are the hot foie gras on rösti potatoes with onion compote, grilled duck au jus accompanied by wonderful country-style fries, and a high and handsome Saint-Honoré pastry. C 275. M 240.

 ## La Marée

1, rue Daru - 01 43 80 20 00, fax 01 48 88 04 04
Closed Sat, Sun, Jul 26-Aug 27. Open until 10:30pm. Priv rm: 32. Air cond. Valet pkg.
Seafood naturally rates top billing at La Marée, a restaurant named for the tide. Cast your eye down the long menu for the langoustines encased in an ideally crisp batter coating, or grilled pikeperch poised on a bed of roasted vegetable julienne. To partner the cellar's fabulous Bordeaux, you'll also find a first-rate tenderloin of Charollais beef, roast pigeon, and veal kidney. Precise, classic cooking for a conservative, well-heeled clientele. C 600.

 ## Marius et Janette

4, av. George V
01 47 23 41 88, fax 01 47 23 07 19
Open daily until 11:30pm. Priv rm: 10. Terrace dining. Air cond. Valet pkg.
Not even a fire could destroy the unsinkable Marius et Jeannette, now shipshape again and back afloat with a seaworthy décor of glowing wood and polished brass. A cosmopolitan crowd watches approvingly as waiters flambé fennel-flavored sea bass (270 F per person) and deliver pricey portions of grilled lobster (480 F). Still, ingredients are of pristine quality (note the exquisitely fresh seafood salad), and not every item is stratospherically priced. To drink, try a wine from Bandol or Cassis. C 450. M 300, 120 (children).

 ## Maxim's

3, rue Royale - 01 42 65 27 94, fax 01 40 17 02 91
Closed Sun (off-seas), Sun & Mon (Jul-Aug). Open until 10:30pm. Priv rm: 80. Air cond. Valet pkg.
Pierre Cardin, owner of Maxim's since 1981, decided that he'd served his last plateful of homard à l'américaine and other such culinary chestnuts. He hired Michel Kerever, a respected Breton chef, to rejuvenate what had become a rather fusty menu. The dining room, thank goodness, is as glorious as ever: Czar Nicholas, the Duke and Duchess of Windsor, Maria Callas and the other legendary denizens of Maxim's in its heyday would surely feel right at home. Kerever's light, exciting menu features rabbit roasted with rosemary and Noirmoutier potatoes, a pan roast of fresh morels and asparagus, and sole on a bed of artichokes, onions, and leeks. Expect to pay a hefty sum, however, to sup in these historic surroundings. Even the cellar's more modest wines are awfully expensive. C 600-1,000.

10/20 Mollard

113, rue Saint-Lazare
01 43 87 50 22, fax 01 43 87 84 17
Open daily until 1am. Priv rm: 130. Air cond. Pkg. No cards.
For its 100th birthday, Mollard finally got the present it needed so badly: a new chef! Joël Renty (trained by Robuchon) is surely more deserving than were his recent predecessors of Mollard's extraordinary Belle Époque décor. Here's hoping that he can bring the menu up to scratch. In the meantime, we can recommend the well-chosen oysters and foie gras and the deliciously flinty '94 Sancerre. Still, the waiters often treat customers with veiled hostility—for heaven's sake, why? C 220. M 130, 192 (wine incl), 65 (children).

 ## L'Obélisque

4, rue Boissy-d'Anglas
01 44 71 15 15, fax 01 44 71 15 02
Closed hols, Aug. Open until 10:30pm. Priv rm: 140. Air cond. Valet pkg.
To eat at the Hôtel de Crillon without breaking the bank, try its other, less formal restaurant.

You'll still benefit from top-notch service and a menu supervised by Christian Constant, chef of Les Ambassadeurs (see above). The food is classic bistro fare: pork sausage with whipped potatoes, pot-au-feu, calf's head sauce gribiche. Sixteen wines are offered by the glass or half-liter jug. C 300-400. M 270 (wine incl).

 Au Petit Montmorency

26, rue Jean-Mermoz or 5, rue Rabelais
01 42 25 11 19
Closed Sat, Sun, Aug. Open until 10pm. Priv rm: 12. Air cond. No pets.
Here is cuisine that flatters one's cravings for rich, generous food. Daniel Bouché coaxes voluptuous flavors out of his superb ingredients; in fall and winter, when the season for truffles, game, and wild mushrooms rolls around Bouché is in his glory, offering grilled cèpes with foie gras spread on toast, warm pigeon pâté, macaroni gratin ennobled with morels and truffles, hare à la royale, or a winy civet of boar flanked by sauerkraut, pears, and chutney. The cellar's venerable vintages are ever-so-tempting, but they'll make the bill even harder to swallow. C 450-800.

12/20 Le Petit Yvan

1 bis, rue Jean Mermoz
01 42 89 49 65, fax 01 42 89 30 95
Closed Sat lunch, Sun. Open until midnight. Air cond. Priv rm: 24. Terrace dining.
Yvan's little annex pulls in a lively, friendly crew with an unbeatable all-in menu that features—for example—scrambled eggs with roasted tomatoes, steak tartare (minced by hand, not by machine) flanked by crispy french fries, and a rum-soaked savarin for dessert. Wine and coffee incur no extra charge. It's all served on bistro tables in a colorful, split-level dining room. M 138.

 Les Princes

Hôtel George V, 31, av. George V
01 47 23 54 00, fax 01 47 20 22 05
Open daily until 10:30pm. Priv rm: 250. No pets. Terrace dining. Air cond. Valet pkg.
In fine weather, book a table on the beautiful flower-covered patio, far more inviting than the cavernous 1930s–style dining room. Wherever you sit, you're sure to savor Jacky Joyeux's crayfish-stuffed artichoke bottoms or grilled sea bass served with a brochette of anise-scented vegetables. The dessert cart is uninspiring, but there's a wide-ranging cellar and several attractive wines are offered by the glass. Impeccable service. C 450-750. M 260 (lunch), 360 (dinner).

 Le Régence

Hôtel Plaza Athénée, 25, av. Montaigne
01 53 67 65 00, fax 01 53 67 66 66
Closed Feb school hols, Jul 21-Aug 10. Open daily until 10:15pm. Garden dining. Air cond. Valet pkg.
Changes have not spared the Plaza Athénée among top hotels of Paris. Young chef Éric Briffard, trained by Meneau and Robuchon, blends colors and flavors in perfect harmony. This style of cooking should work very well for the Plaza's clientele. For example: a John Dory in curry with melting eggplants cooked to perfection with an oriental twist; finish with a sweet roasted peach with pineapple and lavender syrup. Perfect service. C 550-800. M 310 (weekday lunch), 580.

12/20 Le Relais Vermeer

Golden Tulip Saint-Honoré, 218, rue du Fbg-St-Honoré - 01 49 53 03 03, fax 01 40 75 02 00
Closed Sat lunch, Sun, Aug. Open until 10pm. Priv rm: 200. Air cond. Pkg.
A luxurious restaurant for a luxurious hotel, owned by the Dutch Golden Tulip chain. Don't bother looking for an inventive dish on the menu: there aren't any. And the quality of ingredients has declined of late, judging by the crab millefeuille and the peppery sea bream with artichokes. C 220-350. M 180.

 Les Saveurs

Sofitel Champs-Élysées, 8, rue Jean-Goujon
01 43 59 52 41, fax 01 42 25 06 59
Closed Sat, Sun, Aug. Open until 10:30pm. Priv rm: 200. Terrace dining. Air cond. Valet pkg.
If you book a table here, you will able to try Didier Lanfray's fresh cooking: vegetable terrine (pressé de légumes) abetted by a truffle infusion, or the bold, full-flavored lotte with green mangos and fresh pasta. Tempting desserts, too, and attentive service. C 210-250. M 165 (wine incl).

12/20 Sébillon Élysées

66, rue Pierre-Charron
01 43 59 28 15, fax 01 43 59 30 00
Open daily until midnight. Air cond. Valet pkg.
As in the sister establishment in Neuilly (see *The Suburbs*), excellent but expensive shellfish platters are followed by Sébillon's famous leg of lamb, cooked to rosy tenderness and carved before your eyes. Elegant décor, energetic service. C 245. M 180 (wine & coffee incl).

 Shing Jung

7, rue Clapeyron - 01 45 22 21 06
Closed Sat, Sun lunch. Open until 10:30pm. No pets. Pkg. No cards.
The owner of this modest establishment will try to convince you that Koreans are more generous than their Japanese neighbors. Indeed, a colossal assortment of raw fish, listed on the menu as "medium", comprised sea bream, salmon, tuna, brill, and mackerel. For the same money most Japanese places would serve about one-quarter the quantity. Also on hand are jellyfish salad, barbecued beef strips, a hotpot of vegetables and beef, and stuffed lentil-flour crêpes. Delicious and incredibly inexpensive. C 150. M 69 (weekday lunch), 75.

 Shozan

11, rue de La Trémoille
01 47 23 37 32, fax 01 47 23 67 30
Closed Sat lunch, Sun. Open until 11pm. Air cond. Terrace dining. Valet pkg.

Show-biz celebrities and fashion honchos have given this new Japanese restaurant their stamp of approval. They settle into the discreetly handsome brown-and-beige dining room to feast on superb sashimi and lightly grilled fish, or the more complex (and most rewarding) ginger-steamed bass with leeks. Meat eaters are not neglected: the beef tenderloin in dashi broth is delectable. Shozan's owners produce sake in Japan, so there is quite a choice on hand for tasting here. C 400. M 175 (weekday lunch, wine incl).

 ## Le Stresa

7, rue Chambiges - 01 47 23 51 62
Closed Sat dinner, Sun, Aug, Dec 20-Jan 3. Open until 10:30pm. Priv rm: 12. Terrace dining. Air cond. Pkg.
Le Stresa's dining room is always full of press, fashion, and movie people (Sharon Stone was spotted here recently) who love the antipasti drizzled with fruity Tuscan olive oil, the spinach ravioli, calf's liver, and smooth tiramisù prepared by Marco Faiola. Claudio and Toni Faiola seat their guests with a sure social sense of who's up, who's in, who's out. C 450.

La Table du Marché

14, rue de Marignan
01 40 76 34 44, fax 01 40 76 34 37
Closed Sat lunch, Sun. Open until 11pm. Air cond. Valet pkg.
The Paris annex of Christophe Leroy's well-known Saint-Tropez restaurant was launched with considerable media brouhaha. Alas, it provides little in the way of warmth, charm, or good food (a grilled vegetable assortment included cold, oily eggplant; the salade de coquillages et vongoles looked more like plain potato salad...). High prices in line with the smart address, but not with the quality of what's in one's plate. C 200. M 160 (weekdays).

 ## Taillevent

15, rue Lamennais
01 44 95 15 01, fax 01 42 25 95 18
Closed Sat dinner, Sun, Aug. Open until 10:30pm. Priv rm: 32. No pets. Valet pkg.
Refined yet graceful, elegant but never stiff, the tone at Taillevent is set by Jean-Claude Vrinat, a restaurateur whose sole standard is perfection: each detail of the décor and the menu is calculated to provide utter comfort and well-being. While not boldly creative, the kitchen is far from stodgy. Simpler offerings underscore the pristine quality of the ingredients: seared Breton langoustines, for example, in a lightly creamed broth or sea bass anointed with olive oil and accompanied by slow-roasted vegetables. Still, the classic repertoire provides pleasures of its own: why turn down a chance to savor the rich, resonant flavors of a truffled game pie filled with venison, duck and pheasant? The cheese board is exceptional, and desserts invite you to splurge. Incomparable cellar; silken service. C 850.

 ## Chez Tante Louise

41, rue Boissy-d'Anglas
01 42 65 06 85, fax 01 45 65 28 19
Closed Sat, Sun, Aug. Open until 10:15pm. Priv rm: 12. Air cond.
The regulars love being pampered in this snug little spot, where a smiling staff serves Michel Lerouet's lightened versions of traditional French favorites. The single-price menu offers great value, and there is a nicely balanced cellar to boot. C 320. M 190.

 ## Tong Yen

1 bis, rue Jean Mermoz
01 42 25 04 23, fax 01 45 63 51 57
Closed Aug 1-25. Open until 12:15am. Air cond. Terrace dining.'
The quietly attractive dining room, punctuated with fresh flowers, plays host to personalities from stage and screen, who come to enjoy precisely cooked and seasoned Chinese specialties: Peking dumplings, chicken glazed with honey and vinegar, salt-and-pepper shrimp, and the like. To drink, order a cool, white Sancerre. C 300-350.

12/20 Le "30"

"Fauchon," 30, pl. de la Madeleine
01 47 42 56 58, fax 01 47 42 96 02
Closed Sun. Open until 10:30pm. Terrace dining. Air cond.
Whoever dreamed up the name (Le Trente—30—is the building's address) of Fauchon's restaurant won't win any prizes for creativity, but the decorator might, for its "Roman fantasy" interior. Mostly classic, with some bold touches of spice, Bruno Deligne's menu lists very good oysters with celery-root purée (but an otherwise tasty turbot was spoiled by indigestible beans). The stupendous pastries are crafted by Sébastien Gaudard. C 310-450. M 250 (lunch, wine & coffee incl), 250 (dinner).

 ## Chez Vong

"Aux Champs-Élysées," 27, rue du Colisée
01 43 59 77 12, fax 01 43 59 59 27
Closed Sun. Open until midnight. Priv rm: 60. Air cond. Valet pkg.
Here's everyone's dream of a Chinese restaurant: embroidered silk, furniture inlaid with mother-of-pearl, lots of little nooks, an air of mystery, and dishes named "quail in a nest of happiness" or "merry shrimps." The cooking is quite well done. Oddly enough, the cellar is rich in fine (and costly) claret. C 300.

 ## Yvan

1 bis, rue Jean-Mermoz
01 43 59 18 40, fax 01 42 89 30 95
Closed Sat lunch, Sun. Open until midnight. Air cond. Valet pkg.
Yvan Zaplatilek is café society's darling, but he is also a hard-working chef who gives his customers very good food at moderate prices in a

most elegant setting. The menu is primarily French, with an occasional Belgian touch here and there (sole waterzoï, veal kidney braised in dark beer). C 300. M 178 (weekday lunch), 168 & 298 (dinner).

9TH ARRONDISSEMENT

L'Alsaco ❋

10, rue Condorcet - 01 45 26 44 31
Closed Sat lunch, Sun, 1 wk in May, Aug. Open until 11pm. Priv rm: 45.
Beyond the unremarkable façade is an authentic Alsatian *winstub*, decked out in traditional painted wood paneling. L'Alsaco serves generous renditions of choucroute garnie, cream and onion tart, and potatoes with melted Munster cheese, which now deserve a toque. To drink, there are Rieslings galore, and a huge cache of clear fruit brandies. C 150. M 87, 170 (wine incl).

Auberge Landaise ❋

23, rue Clauzel - 01 48 78 74 40, fax 01 48 78 20 96
Closed Sun, Aug 10-20. Priv rm: 50. Pkg.
In a rustic setting conducive to a hearty tuck-in, Dominique and Éric Morin treat their customers to cassoulet, foie gras, braised duck with wild mushrooms, and good grills. Cooking times are not always spot-on, but the flavors are full and robust. Expensive little cellar; superb Armagnacs. C 280. M 130 (dinner), 180.

11/20 Le Bistrot des Deux Théâtres

18, rue Blanche - 01 45 26 41 43, fax 01 48 74 08 92
Open daily until 12:30am. Air cond.
A bistro with a British accent, in an improbable neighborhood. The menu is a pretty good deal, what with its duck liver pâté, saffron-spiced scallops, and iced nougatine with raspberry coulis. M 169 (wine incl).

Bistrot Papillon

6, rue Papillon - 01 47 70 90 03, fax 01 48 24 05 59
Closed Sat, Sun. Open until 10pm. Air cond.
The cozy ambience fits Jean-Yves Guion's soothing menu, made up of long-standing favorites and some good "market specials." Reliably fine ingredients go into his scallop terrine, herbed duck breast, and iced honey vacherin. Balanced cellar. C 210-310. M 140.

La Casa Olympe

48, rue Saint-Georges
01 42 85 26 01, fax 01 45 26 49 33
Closed Sat, Sun, Aug, 1 wk at Christmas. Open until 11pm. Air cond. No pets.
Olympe is at home in the former Casa Miguel, long the city's cheapest deal, with a philanthropically priced 5 F set meal. The current menu reflects Olympe at her best. Her fans fall eagerly onto such warming dishes as cumin-spiced calf's foot sausage, pumpkin soup dotted

with mussels, and roast shoulder of Sisteron lamb. Unpretentious wine list. The premises are small (not to say cramped) though prettily painted in warm tones of yellow and burnt sienna. C 280. M 190.

Charlot

"Roi des Coquillages," 81, bd de Clichy
(pl. de Clichy) - 01 53 20 48 00, fax 01 53 20 48 09
Open daily until 1am. Priv rm: 20. Air cond. Pkg.
A fine view of the Place de Clichy, a warm welcome, and attentive service will take your mind off the overbearing Art Deco interior. Sparkling fresh oysters, plentiful shellfish assortments, bouillabaisse à la marseillaise, and lobsters prepared every possible way are the staples here. C 350. M 169, 185.

Chez Catherine

65, rue de Provence - 01 45 26 72 88
Closed Sat, Sun, Mon dinner, Aug, 1 wk at New Year. Open until 10pm.
It's no easy feat to find a decent restaurant up here near the major department stores. But we did it! Catherine's sleek bistro provides well-wrought classics based on excellent ingredients: minted lamb terrine, salmon with lentils, spiced sea-bass fillet, and duck confit merit your close attention. Frédéric tends the cellar of astutely selected growers' wines. C 180-200.

12/20 Les Diamantaires

60, rue La Fayette - 01 47 70 78 14, fax 01 44 83 02 73
Open daily until 11:30pm. Air cond.
Greek food cooked by Kurds, served by Armenians to a mostly Jewish clientele in a Lebanese-style setting: the mixture is a whole lot more peaceable than it sounds! Delicious Byzantine mezes, meatballs, and skewered lamb, washed down by tasty Greek wines. C 140-200. M 78 (weekday lunch), 125, 150.

I Golosi

6, rue de la Grange-Batelière
01 48 24 18 63, fax 01 45 23 18 96
Closed Sat dinner, Sun, Aug. Open until midnight. Air cond. Pkg.
Enter this bistro from the Passage Verdeau to discover two levels decorated in a style we can only call "1950s Italian." You can order rabbit with wild thyme, chicken dressed with balsamic vinegar, and nettle risotto, accompanied by irresistible Italian wines assembled by a passionate oenophile. A toque this year. C 120-200.

12/20 Le Grand Café Capucines

4, bd des Capucines
01 43 12 19 00, fax 01 43 12 19 09
Open daily 24 hours. Terrace dining. Air cond.
The waiter won't pull a face if you order just one course—a shellfish assortment, salmon tartare, or a grilled pig's trotter. The extravagant décor is a replica of a Roaring Twenties *café*

boulevardier. C 280. M 123 (dinner, after 11pm, wine incl), 169, 185.

 Les Muses

Hôtel Scribe, 1, rue Scribe
01 44 71 24 26, fax 01 44 71 24 64
Closed Sat, Sun, hols, Aug. Open until 10:30pm. Priv rm: 80. Air cond. Valet pkg.
The muse of interior design was off duty the day the Hôtel Scribe's basement restaurant was decorated. And the chef's inspiration has its ups and downs too, judging from our most recent visit (overcooked pikeperch, a fine lobster fricassée served a few degrees too cool). Good cheese board, and there's an array of alluring sweets. Interesting list of growers' wines. C 300-400. M 270.

 L'Œnothèque

20, rue Saint-Lazare
01 48 78 08 76, fax 01 40 16 10 27
Closed Sat, Sun, hols, 2 wks in Aug. Open until 11pm. Priv rm: 40. Air cond.
Daniel Hallée was the sommelier at Jamin before he opened his restaurant-cum-wine shop. Grand vintages at attractive prices and interesting lesser-known growths partner such market-fresh offerings as baby leeks mimosa, smoked-haddock salad, stewed oxtail with al dente vegetables, and excellent grilled fish. Superb collection of Cognacs. C 350.

 Opéra Restaurant

"Café de la Paix," 5, pl. de l'Opéra
01 40 07 30 10, fax 01 40 07 33 86
Closed Sat, Sun, Aug. Open until 11pm. No pets. Valet pkg.
Thanks to the efforts of Christian Le Squer, the cuisine now lives up to the restaurant's opulent Second Empire setting. Suitably luxurious (and delicious) are the cream of cèpes with foie gras and duck cracklings, codfish in a green-olive cream, roast pigeon, and cinnamon-scented roasted figs. Rely on the competent sommelier for help with the wine list. C 340. M 240 (lunch), 345 (wine incl).

12/20 Au Petit Riche

25, rue Le Peletier
01 47 70 68 68, fax 01 48 24 10 79
Closed Sun. Open until 12:15am. Priv rm: 45. Air cond.
The brass trim, mirrors, and woodwork of this nostalgic bistro sparkle and gleam. The cooking is of the honest, satisfying sort: coq au vin de Chinon, calf's head sauce gribiche, sole meunière. Excellent choice of Loire Valley wines. C 250. M 160 (weekday lunch, Sat), 135-175 (weekday dinner, Sat).

 Sinago

17, rue de Maubeuge · 01 48 78 11 14
Closed Sun, Aug. Open until 10:30pm.
Wonderful Cambodian cooking is served in this vest-pocket eatery (there's only room for twenty). Savor the amazing crêpe stuffed with saffron-stained pork, fish spiced with coriander and ginger, or broth perfumed with lemongrass and enriched with plump dumplings. C 150. M 55 (lunch).

 La Table d'Anvers

2, pl. d'Anvers
01 48 78 35 21, fax 01 45 26 66 67
Closed Sat lunch, Sun. Open until 11:30pm. Priv rm: 30. Air cond.
While so many chefs fall back on a "safe," reassuring repertoire of neo-bourgeois and bistro dishes to hide their lack of inspiration, Christian Conticini invents and reinvents flavor combinations with a wizardry that is nothing short of staggering. If you're tempted by the prospect of a real gastronomic adventure, we suggest you trek up to his Table at the foot of Montmartre and prepare for a feast! Choose one of the intriguing "theme" menus (featuring novel vegetables, rare spices, or "just desserts"...), or explore an exciting *carte* that is keyed to the seasons. The options are all so enticing that we usually just close our eyes and pick at random! The astonishing desserts are crafted by Christian's brother, Philippe Conticini. C 500. M 180 (weekday lunch), 250 (weekday dinner).

11/20 La Taverne Kronenbourg

24, bd des Italiens - 01 47 70 16 64, fax 01 42 47 13 91
Open daily until 2am. Priv rm: 100. Terrace dining. Air cond.
The last of the *cafés-concerts* on the Grands Boulevards (live music nightly) serves robust, unpretentious brasserie fare: shellfish, pork knuckle with cabbage, sauerkraut, and fine Alsatian wines. C 200. M 140 (wine incl).

 Venantius

Hôtel Ambassador, 16, bd Haussmann
01 48 00 06 38, fax 01 42 46 19 84
Closed Sat, Sun, 1 wk in Feb, Aug. Open until 10:30pm. Air cond. Valet pkg.
Changes, changes, changes... Jean-Claude Troisville, from the Concorde Saint-Lazare, tries his best to fill up the large dining room which works well with local businessmen at lunch, but somewhat stale for dinner: so is the food. C 350-450. M 220 (weekday lunch), 180 & 280 (weekday dinner).

 Wally le Saharien

36, rue Rodier - 01 42 85 51 90, fax 01 42 86 08 35
Closed Sun. Open until 11:30pm. Priv rm: 60. Air cond. No pets. No cards.
Wally has pitched his tent not far from Pigalle, in a setting accented with carved screens, crimson carpets, and Tuareg-style seating. Topping the list of specialties is his Saharan couscous (no broth, no vegetables), but you can also sample mutton with caramelized skin, pigeon pastilla, and honey cake perfumed with orange-flower water. C 200-300. M 240, 150 (children).

12/20 Brasserie Flo

7, cour des Petites-Écuries
01 42 46 15 80, fax 01 42 47 00 80
Open daily until 1:30am. Air cond. Valet Pkg.
The quintessential Alsatian brasserie, Flo is a jewel: nowhere else will you find the same vivacious atmosphere, superb décor, lively patrons, and delicious sauerkraut, best washed down with carafes of frisky Riesling. C 190-250. M 119 (lunch, wine incl), 189 (dinner, exc Sun), 121 (Sun dinner, wine incl).

Le Canard Laqué Pékinois

34, bd Bonne-Nouvelle
01 47 70 31 65, fax 01 44 79 00 21
Open daily until midnight. Priv rm: 80. Air cond.
We're usually suspicious of these oversized Chinese affairs, but Le Canard Laqué is a find. Good dim-sum, salads, and sautéed shrimp to start, followed by tasty roasted items and a most honorable Peking duck. C 120. M 47 (weekday lunch, wine incl), 58-116 (wine incl).

Le Châteaubriant

23, rue Chabrol - 01 48 24 58 94, fax 01 42 47 09 75
Closed Sun, Mon, Aug. Open until 10:15pm. Air cond. No pets.
From the name you'd never guess that this little dining room tucked away near the Gare de l'Est is a noted Italian restaurant. Save for the rotating roster of daily specials, the menu is immutable. Familiar though they may be, the sardine lasagne with eggplant and the millefeuille de filet de veau are still perfectly delicious and courteously served. Tempting desserts; high prices. C 250-350. M 159.

12/20 Aux Deux Canards

"Chez Catherine," 8, rue du Fbg-Poissonnière
01 47 70 03 23, fax 01 44 83 02 50
Closed Sat lunch, Sun, Jul 20-Aug 20. Open until 10:30pm. Air cond.
This is a place for duck: diners may enjoy the salmon rillettes, magret de canard, canard à l'orange, and tasty desserts in this naively charming bistro with great wines to match. C 220.

12/20 Julien

16, rue du Faubourg-St-Denis
01 47 70 12 06, fax 01 42 47 00 65
Open daily until 1:30am. Air cond. Valet pkg.
For the pleasure of dining in these exuberant surroundings (vintage 1880), we are willing to put up with mediocre food. But if you stick to the oysters, the cassoulet, or eggs poached in red wine, you'll leave with a pleasant memory. C 150-230. M 119 (lunch, wine incl), 121 (dinner, after 10pm, wine incl).

Chez Michel

10, rue Belzunce - 01 44 53 06 20
Closed Sun, Mon, Aug. Open until 11pm.
Scion of a family of restaurateurs, Thierry Breton was just doing what came naturally when he decided to become a chef. Just as naturally, his preference is for Breton cuisine, the backbone of his original 168 F single-price menu, which draws gourmets from all over Paris. It features a daring andouille terrine with buckwheat crêpes, kig ha farz (an Armorican boiled dinner of hog jowls and country-cured bacon), and buttery rich kouign-aman cake. He's even unearthed a cheap and cheerful Breton vin de pays to wash these good things down! M 168.

La P'tite Tonkinoise

56, rue du Fg-Poissonnière - 01 42 46 85 98
Closed Sun, Mon, Aug, 1st wk of Sep. Open until 10pm.
Old Indochina hands come regularly for a whiff of the nostalgia that is virtually palpable here. The chef is a pony-tailed titan, while his wife is indeed a tiny Tonkinoise. Their menu features crisp egg rolls, grilled shrimp in rice sauce (they're not on the menu, so ask for them), duck breast rubbed with five-spice powder, and a savory chicken wing stuffed with onion curry. C 200-240. M 150 (lunch).

11/20 Le Réveil du 10e

35, rue du Château-d'Eau - 01 42 41 77 59
Closed Sat (during school hols), Sun, wk of Aug 15. Open until 8pm (Tue 9:30pm, exc during school hols). Pkg.
A hearty Auvergnat welcome awaits in this modest bistro, along with well-chosen wines, house-made terrines, and robust daily specials. C 120.

12/20 Terminus Nord

23, rue de Dunkerque
01 42 85 05 15, fax 01 40 16 13 98
Open daily until 12:30am. Priv rm: 12. Air cond.
Part of the brasserie group of which Flo (see above) is the flagship, the Terminus serves exactly the same food as the rest of the fleet. Enjoy the atmosphere, the gay 1925 décor, and look no farther than the sauerkraut, oysters, and grills for a satisfying meal. Nimble service. C 150-230. M 119 (lunch exc Sun, wine incl), 121 (dinner from 10pm, wine incl), 180 (dinner, Sun, wine incl), 62 (children, drink incl).

12/20 L'Aiguière

37 bis, rue de Montreuil
01 43 72 42 32, fax 01 43 72 96 36
Closed Sat lunch, Sun. Open until 10:30pm. Priv rm: 50. Air cond. Pkg.
Pascal Viallet is a dab hand with seafood; his repertoire is rooted in tradition but often shows a pleasing contemporary touch. Eclectic wine list; elegant setting overseen by owner Patrick

Masbatin. C 250-320. M 135 (weekdays, wine incl), 175, 248 (wine incl).

 ## Les Amognes

243, rue du Fg-St-Antoine - 01 43 72 73 05
Closed Sun, Mon lunch, 2 wks in Aug. Open until 11pm. Terrace dining.
Thierry Coué has crossed rich and costly ingredients off his shopping list. The food he serves in his country-style dining room is full of earthy character: warm oysters and leeks ravigote, sweetbreads with cumin-spiced cucumber confit, crêpe stuffed with an eggplant compote redolent of cardamom. The cellar is filled with interesting finds. He deserves another toque. M 180.

Astier

44, rue Jean-Pierre-Timbaud - 01 43 57 16 35
Closed 1 wk end Apr, Aug, Dec 23-Jan 2. Open until 11pm. Air cond.
For 135 F, Jean-Luc Clerc will set you up with a slab of savory chicken-liver terrine, followed by rabbit in mustard sauce or a duo of sea whelks and shrimp, nicely aged cheeses, and rich chocolate mousse for dessert. The bistro atmosphere is good-humored and noisy. Intelligent, wide-ranging cellar. M 135.

12/20 Bistrot Lyonnais

8, rue de la Main-d'Or - 01 48 05 77 10
Open until 11pm. No cards.
A genuine Lyonnais bouchon, where you can tuck into terrine beaujolaise, rabbit rillettes, and lots of other regional specialties. Wash them down with a *pot* of Beaujolais. C 65-140.

 ## Chardenoux

1, rue Jules-Vallès - 01 43 71 49 52
Closed Sat lunch, Sun, Aug. Open until 10:30pm. No pets.
In the heart of the old cabinet-makers' district, this graceful corner bistro (a registered Belle Époque building) flaunts its charms of marble, fanciful moldings, and etched glass. It's a setting peculiarly suited to Bernard Passavant's simple, generous cooking: eggs poached in red wine, daube de bœuf à la provençal and the like. Connoisseur's cellar. C 200-270.

Khun Akorn

8, av. de Taillebourg
01 43 56 20 03, fax 01 40 09 18 44
Closed Mon. Open until 11pm. Priv rm: 80. Terrace dining. Pkg.
Thai cooking of rare refinement, served in an evocative, exotic setting. The tong-sai (assorted appetizers) set the mood for what follows. The curries are lighter than their Indian cousins, but Thai chilis make their fiery presence felt elsewhere on the menu. C 250. M 129 (lunch), 195-325.

The prices in this guide reflect what establishments were charging at press time.

 ## Mansouria

11, rue Faidherbe - 01 43 71 00 16, fax 01 40 24 21 97
Closed Mon lunch, Sun. Open until 11:30pm. Terrace dining. Air cond.
The trendy Bastille crowd comes here for a taste of Morocco: honeyed pumpkin purée, Moroccan crêpes, a light and flavorful couscous, and mellow, long-simmered tagines. Charming reception and service. C 250. M 99 & 135 (weekday lunch), 168, 280 (wine incl).

11/20 Jacques Mélac

42, rue Léon-Frot - 01 43 70 59 27
Closed Mon dinner, Sat, Sun, Aug, 1 wk at Christmas-New Year's. Open until 10:30pm. Terrace dining. Air cond.
One of the city's most popular wine bars. The countrified menu proposes charcuteries from the Aveyron region, good cheeses, and exemplary wines. C 200.

11/20 Chez Paul

13, rue de Charonne - 01 47 00 34 57
Open daily until 12:30am. Terrace dining. Pkg.
This traditional bistro stands out from its determinedly hip neighbors. Come here for rillettes, rabbit stuffed with chèvre, and chocolate charlotte. C 200.

 ## Chez Philippe

106, rue de la Folie-Méricourt - 01 43 57 33 78
Closed Sat, Sun, Aug. Open until 10:30pm. Air cond. Garage pkg.
The menu written in purple ink is nothing if not eclectic: herrings Bismarck, grilled lobster, a monumental cassoulet, paella (the best in Paris), York ham with macaroni au gratin, beef bourguignon, turbot Dugléré, and old-fashioned braised hare. Great Burgundies at giveaway prices only add to the gaiety. C 350-450.

 ## Le Repaire de Cartouche

99, rue Amelot or 8, bd des Filles-du-Calvaire
01 47 00 25 86
Closed Sat lunch, Sun. Open until 10:30pm. Priv rm: 45.
Emmanuel Salabert, an experienced, skillful chef, presides over this shrine to Southwestern cuisine. Settle down in the wood-paneled dining room and sample foie gras steamed in a cabbage leaf, mussels in a creamy sauce, pork with prunes and celery, and flaky Landais apple pie laced with Armagnac. Interesting cellar, manageably priced. C 230. M 155 (wine incl).

 ## Le Roudoulié

16, rue de la Vacquerie - 01 43 79 27 46
Closed Sat lunch, Sun, Aug 1-15. Open until 10:30pm. Air cond.
Remember to book in advance (especially for lunch), since Le Roudoulié's charming service, jolly atmosphere and generous, inexpensive food have plenty of fans. The menu has a rustic Southwestern accent: hot duck pâté studded

with cèpes and foie gras, pot-au-feu de canard, and scallops with oyster mushrooms. C 200-300. M 62 (weekday lunch, wine incl), 110, 210.

La Table Richelieu

276, bd Voltaire - 01 43 72 31 23
Closed Sat lunch, Mon. Open until 11pm. Priv rm: 40. Terrace dining. Air cond.
For fresh seafood, you couldn't do much better than this bright, comfortable restaurant, where Daniel Rousseau treats customers to sparkling shellfish assortments and delicious lobster in Sauternes with fresh pasta. Tasty desserts (chocolate millefeuille with morello cherries and pistachio sauce). C 300. M 149 (exc lunch Sun, wine incl), 200, 260.

Thaï Éléphant

43-45, rue de la Roquette
01 47 00 42 00, fax 01 47 00 45 44
Closed Sat lunch, May 1, 3 days at Christmas. Open until midnight (11:45pm Sun). Air cond.
Filled with flowers, pagodas, and cheerful waiters, the Thaï Éléphant is not your run-of-the-mill Asian eatery. The menu is miles long, and many of the dishes are fiercely fiery (the hottest are marked with three red elephants). The shrimp curry is quite fine, and so are the Fomyang soup and the garlicky pork. For dessert, try the delicious jasmine tart. C 280. M 150 (weekday lunch), 275, 300.

Le Villaret

13, rue Ternaux - 01 43 57 75 56
Closed Sun, 10 days in May, Aug, 2 wks at Christmas. Open dinner only until 1am. Air cond.
The former owner of Astier (see above) launched this engaging bistro, where an oft-revised menu of scrupulously prepared cuisine bourgeoise is served with bargain-priced wines. It's a winning formula! C 200.

12TH ARRONDISSEMENT

La Flambée ⚙

4, rue Taine - 01 43 43 21 80
Closed Sun, Aug 3-19. Open until 10:15pm. Terrace dining. Air cond. Pkg.
The dining room shows some signs of wear, but never mind. Michel Roustan warms things up nicely with his traditional Southwestern charcuteries, tasty confit de canard with sautéed potatoes, and excellent warm apple tart. The good wines are moderately priced. C 250. M 125, 199 (wine incl).

La Gourmandise

271, av. Daumesnil - 01 43 43 94 41
Closed Sun, Mon dinner, Aug 3-25. Open until 10:30pm. Garage pkg.
Gourmand or gourmet, you'll be tempted to indulge in Alain Denoual's excellent set meals, the less expensive of which delivers fish terrine with shellfish fumet, saddle of rabbit confit with

cabbage, and a rich triple-chocolate mousse. A la carte, the langoustines with a red-tea infusion and the zippy mango charlotte are both worthy of note. C 340. M 145, 175, 199 (wine incl), 95 (children).

11/20 Les Grandes Marches

6, pl. de la Bastille - 01 43 42 90 32, fax 01 43 44 80 02
Closed 3 wks in Aug. Open until 1am. Terrace dining. Air cond.
Restored around the same time as the Opéra Bastille was built, this posh brasserie is a fine spot for a post-performance supper. Oysters and other shellfish, steaks, and a splendid sea bream roasted in a salt crust deserve a round of applause. C 260. M 138, 175.

12/20 Le Mange Tout

24, bd de la Bastille - 01 43 43 95 15
Closed Sun, 1 wk in Aug. Open until 11:30pm. Priv rm: 18. Terrace dining.
Uncomplicated cooking, served with a smile and a generous hand. Scrambled eggs with morels, skate with capers, andouillette sausage, and clafoutis are the mainstays of a menu rooted in the provinces of France. C 220. M 99, 199 (wine incl).

L'Oulette ⚙

15, pl. Lachambeaudie - 01 40 02 02 12
Closed Sat lunch, Sun. Open until 10:15pm. Terrace dining.
A charmless cohort of office blocks contributes precious little warmth to the surroundings, but happily, Marcel Baudis can be relied upon to kindle a glow with his spirited Southwestern cooking. He ignited our enthusiasm with a spiced duck pâté, tender Pyrenees lamb with country potatoes, and hefty portion of tomme d'Aspe cheese. The cellar is awash in sturdy wines from the Quercy and thereabouts; the service is most attentive. C 300-400. M 165, 245 (wine incl).

La Plantation

5, rue Jules-César - 01 43 07 64 15
Closed Sat lunch, Sun. Open until 11pm. No pets.
Nouvelle cuisine, Creole-style: blaff de bulots (sea whelks marinated in lime juice and chilis), chicken in pan juices deglazed with pineapple vinegar, and fabulous stuffed crab are expertly handled dishes full of vivid tropical flavors. C 220-300. M 90-100 (weekday lunch), 180 (wine incl), 150-235.

Au Pressoir

257, av. Daumesnil
01 43 44 38 21, fax 01 43 43 81 77
Closed Sat, Sun, Aug. Open until 10pm. Priv rm: 40. Air cond. Valet pkg.
Forgotten by most Parisians since the Colonial Exposition closed 60 years ago, the Porte Dorée district is home to a covey of fine restaurants. Le Pressoir numbers among them: chef Henri Séguin cooks with fine ingredients and a generous spirit, shown to advantage in his scal-

lop fricassée with wild mushrooms, codfish brandade with asparagus, or in season a sumptuous hare à la royale. Expensive cellar. C 500-650. M 400.

 ### Le Quincy

28, av. Ledru-Rollin - 01 46 28 46 76
Closed Sat, Sun, Mon, Aug 15-Sep 15. Open until 10pm. Air cond. No cards.
Bobosse, the jovial host, keeps things lively in the dining room, while in the kitchen Jean-Pierre Rouat cooks up zestful bistro dishes rooted in the Berry and Vivarais regions: famously tasty farmhouse terrine, chicken fricassée, boiled crayfish, and the best stuffed cabbage in town. Delicious Rhône and Loire wines. C 300-400.

 ### Le Saint-Amarante

4, rue Biscornet - 01 43 43 00 08
Closed Sat, Sun, Jul 14-Aug 15. Open until 10:30pm. Terrace dining. No pets.
Tucked in a quiet street near the Opéra-Bastille, a remarkable bistro where lusty food and low prices go hand in hand. Kid terrine, artichokes barigoule, lamb's sweetbreads with mushrooms are washed down with growers' wines priced under 100 F in a crowded, lively setting. C 200 (wine incl).

La Sologne

164, av. Daumesnil
01 43 07 68 97, fax 01 43 44 66 23
Closed Sat lunch, Sun, 1 wk in spring, 2 wks in Aug. Open until 10:30pm (Sat & Sun 11:30pm). Terrace dining. Air cond.
Didier and Virginie Maillet spare no pains to make their patrons feel welcome and well fed. The 155 F menu is most attractive (the offerings change often) and the kitchen highlights game in season. M 155, 210.

Le Train Bleu

Gare de Lyon, 20, bd Diderot
01 43 43 09 06, fax 01 43 43 97 96
Open daily until 11pm. Pkg.
The feast is for your eyes only: an extravagant, colossal, delirious, dazzling décor. The food? Don't miss your train for it... High prices. C 300. M 250 (wine incl).

 ### Au Trou Gascon

40, rue Taine - 01 43 44 34 26, fax 01 43 07 80 55
Closed Sat lunch, Sun, Jul 26-Aug 24, Dec 28-Jan 4. Open daily until 10pm. Air cond.
Time marches on, but here the mellow décor and familiar menu remain unchanged. Year in, year out, you can order well-cured Chalosse ham, a warm pâté de cèpes in a bright-green parsley jus, truffled chop of milk-fed veal with macaroni gratin, or rich duck and pork cassoulet. A few dishes from the Carré des Feuillants can also be spotted on the list (red mullet with potatoes and marrow, chestnut bouillon with bits of pheasant...). To accompany this robust cooking, Nicole Dutournier recommends

wonderful wines from Madiran and Jurançon. C 380. M 220 (weekday lunch, 280 (dinner, wine incl).

11/20 **Le Viaduc Café**

43, av. Daumesnil - 01 44 74 70 70
Open daily until midnight (Fri & Sat 12:30am). Terrace dining.
After browsing around the artisans' shops of the Viaduc des Arts, you can enjoy simple French cooking at this arty café. On offer you'll find salmon tartare, grilled duck breast, and vanilla-scented pain perdu (aka French toast). C 150.

11/20 **Les Zygomates**

7, rue de Capri - 01 40 19 93 04
Closed Sat lunch, Sun, Aug, last wk of Dec. Open until 10:30pm. No pets.
For starters, there's an earthy salad of pork tongue, followed by grenadier (a firm-fleshed fish) with red-wine butter or pig's tail with morels. The incredible dining room—formerly a butcher shop—is full of *fin de siècle* details. C 200. M 75 (weekday lunch), 130.

13TH ARRONDISSEMENT

 ### L'Anacréon

53, bd Saint-Marcel - 01 43 31 71 18
Closed Sun, Mon, 1 wk in Feb, Aug. Open until 10:30pm. Air cond. No pets.
No-frills surroundings, but the food is full-flavored and unbeatably priced: soy-marinated salmon bundled up in a crêpe purse, veal kidney with mustard sauce and buttery cabbage, light and lively grapefruit gratin. M 120 (lunch), 180 (menu-carte).

12/20 **Auberge Etchegorry**

Hôtel Vert-Galant, 41, rue Croulebarbe
01 44 08 83 51, fax 01 44 08 83 69
Closed Sun. Open until 10:30pm. Terrace dining.
Come here for hearty Basque food and wines. A cheerful *patron* plates up excellent regional charcuterie, tasty stuffed squid, and generously served quail paupiettes au foie gras. Lots of charm, and a lively atmosphere. C 280. M 135, 210.

Entoto

143, rue Léon-Maurice-Nordman - 01 45 87 08 51
Closed Sun, Mon, 2 wks in Aug. Open until 11pm. No pets. Pkg.
Entoto, or the vegetable kingdom. Spinach, pink lentils with a snap of lime juice, pumpkin, and cracked wheat feature prominently in the generously spiced cuisine of Ethiopia. Meat-eaters will find happiness with lamb's tripe or guinea hen served on a huge crêpe that does double duty as plate and bread. Fabulous coffee. C 150.

Looking for a restaurant? Refer to the **index.**

La Mer de Chine

159, rue Château-des-Rentiers - 01 45 84 22 49
Closed Tue. Open until 1am. Air cond.
The menu features sautéed ducks' tongues, fried soft-shell crabs (imported from Vietnam), oyster beignets, and gingery carp anointed with sesame oil. If chop suey is what you want, look elsewhere! C 180. M 64, 72 (weekday lunch).

12/20 Chez Paul

22, rue de la Butte-aux-Cailles
01 45 89 22 11, fax 01 45 80 26 53
Closed Dec 25, Jan 1. Open daily until midnight. Terrace dining. No pets.
In the heart of the Butte-aux-Cailles district, a corner of old Paris where tourists never go, Chez Paul serves calf's head gribiche, streaky bacon with lentils, sage-scented suckling pig, and other bistro classics. Do stop to admire the magnificent 1930s bar. C 250-290.

 Le Petit Marguery

9, bd de Port-Royal - 01 43 31 58 59
Closed Sun, Mon, Aug, Dec 24-Jan 3. Open until 10:15pm. Priv rm: 20.
The Cousin brothers aren't sticks-in-the-mud: they're willing to leave the beaten path of bistro fare and offer their patrons crispy ravioli stuffed with langoustines and green apples (delicious!). But they also please their faithful public with down-home favorites delivered by fleet-footed waiters: braised wild mushrooms, terrine de boudin, cod gratin with oysters and asparagus, or compote de coq. The single-price menus help keep costs down. M 165 (weekday lunch, Sat), 205, 450.

 Les Vieux Métiers de France

13, bd Auguste-Blanqui
01 45 88 90 03, fax 01 45 80 73 80
Closed Sun, Mon. Open until 10:30pm. Priv rm: 16. Air cond.
Onto an austere modern building, Michel Moisan has grafted the most amazing medieval décor of sculpted wood, stained glass, beams, and paintings. What saves all this quaintness from tipping over into kitsch is Moisan's cuisine: pigeon pâté, braised farm chicken with mushrooms, luscious desserts. Amateur service. C 360-460. M 165, 300.

14TH ARRONDISSEMENT

 L'Amuse Bouche

186, rue du Château - 01 43 35 31 61
Closed Sat lunch, Sun, Aug 7-20. Open until 10:30pm.
A neighborhood crowd comes here for virtuously priced set meals served in a bright, tiny (just 22 seats) dining room. At lunch there's snail fricassée, guinea hen with celery-root purée, and dried fruit-and-nut soup spiced with cinnamon. M 140, 168.

 L'Angélus

12, rue Joannes (corner of rue Boulitte)
01 45 41 51 65
Open daily until 10:30pm.
The two owners used to be magicians,. but there's no hocus-pocus going on in the kitchen. The menu is based on prime ingredients handled with a light touch: try the chicken liver terrine, gutsy andouillette sausage with mustard sauce, and frozen honey nougat. Well-annotated wine list dominated by Burgundy and Bordeaux. M 85-132 (exc Sun, wine incl), 158, 100 (children).

 L'Assiette ❃

181, rue du Château - 01 43 22 64 86
Closed Mon, Tue, 1 wk in May, Aug. Open until 10:30pm.
If Lulu's success were due merely to the fact that her prices are high, her customers chic, and her dining room determinedly "working class," it would surely have faded long ago. No, the high and the mighty come here year after year because they love the food. So do we: the ingredients are magnificent and the portions huge. When Lulu puts truffles in a dish, you can see, smell, and taste them! Try her justly famous boudin parmentier, hare civet, mackerel rillettes, and superb sole meunière (it weighs in at 14 oz). But desserts are not her strong suit, as Lulu owns up herself right on the menu! C 300, 480. M 200 (lunch, wine incl).

12/20 Auberge de l'Argoat

27, av. Reille - 01 45 89 17 05
Closed Sat lunch, Sun, Mon dinner, 1 wk at Aug 15. Open until 10pm.
Here's a welcoming, unpretentious little seafood spot, situated across from the Parc Montsouris. Jeannine Gaulon greets diners warmly, while in the kitchen her chef cooks up soupe de poissons, langoustine and artichoke salad, fresh tuna en daube (a bit dry on our last visit), and grilled sea bream. A few meat dishes round out the bill of fare. C 280-300. M 100 (weekday lunch), 180.

11/20 Le Bar à Huîtres

112, bd du Montparnasse - 01 43 20 71 01
Open daily until 2am. Terrace dining. Pkg.
At this popular oyster bar you can, if you wish, order and eat just one oyster—but that would be a shame. Six or a dozen Belons, fines, or spéciales would surely be more satisfying, as are the gargantuan shellfish platters (200 to 600 F). The cooked fish dishes, however, are skippable. C 220. M 98, 198, 89 (children).

12/20 Bistrot du Dôme

1, rue Delambre - 01 43 35 32 00
Open daily until 11pm. Terrace dining. Air cond.
Flipping-fresh seafood is presented with becoming simplicity at this fashionable spot: featured are crispy fried smelts, tuna with sauce vierge, and lotte in a garlicky cream sauce. A price savvy wine list features all bottles for 99 F, or by the glass at 22 F; merry ambience. C 250.

La Cagouille

Opposite 23 rue de l'Ouest - 12, pl. Constantin-Brancusi - 01 43 22 09 01, fax 01 45 38 57 29
Open daily until 10:30pm. Priv rm: 20. Terrace dining.
At this *bistro du port*, dishes made from the very freshest fish and shellfish (delivered direct from Atlantic ports) are chalked on a blackboard: depending on the day's catch, they might include tiny squid in a garlicky sauce of their own ink, baked black scallops from Brest, fresh fried anchovies, shad in beurre blanc sauce, herbed brill, mackerel with mustard sauce, or thick, juicy sole. If you are content to drink a modest Aligoté or Quincy, your bill will hover around 300 F. But beware if you succumb to the temptations of the finest Cognac collection in Paris (and maybe the world). **C** 300. **M** 150, 250 (wine incl), 60 (children).

 Le Caroubier

122, av. du Maine - 01 43 20 41 49
Closed Mon, Jul 13-Aug 18. Open until 10:30pm. Air cond.
Do you like couscous? Here you'll find the genuine article: homemade, hand-rolled, and fragrant with spices. Also on offer are a lively eggplant salad, savory pastillas, and succulent tagines, simmered in the best Moroccan tradition. Heartwarming welcome. **C** 180-220. **M** 140.

 La Chaumière des Gourmets

22, pl. Denfert-Rochereau - 01 43 21 22 59
Closed Sat lunch, Sun, 1st 3 wks of Aug. Open until 10:30pm. Priv rm: 12. Terrace dining.
The Chaumière's friendly, provincial dining room still features faded fabric on the walls, the staff carries on with imperturbable diligence, the wine list remains small, and the house repertoire invariably classic. But in this case, no news really is good news: the flavorful duck terrine, entrecôte bordelaise, and frozen nougat on the 165 F menu attest to Jean-Paul Huc's unfailing consistency and flair. **C** 350. **M** 165, 245.

12/20 La Coupole

102, bd du Montparnasse
01 43 20 14 20, fax 01 43 35 46 14
Open daily until 2am. Priv rm: 200. Air cond.
This Montparnasse landmark, respectfully restored and run by the Flo brasserie group, survives with its mystique intact. The menu bears Flo's unmistakable stamp: exemplary shellfish assortments, grilled meats, and carafes of sprightly house Riesling are delivered by swift, efficient waiters. **C** 250-350. **M** 89 (lunch, exc Sun), 119 (lunch, exc Sun, wine incl), 121 (dinner, wine incl).

 Le Dôme

108, bd du Montparnasse
01 43 35 25 81, fax 01 42 79 01 19
Closed Mon. Open until 12:30am. Priv rm: 8. Air cond.
Le Dôme is the capital's top seafood brasserie, with a neo–Art Deco interior, booths that provide cozy comfort and privacy for the high-powered patrons, and an appetizing *carte* prepared by chef Franck Graux. In addition to impeccably fresh oysters and the justly famous lobster salad in a truffled dressing, you can choose bouillon de langoustines aux champignons, turbot hollandaise, sea bass in chive vinaigrette, or bouillabaisse that bears comparison with Marseille's best. Precise, cheerful service, and a cellar filled with bottles that incite you to splurge. **C** 400.

 Le Duc

243, bd Raspail - 01 43 20 96 30, fax 01 43 20 46 73
Closed Sun, Mon, hols. Open until 10pm. Air cond.
The respectful, minimalist approach to seafood imposed by Le Duc's founders endures even now that the Minchelli brothers are gone. The kitchen continues to handle only impeccable ingredients, heightening their innate goodness with a little sea salt, a dribble of oil, a brief moment on the fire. A recent dinner brought wild Scottish salmon cured for just a few hours in a bed of salt; perfect raw sardines; expertly grilled sea bream; and red mullet enhanced with fruity olive oil. It deserves another point. But why, we wonder, at a seafood restaurant of this caliber is the supply of white wines so woefully low? We spotted one lonely white Bordeaux on the list! **C** 500-600. **M** 260.

12/20 Giovanna

22, rue Édouard-Jacques - 01 43 22 32 09
Closed Sun lunch, Sun, Aug. Open until 10pm.
You, your companion, and sixteen other diners can tuck into perfectly wrought fresh pasta and other fine Italian dishes in this minute trattoria, popular with the show-biz crowd. Don't overlook the osso buco. **C** 160-220. **M** 65 (weekday lunch).

 Lous Landés

157, av. du Maine - 01 45 43 08 04, fax 01 45 45 91 35
Closed Sat lunch, Sun, Aug. Open until 10:30pm. Priv rm: 12. Terrace dining. Air cond.
Hervé Rumen's Southwestern specialties range from the robust to the refined. Taste his truffled foie gras au jus de canard, Landais squab flavored with three kinds of garlic, or his world-class cassoulet. Desserts are all you would expect from a former colleague of Christian Constant, and the wine list offers some excellent Cahors and Madirans. Marie-Thérèse, a charming hostess, welcomes guests into the pretty green dining room. **C** 300-400. **M** 195, 310.

 Le Moniage Guillaume

88, rue de la Tombe-Issoire
01 43 22 96 15, fax 01 43 27 11 79
Closed Sun. Open until 10:15pm. Priv rm: 30. Terrace dining. Valet pkg.
The regulars (and they are legion) just love this long-established seafood spot. Fish and crustaceans are handled with skill—and priced to

kill, though the set meals provide some relief. Rich cellar, including a reasonably tariffed Menetou-Salon. C 350-400. M 185, 245.

 ## Montparnasse 25

Hôtel Méridien,
19, rue du Cdt-Mouchotte
01 44 36 44 25, fax 01 44 36 49 03
Closed Sat, Sun. Open until 10:30pm. Priv rm: 32. Air cond. No pets. Valet pkg.

Unlike many hotel restaurants which are little more than a convenience for in-house patrons, the Méridien posts a magnetic menu that draws gourmets from all over Paris. The Art Deco interior opens onto a patio, and the well-spaced tables are just what executives desire for their power lunches. Yet even the most intense negotiations come to a halt when the waiter presents chef Jean-Yves Guého's expressively flavorful dishes. This triple-toque winner cooked for years at the Hong Kong Méridien, and it shows in his spiced sole with fried noodles and baby bean sprouts or stupendous suckling pig served in two courses: the rack and leg rubbed with sesame and satay paste, the shoulder and ribs braised with vegetables. A monumental cheese board presents over 150 choice specimens, and the cellar is awash in remarkable growers' wines. C 400-600. M 240 (lunch), 300-390 (dinner).

Pavillon Montsouris

20, rue Gazan - 01 45 88 38 52, fax 01 45 88 63 40
Open daily until 10:30pm. Priv rm: 43. Terrace dining. Valet pkg.

A walk across the Parc Montsouris at sunset will give you an appetite for a fine feast in this turn-of-the-century greenhouse overlooking the park, once the haunt of the beautiful spy, Mata Hari. New comer Gérard Fouché's deft cooking adds sunshine to this charming spot: taste the excellent tatin of red snapper and zucchini and tapenade. Many other dishes harbor his native Southwestern style. Very expensive cellar, and small tables are balanced by gorgeous desserts, and friendly service. C 255-280. M 180, 265, 100 (children).

 ## Les Petites Sorcières

12, rue Liancourt - 01 43 21 95 68, fax 01 42 79 99 03
Closed Sat lunch, Sun. Open until 10:30pm. Priv rm: 14. Terrace dining. Pkg.

Christian Teule fills up his pocket-sized restaurant with an appealing lunch menu that offers house-made jambon persillé followed by herb-poached cod, cheese, and bitter-chocolate mousse. A la carte choices are more elaborate but no less savory: yummy chicken terrine, sautéed lotte with sweet peppers, and spiced pear clafoutis. Good wines are available by the carafe. C 160. M 120 (weekday lunch), 160 (dinner).

11/20 Pinocchio

124, av. du Maine - 01 43 21 26 10, fax 01 43 21 26 37
Closed Sat lunch, Sun. Open until 11pm. Priv rm: 40. Terrace dining. Air cond.

Step past the wooden statue of Pinocchio on the sidewalk, and settle down for some satisfying Sicilian fare: spiced octopus, grilled peppers, lamb-stuffed pansotti, and fragrant bollito misto. C 240. M 120 (weekdays, wine incl).

 ## La Régalade

49, av. Jean-Moulin - 01 45 45 68 58
Closed Sat lunch, Sun, Mon, Jul 20-Aug 25. Open until midnight. Air cond.

Don't fail to book your table way in advance, for La Régalade fills up fast. Here's why: Yves Camdeborde (ex-Crillon, no less) serves up first-rate cooking at incredible prices. Regionally rooted but modern in outlook, the menu proposes a sapid terrine of oxtail and leek, potato and lobster gratin glazed with Parmesan, succulent wood pigeon barded with bacon, and such delectable desserts as pan-roasted burlat cherries. Appealing Southwestern cellar. Another toque. M 165.

 ## Les Vendanges

40, rue Friant - 01 45 39 59 98, fax 01 45 39 74 13
Closed Sat lunch, Sun, Aug 4-25. Open until 10:30pm. Priv rm: 15. Pkg.

Pink napery and antiques lend an old-fashioned charm to the dining room. Guy Tardif cooks up generous classics like pheasant galantine with foie gras, braised beef and vegetables, grilled pikeperch with lentils and bacon, and rhubarb-topped shortbread. Son of a charcutier, he also turns out a bang-up andouillette. Interesting cellar, rich in Bordeaux. M 150, 200, 100 (children).

 ## Au Vin des Rues

21, rue Boulard - 01 43 22 19 78
Closed Sun, Mon, end Feb, Aug. Priv rm: 10. Terrace dining. No cards.

Jean Chanrion's robust Lyonnais-style *plats du jour* are served forth in an authentic bistro setting, and are washed down by jugs of wonderful growers' Mâcons and Beaujolais. C 180-240.

 ## Vin et Marée

108, av. du Maine - 01 43 20 29 50
Open daily until midnight. Air cond. Priv rm: 40.

Jean-Pierre Durand's first seafood brasserie (on Boulevard Murat in the sixteenth arrondissement) is so successful that he decided to reprise that winning formula here, in premises that formerly housed the Armes de Bretagne restaurant. Durand brings home expertly chosen fish and shellfish from the market at Rungis, so that lucky diners can feast on ultrafresh Breton shrimp, tiny squid sautéed with mild garlic, sole cooked in sweet butter, or grilled turbotin. Briny steamed cockles are offered as an amuse-bouche, and for dessert there's a yummy baba au rhum. C 140-225.

Some establishments change their closing times without warning. It is always wise to check in advance.

15TH ARRONDISSEMENT

 L'Agape

281, rue Lecourbe - 01 45 58 19 29
Closed Sat lunch, Sun, Aug. Open until 10:30pm.
Terrace dining.
Marc Lamic's attractive menu brims with bright ideas and flavors: we gobbled up his delicious confit de canard served beneath a fluffy potato blanket, the tasty turbot roasted with fragrant olive oil, potatoes stuffed with ox tail, and hot pineapple gratin. Down-to-earth prices. C 120.

12/20 Le Barrail

17, rue Falguière - 01 43 22 42 61, fax 01 42 79 93 91
Closed Sat, Sun. Open until 10pm. Priv rm: 15. Air cond.
In this attractive spot done up in pastel tones, you make no complaints about the traditional bourgeois cooking. C 250. M 99, 130 (lunch), 165, 170.

 Bistro 121

121, rue de la Convention
01 45 57 52 90, fax 01 45 57 14 69
Open daily until midnight. Air cond. Valet pkg.
Decorated in a now dated "modern" style, but comfortable and bright nonetheless, André Jalbert's bistro is a conservatory of reassuring, traditional French cuisine. You won't leave hungry after feasting on molded anchovies en vinaigrette, veal tenderloin scented with juniper, or the robust game dishes served in season. Attractively priced cellar. C 250. M 121, 168 (weekday lunch), 210 (Sat, Sun, wine incl).

12/20 Casa Alcalde

117, bd de Grenelle - 01 47 83 39 71
Open daily until 10:30pm. Terrace dining. Air cond.
A lively *bodega* offering zesty Basque and Spanish fare. Try the excellent pipérade, marinated anchovies, generously served paella, or codfish à la luzienne. The wine list features fine bottles from beyond the Pyrenees. C 210. M 155.

 Les Célébrités

Hôtel Nikko, 61, quai de Grenelle
01 40 58 20 00, fax 01 40 58 24 44
Closed Aug. Open until 10pm. Priv rm: 22. Air cond. Valet pkg.
No rough edges mar Jacques Sénéchal's virtuoso handling of flawless seasonal foodstuffs. His 350 F single-price menu presents (for example) clams marinière with garlic and parsley, a lusty boiled-beef salad rémoulade, grilled fish of the day, and pasta fired up with capers, herbs, and chilis. Flavors are refined yet definite, cooking times are invariably right. As for the cellar, it's beyond reproach: astutely assembled, appealing and, all in all, affordably priced. C 290-390. M 350.

 Chen

"Au Soleil d'Est," 15, rue du Théâtre
01 45 79 34 34, fax 01 45 79 07 53
Closed Sun. Open until 11:30pm. Priv rm: 14. Air cond. Valet pkg.
Inside a shopping mall, aggressively decorated—Chen does not look promising! But the short menu holds lots of wonderful surprises. The fresh, precisely prepared crab velouté with asparagus, dumplings in a fragrant broth, peppery sautéed crab, and exemplary Peking duck may not be cheap, but they're well worth the money. C 250, 300. M 170 (weekday dinner), 230 (weekdays lunch, wine incl).

 Le Clos Morillons

50, rue des Morillons
01 48 28 04 37, fax 01 48 28 70 77
Closed Sat lunch, Sun. Open until 10pm. No pets.
The French colonial décor of this charming establishment transports you to the tropics. The feeling lingers as you peruse the menu, for Philippe Delacourcelle's repertoire is redolent of exotic spices. Among the original, expertly rendered dishes are sole with sweet lime leaves, calf's liver scented with cinnamon, suavely spiced snails, and gingered veal with puréed almonds. Delectable desserts and a fine selection of wines priced under 100 F complete the picture. He earns another point. C 290-360. C 165, 285.

 Philippe Detourbe

8, rue Nicolas Charlet
01 42 19 08 59, fax 01 45 67 09 13
Closed Sat lunch, Sun, Aug. Open until 11pm. Priv rm: 55. Air cond.
Philippe Detourbe's customers never need to wonder about their bill, since the two moderately priced set meals do the figuring for them. Among the adroitly prepared dishes we've noted lately are cassolette of snails with bacon and mushrooms, grilled red mullet on a bed of ratatouille, and cod with cabbage and a drizzle of hazelnut oil. Affordable cellar, too. M 150 (lunch), 180 (dinner).

 La Dinée

85, rue Leblanc
01 45 54 20 49, fax 01 40 60 74 88
Closed Sat, Sun lunch, 3 wks in Aug. Open until 10:45pm. Priv rm: 20. Air cond.
Christophe Chabanel earned his first toque at the tender age of 22. Here in his digs, a pluperfect neighborhood restaurant, he's won toque number two, for his finely honed technique and inventive, modern menu. Among the excellent options on offer are a warm salad of quail and artichokes in a vivid beet jus, and perfectly roasted pikeperch garnished with a zesty anchoïade and skewered squid. For dessert, go for the spiced pear tempura in red-wine sauce or the apple-caramel chaud-froid. Another point this year. C 350. M 180 (weekday lunch), 290-450 (weekdays, Sun dinner).

Fellini

58, rue de la Croix-Nivert - 01 45 77 40 77
Closed Sat lunch, Sun, Aug. Open until 10:30pm.
Air cond. No pets. No cards.
Giuseppe hails from sunny Napoli, where he learned to cook in a fresh, forthright style. Pull up a seat in his friendly trattoria, and sample a warm salad of baby squid and white beans drizzled with olive oil, or fresh tagliolini with langoustines and tomatoes. His tiramisù is the lightest we've tried. To wash it down, uncork a bottle from the well-stocked Italian cellar. C 260-310. M 130 (weekday lunch).

 ## Le Gastroquet

10, rue Desnouettes - 01 48 28 60 91
Closed Sat, Sun, Aug. Open until 10:30pm.
The *patronne* pampers patrons in the dining room, while her husband, Dany Bulot, cooks up rousing bistro fare in his kitchen. Calf's head, boudin en salade, fresh sausage, and cod marmite are staples on the hearty menu. Moderately priced cellar, with plenty of half-bottles. C 220. M 149 (weekday lunch).

 ## Kim Anh

15, rue de l'Église - 01 45 79 40 96, fax 01 40 59 49 78
Dinner only. Open daily until 11pm. Air cond.
Charming Kim-Anh runs this flower-filled little Vietnamese restaurant while his wife, Caroline, does the cooking in a lilliputian kitchen made for contortionists. Fresh herbs, delectable leaves and shoots, subtle spices enhance her curried shrimp, beef with lemongrass, piquant stuffed crab, and the best egg rolls in town. Steepish prices. C 200. M 220 (dinner).

 ## Restaurant du Marché 🦐

59, rue de Dantzig
01 45 32 26 88, fax 01 48 28 18 31
Closed Sat lunch, Sun. Open until 11pm. Priv rm:
20. Terrace dining. Pkg.
A farmer's cartel sends fresh Southwestern produce straight to Christiane Massia's kitchen door. She transforms this bounty into wonderful cassoulet, beef stewed in Madiran wine, and myriad dishes starring plump Landais ducks. Finish off your feast with a tot of fine Armagnac. C 300. M 190 (weekdays).

 ## Morot Gaudry

8, rue de la Cavalerie
01 45 67 06 85, fax 01 45 67 55 72
Closed Sun. Open until 10:30pm. Priv rm: 24. Terrace dining. Air cond. Pkg.
The thrill is gone. Morot-Gaudry's langoustines with endives, snails with morels and sunchokes, roast lamb with stuffed vegetables, pikeperch with tarragon sabayon are all honorable dishes, but they no longer astonish or surprise. A remarkable chocolate cake en chaudfroid with citrus fruits sounded an optimistic note, however. As always, the cellar holds a trove of moderately priced treasures. From the verdant terrace you can glimpse a corner of the Eiffel Tower. C 320. M 230 (lunch, wine incl), 390, 550.

 ## Le Moulin

70, rue de Vouillé - 01 48 28 81 61
Closed Sat lunch, Sun dinner. Open until 10:30pm.
A quiet, unassuming spot where quality ingredients are handled with care. Roger Buhagiar proposes a fine poached foie gras de canard, roast rack of lamb with fresh vegetables, and a rich double-chocolate dessert. Small list of well-chosen wines; cordial welcome. C 250. M 150 (lunch), 175 (dinner, wine incl).

 ## L'Os à Moelle

3, rue Vasco-de-Gama - 01 45 57 27 27
Closed Sun, Mon, Jul 22-Aug 22. Open until 11pm.
Terrace dining.
Thierry Faucher gives his customers terrific value for their money, with imaginative menus inspired by whatever looks fresh and fine at the market. The 145 F lunch might bring gingerbread-coated foie gras garnished with spinach and beets, veal kidney with celery root purée and bone marrow, cheese, and a chocolate quenelle with saffron sauce. A tour de force, even if portions aren't gigantic. M 145 (lunch), 190 (dinner).

12/20 L'Ostréade

11, bd de Vaugirard
01 43 21 87 41, fax 01 43 21 55 09
Open daily until 11pm (11:30pm in summer). Terrace dining. No cards.
While away an hour before the TGV whisks you out West at this pleasant seafood brasserie. Excellent oysters, ultrafresh fish prepared in clever, uncomplicated ways. C 150-200.

 ## Le Père Claude

51, av. de La Motte-Picquet
01 47 34 03 05, fax 01 40 56 97 84
Open daily until midnight. Priv rm: 50. Air cond.
Claude Perraudin lives like a monk (albeit of the Rabelaisian type), his existence devoted to feeding his faithful patrons. Seven days a week in his jolly brasserie, Father Claude oversees a gargantuan rotisserie where strings of sausages, plump poultry, beef, and racks of lamb spin slowly on the spit until they're done to a turn. There are oceans of tasty wine to wash it all down. The prices? Blessedly low, of course. C 210-350. M 105-160.

 ## Le Petit Plat

49, av. Émile-Zola
01 45 78 24 20, fax 01 45 78 23 13
Closed 3 wks in Aug, 10 days at Christmas. Open daily until 11pm. Terrace dining. Air cond.
A jolly mood pervades this pretty restaurant, owing mostly to the Lampreia brothers' cooking: tomatoes provençales, cockles and mussels in a tasty broth, succulent veal breast with slow-roasted vegetables are typical of their light,

generous fare. The clever wine list was composed by our friend, Henri Gault. C 200. M 130.

 ## Yves Quintard

99, rue Blomet - 01 42 50 22 27, fax 01 42 55 22 27
Closed Sat lunch, Sun, Aug 6-23. Open until 11:30pm. Air cond.
Yves Quintard wins the votes of city workers who gather here to feast on the attractive set meals. The delicious crépinette sausage that combines pig's trotter and sweetbreads is typical of the chef's skillful blending of noble and rustic ingredients. Warm welcome; rather expensive cellar. C 235. C 130 (weekday lunch), 175, 300.

 ## Le Relais de Sèvres

Hôtel Sofitel, 8-12, rue Louis-Armand
01 40 60 33 66, fax 01 45 57 04 22
Closed Sat, Sun, hols, Dec 24-Jan 1. Open until 10pm. Priv rm: 15. Air cond. Valet pkg.
For its flagship restaurant, the Sofitel chain chose a décor that spells good taste in capital letters: blond woodwork; pale-blue fabric on the walls; champagne-colored napery; Louis XV chairs. Newly appointed young chef Bruno Turbot has now found his balance and his way. His quite attractive dinner menu (220 F) comprises grenouilles in a mountain-celery cream, sole filets with pink artichokes enhanced with coriander or a savory oxtail compote with morel mushrooms, along with a full-fledged cheese tray and a choice of dessert. The same menu, including Champagne, wine and mineral water, goes for 320 F. C 420. M 220 (dinner), 320 (lunch, wine incl).

 ## Restaurant de La Tour

"Roger Conticini,"
6, rue Desaix - 01 43 06 04 24
Closed Sat lunch, Sun, Aug. Open until 10:30pm.
Roger Conticini (his sons run the triple-toque Table d'Anvers in the ninth arrondissement) is at the helm of this engaging restaurant. The dishes on his single-price menus change often, but all have an earthy, raffish appeal: hot game pâte, a lusty salad of pig's ear and trotter, tuna braised in red wine with risotto, and gingersnapped duck breast with honey are typical of the house style. Fine little cellar. Nice going, Roger! C 210. M 118 & 138 (weekday lunch), 175 (weekdays, Sat dinner).

 ## Sawadee

53, av. Émile-Zola
01 45 77 68 90, fax 01 77 57 78
Closed Sun. Open until 10:30pm. Priv rm: 80. Terrace dinning. Air cond.
Sawadee is one of the city's best Thais. Spacious, over-decorated, very lively, it offers an immense list of specialties full of unexpected flavors. The salad of pork rinds and fried rice, skewered shellfish, mussels in a fiery sauce, cod with seaweed and wild lemon, duck perfumed with Thai basil, and coconut ice cream all come highly recommended. C 150-200. M 75-175.

 ## Aux Senteurs de Provence

295, rue Lecourbe
01 45 57 11 98, fax 01 45 58 66 84
Closed Sat lunch, Sun, Aug 4-16. Open until 10pm. Terrace dining.
Delicate, freshly fragrant Provençal cuisine. Sun-kissed ingredients lend an authentic savor to the tuna in a tarragon marinade, roast galinette (a Mediterranean fish) à la niçoise, and generous bouillabaisse. The cellar is modest, but the surroundings are neat and cheerful, with cork-covered walls and jaunty nautical prints. C 240-280. M 138.

 ## Pierre Vedel

19, rue Duranton - 01 45 58 43 17, fax 01 45 58 42 65
Closed Sat (lunch Oct-Apr), Sun, 1 week at Christmas. Open until 10:15pm. Priv rm: 12.
Be sure to book your table, because Pierre Vedel's warm Parisian bistro is invariably jam-packed. Little wonder the place is popular, given the delectable house foie gras, authentic bour-ride de lotte à la sétoise (a garlicky monkfish soup), and lush bitter-chocolate charlotte. If you order one of the more modest growers' wines from the interesting list, the bill won't be too bad. C 260-360.

16TH ARRONDISSEMENT

12/20 Amazigh

2, rue La Pérouse - 01 47 20 90 38
Open until 11pm. No cards.
A Moroccan restaurant with an enticing bill of fare: savory briouates (deep-fried pastries) filled with shellfish, eggplant salad sparked with coriander (zalouk), lamb tagine with fried eggplant, and sumptuous "grand couscous." Also worthy of interest are the stuffed sardines, lamb's brains in tomato sauce, and cinnamon-scented oranges. Like the setting, the service is pretty posh. C 250. M 150.

 ## La Baie d'Ha Long

164, av. de Versailles - 01 45 24 60 62
Closed Sun, Aug. Open until 10pm. Priv rm: 20. Terrace dining. Air cond. No pets.
Roger, the proprietor of this small Vietnamese spot, is more interested in his collection of birds and exotic fish than in food. It's his wife, Nathalie, who toils away in the kitchen producing delicious, exotic dishes from her native Vietnam: spicy soups, brochettes perfumed with fresh herbs, duck grilled with ginger. Generous portions; good desserts. C 180. M 105 (weekday lunch).

Bellini

28, rue Le Sueur - 01 45 00 54 20, fax 01 45 00 11 74
Closed Sat lunch, Sun, 1 wk at Christmas. Open until 10:30pm. Air cond.
Comfy banquettes, mirrors, marble, and chamois-toned walls create a cozy setting for

Bellini's somewhat Frenchified Italian fare. Diaphanous slices of prosciutto di Parma lead into such savory dishes as lobster salad with polenta, red mullet with olives, or veal kidney cooked in brawny Barolo wine. The cellar harbors appealing wines from Friulia, Tuscany, and the Veneto. C 250-300. M 180.

 Bertie's

Hôtel Baltimore, 1, rue Léo-Delibes
01 44 34 54 34, fax 01 44 34 54 44
Closed 2 wks in Aug. Open until 10:30pm. Priv rm: 15. Air cond. Valet pkg.

When Le Bertie's opened, a major London daily ran this tongue-in-cheek headline: "Finally! A good meal in Paris!" The dining room cultivates a clubby British look that Parisians adore. And yes, the menu is English: potted crab, Welsh mussel soup, Scottish lamb with mint sauce, bread-and-butter pudding... The maître d' will astound you with his knowledge of Britain's 400 cheeses; the wine steward will amaze you with his list of prime clarets. And after your meal, you can linger contentedly over a rare whisky or vintage Port. C 280-320. M 160 (weekday lunch), 195 (exc Sun), 250 (dinner).

 Bistrot de l'Étoile-Lauriston

19, rue Lauriston - 01 40 67 11 16, fax 01 45 00 99 87
Closed Sat lunch, Sun. Open until midnight. Air cond.

This big, bright bistro continues on its successful career. Chef William Ledeuil handles the neobourgeois repertoire with admirable ease, offering rabbit persillé or a vibrant vegetable salad showered with Parmesan to start, followed by steak à la bordelaise or stuffed veal shank simmered in a sparky vinegar sauce. For dessert, we warmly recommend the apple-rhubarb crumble. C 230.

 La Butte Chaillot

110 bis, av. Kléber
01 47 27 88 88, fax 01 47 04 85 70
Open daily until midnight. Priv rm: 25. Terrace dining. Air cond. Valet pkg.

Chef and restaurateur Guy Savoy turned an unpromising site (a former bank) into a fashionable restaurant with a star-studded clientele. The keys to his success are a clever contemporary décor, a swift and stylish staff, and—best of all—an ever-changing roster of irresistible dishes: succulent spit-roasted poultry with whipped potatoes, veal breast perfumed with rosemary and olive oil, and lots of luscious desserts. C 240. M 150-210.

 Carré Kléber

Hôtel Paris K Palace, 11 bis, rue de Magdebourg
01 47 55 82 08, fax 01 47 55 80 09
Closed Sat lunch, Sun, 3 wks in Aug, 1 wk at Chrismas. Priv rm: 30. Air cond. Pkg.

Provence, as we know, is furiously à la mode. Christophe Delaunay pays homage to the current fashion with a delicious tart of red mullet and baby mackerel on a bed of tomato fondue and tapenade, and other suitably Southern delights. The very pretty modern dining room opens onto a leafy patio. C 220-270. M 185, 80 (children).

 Paul Chène

123, rue Lauriston
01 47 27 63 17, fax 01 47 27 53 18
Closed Sat lunch, Sun, Dec 24-Jan 2. Open until 10:30pm. Priv rm: 30. Air cond. Pkg.

Elbow-room is at a premium in Paul Chène's two faded dining rooms, but the owners are unstinting with their hospitality and the kitchen, too, has a generous spirit. You're sure to relish eggs poached in red wine, quality Parma ham, beef tenderloin béarnaise, and profiteroles napped in chocolate. The cellar boasts a varied, judicious selection, yet the house Bordeaux is not to be neglected. C 300-400. M 200, 250.

 Conti

72, rue Lauriston - 01 47 27 74 67, fax 01 47 27 37 66
Closed Sat, Sun, hols, 1 wk in Jan, Aug. Open until 10:30pm. Air cond.

With Sormani's Jean-Pascal Fayet (see seventeenth arrondissement), Michel Ranvier is a leading French exponent of Italian cooking. Perhaps a shade less creative than Fayet, Ranvier still gives his menu a vigorous zest. Examples? Clams and cockles with fennel in a perfumed broth, a perfect risotto with fresh peas and asparagus, and a fabulous bollito misto with pungent mostarda di Cremona. The Italian cellar is a wonder to behold, and the staff provides silken service. C 360-460. M 198 (lunch).

Le Cuisinier François

19, rue Le Marois - 01 45 27 83 74, fax 01 45 27 83 74
Closed Sun, Mon, Wed dinner, 1 wk in Feb. Open until 10pm.

After stints at La Tour d'Argent, Robuchon, and Boyer in Reims, Thierry Conte did not, as one might expect, open a place with his name in large letters over the door. Instead, he settled for an establishment of modest proportions and a menu that is most moderately priced. Delicious petit-gris snails en sauce and an excellent sole in meat juices are typical of his modern, uncomplicated fare. But desserts are cloying, we find, and the wines too costly. Though Thierry Conte deserves another point for his cuisine. C 250. M 160.

Alain Ducasse

59, av. Raymond-Poincaré
01 47 27 12 27, fax 01 47 27 31 22
Closed Sat, Sun, Jul 4-Aug 4, 1 wk at Christmas-New Year's. Open until 10pm. Valet pkg.

Who else but Alain Ducasse could replace Joël Robuchon? A megachef takes over from a superstar—it couldn't happen any other way. Alain Ducasse faced a two-fold challenge: to take over from the city's foremost chef and maintain the restaurant's stellar rank, and at the same time preserve his own number one rating on the Riviera. For Ducasse, a *patron* is nothing without his team. Sous-chefs are drilled to follow his principles, his precision, his uncompromising approach to ingredients. Paris gives Ducasse the opportunity to play with a palette of northern flavors: Breton fish, Bresse poultry, prime produce from the Loire or Picardy. Olive oil is not absent from his Parisian kitchen, but it somehow feels right, up here in the north, to embellish a turbot with North Sea shrimp and perhaps a spoonful of salted butter from Brittany. To the magnificent cellar that Robuchon left behind, Ducasse has added selections of his own. We'll hold back on rating Ducasse until he's had a chance to prove that he is indeed the leading chef of his generation. C 900-1,500. M 480 (lunch), 890.

 ## Duret Mandarin

34, rue Duret - 01 45 00 09 06
Open daily until 11pm. Air cond. Valet pkg.
The Tang family work hard to deliver (with a smile!) such Chinese classics as crispy egg rolls, deep-fried dumplings, and stuffed crab, and interesting options like steamed scallops with black-bean sauce and "special" roast chicken. Terrific Peking duck, with optimally crisp skin (order it when you book your table). C 160-260. M 79, 95.

 ## Fakhr el Dine

30, rue de Longchamp
01 47 27 90 00, fax 01 47 27 11 39
Open daily until 11:30pm. Priv rm: 60. No pets. Valet pkg.
See *8th arrondissement.* C 290. M 150-360.

 ## Faugeron

52, rue de Longchamp
01 47 04 24 53, fax 01 47 55 62 90
Closed Sat dinner off-seas, Sun, Aug, Dec 23-Jan 3. Open until 10pm. Priv rm: 14. Air cond. No pets. Valet pkg.
Henri Faugeron hails from the Corrèze countryside, where a man is judged by his work, not his pretensions. This modest, even self-effacing chef doesn't go in for bold experiments, but he knows how to use an uncommon spice, or mustard, or vinegar to give traditional dishes a pungent, modern zest. Faugeron pays tribute to his rustic roots with seasonal variations on cèpes and truffles, with tender veal shank heightened with a piquant touch of Brive's violet mustard, or a beef daube braised à l'ancienne for a full ten hours and served with truffled pasta. A pastoral apple flognarde is a final flourish to be savored along with the last drops of a great Bordeaux, Burgundy, or more modest Chinon or Sancerre, chosen by "World's Best Sommelier", in 1986, Jean-Claude Jambon. C 480. M 295 (weekdays), 550 (dinner, wine incl), 650.

Remember to call ahead to reserve your table, and please, if you cannot honor your reservation, be courteous and let the restaurant know.

 ## Les Filaos

5, rue Guy-de-Maupassant - 01 45 04 94 53
Closed Sun, Aug. Open until 11pm. Priv rm: 45.
Spicy savors from Mauritius: try the palate-tingling stuffed crab seasoned with ginger and coriander, or tamarind-flavored codfish beignets, octopus in a saffron marinade, or smoked sausages with fiery rougail. C 220.

 ## Le Flandrin

80, av. Henri Martin - 01 45 04 35 69
Open daily until 11:30pm. Terrace dining.
This chic brasserie now boasts a much-improved *carte*, thanks to the efforts of young Olivier Denis (trained by mega-chef Alain Passard). We like the shrimp beignets, macaroni and ricotta gratin, crab ravioli, langoustines grilled with wild thyme, and the warming lamb curry. Oysters and other fresh shellfish in season; good service. C 250.

 ## Gastronomie Quach

47, av. Raymond-Poincaré - 01 42 27 98 40
Open daily until 11pm. Priv rm: 20. Air cond.
Aquariums decorate the posh dining room where Monsieur Quach serves Cantonese and Vietnamese dishes that now have more good days than bad: prawns grilled with lemongrass, squid with red peppers, and grilled lamb with five spices are more precisely turned out than in the past. And the fine Peking duck keeps the glossy patrons coming back for more. C 230-310. M 92 (weekdays, Sat lunch), 109.

 ## La Grande Cascade

Bois de Boulogne, near the racetrack
01 45 27 33 51, fax 01 42 88 99 06
Closed end Dec-mid Jan. Open until 10:30pm. Priv rm: 50. Terrace dining. Valet pkg.
The setting of this former pleasure pavillion is exuberantly Belle Époque, and up until recently, the cuisine was discreetly classic. But super-chef Alain Ducasse has commissioned one of his best lieutenants, Jean-Louis Nomicos, to revamp the menu. As a result, the Cascade now shines with exciting tastes: fine potato raviolis; greens with a Parmesan tuile; sea-bass steak with fennel seeds and black pepper served with ground tomatoes in olive oil; and corn-fed chicken stuffed with fresh herbs accompanied by succulent mushrooms gnocchi. Go for the satisfying 285 F menu. C 550-820. M 285.

 ## Lac Hong

67, rue Lauriston - 01 47 55 87 17
Closed Sun, Aug. Open until 10:45pm. Air cond. No pets.
Vietnam's cuisine may be the most delicately flavorful in all of Southeast Asia. To test that proposition, just taste Lé Thi Lanh's remarkable salad of grilled scampi and green papaya, ginger-roasted lobster, shrimp-stuffed rice pancakes, steamed smoked duck with fish sauce, or lamb redolent of curry and star anise. Even the Cantonese rice is exquisite: flawlessly cooked

and bursting with flavor. C 250. M 98 (weekday lunch, Sat).

Jamin

32, rue de Longchamp - 01 45 53 00 07
Closed Sat, Sun, Jul 11-Aug 4. Open until 10:30pm. Air cond. Pkg.
Joël Robuchon's old Jamin has opened its doors again, after a three-year interruption, with Robuchon pupil Benoit Guichard in the kitchen. Prices are considerably lower nowadays, with a 375 F set meal served at lunch and dinner, and an à la carte average of 500F. The current menu proposes duck and fig terrine, a warm salad of langoustines and cuttlefish spiked with ginger, braised beef with cumin-spiced carrots, and wine-dark stewed rabbit with fresh pasta and cèpes. We'll give the new staff time to learn the ropes before we weigh in with our rating. Stay tuned! C 500. M 280 (lunch), 375.

12/20   Chez Ngo

70, rue de Longchamp
01 47 04 53 20, fax 01 47 04 53 20
Open daily until 11:45pm. Priv rm: 7. Air cond. No pets. Pkg.
An elegant Chinese table (pretty décor, lovely dishes). Look beyond the menu's classic dishes to the more interesting grilled frogs' legs, delectable steamed fish, curried eel, and zippy salt-and-pepper shrimp showered with herbs. C 250. M 97 (lunch), 98 (lunch, wine incl), 168 (wine incl), 398 (for 2 pers).

 Nikita

6, rue Faustin Hélié
01 45 04 04 33, fax 01 47 53 92 10
Closed Aug. Open until 12:30am. Air cond. Valet pkg.
The décor of red velvet and gilt mirrors is typical of the city's posher Russian restaurants. What's different about this one, though, is that the prices are not high-hat! Yes, there's a gypsy violinist and a sloe-eyed singer; but for once the shashlik and potato dumplings are creditably prepared, and diners aren't made to feel like cheapskates if they don't order caviar. Take note of the 290 F set meal: it's worthy of a celebration. C 350. M 120 (lunch, wine incl), 290, 490.

 Oum el Banine

16 bis, rue Dufrenoy
01 45 04 91 22, fax 01 45 03 46 26
Closed lunch Sat & Sun. Open until 11pm. Air cond.
To enter, knock on the heavy wooden door, just as you would in Morocco. Maria Seguin, a native of Fès, practices authentic Fassi cuisine, whose secrets are handed down from mother to daughter. Five types of couscous are on offer, as well as eight tagines (with olives and pickled lemons, peppers and tomato, zucchini and thyme, etc.). More rarely seen, but typically Moroccan, are brains in a piquant tomato sauce, spiced tripe, and calf's foot with chickpeas. C 275.

 Le Pergolèse

40, rue Pergolèse - 01 45 00 21 40, fax 01 45 00 81 31
Closed Sat, Sun, Aug. Open until 10:30pm. Priv rm: 32. Valet pkg.
Local stockbrokers are bullish on Le Pergolèse. They've adopted Albert Corre's plush and intimate (indeed, slightly cramped) dining room as their unofficial headquarters. But it may be that Corre is spending too much time at the tables and not enough at the stove, for the cooking has dipped below its previous high. Our carpaccio of salt-cured lamb lacked character, for instance, and an overcooked sea bass was further marred by a dubious sauce. Happily, an unctuous chocolate dessert saved the toque—but only just! C 400-500. M 230, 320.

 Le Port Alma

10, av. de New-York - 01 47 23 75 11
Closed Sun, Aug. Open until 10:30pm. Air cond.
Paul Canal isn't one to blow his own horn, but he has few peers when it comes to cooking fish and crustaceans. Count on Canal to pick the best of the day's catch, and prepare his prime specimens with a skilled hand and no superfluous sauces to mask their flavors. Bourride and bouillabaisse are featured on Fridays, or upon reservation. Balanced cellar, with plenty of half-bottles. C 300-500. M 200 (lunch).

 Le Pré Catelan

Bois de Boulogne, route de Suresnes
01 44 14 41 14, fax 01 45 24 43 25
Closed Sun dinner, Mon, Feb school hols. Open until 10:30pm. Priv rm: 50. Terrace dining. Valet pkg.
The Pré Catelan comes in two versions: summer, with tables set in a leafy garden amid fluttering parasols; and winter, an elegant dining room warmed by a crackling fire. The versatile talent of the chef suits both settings, with dishes that are by turns urbane or rustic. In season, you'll discover an extraordinary "menu truffe et cochon," which demonstrates that with the right perfume—truffles, for example—one can indeed turn a sow's ear into something sublime: in this case a croquant d'oreille with langoustines. Sophisticated spicing marks the black risotto with Thai basil, and lamb's brain salad with its exquisite saffron aspic. Desserts are divine (ah! the hot chocolate-praline pastilla!), and the cellar is well served by a first-rate sommelier. C 650-900. M 280 (weekday lunch), 550, 750.

Prunier Traktir

16, av. Victor-Hugo
01 44 17 35 85, fax 01 44 17 90 10
Closed Sun, Mon lunch, Jul 15-Aug 15. Open until 11pm. Priv rm: 10. Air cond. Valet pkg.
The rebirth of Prunier Traktir caused great rejoicing among Paris's pearls-and-tweed set, who regarded the demise of this once-brilliant seafood house as a personal loss. The man behind the revival is Jean-Claude Vrinat of Taillevent. From the moment he opened the doors of the gorgeously restored Art Deco interior,

Parisians took the dining room by storm. Handsome rooms are fitted up on the second floor as well, and Prunier is regularly packed with the sleek and famous. In the kitchen, Gabriel Biscay balances Prunier classics (lobster bisque, codfish brandade, marmite dieppoise) with such contemporary items as fish tartare with oysters, red mullet à l'orientale, and langoustines royales au naturel. C 580.

 ## Le Relais d'Auteuil

31, bd Murat - 01 46 51 09 54, fax 01 40 71 05 03
Closed Sat lunch, Sun, 3 wks of Aug. Open until 10:30pm. Air cond. Valet pkg.
Patrick Pignol's imaginative, resolutely modern cuisine is a treat to discover. Uncompromising in his choice of ingredients, he follows the seasons to obtain the very freshest, finest produce. In summer, he'll feature zucchini blossoms and other vegetables at the peak of their flavor; in fall, look for sage-scented braised partridge; winter might bring a mammoth sole in a sauce of lightly salted butter and fiery Szechuan pepper. If only Pignol would keep a tighter rein on his prices...! C 500. M 250 (lunch), 410, 520.

12/20 Le Relais du Bois de Boulogne

Bois de Boulogne, Croix-Catelan, route de Suresnes
01 42 15 00 11, fax 01 42 15 03 52
Closed Sun dinner, Mon. Open until 10:30pm. Terrace dining. Pkg.
This Second Empire hunting pavilion where naughty ladies and gentlemen once engaged in rather outrageous behavior is now the backdrop for tame family parties and quiet lunches. In summer, nab a table in the garden and enjoy duck carpaccio with balsamic vinegar or fish en papillote. C 200. M 120, 150 (wine incl), 165, 78 (children).

 ## Le Relais du Parc

Hôtel Le Parc, 55-57, av. Raymond-Poincaré
01 44 05 66 10, fax 01 44 05 66 00
Open daily until 10:30pm. Terrace dining. Air cond. Valet pkg.
Le Relais du Parc holds a winning hand. Set in the luxurious Le Parc hotel, it sports a British colonial setting and is now under the supervision of Alain Ducasse (who also has taken over Robuchon next door). Ducasse has kept such Robuchon dishes as the aerial creamy soup in a crustacean gelée, but he has also added Southwestern dishes: cod-stuffed bell peppers; tomatoes stuffed with vegetables; John Dory on a bed of fennel; melon soup in Jurançon wine. Reservations are a must. C 330.

 ## La Salle à Manger

17, av. Kléber - 01 44 28 00 17, fax 01 45 01 54 21
Closed Sat, Sun, hols. Open until 10pm. Priv rm: 60. Air cond. Valet pkg.
In an auspicious new departure, the ever-so-swank Hôtel Raphaël has renovated its dining room, and entrusted the kitchen to chef Philip Delahaye. The menu entices with such sophisticated fare as langoustine fricassée flanked by a crisp craquant of apples and pig's trotter, roasted sea bass served en soupière with mild garlic and star anise, or breast of guinea hen with marble-sized potatoes and morsels of smoky sausage set in a pool of green-pea cream. Desserts are equally dainty; indeed, the only quibble we have is that the food occasionally edges awfully close to preciousness. C 450. M 290 (dinner), 295 (lunch).

 ## Le Toit de Passy

94, av. Paul-Doumer
01 45 24 55 37, fax 01 45 20 94 57
Closed Sat lunch, Sun. Open until 10:30pm. Priv rm: 25. Terrace dining. Air cond. Pkg.
On a fine day the terrace is unquestionably the place to sit for the unimpeded view of Passy's rooftops. Yet the dining room, accented with plants and partitions, is also an elegant setting for Yannick Jacquot's cuisine. The cellar holds no fewer than 45,000 bottles, so the wine list will take some perusing. C 500 (wine incl). M 195 (weekday lunch), 280-350 (lunch, wine incl), 395-510 (weekdays).

 ## Vivarois

192, av. Victor-Hugo
01 45 04 04 31, fax 01 45 03 09 84
Closed Sat, Sun, Aug. Open until 10pm. Air cond. Valet pkg.
Claude Peyrot imperturbably polishes a concise, unchanging *carte* which he supplements daily with a half-dozen dishes created on the spur of the moment. In the latter category, we fondly recall a sublime wild-mushroom terrine with foie gras; in the former, we recommend the sweet-pepper bavaroise heightened with an uncommonly fragrant walnut oil. Peyrot's pared-down style leaves little room for error. When a dish is perfectly done, its purity elicits admiration; but the slightest flaw makes simplicity look suspiciously like skimping... Exemplary service in a handsome contemporary dining room. The fine cellar is run by Jean-Claude Vinadier, sommelier extraordinaire. C 650. M 345 (weekday lunch).

 ## Woo Jung

8, bd Delessert - 01 45 20 72 82
Closed Sun, Aug 17-30, Dec 21-Jan 4. Open until 10:30pm. Priv rm: 24. Air cond. No pets.
A Korean restaurant filled with Koreans (a good sign) in the chic Passy district. Adventurous diners can opt for a mustardy jellyfish salad, beef tartare with sesame seeds, or pearly-fresh raw sea bream. Every dish is beautifully served. C 250.

Zébra Square

3, pl. Clément-Ader
01 44 14 91 91, fax 01 45 20 46 41
Open daily until 1am. Priv rm: 8. Terrace dining.
Air cond. No pets. Pkg.
   Good food at reasonable prices in an
"American-style" setting. Assorted warm
vegetables drizzled with Provençal olive oil,
crab with sweet-pepper coulis, and sea bream
with roasted artichokes and a touch of
lemongrass all succeed in revving up the appetite. Brunch is served on weekends. C 250. M
110 (weekday lunch).

17TH ARRONDISSEMENT

 ## Albert-Albert

24, rue de Tilsitt - 01 45 72 25 14, fax 01 45 72 25 48
Closed Sat lunch, Sun, Aug 10-20. Open until mid-
night. Priv rm: 50. Air cond. Valet pkg.
   Albert Nahmias not only has a flair for public
relations, he is also a highly professional restaurateur. His handsome premises (salmon-
colored walls, blue banquettes, modern
paintings...) are in a high-rent district, but he
manages to offer a 180 F single-price menu based
on very good ingredients: among the choices are
Breton oysters, sea bream roasted with fresh
thyme, lamb with sweet peppers, a delicious
dish of streaky bacon in a sauce spiked with
truffle juice, and mango tarte Tatin to finish. All
are capably prepared by a young chef trained by
Chapel. Excellent cellar, with wines from 70 F. C
200. M 150 (weekday lunch, wine incl), 180
(weekdays, Sat dinner).

 ## Amphyclès

"Phillipe Groult", 78, av. des Ternes
01 40 68 01 01, fax 01 40 68 91 88
Closed Sat lunch, Sun. Open until 10:30pm. Priv
rm: 25. Air cond. Valet pkg.
   Joël Robuchon imbued his star pupil, Philippe
Groult, with a passion for perfection. Superb
ingredients, which Groult chooses with discriminating care, are the basis of colorful, flavorful dishes that delight both eye and palate. To
wit: a scarlet spider crab stuffed with a blend of
its own meat, tourteau crab, and lobster; pearly
white John Dory topped with slow-roasted
tomatoes and glossy black olives; or golden
sweetbreads with dried fruits and nuts and a
brilliant green snow-pea fondue. Only the best
growers are admitted to the select and expensive
wine list. C 550-900. M 720, 820.

 ## Apicius

122, av. de Villiers
01 43 80 19 66, fax 01 44 40 09 57
Closed Sat, Sun, Aug. Open until 10pm. Air cond.
Valet pkg.
   We know lots of high-class restaurants where
the food is perfectly fine—but the ambience is
stuffy and dull. At Jean-Pierre Vigato's Apicius,
not only is the food simply fabulous, the atmosphere is as warm as can be. The charm begins to
work from the moment Madeleine Vigato welcomes you into the lavishly flower-decked
dining room. Though Vigato's core repertoire
doesn't vary much from one year to the next, he
stays sharp by offering a half-dozen different
starters and entrées each day (which Madeleine
describes at each table in luscious detail). If
they're on hand, do try the langoustine tartare
seasoned with olive oil, a hint of meat juice,
pepper, and a whisper of garlic; or the tiny artichokes flavored with aged Parmesan and white
truffles; or (in autumn) the sumptuous duck pie,
a performance worthy of Escoffier! C 550-750. M
520 (weekdays).

 ## Augusta

98, rue de Tocqueville
01 47 63 39 97, fax 01 42 27 21 71
Closed Sun, Aug 4-25. Open until 10pm. Air cond.
   Scrupulously seasonal, rigorously precise,
based on the freshest seafood: Philippe de Saint-
Étienne's cuisine is all this and more. The clear,
direct flavors of his sweet-and-sour scampi,
rockfish soup, fricassée of sole and artichokes,
seared sea bass with sea salt, or roast John Dory
with a shellfish jus incite us to unashamed gorg-
ing! Remarkable wine list; young, eager staff. C
400-600.

 ## 12/20 Le Ballon des Ternes

103, av. des Ternes
01 45 74 17 98, fax 01 45 72 18 84
Closed Aug 1-21. Open until 12:30am. Priv rm: 40.
Terrace dining. Air cond.
   Shellfish assortments, tuna carpaccio
showered with sesame seeds, veal kidney with
mustard sauce, and house-made apple tart are
served with top-quality wines at this likeable
Belle Époque brasserie. C 250.

 ## Baumann Ternes

64, av. des Ternes - 01 45 74 16 66, fax 01 45 72 44 32
Open daily until midnight. Priv rm: 27. Terrace
dining. Air cond. Pkg.
   A bastion of the Baumann restaurant empire,
where you can savor first-class choucroutes and
other Alsatian specialties, as well as tasty tar-
tares and grills. Wonderful wines; lively ambience. C 230. M 112 (beer incl), 163.

Billy Gourmand

20, rue de Tocqueville - 01 42 27 03 71
Closed Sat lunch, Sun, hols, 3 wks in Aug. Open until
10pm. Priv rm: 14.
   Chef Philippe Billy presents his polished, prettily presented cuisine in a spacious dining room
decorated with mirrors and plants. On a recent
visit we tucked into crab ravioli with mussels
and baby broad beans, a tender lamb chop
topped with seasoned butter, and a delicate
morello cherry cake. The engaging *patronne*
oversees a fine cellar of Loire Valley wines. C
280. M 160.

Le Bistrot d'à Côté

10, rue Gustave-Flaubert
01 42 67 05 81, fax 01 47 63 82 75
Open daily until 11:30pm. Terrace dining. Air cond. Valet pkg.
All you want from a bistro: hustle, bustle, and cheeky waiters. Who wouldn't be won over by the simple, savory pleasures of the menu's French provincial specialties? The wines, however, are awfully expensive for this sort of place. C 250-330.

 ## Le Bistrot de l'Étoile-Niel

75, av. Niel - 01 42 27 88 44, fax 01 42 27 32 12
Closed Sun lunch. Open until midnight. Terrace dining. Air cond. Valet pkg.
Here's your typical cheerful neighborhood bistro—except that it's owned and supervised by Guy Savoy. Handily prepared and served with a smile, the tuna carpaccio with shellfish vinaigrette, chicken with pickled lemons, vanilla-chocolate chaud-froid, and house Merlot have won a loyal following. C 230. M 180.

 ## Le Bistrot de l'Étoile-Troyon

13, rue Troyon - 01 42 67 25 95, fax 01 46 22 43 09
Closed Sat, Sun lunch. Open until 11:30pm. Terrace dining. Air cond. Valet pkg.
Guy Savoy can keep a close eye on the first-born of his bistro annexes, for it stands just across the street from his three-toque restaurant. In the small, convivial dining room you can treat yourself to such heartwarming bourgeois classics as leek and chicken-liver terrine, roast veal with onion marmalade, coffee parfait, and lush chocolate quenelles. Good growers' wines; democratic prices. C 170. M 160.

 ## Les Bouchons de François Clerc

22, rue de la Terrasse - 01 42 27 31 51
Open daily until 11pm. Air cond. Terrace dining.
See *5th arrondissement.* M 117 (weekday lunch), 219.

 ## Caves Pétrissans

30 bis, av. Niel - 01 42 27 52 03, fax 01 40 54 87 56
Closed Sat, Sun, hols, Aug 4-24. Open until 10:30pm. Priv rm: 10. Terrace dining.
Four generations of Pétrissans have overseen this wine shop-cum-restaurant, where patrons linger happily over Denis Bischoff's deft cooking. The quality ingredients are simply prepared and generously served; try the terrine maison served with onion marmalade, tête de veau sauce ravigote, and flaky fruit tarts. Fabulous wine list. C 200. M 165.

12/20 Charly de Bab-el-Oued

95, bd Gouvion-Saint-Cyr
01 45 74 34 62, fax 01 45 74 35 36
Closed mid Jul-mid Aug. Open until 11:30pm. Air cond. No pets.
An inviting place to dream of the *Arabian Nights* amid colorful tiles, cedarwood, and palm trees. Feast on excellent couscous, pastillas, and tagines, followed by sweet Eastern pastries made on the premises. Perfect service. C 230-280.

 ## 12/20 Les Cigales

127, rue Cardinet - 01 42 27 83 93
Closed Sat, Sun, Aug. Open until 10pm. Pkg.
The décor plays the Provençal card to the hilt (sun-yellow walls, photos of the Riviera...), and so does the bright bill of fare: tomatoes stuffed with creamy goat cheese, grilled sea bream anointed with virgin olive oil, pasta dressed with pistou are all handily turned out. C 200. M 150 (lunch).

 ## Clos Longchamp

Hôtel Méridien, 81, bd Gouvion-St-Cyr
01 40 68 30 40, fax 01 40 68 30 81
Closed Sat, Sun, Aug 4-24, last wk of Dec. Open until 10:30pm. Priv rm: 18. Air cond. Valet pkg.
Jean-Marie Meulien's elegant menu combines the flavors of the Mediterranean with the spices of Southeast Asia. Plump pink shrimp are perfumed with Thai herbs; tender lamb and vegetables are given a spicy tandoori treatment; a thick chop of milk-fed veal is paired with wild mushrooms. A similarly exotic mood inspires the desserts (coconut blancmange). Award-winning sommelier Didier Bureau administers a remarkable cellar. C 450-600. M 250 (weekday lunch), 340, 470.

 ## L'Écrin d'Or

35, rue Legendre - 01 47 63 83 08
Closed Sat lunch, Mon, Aug. Open until 11pm. Priv rm: 16.
Huge mirrors, moldings, chandeliers, and great swathes of velvet hangings make a precious setting for Gilles Cendres's warm beef salad, scallop fricassée with fresh pasta, and Grand Marnier soufflé. Intelligently chosen wines; friendly welcome. C 260-350. M 95, 115.

Épicure 108

108, rue Cardinet - 01 47 63 50 91
Closed Sat lunch, Sun, Feb school hols, 2 wks in Aug. Open until 10pm.
A quiet restaurant with a pastel interior (in need, we think, of a brush-up) where chef Tetsu Goya presents hearty Alsatian-style dishes. The 180 F menu brings a salad of quail and foie gras, fish simmered with sauerkraut, and chocolate puffs with pear marmalade. Nice little cellar, with some fine Rieslings. M 180, 250.

 ## L'Étoile d'Or

Hôtel Concorde La Fayette, 3, pl. du Général-Kœnig
01 40 68 51 28, fax 01 40 68 50 43
Closed Sat, Sun. Open until 10:30pm. Priv rm: 40. Air cond. Valet pkg.

Jean-Claude Lhonneur has made L'Étoile d'Or one of the best hotel restaurants in town. Bold harmonies of flavors, split-second timing, and feather-light sauces are the three solid bases of his alluring repertoire. We know: it isn't easy to find this handsome, wood-paneled dining room, hidden in the labyrinth of the Hôtel Concorde; paying the bill isn't so simple either. But if you make the effort, your reward will be (for example) meltingly savory duck liver in a Banyuls wine jus, smothered sea bass perfumed with truffled oil, or savory stewed ox jowls en ravigote, and a chocolate soufflé that the waiter swears is the best in Paris! C 400-675. M 270.

 Faucher

123, av. de Wagram
01 42 27 61 50, fax 01 46 22 25 72
Closed Sat lunch, Sun. Open until 10pm. Terrace dining. Valet pkg.
Gérard Faucher keeps prices down to keep customers coming. He's crossed a few costly items off of his shopping list, but otherwise his menu is as vivid and modern as ever. He's even managed to preserve some signature dishes, like the millefeuille of thinly sliced raw beef and spinach leaves, and the short ribs with a truffled jus. You'll also find a wickedly tasty combination of foie gras, fried egg, and grilled coppa, and crackling lacquered duck breast. Wines from a revised, less expensive cellar complete the picture. Nicole Faucher greets guests with a smile in the cheerful yellow dining room. C 250. M 385.

 La Gazelle

9, rue Rennequin - 01 42 67 64 18, fax 01 42 67 82 77
Closed Sun. Open until 11:30pm.
The prettiest African restaurant in Paris, La Gazelle boasts a range of intensely tasty dishes prepared by owner-chef Marie Koffi-Nketsin, who comes from Cameroon: try her shrimp fritters, lemon chicken yassa, and marinated kid baked en papillote with African corn. Crocodile also features on the menu—connoisseurs, take note! Heartwarming ambience. C 180. M 130, 150.

 Chez Georges

273, bd Pereire - 01 45 74 31 00, fax 01 45 74 02 56
Closed Aug 1-21. Open until 11:30pm. Priv rm: 30. Terrace dining. Pkg.
Trends may come and go, but the bustling bistro atmosphere and comforting cuisine (ribs of beef with gratin savoyard, cheese ravioli in chive cream, hachis parmentier...) at Chez Georges remain the same. And so do the high prices. C 240-350.

12/20 Goldenberg

69, av. de Wagram
01 42 27 34 79, fax 01 42 27 98 85
Open daily until 11:30pm. Terrace dining.
Patrick Goldenberg creates a typically Yiddish atmosphere of good humor and nostalgia in which to savor Kosher cooking rooted in the traditions of Russia, Hungary, Romania...

There's pastrami, corned goose breast, kneidler in chicken broth, veal sausage, and other Central European classics. For dessert, try the poppyseed strudel. C 160-260. M 98 (wine incl).

 Graindorge

15, rue de l'Arc-de-Triomphe
01 47 54 00 28, fax 01 44 09 84 51
Closed Sat lunch, Sun. Open until 11pm. Priv rm: 30. Garage pkg.
When Bernard Broux (long-time chef at Le Trou Gascon) opened a place of his own, he forsook the Southwest in favor of the cuisine of his native Flanders. Broux's menu assembles hearty Northern savors with creamy beer soup, waterzoï of scallops and shellfish in shrimp fumet, carbonnade of ox jowls laced with gin, and strawberries in a sabayon spiked with raspberry-flavored kriek beer. Good wine list, but beer lovers will be knocked out by the selection of rare brews. The 165 F lunch is a bargain. C 210. M 135, 165 (weekday lunch), 188, 230, 60 (children)

 Guyvonne

14, rue de Thann - 01 42 27 25 43, fax 01 42 27 25 43
Closed Sat, Sun, Aug 4-Sep 1, Dec 23-Jan 1. Open until 10pm. Priv rm: 10. Terrace dining. No pets.
Guy Cros's menu balances tradition and modernity, with basil-scented sautéed squid, herbed roast salmon, and veal sweetbreads in a lush cream sauce laced with Port. Fine wine list; peaceful, provincial setting. C 290. M 150, 180, 95 (children).

 Kifune

44, rue Saint-Ferdinand - 01 45 72 11 19
Closed 2 wks in Aug, Dec-Jan. Open until 10pm. No pets. Pkg.
In the best Japanese tradition, large sums are demanded for tiny portions of food. But at Kifune the quality is irreproachable: sparkling fresh sashimi and sushi, shrimp tempura, whiting in soy sauce, ethereal fried chicken. C 300-400. M 135 (weekday lunch, Sat).

 Le Manoir de Paris

6, rue Pierre-Demours
01 45 72 25 25, fax 01 45 74 80 98
Closed Sat lunch, Sun. Open until 10:30pm. Priv rm: 60. Air cond. Valet pkg.
Owner Francis Vandenhende and chef Daniel Hébert steer a skillful course between classicism and culinary daring, with nods to Provence (in honor of Vandehende's Niçoise wife). Their pleasingly eclectic menus propose brandade de morue (a purée of codfish and potatoes) swirled inside a sweet red pepper; a traditional bouchée à la reine filled with morsels of kidney, cock's comb, and prawns; coalfish escorted by fried garlic and a delicate white-bean purée studded with chorizo; and fragrant, cumin-spiced rack of lamb. Careful: the desserts are swoon-inducing (just spoon into that coffee mousse...). Rémi

Aspect oversees the splendid cellar. **C** 450. **M** 195-295 (lunch), 195-350 (dinner).

 ## Les Marines de Pétrus

27, av. Niel - 01 47 63 04 24, fax 01 44 15 92 20
Open daily until 11pm. Air cond. Terrace dining. No cards.
The nautical décor charms us less than Souad Barrié, the gracious *patronne*, or the menu of tasty seafood: tartare prepared with a trio of fresh fish, empereur (a mild white fish) au curry, or cod with spicy condiments. Meat-eaters can plump for beef tenderloin béarnaise or pig's trotter en crépinette. A buttery brioche feuilleté served with caramel ice cream rounds things off on a satisfyingly rich note. There are two wine lists: one is modest, the other (which you must ask to see) quite grand. **C** 230-260.

 ## La Niçoise

4, rue Pierre-Demours
01 45 74 42 41, fax 01 45 74 80 98
Closed Sat lunch, Sun. Open until 11pm. Priv rm: 60. Air cond. Valet pkg.
Sunny Niçois specialties served in a picture-postcard setting that's reminiscent of Nice at holiday time. Prime ingredients are prepared with touching sincerity to yield ricotta ravioli in a creamy pistou sauce, veal sauté with green olives, and sweet polenta with pears. Perfect Provençal cellar. **M** 90, 125 (wine incl), 165.

 ## Le Petit Colombier

42, rue des Acacias
01 43 80 28 54, fax 01 44 40 04 29
Closed Sat, Sun lunch, Aug 1-18. Open until 10:45pm. Priv rm: 35. Air cond. Pkg.
With loving devotion, Bernard Fournier watches over his "provincial" inn, a family heirloom which he runs with the energy of three men. The reward for his vigilance is a loyal clientele of contented gourmands who tuck in joyfully to such spirited, full-bodied dishes as hare terrine enriched with foie gras, lobster quenelles, or veal chops tenderly braised en cocotte. Each day also brings a roast—succulent ribs of beef, for example, or poularde truffée aux petits légumes—carved and served at the table. To toast these delights, there is a splendiferous cellar with some 50,000 bottles. **C** 480. **M** 200 (weekday lunch), 360 (dinner).

 ## Paolo Petrini

6, rue du Débarquadère
01 45 74 25 95, fax 01 45 74 12 95
Closed Sat lunch, Sun, 3 wks in Aug. Open until 11pm. Air cond.
Paolo Petrini hails from Pisa, he's a genuine Italian chef (Paris has so few)! His cooking is spare and stylized, yet the full spectrum of Italy's seductive savors are present in his warm, basil-scented salad of squid, clams, and cannellini beans, his delectable risotto ai porcini, grilled beef fillet dressed with balsamic vinegar, pappardelle napped with a rich, winy hare sauce, or

tagliarini swathed in melted Fontina. Superb Italian cellar. **C** 300-350. **M** 150, 190.

 ## Petrus

12, pl. du Maréchal-Juin
01 43 80 15 95, fax 01 43 80 06 96
Closed Aug. Open until 11pm. Priv rm: 20. Air cond. Valet pkg.
Jacky Louazé is the skipper aboard the good ship Petrus, who deserves another point this year. He handles seafood with discretion and restraint, serving forth a superb carpaccio of sea bream, bass, and salmon, a golden heap of crisp-fried whitebait, gingered tuna cooked as rare as you like, and a sole of pristine freshness. To begin, we always choose a dozen or so glossy Marennes oysters, and to finish, we just as invariably order the chocolate soufflé. Fine selection of white wines. **C** 400. **M** 250 (dinner).

 ## Il Ristorante

22, rue Fourcroy - 01 47 63 34 00
Closed 2 wks in Aug. Open until 10:45pm. Air cond. Pkg.
The Anfuso clan welcomes guests into their Venetian-style dining room to savor Rocco Anfuso's vibrant, high-spirited *cucina*. Outstanding features of a recent feast were sea bass ravioli perfumed with basil, beef fillet paired with peppery arugula, and an authentic tiramisù. Watch out, though: the fine Italian wines can send your bill soaring! **C** 280. **M** 165 (lunch).

 ## Michel Rostang

20, rue Rennequin
01 47 63 40 77, fax 01 47 63 82 75
Closed Sat lunch, Sun, Aug 1-18. Open until 10:30 pm. Priv rm: 30. Air cond. Valet pkg.
Why is Michel Rostang down to two toques from four? His creativity isn't in question: his menu lists hot foie gras infused with mocha and pepper, a fricassée of lamb's sweetbreads and lobster with spiced carrots, and sea bass roasted with pickled lemons, proof that Rostang is still touched by inspiration. But save for a perfectly aged and cooked rib steak in red-wine jus, and a fabulous biscuit au chocolat with a rich, molten center, we were puzzled and disappointed by flavors so evanescent that, had we closed our eyes, we mightn't have known what we were eating. Given Rostang's reputation—and prices—we think diners are entitled to greater gustatory thrills. Marie-Claude Rostang remains a gracious hostess, and Alain Ronzatti still presides over a connoisseur's cellar. **C** 650. **M** 298 (weekday lunch), 540, 720.

 ## Rôtisserie d'Armaillé

6, rue d'Armaillé - 01 42 27 19 20, fax 01 40 55 00 23
Closed Sat, Sun. Open until 11pm (Fri & Sat 11:30pm). Air cond. Pkg.
Jacques Cagna reprises the bistro formula he successfully inaugurated at La Rôtisserie d'en Face (sixth arrondissement). For 198 F. you can

choose from a wide array of starters and desserts as well as a main course of spit-roasted poultry or meat. Interesting cellar. C 300. M 150 (weekday lunch), 198 (weekdays, Sat dinner).

 Guy Savoy

18, rue Troyon
01 43 80 40 61, fax 01 46 22 43 09
Closed Sat lunch, Sun. Open until 10:30pm. Priv rm: 35. Air cond. Valet pkg.
Guy Savoy is a real cook, a real artisan—a man who likes simple things. The flower arrangments in a bare Japanese style show his taste for simplicity; his cooking follows the same pattern. Savoy has stripped it of unecessary frills, retaining as much as possible a rustic, yet still elegant, style. He likes strong contrasts and does not hesitate, for instance, to serve as finger-food beets as opposed to cèpes mushrooms. Savoy uses his own products from the terroir to create a vivid and robust cooking with a rural accent, which for us is quite a compliment. A fantastic cellar with a large selection of the best. Wines of all regions—with prices in consequence. C 650-900. M 880.

 Sormani

4, rue du Général-Lanrezac
01 43 80 13 91, fax 01 40 55 07 37
Closed Sat, Sun, Aug 4-22. Open until 10:30pm. Priv rm: 18. Terrace dining. Air cond. Valet pkg.
Jean-Pascal Fayet's Italian cuisine is emphatically not the textbook version. His menu fairly crackles with such delectable inventions as diaphanous ravioli stuffed with sea urchins in a creamy ricotta sauce; a "pizza" topped with onion purée, lobster, and arugula; tender tagliatelle enriched with bacon and white beans; a sumptuous white-truffle risotto. True, spooning caviar onto leek ravioli may be a mite decadent, but Fayet's taste is more often faultless and his technique is admirably sure. The cellar boasts fabulous bottles from Piedmont, Sicily, and Tuscany. C 400-600. M 300 (lunch), 350 (lunch, wine incl), 400 (wine incl).

 La Soupière

154, av. de Wagram - 01 42 27 00 73
Closed Sat lunch, Sun, Aug 11-18. Open until 10:30pm. Terrace dining.
Christian Thuillart pampers his patrons in a pretty *trompe-l'œil* dining room. There's nothing deceptive about Thuillart's classic repertoire, however. A passionate connoisseur of rare and expensive mushrooms, he has built special menus around truffles and morels, served when their season is at its height. C 260. M 138, 165, 240.

 Le Sud Marocain

10, rue Villebois-Mareuil - 01 45 72 39 30
Closed Aug. Open until 10:30pm. Priv rm: 10. Air cond.
Here's a find! This tiny restaurant (it holds just 25) run by a *patron* who looks just like Chico

Marx serves sensational marinated sardines with ratatouille, a light, fragrantly herbal harira soup, excellent tagines (chicken and olives, lamb with prunes...), and a first-rate couscous royal. C 180-215.

 La Table de Pierre ♻

116, bd Pereire - 01 43 80 88 68, fax 01 47 66 53 02
Closed Sat lunch, Sun. Open until 11pm. Terrace dining. Air cond.
Pierre Darrieumerlou's table fairly groans beneath the weight of generously served Basco-Béarnais fare. Bring along a healthy appetite and order the codfish-stuffed peppers, confit de canard aux cèpes, or Pyrenees lamb with beans. Warm welcome; jolly atmosphere. Another point. C 210.

 Taïra

10, rue des Acacias
01 47 66 74 14, fax 01 47 66 74 14
Closed Sat lunch, Sun, 1 wk in Aug. Open until 10pm. Air cond.
Taïra is not a Japanese restaurant, but its chef is Japanese. What does that mean? Since chef/owner Taïra Kurihara's training is western but his roots are oriental, he has his own unique interpretation of bouillabaisse, and his sardines in oil are a summit. Try the aerial spring rolls stuffed with langoustines, the grilled sea-scallops on a potato purée, the John Dory finished with an unusual prawn sauce, the cuttle fish perfumed with basil. One of the best seafood restaurants of Paris and they are so nice... C 300-400. M 150, 170, 330 (dinner).

11/20 Timgad

21, rue Brunel - 01 45 74 23 70, fax 01 40 68 76 46
Open daily until 11pm. Priv rm: 10. No pets. Air cond. Pkg.
All the fragrant specialties of the Maghreb are on offer in this elegant restaurant, where you can sample hand-rolled couscous, crispy brik pastries, and a wide range of tagines. C 270-350.

 La Toque

16, rue de Tocqueville
01 42 27 97 75, fax 01 47 63 97 69
Closed Sat, Sun, Jul 20-Aug 20. Open until 10pm. Air cond.
The pretty dining room is tiny and so are the tables at Jacky Joubert's little Toque. Never mind: the good classic cooking is generously apportioned and attractively served. It earns another point. C 280. M 150, 210.

18TH ARRONDISSEMENT

A. Beauvilliers

52, rue Lamarck - 01 42 54 54 42, fax 01 42 62 70 30
Closed Sun, Mon lunch. Open until 10:45pm. Priv rm: 34. Terrace dining. Air cond.
If ever a restaurant was designed for celebrations, this is it. Indeed, show-business per-

sonalities, celebrities, and politicos regularly scale the Butte Montmartre to toast their triumphs with Beauvilliers's best bubbly. But more care goes into the elegant setting than into the food. A recent visit brought us some decent but unexceptional dishes (chicken en cocotte, red mullet en escabèche, stuffed sweetbreads in aspic...) and one unmitigated disaster. Sea bass in a salt crust, the most expensive item on the menu, arrived horribly overcooked, with greasy fried chayote squash. Adequate desserts; goodish cellar, with a superb selection of Champagnes. C 400-500. M 185 (weekday lunch), 285 (weekday lunch, Sat), 400 (weekday dinner).

 Le Cottage Marcadet

151 bis, rue Marcadet - 01 42 57 71 22
Closed Sun, Aug. Open until 10pm. Air cond. No pets.
This little Cottage has nothing in common with the tourist traps farther up the Butte Montmartre. Here, chef Jean-François Canot pleases his patrons with personalized cooking full of bold, frank flavors. We loved the juniper-spiced calf's foot, the smoked-fish terrine, grilled sea bream dressed with oyster vinaigrette, and duck confit en chartreuse. The 210 F set meal is practically a gift. C 350. M 120 (lunch), 150, 210 (wine incl).

 Langevin

"Au Poulbot Gourmet,"
39, rue Lamarck - 01 46 06 86 00
Closed Sun dinner. Open until 10:15pm.
A glassed-in terrace gives patrons a wide-angle view of this picturesque corner of Montmartre. Jean-Paul Langevin serves forth appetizing versions of traditional country fare: tomatoes stuffed with curried snails, sole with mussels in sauce poulette, and iced charlotte aux deux chocolats sauce pistache. Tempting cellar. C 260. M 115 (lunch, exc Sun, wine incl), 160.

11/20 Chez Marie-Louise

52, rue Championnet - 01 46 06 86 55
Closed Sun, Mon, hols, Aug. Open until 10pm. No pets.
Lobster salad, veal chop grand'mère, lotte with fresh pasta, clafoutis of seasonal fruits—here's honest bistro cooking, unchanged for 35 years, served amid copper saucepans and prints of carousing monks. C 200-240. M 130.

 Le Restaurant

32, rue Véron - 01 42 23 06 22, fax 01 42 23 36 16
Closed lunch Sat & Mon, Sun. Open until 11:30pm.
Yves Péladeau worked his way up from busboy to owner-chef of his Restaurant in the trendy Abbesses section of Montmartre. The dining room is as modern, bright, and *à la mode* as the imaginative menu. Give your taste buds a treat with grilled leeks and potatoes with Cantal cheese, gingered pork with soy sauce, and honey-roasted duck spiced with coriander. Small but intelligent wine list (Minervois from Jacques Maris). M 120, 45 (children).

11/20 Le Sagittaire

77, rue Lamarck - 01 42 55 17 40
Closed Sun dinner, Mon. Open until 10:30pm.
In an old-fashioned Belle-Époque dining room adorned with a magnificent carved-wood bar, fill up on the generous all-in menu of homey French favorites. M 100 (lunch, wine incl, exc Sun), 165 (wine incl), 65 (children).

12/20 Wepler

14, pl. de Clichy - 01 45 22 53 24, fax 01 44 70 07 50
Open daily until 1am. Air cond. Pkg.
A deluxe brasserie providing reliable food and good service. The shellfish are glossy and ultrafresh; other worthwhile options are the grilled salmon béarnaise, choucroute garnie, and bouillabaisse. C 190. M 92, 105 (weekday lunch), 150 (exc weekday lunch), 80 (children).

19TH ARRONDISSEMENT

12/20 Dagorno

190, av. Jean-Jaurès
01 40 40 09 39, fax 01 48 03 17 23
Open daily until 1:15am. Priv rm: 230. Air cond. Valet pkg.
Quite a contrast with the futuristic Cité des Sciences, this opulent brasserie cultivates an old-fashioned image, offering decent, uncomplicated food. You won't be disappointed by the fresh shellfish, calf's head sauce gribiche, or the enormous côte de bœuf sauce bordelaise. C 300. M 157, 40 (children).

12/20 La Pièce de Bœuf

7, av. Corentin-Cariou
01 40 05 95 95, fax 01 40 34 67 78
Closed Sat, Sun, Jul 27-Aug 25. Open until 10:30pm. Air cond.
Well-wrought traditional brasserie fare; despite the name, we find that seafood is the menu's strong suit. The wine list favors Bordeaux and Champagnes. C 250. M 155.

 La Verrière d'Éric Fréchon

10, rue du Général-Brunet
01 40 4 03 30, fax 01 40 40 03 30
Closed Sun, Mon, Aug. Open until 11pm. Priv rm: 30. No pets. Terrace dining.
There's nothing mysterious about it: when you serve fine food for reasonable prices, gourmets will beat a path to your door, no matter how remote your restaurant! In his neat and tidy little bistro, Éric Fréchon (a former second-in-command to Christian Constant at the Crillon) proposes a dazzling single-price menu for just 190 F. Market-fresh ingredients, balanced flavors, and cutting-edge technique distinguish Fréchon's cream of white bean soup showered with croûtons and shavings of Spanish ham; his langoustine croquants served with a lovely honey-dressed salad of tender lamb's lettuce; or cod stuffed with salt-cod purée and roasted in a spicy herbal crust; or an earthy sausage of pig's

trotter enriched with foie gras and presented with whipped potatoes. For dessert, there's a superb mango feuilleté enhanced by lashings of almond cream. Interesting cellar of growers' wines; warm welcome from Sylvie Fréchon. In short, this is one of the year's top tables. M 190.

11/20 Au Rendez-Vous de la Marine

14, quai de la Loire - 01 42 49 33 40
Closed Sun, Mon, 1 wk in Aug. Open until 10pm. Terrace dining.
Sit down to a hearty omelette aux cèpes, confit de canard, or monkfish fillet at this friendly address by the canal. C 130-140.

 ## Chez Vincent

5, rue du Tunnel - 01 42 02 22 45
Closed Sat lunch, Sun. Open until 11pm.
Our friend Henri Gault calls this the "best trattoria in France." Reserve your table well in advance to savor Vincent's beef or salmon carpaccio showered with wonderful vegetables, warm shellfish marinière, deep-fried sardines, squid, and eggplant, or his silky fresh pasta. C 180-200. M 130, 160, 200 (dinner).

20TH ARRONDISSEMENT

 ## Les Allobroges

71, rue des Grands-Champs - 01 43 73 40 00
Closed Sun, Mon, 1 wk at easter, Aug. Open until 10pm. Pkg.

It's worth the trip out to the twentieth arrondissement to taste Olivier Pateyron's langoustines with ratatouille, braised lamb with garlic confit, and cherry-pistachio dessert. The little 92 F set meal has its charms, and à la carte prices are clement too, inciting one to splurge on lobster and lotte with tarragon or spiced Barbary duck (order both in advance). Only the wine list needs improvement. C 250. M 92, 164.

12/20 A la Courtille

1, rue des Envierges
01 46 36 51 59, fax 01 46 36 65 56
Open daily until 10:45pm. Terrace dining.
Enjoy a spectacular view of the city from the terrace of this elegant bistro. Even better than the food (which is pretty good: marinated sardines, duck breast with fresh figs, crème brûlée...) is the wine list, compiled by Bernard Pontonnier and Francis Morel. C 160-200. M 70, 100 (lunch), 140.

11/20 Le Saint-Amour

2, av. Gambetta - 01 47 97 20 15
Closed Aug 15-23. Open until 10pm. Priv rm: 30. Terrace dining.
The owner, an Auvergne native, serves first-rate regional charcuteries and cheeses alongside a few unpretentious hot dishes. Wines by the glass or the carafe. Good-humored ambience, a blessing in this gray, gloomy district. C 140-210. M 60-75 (exc Sat dinner & Sun, wine incl), 90-120 (wine incl).

A DISCLAIMER

Readers are advised that prices and conditions change over the course of time. The restaurants, hotels, shops, and other establishments reviewed in this book have been reviewed over a period of time, and the reviews reflect the personal experiences and opinions of the reviewers. The reviewers and publishers cannot be held responsible for the experiences of the reader related to establishments reviewed. Readers are invited to write to the publisher with ideas, comments, and suggestions for future editions.

PARIS: HOTELS

LUXURY

 Le Bristol

8th arr. - 112, rue du Faubourg-Saint-Honoré
01 53 43 43 00, fax 01 53 43 43 01
*Open year-round. 40 stes 6,500-34,000. 153 rms
2,500-4,500. Bkfst 165-260. Restaurant. Rm ser.
Air cond. Conf. Pool. No pets. Valet pkg.*
An elegant décor (genuine period furniture,
fine pictures), comfortable rooms, lavish suites,
and a prestigious clientele make Le Bristol one of
the rare authentic luxury hotels in Paris (as well
as one of the most expensive). An elegant restaurant (Le Bristol) opens onto a formal French
garden, see *Restaurants*. The staff is both cordial
and impressively trained.

 Castille

1st arr. - 37, rue Cambon
01 44 58 44 58, fax 01 44 58 44 00
*Open year-round. 8 stes 3,300-3,700. 99 rms 1,750-
2,400. Bkfst 125. Rms for disabled. Restaurant. Air
cond. Conf. Valet pkg.*
Venetian-style elegance, decked out in
brocades, damask, and marble. Next door to
Chanel and just opposite the Ritz, the Castille
provides luxurious amenities and impeccably
stylish service. Restaurant: Il Cortile, see *Restaurants*.

 Hôtel de Crillon

8th arr. - 10, place de la Concorde
01 44 71 15 00, fax 01 44 71 15 02
*Open year-round. 43 stes 4,900-29,000. 120 rms
2,550-4,100. Restaurants. Rm ser. Air cond. Conf.
Valet pkg.*
The Crillon is housed in an honest-to-goodness
eighteenth-century palace. Indeed, the accommodations are truly fit for a king, with terraces
overlooking the Place de la Concorde,
sumptuous public rooms, and an exquisitely
trained staff. The guest rooms are beautifully
decorated; the suites offer all the splendor one
could hope for. Everywhere the eye rests on silk
draperies, woodwork ornamented with gold
leaf, Aubusson rugs, and polished marble. Relais
et Châteaux. Restaurants: Les Ambassadeurs
and L'Obélisque, see *Restaurants*.

 George V

8th arr. - 31, av. George-V
01 47 23 54 00, fax 01 47 20 22 05
*Open year-round. 44 stes 5,700-15,500. 214 rms
1,800-3,900. Bkfst 140-210. Rms for disabled. Restaurant. Rm ser. Air cond. Conf.*

The management has made Herculean efforts
to instill new life and spirit into this landmark.
The bar and the restaurant (Les Princes, see *Restaurants*) have been redecorated, a Grill has been
added, and the rooms have been renovated, with
as much concern for elegance as for modernity
(electronic panels located at the head of the beds
allow guests to close the venetian blinds, control
TV and air conditioning, call room service...).
The pictures, rare ornaments, and lovely furniture in the public rooms radiate the legendary
George-V charm. And the service is once again
all it should be.

 **Le Grand Hôtel
Inter Continental**

9th arr. - 2, rue Scribe
01 40 07 32 32, fax 01 42 66 12 51
*Open year-round. 35 stes 3,500-14,000. 479 rms
1,700-2,800. Bkfst 125-160. Rms for disabled. Restaurant. Rm ser. Air cond. Conf. No pets. Valet pkg.*
The monumental Second Empire building has
recovered all the splendor it displayed when
Empress Eugénie inaugurated it in 1862. The
huge central lobby, capped by a glittering glass
dome, is a wonder to behold. Guest rooms provide everything the international traveler could
require in the way of amenities, as well as the
most up-to-date business equipment, a health
club, and much more. Excellent bar; for the
Opéra Restaurant, see *Restaurants*.

 Inter Continental

1st arr. - 3, rue de Castiglione
01 44 77 11 11, fax 01 44 77 14 60
*Open year-round. 79 stes 4,200-20,000. 371 rms
2,500-2,700. Bkfst 100-150. Rm ser. Restaurants.
Air cond. Conf. Valet pkg.*
A three-year renovation program has started at
the Inter Continental. The 450 rooms and conference rooms of this monumental Second Empire hotel are being progressively refurbished.
The restaurant and patio are also under
reconstruction. In the meantime, the hotel
remains open and is hosting a series of cultural
and culinary events.

 Hôtel du Louvre

1st arr. - Pl. André Malraux
01 44 58 38 38, fax 01 44 58 38 01
*Open year-round. 4 stes 3,000. 195 rms 1,350-1,950.
Bkfst 110. Rms for disabled. Restaurant. Rm ser.
Air cond. Valet pkg.*
Here is a remarkable example of Second Em-
pire architecture, conveniently situated near
Palais-Royal and the Louvre. Tradition and con-
temporary comforts combine to excellent effect
in the posh guest rooms. Business travelers will

appreciate the range of services placed at their disposal.

 Hôtel Meurice

1st arr. - 228, rue de Rivoli
01 44 58 10 10, fax 01 44 58 10 15
Open year-round. 35 stes 6,000-15,000. 152 rms 2,250-3,100. Bkfst 150-195. Rms for disabled. Restaurant. Rm ser. Air cond. Conf. Valet pkg.
The Meurice has undergone substantial renovation in the past few years to restore its glamour and prestige. The admirable salons on the main floor were refurbished; the guest rooms and suites (which offer a view of the Tuileries) were equipped with air conditioning and tastefully redecorated; and the pink-marble bathrooms are ultramodern. The Meurice ranks as one of the best grand hotels in Paris. An elegant restaurant, Le Meurice, see *Restaurants*, is lodged in the Salon des Tuileries, overlooking the gardens.

 Plaza Athénée

8th arr. - 25, av. Montaigne
01 53 67 66 65, fax 01 53 67 66 66
Open year-round. 40 stes 2,500-13,500. 166 rms 2,500-4,650. Bkfst 160-250. Restaurant. Air cond. Valet pkg.
Discretion, efficiency, and friendly courtesy are the Plaza's trademarks. The accommodations are bright, generous in size, and fitted with every amenity. The rooms overlooking Avenue Montaigne are perfectly soundproofed. At about 11am, guests gather in the Plaza Bar Anglais (where Mata Hari was arrested); and from 4pm to 7pm you'll see them in the gallery (of which Marlene Dietrich was particularly fond). The Régence restaurant is located across from the patio, where tables are set in the summer among cascades of geraniums and ampelopsis vines, see *Restaurants*.

 Prince de Galles

8th arr. - 33, av. George-V
01 47 23 55 11, fax 01 47 20 61 05
Open year-round. 30 stes 3,650-12,000. 138 rms 1,900-2,900. Bkfst 145-175. Restaurant. Rm ser. Air cond. Conf. Valet pkg.
Extensive renovations have restored the brilliance of this renowned hotel, built in the Roaring Twenties. Marble expanses stretch as far as the eye can see, walls sport handsome prints, and guest rooms are outfitted with minibars, safes, and a flock of new facilities. We only wish that the lovely old mosaics had been preserved. As ever, the hotel's open-roofed patio is a delightful place to have lunch on a warm day; the paneled Regency Bar is another pleasant spot, distinguished by excellent service. For Le Jardin des Cygnes, see *Restaurants*.

 Raphaël

16th arr. - 17, av. Kléber
01 44 28 00 28, fax 01 45 01 21 50

Open year-round. 25 stes 3,950-24,000. 65 rms 1,850-2,950. Bkfst 120-160. Restaurant. Rm ser. Air cond. Conf. Valet pkg.
Built between the wars, the Raphaël has maintained an atmosphere of rare refinement and elegance, that you only find in a very few hotels throughout the world. Oriental rugs on the marble floors, fine woodwork, old paintings and period furniture make Le Raphaël a very luxurious place to stay, preferred by a wealthy, well-bred clientele. The spacious rooms are richly furnished in various styles; the wardrobes and bathrooms are immense. A truly extraordinary and splendid new addition is a three-level suite that boasts an eye-popping panoramic view from the terrace (the terrace, by the way, is at the same level as the Arc de Triomphe). The suite is a glittering showcase for the finest in French craftsmanship. Or ask for the duplex suite 515— the bathroom is unbelievable! Top-drawer reception and service, of course. Intimate (and star-studded) English bar. Sumptuous conference facilities. For La Salle à Manger, see *Restaurants*.

 Résidence Maxim's de Paris

8th arr. - 42, av. Gabriel
01 45 61 96 33, fax 01 42 89 06 07
Open year-round. 33 stes 2,750-15,000. 4 rms 2,000-2,250. Restaurant. Air cond. Conf. Valet pkg.
Pierre Cardin himself designed the hotel of his dreams, a small but palatial establishment that may well be the world's most luxurious. The landings of each floor are decorated like elegant salons, with beautiful and unusual antique pieces and paintings. Polished stone and sumptuous murals adorn the bathrooms. The suites must be seen to be believed, particularly those on the top floor, which are lacquered in vivid colors and furnished with pieces designed by Cardin. Obviously, accommodations like these are well beyond the bank balances of most mortals.

 Ritz

1st arr. - 15, place Vendôme
01 43 16 30 30, fax 01 43 16 36 68
Open year-round. 45 stes 5,500-25,700. 142 rms 2,800-4,300. Bkfst 180-230. Rms for disabled. Restaurant. Rm ser. Conf. Heated pool. Valet pkg.
The world's most famous hotel is poised to enter the 21st century with highest-tech facilities, but without having betrayed the character that won the Ritz its reputation. Even if nowadays you can change the video program or make a phone call without leaving your bed or marble bath (Charles Ritz was the first to provide private bathrooms for his clients), nothing has altered the pleasure of stretching out on a wide brass bed surrounded by fine antiques. Add to that an atmosphere of luxury so enveloping that a new word ("ritzy") had to be coined for it. Impeccable staff. The new health club was modeled on a thermal spa of antiquity, and L'Espadon, see *Restaurants*, has its own garden.

Royal Monceau

8th arr. - 35, av. Hoche
01 42 99 88 00, fax 01 42 99 89 90
Open year-round. 39 stes 3,650-16,000. 180 rms 2,150-3,350. Bkfst 140-190. Rms for disabled. Restaurants. Rm ser. Air cond. Conf. Heated pool. Valet pkg.
Politicians, foreign business people and entertainers appreciate the Royal Monceau's spacious rooms, magnificent marble bathrooms, and luxurious amenities (excellent room service). Extras include a fashionable piano bar, a prestigious health club, Les Thermes, (with sauna, Jacuzzi, swimming pool, and a massage service), ultramodern conference rooms and a well-equipped "business club." The rooms overlooking the charming flowered patio are the most sought-after by the hotel's habitués. Restaurants: Le Carpaccio and Le Jardin du Royal Monceau, see *Restaurants*.

 Westminster

2nd arr. - 13, rue de la Paix
01 42 61 57 46, fax 01 42 60 30 66
Open year-round. 18 stes 3,600-5,500. 84 rms 1,650-2,450. Bkfst 110-130. Restaurant. Rm ser. Air cond. Conf. Valet pkg.
Here is a charming mid-size luxury hotel advantageously situated between the Opéra and Place Vendôme. The pink-and-beige marble lobby is splendid and luxurious; the bar (with piano) is more than comfortable. Conference rooms are superbly equipped. As for the guest rooms, they are handsomely decorated with attractive fabrics, chandeliers, and Louis XV–style furnishings and are fitted with minibars, safes, and satellite TV. The marble bathrooms and suites have been totally refurbished. Restaurant: Le Céladon, see *Restaurants*.

FIRST CLASS

 Ambassador

9th arr. - 16, bd Haussmann
01 44 83 40 40, fax 01 42 46 19 84
Open year-round. 9 stes 2,000-3,800. 289 rms 1,300-1,800. Restaurant. Rm ser. Air cond. Conf. Valet pkg.
A fine traditional hotel. The guest rooms have been modernized in excellent taste with sumptuous fabrics, thick carpeting, and Art Deco furniture. Nearly all are air conditioned. The lobby and public rooms boast pink-marble columns topped with gilded Corinthian capitals, marble floors, and Aubusson tapestries on the walls. The penthouse suites look out over Sacré-Cœur. Restaurant: Venantius, see *Restaurants*; and a handsome Art Deco bar.

 Astor Madeleine

8th arr. - 11, rue d'Astorg
01 53 05 05 20, fax 01 53 05 05 30
Open year-round. 5 stes 2,950-8,000. 130 rms 1,590-2,650. Bkfst 120-195. Rms for disabled. Restaurant. Rm ser. Air cond. Valet pkg.
The Astor has just completed an ambitious, two-year renovation program directed by architect Frédéric Méchiche. The lobby is resplendent with fine woodwork, and the quiet rooms, arranged around a white courtyard, are decorated in English or Empire style, with striped fabrics in shades of lavender, green, or blue. Though not huge, the guest quarters provide plenty of comfort and luxury. Two suites offer terraces with views over the city's rooftops. See *Restaurants* for the restaurant.

 Baltimore

16th arr. - 88 bis, av. Kléber
01 44 34 54 54, fax 01 44 34 54 44
Open year-round. 1 ste 3,500. 104 rms 1,790-2,950. Half-board 2,040-3,250. Bkfst 120-195. Restaurant. Air cond. Conf. Pkg.
Six fully equipped meeting rooms are located on the lower level; the largest and most luxurious is the former vault room of the Banque Nationale de Paris. The bright lobby is quite imposing; the rooms less so, owing to overdecoration. Some are on the small side, too, but amenities abound. Restaurant: Le Bertie's, see *Restaurants*.

 Balzac

8th arr. - 6, rue Balzac
01 44 35 18 00, fax 01 44 35 18 05
Open year-round. 14 stes 3,200-6,000. 56 rms 1,700-2,200. Bkfst 90-150. Restaurant. Rm ser. Air cond. Valet pkg.
A quietly luxurious establishment near the Place de l'Étoile, frequented by celebrities and jet-setters. The huge rooms have been redecorated by Nina Campbell in delicate tones with lovely furniture, beautiful chintzes, and thick carpeting. Most have king-size beds, all have superb modern bathrooms. Unobtrusive yet attentive staff. And let us no forget the arrival of Pierre Gagnaire at the restaurant, see *Restaurants*.

 Beverly Hills

8th arr. - 35, rue de Berri
01 53 77 56 01, fax 01 42 56 52 75
Open year-round. 14 stes 2,000-9,000. Air cond. Conf.
The extravagant décor of marble, mirrors, and precious woods reeks of money: this apartment-hotel is designed for millionaires, emirs, and merchant princes who want to wallow in luxury. Security is provided for with total electronic surveillance. The huge suites offer every imaginable amenity, from dining rooms to wide-screen TV.

Caron de Beaumarchais

4th arr. - 12, rue Vieille-du-Temple
01 42 72 34 12, fax 01 42 72 34 63
Open year-round. 19 rms 620-730. Bkfst 48-78. Air cond. Conf.
Here's a find: a hotel overflowing with charm, set in the heart of the Marais. The lobby's eighteenth-century atmosphere is underscored by a Louis XVI fireplace, beamed ceilings, and handsome antiques. The perfectly comfortable rooms are equipped with air conditioning and double glazing for cool quiet in summer.

 ## Château Frontenac

8th arr. - 54, rue Pierre-Charron
01 53 23 13 13, fax 01 53 23 13 01
Open year-round. 4 stes 1,600-1,700. 102 rms 950-1,450. Bkfst 85. Air cond. Conf. No pets.
A reasonably priced hotel (given the location), with various sizes of rooms done in vaguely Louis XV style. Superb marble bathrooms. The soundproofing is effective, but the rooms overlooking the Rue Cérisole are still the quietest. Attentive reception staff; excellent service. Restaurant: Le Pavillon Frontenac.

 ## Clarion Saint-James et Albany

1st arr. - 202, rue de Rivoli
01 44 58 43 21, fax 01 44 58 43 11
Open year-round. 13 stes 1,800-2,500. 198 rms 980-1,500. Restaurant. Half-board 200. Rm ser. Conf.
The Clarion Saint James et Albany enjoys an exceptional location across from the Tuileries, and provides studios, two-room apartments, suites, and bilevel suites equipped with kitchenettes. The rooms overlook a courtyard or an inner garden and are perfectly quiet. Modern décor.

 ## Concorde La Fayette

17th arr. - 3, place du Général-Kœnig
01 40 68 50 68, fax 01 40 68 50 43
Open year-round. 32 stes 3,000. 938 rms 1,250-1,650. Bkfst 98-122. Restaurants. Rm ser. Conf. No pets. Valet pkg.
The Concorde La Fayette is immense: a huge oval tower that houses the Palais des Congrès, banquet rooms, scores of boutiques, cinemas, and nightclubs. The hotel's rooms meet the chain's usual standards, with all the modern amenities. Panoramic bar, three restaurants, including L'Étoile d'Or, see *Restaurants*. Airport shuttles.

 ## Concorde Saint-Lazare

8th arr. - 108, rue Saint-Lazare
01 40 08 44 44, fax 01 42 93 01 20
Open year-round. 27 stes 2,450-3,500. 273 rms 1,200-1,500. Bkfst 105. Restaurant. Rm ser. Air cond. Conf. Valet pkg.
An enormous hotel, built in 1889 by Gustave Eiffel, with superb rooms and services. The most arresting feature is the lobby, a listed architectural landmark, that soars three storeys up to coffered ceilings aglitter with gilt, marble, and crystal chandeliers. A magnificent billiard room on the main floor is open to the public. Restaurant: Café Terminus, see *Restaurants*.

 ## Édouard VII

2nd arr. - 39, av. de l'Opéra
01 42 61 56 90, fax 01 42 61 47 73
Open year-round. 4 stes 2,000. 65 rms 950-1,400. Bkfst 90. Restaurant. Rm ser. Air cond. Conf.
A luxurious place to stay, with individually styled rooms and beautifully crafted furniture. From the upper storeys there is a wonderful view of the Opéra. Restaurant: Delmonico, see *Restaurants*.

 ## Golden Tulip Saint-Honoré

8th arr. - 218, rue du Faubourg-Saint-Honoré
01 49 53 03 03, fax 01 40 75 02 00
Open year-round. 20 stes 2,400-3,900. 52 rms 1,500-1,800. Bkfst 110. Rms for disabled. Restaurant. Air cond. Pool. Garage pkg.
This comfortable hotel is decorated in modern style using traditional materials (marble, wood, quality fabrics, *trompe-l'œil* paintings). The bright, spacious rooms offer every amenity; all are air conditioned, with splendid marble bathrooms, and kitchenettes. Restaurant: Le Relais Vermeer, see *Restaurants*.

 ## Hilton

15th arr. - 18, av. de Suffren
01 43 38 56 00, fax 01 44 38 56 10
Open year-round. 26 stes 3,700-12,000. 436 rms 1,595-2,365. Bkfst 85-120. Rms for disabled. Restaurants. Rm ser. Air cond. Conf. Valet pkg.
The city's first postwar luxury hotel is still living up to Hilton's high standards. Rooms are airy and spacious, service is courteous and deft, and children—of any age—can share their parents' room at no extra charge. Restaurants, bars, boutiques.

 ## Lancaster

8th arr. - 7, rue de Berri
01 40 76 40 76, fax 01 40 76 40 00
Open year-round. 7 stes 3,000-7,300. 51 rms 1,850-2,650. Bkfst 120-170. Restaurant. Rm ser. Conf. Valet pkg.
Inhale the perfume of the immense bouquet of flowers in the lobby, then admire the general setting—furniture, wall hangings, paintings, ornaments—of this refined and luxurious hotel. The ravishing indoor garden, with its flowers, fountains, and statues (meals are served there on sunny days) lends an unexpected bucolic touch to this hotel, only steps from the Champs-Élysées.

 ## Littré

6th arr. - 9, rue Littré
01 45 44 38 68, fax 01 45 44 88 13
Open year-round. 4 stes 1,350-1,550. 93 rms 695-1,000. Rm ser. Conf. No pets. Pkg.

The style and décor of this four-star hotel are stiff and starchy, but the Littré's habitués find the old-fashioned comfort and service entirely satisfactory. In the spacious, recently renovated rooms you'll find high, comfortable beds, ponderous furniture, huge armoires, and big marble bathrooms. English bar.

 ## Lotti

1st arr. - 7, rue de Castiglione
01 42 60 37 34, fax 01 40 15 93 56
Open year-round. 2 stes 4,900-6,500. 129 rms 1,410-3,330. Bkfst 120. Restaurant. Conf. Valet pkg.
An elegant hotel, popular with European aristocracy. Each of the spacious rooms is individually decorated and offers excellent facilities. The restaurant, the lobby, and all the rooms were recently redecorated. The bathrooms are under renovation, and will then feature Jacuzzis. The charming attic rooms are reserved for non-smokers.

 ## Hôtel Lutétia

6th arr. - 45, bd Raspail
01 49 54 46 46, fax 01 49 54 46 00
Open year-round. 30 stes 2,200-12,000. 225 rms 990-1,990. Bkfst 65. Rms for disabled. Restaurants. Air cond. Conf. Valet pkg.
A Left Bank landmark, in the Art Deco style. Marble, gilt, and red velvet grace the stately public areas where well-heeled travelers come and go. Leading off the imposing entrance are the lounge, a bar, a brasserie, a restaurant (Brasserie Lutétia and Le Paris, see *Restaurants*), and conference rooms. The large suites are done up in pink, with understated furniture and elegant bathrooms—the overall look is very 1930s.

 ## Marignan

8th arr. - 12, rue Marignan
01 40 76 34 56, fax 01 40 76 34 34
Open year-round. 16 stes 2,650. 57 rms 1,690-1,990. Bkfst 120. Restaurant. Air cond. Conf. Valet pkg.
Strategically situated in the heart of the "Golden Triangle," between the Champs-Élysées and Avenue Montaigne, this charming establishment with its listed Art Deco façade and lobby draws a haute-couture crowd. Magnificent rooms done up in marble and expensive fabrics, with every modern comfort; some even boast a little terrace.

 ## Montalembert

7th arr. - 3, rue de Montalembert
01 45 49 68 68, fax 01 45 49 69 49
Open year-round. 5 stes 2,700-3,700. 51 rms 1,675-2,140. Bkfst 100. Restaurant. Rm ser. Air cond. Conf.
Restored to its former splendor, this 1926 hotel sports luxurious materials (marble, ebony, sycamore, leather), designer fabrics and linens. Guests love the huge towels, cozy dressing gowns, and premium toiletries they find in the spectacular blue-gray bathrooms. The eighth-

floor suites afford an enchanting view of the city. The hotel bar is a favorite with writers and publishers.

 ## Le Parc

16th arr. - 55-57, av. R.-Poincaré
01 44 05 66 66, fax 01 44 05 66 00
Open year-round. 20 stes 3,200-3,500. 100 rms 1,990-2,650. Bkfst 120. Rms for disabled. Restaurants. Air cond. Conf. Valet pkg.
Celebrity decorators were called in to refurbish this elegant hotel. Supremely comfortable, the rooms boast the most refined appointments and every imaginable amenity. The public rooms are accented with beautiful sculpture. A glorious indoor garden is planted with rare specimens. Restaurant: Le Relais du Parc, see *Restaurants*.

 ## Pergolèse

16th arr. - 3, rue Pergolèse
01 40 67 96 77, fax 01 45 00 12 11
Open year-round. 40 rms 890-1,590. Air cond.
The Pergolèse provides a top-class address as well as smiling service and first-rate amenities for what are still (relatively) reasonable prices. Elegant furnishings and vivid, modern, décor by Rena Dumas.

 ## Régina

1st arr. - 2, place des Pyramides
01 42 60 31 10, fax 01 40 15 95 16
Open year-round. 15 stes 2,700-3,900. 121 rms 1,600-2,200. Bkfst 95-145. Restaurant. Air cond. Conf. Valet pkg.
Opposite the Tuileries is one of the city's most venerable luxury hotels, with immense rooms, precious furniture (Louis XVI, Directoire, Empire) and—a practical addition—double-glazed windows. The grandiose lobby is graced with handsome old clocks that give the time of all the major European cities. Pretty indoor garden; English bar. Restaurant: Le Pluvinel, see *Restaurants*.

 ## Royal Saint-Honoré

1st arr. - 221, rue Saint-Honoré
01 42 60 32 79, fax 01 42 60 47 44
Open year-round. 5 stes 2,350. 67 rms 1,250-1,950. Bkfst 90. Restaurant. Rm ser. Conf. No pets.
Closed for over a year, the Royal Saint-Honoré is back with a brighter, fresher look. The attentive staff does its utmost to make your stay enjoyable. All of the rooms are spacious; some boast terraces overlooking the Tuileries. Marble bathrooms, and a new bar.

 ## Saint James Paris

16th arr. - 43, av. Bugeaud
01 44 05 81 81, fax 01 44 05 81 82
Open year-round. 24 stes 2,400-3,600. 24 rms 1,550-1,980. Bkfst 95-110. Restaurant. Rm ser. Air cond. Conf. Valet pkg.
A large staff looks after the 48 rooms and suites—a luxury level of attention with prices fixed accordingly. The huge rooms are decorated

in a low-key 1930s style with flowers and plants, and feature bathrooms clad in gray mosaic tile. Don't miss the magnificent library, which also houses the hotel's piano bar. Very luxurious health club with sauna, and a Jacuzzi.

 ## Scribe

9th arr. - 1, rue Scribe
01 44 71 24 24, fax 01 44 71 24 42
Open year-round. 11 stes 1,950-6,400. 206 rms 1,950-2,450. Bkfst 105-125. Rms for disabled. Air cond. Conf. Valet pkg.
Behind the Scribe's Napoléon III façade stands a prime example of the French hotelier's art. All the rooms, suites, and two-level suites are furnished in classic style, and offer huge bathrooms. A multitude of TV channels is on tap, as well as 24-hour room service. Restaurant: Les Muses, see *Restaurants;* and a bar.

 ## La Trémoille

8th arr. - 14, rue de La Trémoille
01 47 23 34 20, fax 01 40 70 01 08
Open year-round. 14 stes 2,780-5,170. 93 rms 1,400-2,930. Bkfst 100-120. Rms for disabled. Restaurant. Rm ser. Air cond. Conf. Valet pkg.
Cozy comfort, antique furniture, balconies with bright flower-filled window-boxes, and service worthy of a grand hotel. Several suites are quite new and remarkably comfortable; all the rooms have lovely bathrooms and modern amenities. The delightful dining room/salon is warmed by a crackling fire in winter.

 ## Hôtel Vernet

8th arr. - 25, rue Vernet
01 44 31 98 00, fax 01 44 31 85 69
Open year-round. 3 stes 3,500. 54 rms 1,650-2,250. Bkfst 120-150. Restaurant. Rm ser. Air cond. Conf. No pets. Valet pkg.
An admirable hotel, the Vernet combines the best of modern and traditional comforts. The rooms and suites are handsomely decorated with genuine Louis XVI, Directoire, or Empire furniture, and walls are hung with sumptuous fabrics. Jacuzzi in all the bathrooms. Free access to the beautiful Royal Monceau' health club. Restaurant: Les Élysées du Vernet, see *Restaurants.*

 ## Vigny

8th arr. - 9, rue Balzac
01 40 75 04 39, fax 01 40 75 05 81
Open year-round. 12 stes 2,600-5,000. 25 rms 1,900-2,200. Bkfst 90-150. Restaurant. Rm ser. Air cond. No pets. Pkg.
A romantic hotel, the Vigny offers English mahogany furniture, comfortable beds, and fine marble bathrooms: the virtues of another age simplified and brought up to date. The suites provide all-out luxury. Excellent service. Bar.

 ## Warwick

8th arr. - 5, rue de Berri
01 45 63 14 11, fax 01 43 59 00 98
Open year-round. 21 stes 4,200-8,500. 126 rms 1,790-2,650. Bkfst 105-150. Restaurant. Rm ser. Conf. Valet pkg.
Luxurious and modern, just off the Champs-Élysées, this hotel offers bright, spacious, freshly refurbished rooms done in pastel colors and chintz. Efficient soundproofing and air conditioning. There is an attractive bar with piano music in the evening and a pleasant rooftop terrace. Restaurant: La Couronne, see *Restaurants.*

CLASSIC

 ## Hôtel de l'Arcade

8th arr. - 9, rue de l'Arcade
01 53 30 60 00, fax 01 40 07 03 07
Open year-round. 4 stes 1,100. 37 rms 770-940. Bkfst 55. Rms for disabled. Air cond. Conf.
Here you'll revel in truly spacious, prettily decorated quarters, conveniently sited in the shoppers' mecca between the Madeleine and the major department stores. The perfectly quiet rooms sport pastel fabrics and cherrywood furniture; bathrooms are clad in white marble.

 ## Britannique

1st arr. - 20, avenue Victoria
01 42 33 74 59, fax 01 42 33 82 65
Open year-round. 40 rms 645-888. Bkfst 52. No pets.
A warm welcome and good service characterize this family-run hotel. The rooms are decorated with pale walls, dark carpeting and comfortable modern furniture. Rooms on the second and fifth floors have balconies with views of the Châtelet.

 ## Buci Latin

6th arr. - 34, rue de Buci
01 43 29 07 20, fax 01 43 29 67 44
Open year-round. 2 stes 1,590-1,690. 25 rms 900-1,170. Rms for disabled. Restaurant. Rm ser. Air cond.
Decorator Alain Perrier turned this small hotel into a showcase of contemporary style. On the ground floor you'll find a pleasant American-style coffee shop.

 ## Cayré

7th arr. - 4, bd Raspail
01 45 44 38 88, fax 01 45 44 98 13
Open year-round. 118 rms 900-1,200. Bkfst 50-65. Restaurant. Rm ser.
A pink-and-gray marble floor, glass pillars and red-leather furniture lend an air of luxury to the lobby. The modern, thoroughly soundproofed rooms are impersonal but well equipped, with marble bathrooms. Good service, too.

Looking for a hotel? Refer to the index.

Colisée

8th arr. - 6, rue du Colisée
01 43 59 95 25, fax 01 45 63 26 54
Open year-round. 45 rms 655-870. Bkfst 45.
Discreetly modern rooms, mostly on the small side (those with numbers ending in an 8 are more spacious), but quite comfortable. Some are soundproofed. The four attic rooms have beamed ceilings and considerable charm. Inviting bar, but no restaurant.

 Commodore

9th arr. - 12, bd Haussmann
01 42 46 72 82, fax 01 47 70 28 81
Open year-round. 11 stes 2,300-3,600. 151 rms 1,250-1,650. Bkfst 110-140. Restaurant. Conf.
A recently renovated establishment located a few steps away from the Drouot auction house. Good-sized rooms, convenient for business travelers.

 Duminy Vendôme

1st arr. - 3, rue du Mont-Thabor
01 42 60 32 80, fax 01 42 96 07 83
Open year-round. 77 rms 525-870. Bkfst 65. Rms for disabled. Rm ser. Conf. Valet pkg.
Duminy Vendôme's rooms have good bathrooms and 1920s–style furnishings. Rooms on the sixth and seventh floors have slightly sloping ceilings, and those with numbers ending in 10 are larger than the rest. A small summer patio is located on the main floor. Charming reception. Some rooms have been renovated.

 Élysa

5th arr. - 6, rue Gay-Lussac
01 43 25 31 74, fax 01 46 34 56 27
Open year-round. 30 rms 450-720. Bkfst 45. Restaurant. Rm ser. Conf. No pets.
In the heart of the Latin Quarter, near the Luxembourg Gardens. The small, inviting rooms are regularly renovated. Gray-marble bathrooms.

 Élysées Maubourg

7th arr. - 35, bd de Latour-Maubourg
01 45 56 10 78, fax 01 47 05 65 08
Open year-round. 30 rms 560-1,000. Bkfst 45. Conf.
The 30 rooms of this hotel are decorated in classic good taste. Adequately sized, they are superbly equipped and comfortable. There is a Finnish sauna in the basement, a bar, and a flower-filled patio.

 Hôtel Étoile Friedland

8th arr. - 177, rue du Faubourg-Saint-Honoré
01 45 63 64 65, fax 01 45 63 88 96
Open year-round. 40 rms 650-1,100. Bkfst 75. Rms for disabled. Rm ser.
The bright yellow lobby is not at all typical of the hotel's décor. Indeed, the rooms are lovely, done up in soft, delicate shades. Excellent soundproofing.

 Frantour-Paris-Suffren

15th arr. - 20, rue Jean-Rey
01 45 78 50 00, fax 01 45 78 91 42
Open year-round. 11 stes 1,990-3,450. 396 rms 890-1,075. Bkfst 80. Rms for disabled. Restaurant. Air cond. Conf. Pkg.
The Frantour Suffren is a large, modern hotel located next to the Seine and the Champ-de-Mars. Though somewhat impersonal, the simple rooms are regularly refurbished and offer excellent equipment. Friendly service. Meals are served in the enclosed garden.

 Grand Hôtel de Champagne

1st arr. - 17, rue Jean-Lantier
01 42 36 60 00, fax 01 45 08 43 33
Open year-round. 3 stes 990-1,230. 40 rms 590-800. Bkfst 55.
A welcoming hotel, with exposed stone walls and ancient beams for atmosphere. The rooms are individually decorated, sometimes in exuberant fashion; some give onto a pretty terrace.

 Holiday Inn

19th arr. - 216, avenue Jean-Jaurès
01 44 84 18 18, fax 01 44 84 18 20
Open year-round. 8 stes 1,490. 174 rms 890-1,050. Bkfst 75. Rms for disabled. Restaurant. Rm ser. Air cond. Conf. Garage pkg.
The contemporary architecture and modern comforts of this Holiday Inn are in keeping with the urban environment of La Villette. Many of the perfectly quiet rooms look out onto the Cité de la Musique, an impressive building by noted architect Christian de Portzamparc.

 Holiday Inn Saint-Germain-des-Prés

6th arr. - 92, rue de Vaugirard
01 42 22 00 56, fax 01 42 22 05 39
Open year-round. 22 stes 930-1,030. 112 rms 840-940. Bkfst 75. Rms for disabled. Air cond. Conf. Garage pkg.
This is a quiet, functional establishment. Well-equipped rooms with minibar and satellite TV, some furnished in cruise-liner style. Piano bar filled with plants. American buffet breakfasts, Gregory's Restaurant. Impeccable service.

 Holiday Inn République

11th arr. - 10, place de la République
01 43 55 44 34, fax 01 47 00 32 34
Open year-round. 7 stes 1,950-2,995. 311 rms 1,395-1,625. Bkfst 105. Rms for disabled. Restaurant. Rm ser. Air cond. Conf.
The architect Davioud, who designed the Châtelet, built this former Modern Palace in 1867. Today it belongs to the largest hotel chain in the world, which completely restored and modernized it. The rooms and suites are functional, pleasant, and well soundproofed; the

most attractive ones overlook the flower-filled, covered courtyard.

 ## Libertel Terminus Nord

10th arr. - 12, bd de Denain
01 42 80 20 00, fax 01 42 80 63 89
Open year-round. 4 stes 1,600. 239 rms 600-1,000. Bkfst 80. Rms for disabled. Restaurant. Air cond. Garage pkg.
A successful renovation has transformed this hotel into a fine place to stay. The spacious, fully equipped rooms are decorated in a Victorian style; good value for the category.

 ## Madison

6th arr. - 143, bd Saint-Germain
01 40 51 60 00, fax 01 40 51 60 01
Open year-round. 55 rms 760-1,500.
A smart, comfortable hotel in the heart of Saint-Germain, decorated with a sprinkling of antique pieces; the bathrooms are done up in pretty Provençal tiles. Quiet, very well equipped rooms.

 ## Méridien Étoile

17th arr. - 81, bd Gouvion-Saint-Cyr
01 40 68 34 34, fax 01 40 68 31 31
Open year-round. 18 stes 3,800-8,000. 1,008 rms 1,350-2,050. Bkfst 85. Restaurants. Rm ser. Air cond. No pets. Valet pkg.
This Méridien is the largest hotel in Western Europe, and one of the busiest in Paris. The rooms are small but prettily furnished. A variety of boutiques, a nightclub, the Hurlingham Polo Bar, and four restaurants liven things up (for the excellent Clos Longchamp, see *Restaurants*), as does the popular cocktail lounge where top jazz musicians play (Club Lionel Hampton).

 ## Méridien Montparnasse

14th arr. - 19, rue du Commandant-Mouchotte
01 44 36 44 36, fax 01 44 36 49 00
Open year-round. 37 stes 3,500-4,500. 916 rms 1,250-1,550. Bkfst 85-115. Rms for disabled. Restaurants. Rm ser. Air cond. Conf. Valet pkg.
Luxurious, soigné, and comfortable—that's the Méridien in a nutshell. Try to reserve one of the newer rooms, which are particularly bright and spacious. Or the Presidential Suite, if your means permit. Certain rooms are for non-smokers only; all afford good views of the city. Fine dining at the Montparnasse 25, see *Restaurants*.

 ## Montana Tuileries

1st arr. - 12, rue Saint-Roch
01 42 60 35 10, fax 01 42 61 12 28
Open year-round. 25 rms 580-1,090. Bkfst 55.
This very chic little hotel doesn't actually overlook the Tuileries, but they are only a stone's throw away. All double rooms, well equipped. Some rooms have balconies.

 ## Napoléon

8th arr. - 40, avenue de Friedland
01 47 66 02 02, fax 01 47 66 82 33
Open year-round. 2 stes 3,500-4,500. 100 rms 1,250-1,950. Bkfst 90-110. Restaurant. Rm ser. Air cond. Conf. Valet pkg.
Admirably situated, just renovated from stem to stern, this fine hotel provides top-flight service along with excellent equipment and amenities. The spacious rooms have classic décor, and offer good value in this up-market neighborhood.

 ## Nikko

15th arr. - 61, quai de Grenelle
01 40 58 20 00, fax 01 45 75 42 35
Open year-round. 12 stes 2,500-8,700. 764 rms 1,480-1,980. Bkfst 85-130. Restaurants. Rm ser. Air cond. Conf. Heated pool. Valet pkg.
Thirty-one floors piled up to resemble an immense beehive, housing ultrafunctional rooms whose large porthole windows overlook the Seine and the Pont Mirabeau. You'll also find an inviting bar, restaurants (Les Célébrités, see *Restaurants*), and a brasserie within the complex.

 ## Novotel Les Halles

1st arr. - Pl. Marguerite-de-Navarre
01 42 21 31 31, fax 01 40 26 05 79
Open year-round. 5 stes 1,500. 280 rms 860-915. Bkfst 62. Rms for disabled. Restaurant. Rm ser. Air cond. Conf. Pkg.
This ultramodern building constructed of stone, glass, and zinc is located in the heart of the former market district, near the Pompidou Center and the Forum des Halles. The bright, quiet rooms are impeccably equipped. Loads of services on offer; piano bar until midnight.

 ## Opéra Richepanse

1st arr. - 14, rue de Richepanse
01 42 60 36 00, fax 01 42 60 13 03
Open year-round. 3 stes 1,600-1,900. 35 rms 750-1,400. Bkfst 65-85. Rm ser. Air cond.
The cozy, inviting guest rooms are elaborately decorated in shades of blue, with solid-wood furnishings in Art Deco style. Top-floor suites enjoy a wide-angle view of the Madeleine church. On the basement level is a lovely breakfast room, as well as a little sauna for relaxing steam baths.

 ## Paris K Palace

16th arr. - 11 bis, rue de Magdebourg
01 44 05 75 75, fax 01 44 05 74 74
Open year-round. 15 stes 2,610. 68 rms 1,510-1,910. Bkfst 105. Restaurant. Rm ser. Air cond. Conf. Pool. Garage pkg.
Ricardo Bofill designed this sleek, contemporary structure situated between the Trocadéro and Arc de Triomphe. Guests enjoy bright, spacious quarters with sophisticated designer furniture and equipment. There's a fitness center, sauna, and Jacuzzi, too, as well as a covered pool surrounded by a teak deck. For the Carré Kléber, see *Restaurants*.

La Perle

6th arr. - 14, rue des Canettes
01 43 29 10 10, fax 01 46 34 51 04
Open year-round. 38 rms 850-1,350. Rms for disabled. Rm ser. Air cond. Bkfst 70.
The hotel's courtyard shields guests from the neighborhood's unending hustle and bustle. Inside, you'll find a large marble-clad lobby and nicely fitted rooms with goose-down comforters on the beds.

 Résidence Saint-Honoré

8th arr. - 214, rue du Fg-St-Honoré
01 42 25 26 27, fax 01 45 63 30 67
Open year-round. 8 stes 1,200-1,400. 77 rms 770-1,100. Bkfst 50. Air cond. Conf. Pkg.
A smart hotel with elegant rooms and fine furnishings. The public rooms and bar are a shade less tastefully done. Dynamic management, uncommonly courteous staff; piano bar. On the lower level, there is an antique store.

 Rochester Champs-Élysées

8th arr. - 92, rue de la Boétie
01 43 59 96 15, fax 01 42 56 01 38
Open year-round. 10 stes 1,380. 80 rms 880-1,200. Bkfst 85. Rms for disabled. Air cond. No pets.
A glitzy hotel that suits the district's flashy clientèle to a T. The rooms are very comfy, with thoughtfully chosen appointments and marble bathrooms. We suggest that you ask to be accommodated in one of the rooms overlooking the indoor garden and fountain. A meeting room is available for business or social occasions.

 Sofitel Arc de Triomphe

8th arr. - 14, rue Beaujon or 4, av. Bertie-Albrecht
01 45 63 04 04, fax 01 42 25 36 81
Open year-round. 6 stes 2,300-2,550. 129 rms 1,650-2,150. Bkfst 65-100. Restaurant. Rm ser. Air cond. Conf. Valet pkg.
This solid, austere building dating from 1925 houses a comfortable hotel that is not long on charm. But the facilities (ultramodern equipment for the business clientele) are first-rate, and are constantly being updated. The largish, bright rooms are functionally decorated. Restaurant: Clovis, see *Restaurants.*

Sofitel Champs-Élysées

8th arr. - 8, rue Jean-Goujon
01 40 74 64 64, fax 01 40 74 64 99
Open year-round. 2 stes 1,800. 38 rms 1,500. Bkfst 85-100. Rms for disabled. Restaurant. Rm ser. Air cond. Conf. Valet pkg.
This hotel is quietly luxurious, with rooms that are impeccably decorated and equipped. Lots of thoughtful little extras and a cheerful efficient staff make staying here a pleasure. Delicious breakfasts. Restaurant: Les Saveurs, see *Restaurants.*

 Sofitel Paris Saint-Jacques

14th arr. - 17, bd Saint-Jacques
01 40 78 79 80, fax 01 40 78 79 04
Open year-round. 14 stes 2,000-2,500. 783 rms 1,000-1,500. Bkfst 95. Rms for disabled. Restaurant. Rm ser. Air cond. Conf. Valet pkg.
The Sofitel Saint-Jacques is conveniently close to Orly airport. It offers good-sized rooms (about half have just been redecorated) with comfortable bathrooms, air conditioning, and blackout blinds that allow long-distance travelers to sleep off their jet lag. Over 100 rooms for non-smokers. A new bar, the Nelli's; and regional culinary events at the restaurant Le Français.

 Sofitel Paris Sèvres

15th arr. - 8-12, rue Louis-Armand
01 40 60 30 30, fax 01 45 57 04 22
Open year-round. 14 stes 1,850-2,300. 524 rms 1,450-1,550. Bkfst 95-105. Restaurants. Air cond. Conf. Heated pool. Valet pkg.
The rooms are perfectly functional, very comfortable, with huge bathrooms. A plethora of meeting and conference rooms (with simultaneous translation available in five languages) are connected to a central administration office. Guests enjoy free admittance to the Vitatop gym club on the 23rd floor. Restaurant: Le Relais de Sèvres, see *Restaurants.*

 Terrass Hôtel

18th arr. - 12, rue Joseph-de-Maistre
01 46 06 72 85, fax 01 42 52 29 11
Open year-round. 13 stes 1,650. 88 rms 830-1,090. Bkfst 75. Restaurant. Air cond. Conf. Pkg.
Located at the foot of the Butte Montmartre, this fine hotel offers a majestic view of almost all of Paris. Rooms are comfortable and nicely fitted. Up on the seventh floor, the panoramic terrace doubles as a bar in summer.

 Victoria Palace

6th arr. - 6, rue Blaise-Desgoffe
01 45 44 38 16, fax 01 45 49 23 75
Open year-round. 3 stes 2,500. 80 rms 890-2,000. Air cond. Conf. Garage pkg.
A reliable establishment, with a certain British charm, has been completely refurbished. The rooms are soothing and spacious, with really generous closets and good bathrooms. Bar and restaurant. The welcome is always most courteous.

 Yllen

15th arr. - 196, rue de Vaugirard
01 45 67 67 67, fax 01 45 67 74 37
Open year-round. 1 ste 910-995. 39 rms 490-695. Bkfst 45. Rms for disabled.
Yllen's modern, functional rooms have understated décor and are well soundproofed—but they are quite small. Corner rooms (those with

numbers ending in 4) on the upper floors are the best. Energetic management, friendly reception.

 ## Waldorf Madeleine

8th arr. - 12, bd Malesherbes
01 42 65 72 06, fax 01 40 07 10 45
Open year-round. 7 stes 1,400. 35 rms 1,100. Bkfst 50. Air cond. Pkg.
This handsome freestone building houses an elegant lobby (notice the Art Deco ceiling) and rooms of exemplary comfort, with double glazing and air conditioning. You can count on a smiling reception.

CHARMING

 ## Abbaye Saint-Germain

6th arr. - 10, rue Cassette
01 45 44 38 11, fax 01 45 48 07 86
Open year-round. 4 stes 1,800-1,900. 42 rms 900-1,500. Air cond. No pets.
Set back from the street, this serene eighteenth-century residence located between a courtyard and a garden offers well-kept, conventionally decorated rooms which are not particularly spacious; the most delightful are on the same level as the garden (number 4 even has a terrace). Very quiet; lovely public rooms.

 ## Alba Opéra

9th arr. - 34 ter, rue La Tour-d'Auvergne
01 48 78 80 22, fax 01 42 85 23 13
Open year-round. 6 stes 1,400-1,500. 18 rms 500-700. Bkfst 40.
Georges Bizet, the author of *Carmen*, was born in this street. He would surely have approved the Alba's elegant décor, enhanced with artworks and mirrors. On the top floor an authentic painter's studio has been installed.

 ## Angleterre

6th arr. - 44, rue Jacob
01 42 60 34 72, fax 01 42 60 16 93
Open year-round. 3 stes 1,400. 24 rms 550-1,200. Bkfst 55. Rms for disabled. No pets.
Hemingway once lived in this former British Embassy, built around a flower-filled patio. The impeccable rooms are fresh and appealing; some are quite spacious, with high beamed ceilings. Large, comfortable beds; luxurious bathrooms. Downstairs, there is a bar and lounge with a piano.

 ## Atala

8th arr. - 10, rue Chateaubriand
01 45 62 01 62, fax 01 42 25 66 38
Open year-round. 1 ste 1,000-1,600. 47 rms 850-1,400. Bkfst 60-120. Air cond. Conf. Pkg.
In a quiet street near the Champs-Élysées, this hotel provides cheerfully decorated rooms that open onto a verdant garden. Balconies and terraces come with rooms on the sixth and eighth floors. Beautiful indoor garden; excellent service.

 ## L'Atelier Montparnasse

6th arr. - 49, rue Vavin
01 46 33 60 00, fax 01 40 51 04 21
Open year-round. 1 ste 950. 16 rms 600-750. Bkfst 45. Restaurant. Rm ser. Garage pkg.
A smart little address done up in modern style, with pretty mosaics in the bathrooms. The rooms themselves are quiet and cozy. Art exhibits are hosted regularly in the hotel's lobby.

 ## De Banville

17th arr. - 166, bd Berthier
01 42 67 70 16, fax 01 44 40 42 77
Open year-round. 39 rms 635-760. Bkfst 50-80. Restaurant. Rm ser. Air cond.
A fine small hotel that dates from the 1930s. There are flowers at the windows (some of which open to panoramic views of Paris) and all manner of pleasing details in the large, bright rooms. Marble or tile bathrooms. Excellent English breakfasts.

 ## Beau Manoir

8th arr. - 6, rue de l'Arcade
01 42 66 03 07, fax 01 42 68 03 00
Open year-round. 3 stes 1,350-1,465. 29 rms 995-1,155. Rms for disabled. Rm ser. Air cond. Pkg.
The opulent décor—it features *Grand Siècle* wall hangings—is somehow reminiscent of Versailles. But the Beau Manoir is just steps away from the Madeleine, in the city's fashionable shopping district. Uncommonly delicious breakfasts are served in the hotel's vaulted cellar.

 ## Bersoly's Saint-Germain

7th arr. - 28, rue de Lille
01 42 60 73 79, fax 01 49 27 05 55
Closed Aug 10-20. 16 rms 580-680. Bkfst 50. Garage pkg.
Writers, artists, and antique dealers frequent this hotel, whose furniture is largely provided by the nearby "golden triangle" of antique shops. Rooms are named for famous artists, and reproductions of their paintings adorn the walls. Breakfast is served in the attractive vaulted basement. Faultless reception.

 ## Bradford Élysées

8th arr. - 10, rue St-Philippe-du-Roule
01 45 63 20 20, fax 01 45 63 20 07
Open year-round. 50 rms 650-1,190. Bkfst 65. Air cond. No pets.
A traditional hotel with comfortable, spacious accommodations decorated in understated good taste. Attractive singles; rooms ending with the numbers 6 and 7 are the largest. You can expect a cheerful welcome.

Hôtel de la Bretonnerie

4th arr. - 22, rue Sainte-Croix-de-la-Bretonnerie
01 48 87 77 63, fax 01 42 77 26 78
Closed Jul 28-Aug 24. 3 stes 950. 27 rms 650-780. Bkfst 45. No pets.
A seventeenth-century town house, charmingly decorated. The rooms are made cozy with exposed wood beams and antique furniture (some canopied beds); the large bathrooms are perfectly modern. Look forward to a friendly reception.

Hôtel de Buci

6th arr. - 22, rue de Buci
01 43 26 89 22, fax 01 46 33 80 31
Open year-round. 24 rms 900-1,300. Bkfst 70-110. Rms for disabled. No pets.
Here's a beautiful, spanking-new hotel opposite the Buci street market. The place simply overflows with charm: the cozy rooms are graced with antique furnishings and a wealth of tasteful touches. Excellent breakfasts are served in the hotel's vaulted cellar.

California

8th arr. - 16, rue de Berri
01 43 59 93 00, fax 01 45 61 03 62
Open year-round. 13 stes 3,000-6,000. 160 rms 1,400-2,200. Bkfst 120. Restaurant. Rm ser. Conf. Valet pkg.
What sets this hotel apart from other similar establishments near the Champs-Élysées is a collection of some 3,000 artworks. As you might imagine, that's a lot of paintings per square yard (and alas, not all are in the best of taste). But the bright patio, with its tiled fountain, provides a welcome respite.

Centre Ville Matignon

8th arr. - 3, rue de Ponthieu
01 42 25 73 01, fax 01 42 56 01 39
Open year-round. 4 stes 990-1,500. 19 rms 590-690. Bkfst 55. Restaurant. Rm ser.
A 1930s feel floats about this hotel, perhaps owing to the lobby's mosaics and boxy armchairs. The rooms are small but attractively decorated, and there is a patio for relaxing.

Chateaubriand

8th arr. - 6, rue Chateaubriand
01 40 76 00 50, fax 01 40 76 09 22
Open year-round. 28 rms 1,100-1,400. Bkfst 65. Rms for disabled. Restaurant. Rm ser. Air cond. Garage pkg.
Built in 1991, this luxury hotel tucked away behind the Champs-Élysées boasts a polychrome-marble lobby and a courteous, professional staff. Classically elegant rooms; beautiful bathrooms.

Claridge Bellman

8th arr. - 37, rue François-Ier
01 47 23 54 42, fax 01 47 23 08 84

Open year-round. 40 rms 800-1,350. Bkfst 70. Restaurant. Rm ser. Air cond. No pets.
A small hotel with quietly attractive rooms of reasonable size, each of which boasts a special feature, be it a crystal chandelier, antique furniture, a fine print or painting, or a marble fireplace.

Hôtel Costes

1st arr. - 239, rue Saint-Honoré
01 42 44 50 00, fax 01 42 44 50 01
Open year-round. 29 stes 2,490-3,450. 56 rms 1,590-1,990. Restaurant. Pool. Fitness center.
An opulent atmosphere prevails at this richly decorated hotel near Place Vendôme, now one of the capital's most sought-after places to stay. Entirely renovated, artistically decorated rooms are both comfortable and blessedly quiet. Duplex suites; gorgeous enclosed courtyard where meals are served in fine weather. There is a fitness center with a pool on the basement level.

Danemark

6th arr. - 21, rue Vavin
01 43 26 93 78, fax 01 46 34 66 06
Open year-round. 15 rms 590-790. Bkfst 55.
This small hotel was carefully renovated in 1930s style. Although the rooms are not very large, they are elegantly furnished, with pleasant lighting, mahogany, ash, or oak furniture and gray-marble bathrooms (number 10 has a Jacuzzi).

Les Deux Iles

4th arr. - 59, rue St-Louis-en-l'Ile
01 43 26 13 35, fax 01 43 29 60 25
Open year-round. 17 rms 700-830. Bkfst 45.
This particularly welcoming hotel, like many buildings on the Ile-Saint-Louis, is a lovely seventeenth-century house. You'll sleep close to the Seine in small, pretty rooms decorated with bright fabrics and painted furniture.

Duc de Saint-Simon

7th arr. - 14, rue Saint-Simon
01 44 39 20 20, fax 01 45 48 68 25
Open year-round. 5 stes 1,800-1,850. 29 rms 1,025-1,425. Bkfst 70. Rm ser. Air cond. No pets.
Set back from the street between two gardens, this quiet, elegant nineteenth-century hotel provides discreet luxury and comfort, with antiques, fine paintings and objets d'art, good lighting, and enchanting décor. The four rooms have terraces that overlook the garden. Room 41, in the annex, boasts an imposing canopied bed. There is a bar, but no restaurant.

Ducs d'Anjou

1st arr. - 1, rue Sainte-Opportune
01 42 36 92 24, fax 01 42 36 16 63
Open year-round. 38 rms 480-592. Bkfst 44. Conf.
Located on the delightful small Place Sainte-Opportune, this ancient building has been restored from top to bottom. The rooms are small (as are the bathrooms) but quiet; rooms 61 and 62 are larger, and can comfortably accommodate

three people. Those overlooking the courtyard are a bit gloomy.

 ## Éber Monceau

17th arr. - 18, rue Léon-Jost
01 46 22 60 70, fax 01 47 63 01 01
Open year-round. 5 stes 1,050-1,360. 13 rms 500-660. Bkfst 50. Rm ser. No pets.
A quiet charming hotel, "adopted," so to speak, by people in fashion, photography, and the movies. Rooms are on the small side, and all have cable TV. A large, two-level suite on the top floor has a lovely terrace. The lobby impresses with its Henri II fireplace and Renaissance beams. Breakfast, which can be served in the patio in summer, is wonderful. A bar and a small lounge.

 ## Grand Hôtel Malher

4th arr. - 5, rue Malher
01 42 72 60 92, fax 01 42 72 25 37
Open year-round. 1 ste 880-990. 30 rms 470-720. Bkfst 45. Conf. No pets.
Now freshly refurbished, this family-owned hotel in the historic Marais sports a welcoming country-style décor. After a good night's sleep in one of the pretty guest rooms, you can go down to hearty breakfast, served with a smile in a vaulted seventeenth-century cellar.

 ## L'Hôtel

6th arr. - 13, rue des Beaux-Arts
01 44 41 99 00, fax 01 43 25 64 81
Open year-round. 2 stes 2,800-3,500. 25 rms 1,000-2,500. Rm ser. Air cond.
"L'Hôtel" provides top-notch amenities and service, of course, but it's the charm of the place that accounts for its enduring popularity. The décor resembles no other—whether it's number 16, once occupied by Oscar Wilde, the neo-Egyptian Imperial room, the purple-swathed Cardinale room, or number 36, which contains the Art Deco furniture of music-hall star Mistinguett. Bar: Le Bélier.

 ## Hôtel du Jeu de Paume

4th arr. - 54, rue St-Louis-en-l'Ile
01 43 26 14 18, fax 01 40 46 02 76
Open year-round. 32 rms 895-1,450. Bkfst 80. Rms for disabled. Rm ser. Conf. Sauna.
This is a seventeenth-century building with a splendid wood-and-stone interior, featuring a glass elevator that ferries guests to bright, quiet rooms with marble baths. There is a pleasant little garden, too, and a music room.

Left Bank Saint-Germain

6th arr. - 9, rue de l'Ancienne Comédie
01 43 54 01 70, fax 01 43 26 17 14
Open year-round. 32 rms 850-990. Bkfst 30. Rms for disabled. Air cond.

Housed in a seventeenth-century building next to the historic Café Procope, this engaging hotel offers intimate rooms decorated with Jouy-print fabrics. Some lodgings afford views of Paris rooftops and Notre-Dame; all have nicely equipped little bathrooms.

 ## Lenox

7th arr. - 9, rue de l'Université
01 42 96 10 95, fax 01 42 61 52 83
Open year-round. 2 stes 1,500. 32 rms 650-1,100. Bkfst 45.
These petite but most attractive rooms are decorated with elegant wallpaper and stylish furniture; numbers 51, 52, and 53 are the most enchanting. On the top floor are two split-level suites with exposed beams and flower-filled balconies. The elegant bar stays open until 2am.

 ## Lenox Montparnasse

14th arr. - 15, rue Delambre
01 43 35 34 50, fax 01 43 20 46 64
Open year-round. 6 stes 980. 46 rms 540-650. Bkfst 45. Rm ser.
In the heart of Montparnasse, a peaceful hotel with a cozy sort of charm. The penthouse suites are awfully attractive—they even have fireplaces. Rooms vary in size, yet are uniformly comfortable and well maintained. Smiling staff; elegant bar (open until 2am).

 ## Lido

8th arr. - 4, passage de la Madeleine
01 42 66 27 37, fax 01 42 66 61 23
Open year-round. 32 rms 830-980. Air cond.
A laudable establishment, situated between the Madeleine and the Place de la Concorde. The lobby is most elegant, with Oriental rugs on the floor and tapestries on the stone walls. The guest rooms, decorated in pink, blue, or cream, have comfortable beds, modern bathrooms, and double-glazed windows. Thoughtful, courteous staff.

 ## Lutèce

4th arr. - 65, rue St-Louis-en-l'Ile
01 43 26 23 52, fax 01 43 29 60 25
Open year-round. 23 rms 710-980. Bkfst 45. Air cond.
A tasteful, small hotel for people who love Paris, this handsome old house has some little twenty rooms (there are two charming mansards on the sixth floor), with whitewashed walls and ceiling beams, decorated with bright, cheerful fabrics. The bathrooms are small but modern and impeccably kept. The lobby features lavish bouquets and a stone fireplace which is often used in winter.

Luxembourg

6th arr. - 4, rue de Vaugirard
01 43 25 35 90, fax 01 43 26 60 84
Open year-round. 33 rms 700-800. Bkfst 60. Air cond. Conf.

Near the Luxembourg Gardens, in the heart of the Latin Quarter. The pleasant rooms have good equipment but small bathrooms. And there is a beautiful vine-covered patio.

 ## Majestic

16th arr. - 29, rue Dumont-d'Urville
01 45 00 83 70, fax 01 45 00 29 48
Open year-round. 3 stes 1,520-1,920. 27 rms 920-1,470. Bkfst 60. Air cond.
The big rooms in this exemplary hotel are redecorated by turns, and all boast comfortable beds, fine furniture, and thick carpeting. On the top floor, a lovely penthouse features a small balcony filled with flowers. Old-World atmosphere.

 ## Hôtel Mansart

1st arr. - 5, rue des Capucines
01 42 61 50 28, fax 01 49 27 97 44
Open year-round. 6 stes 1,200-1,500. 51 rms 580-950. Bkfst 55. Rm ser. No pets.
The lobby looks for all the world like an art gallery; the rooms are positively charming, arrayed in elegant furnishings with all the modern comforts and equipment one could wish. If you book well in advance, you can request the "Mansart" room, which overlooks Place Vendôme.

 ## Hôtel de Notre-Dame

5th arr. - 19, rue Maître-Albert
01 43 26 79 00, fax 01 46 33 50 11
Open year-round. 34 rms 690-750. Bkfst 40. No pets.
Some of the beamed rooms are rather small, but all are comfy and prettily fitted out, with impeccable marble bathrooms. Situated on a quiet street near the river, this hotel is managed by a cheerful staff.

 ## Nouvel Hôtel

12th arr. - 24, av. du Bel-Air
01 43 43 01 81, fax 01 43 44 64 13
Open year-round. 28 rms 360-530. Bkfst 40.
The rooms of the Nouvel Hôtel are peaceful and attractive, and all were just freshly renovated and redecorated (the prettiest is number 10 9, on the same level as the garden). Good bathrooms; hospitable reception. Old-fashioned hot chocolate is served at breakfast.

 ## Panthéon

5th arr. - 19, pl. du Panthéon
01 43 54 32 95, fax 01 43 26 64 65
Open year-round. 34 rms 635-780. Bkfst 45. Air cond. Conf. No pets. Pkg.
Clever use of mirrors makes the entrance, lounge, and bar of this eighteenth-century building seem bigger. The elegant rooms are quite spacious, decorated in Louis XVI or Louis-Philippe style, with pastel wallcoverings. Room 33 has a grand canopied bed. Buffet breakfast; friendly welcome.

 ## Parc Saint-Séverin

5th arr. - 22, rue de la Parcheminerie
01 43 54 32 17, fax 01 43 54 70 71
Open year-round. 27 rms 500-1,500. Bkfst 50. No pets.
The rooms on the sixth and seventh floors of this 1930s-vintage hotel boast balconies with a view over the church and cloister of Saint-Séverin. All the accommodations are bright and spacious, enhanced with antiques and contemporary art objects.

 ## Le Pavillon Bastille

12th arr. - 65, rue de Lyon
01 43 43 65 65, fax 01 43 43 96 52
Open year-round. 1 ste 1,200-1,375. 23 rms 650-955. Bkfst 65. Rms for disabled. Rm ser. Air cond.
Across from the Bastille opera house, here are all the comforts of a luxury hotel, with the charm of a private town house. The bright rooms and lobby are decorated in a bold, high style; the owner welcomes guests with a glass of white wine. Minibar; sumptuous buffet breakfasts.

  ## Pavillon de la Reine

3rd arr. - 28, pl. des Vosges
01 42 77 96 40, fax 01 42 77 63 06
Open year-round. 22 stes 2,300-3,500. 33 rms 1,500-2,100. Bkfst 95-140. Rms for disabled. Rm ser. Air cond. Valet pkg.
Part of the hotel dates from the seventeenth century, while the rest is a clever "reconstitution." The rooms and suites, all with marble bathrooms, are tastefully decorated. The furnishings are an artful blend of authentic antiques and lovely reproductions. Accommodations overlook either the back of the Place des Vosges or a quiet inner patio filled with flowers.

 ## Prince de Conti

6th arr. - 8, rue Guénégaud
01 44 07 30 40, fax 01 44 07 36 34
Open year-round. 3 stes 1,000-1,250. 23 rms 750-990. Bkfst 60. Rms for disabled. Air cond. Conf. No pets.
Probably the handsomest *hôtel de charme* on the Left Bank. Chintzes, stripes, and tartans give the superbly decorated rooms a distinctive British feel. Splendid split-level suites; attentive service.

 ## Regent's Garden Hotel

17th arr. - 6, rue Pierre-Demours
01 45 74 07 30, fax 01 40 55 01 42
Open year-round. 39 rms 640-930. Bkfst 45. Garage pkg.
This handsome Second Empire building, just a stone's throw from the Place de l'Étoile, offers large, nicely proportioned rooms with high, ornate ceilings; some have fireplaces. Comfortable and well kept, the hotel also boasts a gorgeous flower garden.

Looking for a hotel? Refer to the **index.**

Relais Christine

6th arr. - 3, rue Christine
01 43 26 71 80, fax 01 43 26 89 38
Open year-round. 15 stes 2,600-3,200. 36 rms 1,630-1,800. Bkfst 95. Rm ser. Air cond. Conf. Valet pkg.
This Renaissance cloister has retained some of the peace of its earlier vocation, but this luxurious hotel also possesses all the comforts of the present age, from double glazing to perfect service. The rooms are decorated with Provençal prints and pink Portuguese marble baths. The best rooms are the two-level suites and the ground-floor room with private terrace, but all are spacious, quiet, and air conditioned. Courteous reception.

 ## Le Relais du Louvre

1st arr. - 19, rue des Prêtres-St-Germain-l'Auxerrois
01 40 41 96 42, fax 01 40 41 96 44
Open year-round. 2 stes 1,280-1,450. 18 rms 600-960. Bkfst 50. Restaurant. Rm ser.
The original façade of this historic building opposite the Tuileries has been preserved, but the interior is fully modernized. The comfortable rooms, elegantly decorated by Constance de Castelbajac, overflow with charm; they all have marble bathrooms, too. Rooms with numbers ending in 1 are slightly smaller than the rest. Wonderfully hospitable reception.

 ## Le Relais Médicis

6th arr. - 23, rue Racine
01 43 26 00 60, fax 01 40 46 83 39
Open year-round. 16 rms 930-1,495. Air cond. Conf.
Bright colors adorn the walls of each room: yellow, blue, red... The effect is cheerful and charming, enhanced by ancient beams, pictures, vintage photos. A quiet patio and fountain are conducive to relaxation. The staff visibly cares about guests' comfort and well-being.

 ## Relais Saint-Germain

6th arr. - 9, carrefour de l'Odéon
01 43 29 12 05, fax 01 46 33 45 30
Open year-round. 1 ste 1,950. 21 rms 1,280-1,700. Rm ser.
All the accommodations are personalized and decorated in luxurious style, with superb furniture, lovely fabrics, exquisite lighting, and beautiful, perfectly equipped marble bathrooms. The tall, double-glazed windows open onto the lively Carrefour de l'Odéon. You are bound to fall in love with Paris staying at this tiny jewel of an establishment. Exemplary service.

 ## Les Rives de Notre-Dame

5th arr. - 15, quai Saint-Michel
01 43 54 81 16, fax 01 43 26 27 09
Open year-round. 1 ste 2,600. 9 rms 995-1,650. Bkfst 60-85. Rms for disabled. Restaurant. Rm ser. Air cond. Conf.

From the roomy, bright accommodations in this seventeenth-century hotel, you'll enjoy a pretty view of the Seine. The rooms all have fresh, personalized décor in Tuscan or Provençal styles.

 ## Rond Point de Longchamp

16th arr. - 86, rue de Longchamp
01 45 05 13 63, fax 01 47 55 12 80
Open year-round. 57 rms 510-1,500. Bkfst 65-100. Restaurant. Air cond. Conf.
The sizeable, comfortable rooms are nicely fitted and prettily decorated (gray carpeting, burr-walnut furniture), and have marble bathrooms. A bar, as well as a billiard room.

 ## Hôtel Saint-Germain

7th arr. - 88, rue du Bac
01 45 48 62 92, fax 01 45 48 26 89
Open year-round. 29 rms 415-730. Bkfst 45. No pets.
In the best Rive Gauche tradition, this posh yet discreet little hostelry charms guests with beamed and vaulted ceilings, elegant décor, and period furnishings. The atmosphere is somehow provincial (in the best sense of the word); rooms offer space and comfort as well as all modern conveniences.

 ## Saint-Grégoire

6th arr. - 43, rue de l'Abbé-Grégoire
01 45 48 23 23, fax 01 45 48 33 95
Open year-round. 1 ste 1,390. 19 rms 790-990. Bkfst 60.
The cozy lounge is warmed in winter by a fireplace and there's a small garden for fine days. The rooms are painted in subtle shades of yellow and pink, with matching chintz curtains, white damask bedspreads, and some fine antique furniture. Double glazing and modern bathrooms. Expensive.

Saint-Louis

4th arr. - 75, rue St-Louis-en-l'Ile
01 46 34 04 80, fax 01 46 34 02 13
Open year-round. 21 rms 595-795. Bkfst 45.
Elegant simplicity characterizes this appealing hotel, where attention to detail is evident in the gorgeous flower arrangements and polished antiques. Small, perfectly soundproofed rooms offer comfortable beds and thick carpeting underfoot. The modern bathrooms are pretty indeed.

Saint-Louis-Marais

4th arr. - 1, rue Charles-V
01 48 87 87 04, fax 01 48 87 33 26
Open year-round. 16 rms 350-710. Bkfst 40.
Reasonable prices and a delightful reception at this former convent annex in the heart of historic Paris. Each little room is different; all are charming and comfortable. Some rooms have been redecorated.

Saint-Merry

4th arr. - 78, rue de la Verrerie
01 42 78 14 15, fax 01 40 29 06 82
*Open year-round. 1 ste 2,000. 11 rms 400-1,100.
Bkfst 50.*
A former presbytery, this seventeenth-century building is home to an original collection of Gothic furniture, which the owner has been buying at auctions for many years. The telephone booth near the reception desk is a former confessional! Rooms are mostly small, with bathrooms not much bigger than closets, but the charm of the place is such that you have to book well in advance for the summer.

 Sainte-Beuve

6th arr. - 9, rue Sainte-Beuve
01 45 48 20 07, fax 01 45 48 67 52
Open year-round. 5 stes 1,550-1,700. 18 rms 700-1,300. Bkfst 80. Rm ser.
The Sainte-Beuve is a tasteful, harmonious example of the neo-Palladian style of decoration, promoted in particular by David Hicks. In the guest rooms soft colors, chintzes and the odd antique create a soothing atmosphere. Most attractive marble-and-tile bathrooms; elegant lobby with comfortable sofas arranged around the fireplace.

 **Hôtel
des Saints-Pères**

6th arr. - 65, rue des Saints-Pères
01 45 44 50 00, fax 01 45 44 90 83
*Open year-round. 3 stes 1,650. 35 rms 750-1,250.
Bkfst 55. No pets.*
Situated in two buildings, with all the quiet, elegantly furnished rooms overlooking a garden. Suite 205 is particularly attractive. Downstairs is a pretty breakfast room, and a bar that opens onto the garden.

 San Régis

8th arr. - 12, rue Jean-Goujon
01 44 95 16 16, fax 01 45 61 05 48
Open year-round. 10 stes 3,200-5,500. 34 rms 1,650-2,850. Bkfst 100. Restaurant. Rm ser. Air cond. No pets. Valet pkg.
This jewel of a hotel, much appreciated by celebrities from the worlds of show business and *haute couture*, provides a successful mix of traditional comfort and the latest technology. Beautiful, newly decorated rooms boast splendid period furniture and paintings, sumptuous bathrooms, and lots of space, light, and character. The staff is irreproachable.

 Select Hotel 🌲🌹

5th arr. - 1, pl. de la Sorbonne
01 46 34 14 80, fax 01 46 34 51 79
*Open year-round. 1 ste 980-1,250. 67 rms 530-890.
Bkfst 30. Air cond. Conf.*
A glass-roofed atrium with an abundance of plants has been built at the heart of this attractive hotel next door to the Sorbonne. The pleasant, spacious rooms are functionally furnished; some open onto a lively square.

 Solférino

7th arr. - 91, rue de Lille
01 47 05 85 54, fax 01 45 55 51 16
*Closed Dec 22-Jan 4. 33 rms 269-639. Bkfst 39.
24 rms 510-690. Pkg.*
Almost opposite the Musée d'Orsay, here are simple rooms done in fresh colors, with bath or shower. There is a cozy little lounge, a sky-lit breakfast room, and pretty ornaments everywhere.

 Université

7th arr. - 22, rue de l'Université
01 42 61 09 39, fax 01 42 60 40 84
Open year-round. 27 rms 600-1,300. Bkfst 45. Air cond. No pets.
Comfortable beds and pink-marble bathrooms in an intelligently renovated seventeenth-century residence, most appealing with its beams, half-timbering, and period furniture. Rooms on the first floor have high ceilings, while the fifth-floor suites boast flower-decked terraces.

 Vert Galant

13th arr. - 41, rue Croulebarbe
01 44 08 83 50, fax 01 44 08 83 69
Open year-round. 15 rms 400-500. Bkfst 40. Rms for disabled. Conf. No pets. Garage pkg.
Now for something completely different: this delightful country *auberge* provides adorable rooms (with kitchenette) overlooking an indoor garden where grapes and tomatoes grow! Quiet; good value. Restaurant: Auberge Etchegorry, see *Restaurants*.

 Vieux Paris 🌲🌹

6th arr. - 9, rue Gît-le-Cœur
01 43 54 41 66, fax 01 43 26 00 15
Open year-round. 7 stes 1,550-1,650. 13 rms 990-1,770. Bkfst 70-80. No pets. Garage pkg.
Here's a hotel that wears its name well, for it was built in the fifteenth century. A recent overhaul turned the Vieux Paris into a luxurious stopover, whose comfort and first-rate amenities fully justify the high rates. Rooms are handsomely furnished and perfectly quiet, with Jacuzzis in every bathroom. Warm reception.

 **La Villa
Saint-Germain**

6th arr. - 29, rue Jacob
01 43 26 60 00, fax 01 46 34 63 63
Open year-round. 4 stes 2,000-3,000. 28 rms 900-1,800. Bkfst 80. Rm ser. Air cond.
A laser beam projects room numbers onto the doors; the bathroom sinks are crafted of chrome and sanded glass; orange, violet, green, and red leather furniture stands out vividly against the subdued gray walls: a high-tech environment that attracts a trendy, moneyed clientele. Jazz club on the lower level (La Villa), with name performers.

PRACTICAL

 ## Acacias Saint-Germain

6th arr. - 151 bis, rue de Rennes
01 45 48 97 38, fax 01 45 44 63 57
Open year-round. 4 stes 480-1,130. 37 rms 380-800.
Bkfst 40-65.
Some of the small, pleasant rooms of this good
hotel have been redecorated. There is a pretty
summer garden, too, and the staff is most obliging.

 ## Adagio

15th arr. - 257, rue de Vaugirard
01 40 45 11 40, fax 01 40 45 10 10
Open year-round. 3 stes 1,400. 184 rms 590-835.
Bkfst 75. Rms for disabled. Restaurant. Rm scr. Air
cond. Conf. Garage pkg.
An ultramodern hotel with a bright lobby and
comfortable, functional rooms. From the terrace,
guests can admire the Eiffel Tower.

 ## Alliance Saint-Germain

6th arr. - 7-11, rue Saint-Benoît
01 42 61 53 53, fax 01 49 27 09 33
Open year-round. 117 rms 895-1,070. Bkfst 75. Rms
for disabled. Conf. No pets.
This large, modern hotel, formerly a printing
works, is located in the heart of Saint-Germain-
des-Prés; its gracious turn-of-the-century façade
has been preserved. The spacious rooms are
functional and well equipped; each floor is
decorated in a different color. A cellar jazz club
provides hot and cool live music every night
except Sunday, and Monday.

 ## Atlantis Saint-Germain-des-Prés

6th arr. - 4, rue du Vieux-Colombier
01 45 48 31 81, fax 01 45 48 35 16
Open year-round. 34 rms 380-585. Bkfst 30. No pets.
A typical little Left Bank hotel just steps from
Saint-Sulpice, with attractive rooms and a
flower-filled breakfast room. On the walls hang
works by amateur painters for an arty touch.

 ## Bergère Opéra

9th arr. - 34, rue Bergère
01 47 70 34 34, fax 01 47 70/36 36
Open year-round. 134 rms 590-990. Rm scr. Air
cond. Conf. No pets.
All the quiet rooms (most of which overlook a
courtyard garden) have been freshened up and
modernized, including the bathrooms.

 ## Best Western Folkestone Opéra

8th arr. - 9, rue Castellane
01 42 65 73 09, fax 01 42 65 64 09

Open year-round. 50 rms 605-800. Bkfst 45. Air
cond.
The beamed rooms have Art Deco armchairs
and comfortable beds. Rooms on the first floor
are air-conditioned. Generous buffet breakfasts;
gracious reception.

 ## Hôtel Boileau

16th arr. - 81, rue Boileau
01 42 88 83 74, fax 01 45 27 62 98
Open year-round. 30 rms 360-425. Rms for dis-
abled. Conf.
This establishment is warm and bright, with
small, simply furnished rooms. A skylight
covers the little garden-courtyard.

 ## Brighton

1st arr. - 218, rue de Rivoli
01 47 03 61 61, fax 01 42 60 41 78
Open year-round. 1 ste 1,400. 69 rms 450-920. Bkfst
30. Restaurant. Rm scr. No pets.
A dream setting opposite the Tuileries, near
the Louvre, is offered at very reasonable prices.
The rooms on the Rue de Rivoli have wonderful
views, high molded ceilings, brass beds, and
good-sized bathrooms. The little attic rooms are
especially good value. Tiny elevator, though,
and unsmiling staff.

 ## Hôtel de Châteaudun

9th arr. - 30, rue de Châteaudun
01 49 70 09 99, fax 01 49 70 06 99
Open year-round. 26 rms 620-760. Bkfst 50. Rm scr.
Air cond. Conf.
The chilly reception area and graceless furniture are only part of the picture here. For the
comfortable rooms are perfectly soundproofed,
and the staff is warm and friendly. Buffet breakfasts.

 ## Hôtel des Chevaliers

3rd arr. - 30, rue de Turenne
01 42 72 73 47, fax 01 42 72 54 10
Open year-round. 24 rms 590-820. Bkfst 50.
In the heart of the Marais, a small hotel frequented by actors and movie folk. The small
rooms are bright and pleasantly furnished, with
good bathrooms. Warm reception.

 ## Claret

12th arr. - 44, bd de Bercy
01 46 28 41 31, fax 01 49 28 09 29
Open year-round. 52 rms 350-650. Bkfst 50. Half-
board 450. Restaurant. Rm scr. Air cond. Pkg.
This neat, modernized hotel (formerly a *relais*
de poste) offers a family atmosphere and a wine
bar in the basement. Each meticulously maintained room is named for a wine region of
France. Good value.

Hôtel du Collège de France

5th arr. - 7, rue Thénard
01 43 26 78 36, fax 01 46 34 58 29

Open year-round. 2 stes 1,030. 29 rms 480-580.
Bkfst 33. Rms for disabled. No pets.
The simple rooms of the Hôtel du Collège de
France, located on a quiet little street, are tidy
and comfortable. Most charming are the attic
rooms, with their wooden beams and a view of
the towers of Notre-Dame.

 ## Hôtel du Danube

6th arr. - 58, rue Jacob
01 42 60 34 70, fax 01 42 60 81 18
Open year-round. 6 stes 1,000. 34 rms 450-800.
Bkfst 45.
Each room is different, hung with floral
wallpaper and furnished with antiques (including some canopied beds). And prices are
reasonable, considering the neighborhood.

 ## Ermitage Hôtel

18th arr. - 24, rue Lamarck
01 42 64 79 22, fax 01 42 64 10 33
Open year-round. 12 rms 330-460. No pets. Pkg.
This charming hotel occupies a little white
building behind the Basilica of Sacré-Cœur. The
personalized décor in each room is punctuated
by an antique or *bibelot*. Pretty bathrooms; no TV.
There is a garden and a terrace for relaxing, and
you can expect a friendly reception.

 ## Étoile Park Hotel

17th arr. - 10, avenue Mac-Mahon
01 42 67 69 63, fax 01 43 80 18 99
*Closed Dec 24-Jan 1. 2 stes 610-690. 28 rms 380-
710. Bkfst 52. No pets.*
Modern and decorated in impersonal good
taste, this hotel offers freshly refurbished guest
rooms and comfortable, well-designed
bathrooms—everything, in a word, but charm.

 ## Étoile Pereire

17th arr. - 146, bd Pereire
01 42 67 60 00, fax 01 42 67 02 90
Open year-round. 5 stes 1,000. 21 rms 600-760.
Bkfst 54. Rms for disabled. Rm ser. No pets.
Attention to detail is a priority at this welcoming hotel, owned by a former pianist. Located at
the back of a quiet courtyard, the spacious, pastel
rooms are most attractive, with garden views.
Both the atmosphere and service are charming
and cheerful.

 ## Familia Hotel

5th arr. - 11, rue des Écoles
01 43 54 55 27, fax 01 43 29 61 77
Open year-round. 30 rms 380-490.
The management of this modest two-star hotel
strives to make guests comfortable. Rooms are
small but decently equipped; reasonable rates.

 ## Ferrandi

6th arr. - 92, rue du Cherche-Midi
01 42 22 97 40, fax 01 45 44 89 97
Open year-round. 1 ste 980-1,280. 41 rms 480-980.
Bkfst 60-70. Air cond. Pkg.

In a quiet street near Montparnasse, with a
reception area that matches the charm of the
rooms. Some of the guest rooms have four-
poster beds, others a fireplace (many could use
a fresh coat of paint). All have good bathrooms
(with hairdryers) and double glazing. Delightful
welcome.

 ## Fleurie

6th arr. - 32-34, rue Grégoire-de-Tours
01 43 29 59 81, fax 01 43 29 68 44
Open year-round. 3 stes 1,200. 26 rms 650-850.
Bkfst 50. Air cond. No pets.
From the welcoming dark-green entrance to
the period rooms decorated with quality furniture and warm colors, this hotel in the heart of
Saint-Germain exudes Left Bank charm. Plants
and flower bouquets lend a pleasing, springlike
touch.

 ## Forest Hill

19th arr. - 28 ter, av. Corentin-Cariou
01 44 72 15 30, fax 01 44 72 15 80
*Open year-round. 13 stes 850-1,250. 246 rms 495-
940. Bkfst 40-68. Half-board 615-1,060. Rms for
disabled. Restaurant. Rm ser. Air cond. Conf.
Garage pkg.*
A mammouth concrete structure opposite the
Cité des Sciences, the Forest Hill houses functional rooms (with small windows!) that have
the virtue of being absolutely quiet.

 ## Hôtel Français

10th arr. - 13, rue du 8-Mai-1945
01 40 35 94 14, fax 01 40 35 55 40
*Open year-round. 71 rms 375-460. Bkfst 30. Garage
pkg.*
You'll appreciate the good value of this convenient hotel, situated opposite the Gare de l'Est.
Old-fashioned charm combines with modern
comforts (iron and ironing board, hairdryer, and
safe in all the rooms).

 ## Galileo

8th arr. - 54, rue Galilée
01 47 20 66 06, fax 01 47 20 67 17
*Open year-round. 27 rms 800-950. Bkfst 60. Rms
for disabled. Rm ser. Air cond. No pets.*
Just steps from the Champs-Élysées, the
Galileo offers an elegant lobby and public rooms,
an Italian-style garden, and bright guest rooms
done in understated good taste, with gray-
marble bathrooms. Effective soundproofing and
air conditioning.

 ## Grand Hôtel de Besançon

2nd arr. - 56, rue Montorgueil
01 42 36 41 08, fax 01 45 08 08 79
Open year-round. 10 stes 620-650. 10 rms 550-590.
Bkfst 40-60. No pets. Garage pkg.
After a full-dress overhaul, the Besançon
provides soundproofed rooms furnished with
Louis-Philippe–style pieces. Convenient to the
Louvre and to the Forum des Halles.

Grand Hôtel des Gobelins

13th arr. - 57, bd St-Marcel - 01 43 31 79 89
Open year-round. Rms 320-430. Bkfst 36. No pets.
Situated on the edge of the fifth arrondissement, this hotel offers exceptional value for money. Some of the rooms look out onto the Panthéon. Double-glazed windows; dry cleaning service daily, even on weekends.

 ## Grands Hommes

5th arr. - 17, pl. du Panthéon
01 46 34 19 60, fax 01 43 26 67 32
Open year-round. 2 stes 860-1,220. 30 rms 635-780. Bkfst 45. Conf. No pets.
An eighteenth-century building opposite the Panthéon. The fairly spacious rooms are decorated in ocher and orange tones; room 22 has a canopied brass bed, 60 and 61 boast balconies and pleasant views. The staff is friendly and efficient.

 ## Hameau de Passy

16th arr. - 48, rue de Passy
01 42 88 47 55, fax 01 42 30 83 72
Open year-round. 32 rms 450-530. Bkfst 30-57. Rms for disabled.
Tucked away in a flower-filled cul-de-sac, this exceptionally quiet hotel was recently modernized. Roughcast walls and stained-wood furniture decorate the comfortable rooms (some connecting) that overlook the garden. Bright, tidy bathrooms; smiling service and reception.

 ## Istria

14th arr. - 29, rue Campagne-Première
01 43 20 91 82, fax 01 43 22 48 45
Open year-round. 26 rms 420-590. Bkfst 45.
Elm furniture and pastel colors grace the rooms and bathrooms of this well-kept hotel, where Mayakovski, Man Ray, and Marcel Duchamp once slept. The building is fully modernized.

 ## Le Jardin de Cluny

5th arr. - 9, rue du Sommerard
01 43 54 22 66, fax 01 40 51 03 36
Open year-round. 40 rms 540-800. Bkfst 50. No pets.
A perfectly functional hotel in the heart of the Latin Quarter, with comfortable, cheerful rooms (some are air conditioned) and spotless bathrooms. Professional desk staff.

 ## Les Jardins d'Eiffel

7th arr. - 8, rue Amélie
01 47 05 46 21, fax 01 45 55 28 08
Open year-round. 80 rms 560-960. Bkfst 60. Rms for disabled. Air cond. Conf. Garage pkg.
A handsome old-fashioned hotel that dates from the turn of the century. Attractive, well-equipped rooms: those on the upper floors overlook the Eiffel Tower. Charming reception.

 ## Hôtel du Léman

9th arr. - 20, rue de Trévise
01 42 46 50 66, fax 01 48 24 27 59
Open year-round. 24 rms 390-660. Bkfst 40. Conf.
This charming, out-of-the-ordinary small hotel has been tastefully renovated. Tuscany marble inlays enhance the modern décor in the lobby. The tiny rooms are pleasantly decorated with attractive bedside lamps and original drawings and watercolors. A generous buffet breakfast is served in the vaulted basement. The staff does its utmost to make guests feel at home.

 ## Louvre Saint-Honoré

1st arr. - 141, rue Saint-Honoré
01 42 96 23 23, fax 01 42 96 21 61
Open year-round. 40 rms 496-862. Bkfst 45. Rms for disabled. Rm ser. Air cond.
Convenient to the Louvre, with quiet, functional accommodations. Rooms open onto a patio embellished with wood sculptures and plants.

 ## Jardins du Luxembourg

5th arr. - 5, impasse Royer-Collard
01 40 46 08 88, fax 01 40 46 02 28
Open year-round. 25 rms 850. Bkfst 50. Rms for disabled. Air cond. No pets.
Fresh from a successful year-long renovation, the small rooms sport a cozy Mediterranean look and the tiled bathrooms are immaculate and bright. The basement breakfast room is a mite gloomy, though, and parking is most problematic!

 ## Hôtel Le Laumière

19th arr. - 4, rue Petit
01 42 06 10 77, fax 01 42 06 72 50
Open year-round. 54 rms 265-350. Bkfst 32. Pkg.
This meticulously-kept small hotel is located a few steps away from the Buttes-Chaumont park, in a district where modern hotels are not exactly plentiful. Convenient for the La Villette exhibition center. Rooms are small (those on the courtyard are larger), fully renovated, and moderately priced.

 ## Magellan

17th arr. - 17, rue Jean-Baptiste-Dumas
01 45 72 44 51, fax 01 40 68 90 36
Open year-round. 75 rms 430-630. Bkfst 40-55. Restaurant. Rm ser. No pets. Garage pkg.
The elegant lobby and lounge were just redecorated, but not the rooms (though some of them could use a rehab). It is preferable to choose a room in the quiet annex which gives onto a garden.

 ## Modern Hotel Lyon

12th arr. - 3, rue Parrot
01 43 43 41 52, fax 01 43 43 81 16
Open year-round. 1 ste 750-855. 47 rms 495-580. Bkfst 39. No pets.

The location is most convenient (near the Gare de Lyon), and the building is attractive. Comfortable, unpretentious rooms; skimpy breakfasts.

 ## Hôtel Le Montana

6th arr. - 28, rue St-Benoît - 01 44 39 71 00
Open year-round. 1 ste 962. 16 rms 556-762. Bkfst 50. Restaurant. Rm ser.
Streetside rooms are nice and bright, while rooms at the back can be gloomy. All are decorated in a rather stark contemporary style. Hotel guests are offered a free second drink at the bar of the well-known Montana jazz club.

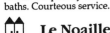 ## Hôtel des Nations

5th arr. - "Neotel", 54, rue Monge
01 43 26 45 24, fax 01 46 34 00 13
Open year-round. 38 rms 560-630. Bkfst 56.
Across from the Arènes de Lutèce, this hotel is pretty and modern. The comfortable, pleasant rooms are prettily decorated and sport marble baths. Courteous service.

 ## Le Noailles

2nd arr. - 9, rue de la Michodière
01 47 42 92 90, fax 01 49 24 92 71
Open year-round. 58 rms 580-860. Bkfst 45-80. Rm ser. Conf.
Metal, glass, and wood compose this hotel's riveting contemporary architecture. The functional rooms are bright, cheerful, and fully soundproofed. The Noailles features a restful central patio, charming lounges, a bar, and pleasant little library.

 ## Novanox

6th arr. - 155, bd du Montparnasse
01 46 33 63 60, fax 01 43 26 61 72
Open year-round. 27 rms 550-680. Bkfst 50.
The owner of this hotel, opened in 1989, has used an amusing mixture of 1920s, 1930s, and 1950s styles for the décor. On the ground floor, a large, cheerful room serves as lounge, bar, and breakfast room.

 ## Novotel-Bercy

12th arr. - 85, rue de Bercy
01 43 42 30 00, fax 01 43 45 30 60
Open year-round. 1 ste 1,250. 128 rms 690-720. Bkfst 62. Rms for disabled. Restaurant. Rm ser. Air cond. Conf.
This classic chain hotel is located just minutes from the Palais Omnisports and Finance Ministry. Standard rooms and service.

L'Orchidée

14th arr. - 65, rue de l'Ouest
01 43 22 70 50, fax 01 42 79 97 46
Open year-round. 40 rms 450-500. Bkfst 35. Sauna. Jacuzzi. No pets. Garage pkg.
Tucked behind the attractive façade are an inviting lobby furnished with wicker pieces and a small garden-courtyard. Rooms look out over the garden or a square; some have balconies. Impeccable bathrooms.

 ## Opéra Cadet

9th arr. - 24, rue Cadet
01 48 24 05 26, fax 01 42 46 68 09
Open year-round. 3 stes 1,500. 82 rms 710-990. Bkfst 65. Rms for disabled. Air cond. Conf. Garage pkg.
A functional, modern hotel in the heart of the city, offering comfortable accommodations. Double-glazed windows; winter garden.

 ## Orléans Palace Hôtel

14th arr. - 185, bd Brune
01 45 39 68 50, fax 01 45 43 65 64
Open year-round. 92 rms 510-580. Bkfst 55. Restaurant. Conf.
A quiet and comfortable traditional hotel that offers good value. The well-equipped and soundproofed rooms are decorated in contemporary style, and there is a pretty *jardin intérieur.*

 ## Parc Montsouris

14th arr. - 4, rue du Parc-Montsouris
01 45 89 09 72, fax 01 45 80 92 72
Open year-round. 2 stes 480. 35 rms 310-420. Bkfst 30. Rms for disabled.
This good little hotel features quiet rooms done up in pastel tones and bright, new bathrooms. The lovely Parc Montsouris is just a short walk away.

Le Parnasse

14th arr. - 79-81, av. du Maine
01 43 20 13 93, fax 01 43 20 95 60
Closed Jul. 79 rms 515-560. Bkfst 42. Rms for disabled. Air cond. Conf.
The Parnasse is lodged in a pretty, white building; it offers large, bright rooms and complete bathrooms. Double glazing ensures peaceful nights. There are views—of the Tour Montparnasse...and the cemetery!

 ## Hôtel de la Place du Louvre

1st arr. - 21, rue des Prêtres-St-Germain-l'Auxerrois
01 42 33 78 68, fax 01 42 33 09 95
Open year-round. 20 rms 496-812. Bkfst 50.
Lodged in a Renaissance building, this hotel is decorated with paintings and sculptures throughout. The fairly large rooms are all comfortably furnished, with good bathrooms, and there are five charming split-level rooms under the eaves. Breakfast is served in a vaulted cellar.

Plaza La Fayette

10th arr. - 175, rue La Fayette
01 44 89 89 10, fax 01 40 36 00 30
Open year-round. 48 rms 595-890. Bkfst 50-65. Rms for disabled. Restaurant. Air cond. Pkg.
Here's a fine, brand-new hotel with well-equipped, soundproofed rooms. Breakfast is served on the terrace on warm days. Private bar and restaurant for hotel residents.

Hôtel du Pré

9th arr. - 10, rue Pierre-Sémard
01 42 81 37 11, fax 01 40 23 98 28
Open year-round. 40 rms 445-575. Bkfst 50. No pets.
Comfortable and close to the Gare du Nord and the Gare de l'Est. Downstairs, guests have the use of a bar, a bright lounge, and a pleasant breakfast room (good breakfasts). The cheerful, spacious guest rooms sport pink, green or white wicker furniture.

 ## Queen Mary

8th arr. - 9, rue de Greffulhe
01 42 66 40 50, fax 01 42 66 94 92
Open year-round. 1 ste 1,200. 35 rms 725-895. Rms for disabled. Rm ser. Air cond.
On a quiet street in the Haussmann district, this Queen Mary is an adorable, recently refurbished hotel. The cozy little rooms are furnished in the English style, right down to the decanter of Sherry placed on the table.

 ## Résidence Bassano

16th arr. - 15, rue de Bassano
01 47 23 78 23, fax 01 47 20 41 22
Open year-round. 3 stes 1,600-1,950. 28 rms 750-1,150. Bkfst 65. Restaurant. Rm ser. Air cond.
Housed in a building of Haussmann vintage, the rooms are summarily furnished, yet most are bright and all are thoughtfully designed and equipped. Delightful cocktail bar.

 ## Résidence des Gobelins

13th arr. - 9, rue des Gobelins
01 47 07 26 90, fax 01 43 31 44 05
Open year-round. 32 rms 320-430. Bkfst 36. No pets.
A delightful small hotel in a quiet street not far from the Latin Quarter and Montparnasse with congenial young owners. Rooms are decorated in blue, green, or orange, a different color for each floor. Some give onto a terrace.

 ## Résidence Monceau

8th arr. - 85, rue du Rocher
01 45 22 75 11, fax 01 45 22 30 88
Open year-round. 1 ste 865. 50 rms 700. Bkfst 50. Rms for disabled. Restaurant. No pets.
Though it lacks atmosphere, the Résidence Monceau is functional and well kept, and employs a helpful, courteous staff. All the rooms and corridors have just been freshly redecorated.

 ## Résidence Saint-Lambert

15th arr. - 5, rue Eugène-Gibez
01 48 28 63 14, fax 01 45 33 45 50
Open year-round. 48 rms 380-570. Bkfst 42.
This pleasant, quiet hotel near the exhibition center at Porte de Versailles has tidy, smallish but nicely equipped rooms (double glazing), some overlooking the garden. A laundry and bar are on the premises.

 ## Résidence Trousseau

11th arr. - 13, rue Trousseau
01 48 05 55 55, fax 01 48 05 83 97
Open year-round. 2 stes 1,350-1,500. 64 rms 300-550. Bkfst 50. Conf. Pkg.
A modern hotel not far from the Bastille. The suites have refurbished with kitchenettes, a practical touch. The quiet rooms are set around an enclosed garden.

 ## Saint-Christophe

5th arr. - 17, rue Lacépède
01 43 31 81 54, fax 01 43 31 12 54
Open year-round. 36 rms 450-600. Bkfst 50. Rms for disabled.
If you like bright pink, you'll love the décor of this quiet, well-maintained hotel. Remarkably warm, courteous reception.

 ## Saint Ferdinand

17th arr. - 36, rue Saint-Ferdinand
01 45 72 66 66, fax 01 45 74 12 92
Open year-round. 42 rms 750-900. Bkfst 50. Air cond.
This small, functional hotel is of recent vintage. The rooms are tiny (the bathrooms even more so), and the décor is fading fast. Obliging staff, however, and good equipment.

 ## Hôtel de Saint-Germain

6th arr. - 50, rue du Four
01 45 48 91 64, fax 01 45 48 46 22
Open year-round. 30 rms 415-695. Bkfst 45-60.
This small hotel with its doll-sized rooms and white-wood furniture has finished its renovation. Many services.

 ## Hôtel de Seine

6th arr. - 52, rue de Seine
01 46 34 22 80, fax 01 46 34 04 74
Open year-round. 30 rms 695-980. No pets.
Just a stone's throw from the Buci open-air market, this establishment provides quiet, well-kept rooms with an old-fashioned feel. Cheerful staff.

 ## Sénateur

6th arr. - 10, rue de Vaugirard
01 43 26 08 83, fax 01 46 34 04 66
Open year-round. 42 rms 720-750. Bkfst 50. Rms for disabled. Conf.
A comfortable, modern hotel with a huge mural and plenty of greenery brightening up the ground floor. Fine views from the top floor. Attentive service.

Suède

7th arr. - 31, rue Vaneau
01 47 05 00 08, fax 01 47 05 69 27
Open year-round. 1 ste 1,000. 38 rms 400-900. Bkfst 50. Restaurant. No pets.
Decorated in tones of blue in a refined but rather austere Directoire style, the guest rooms are quiet and nicely equipped. Streetside rooms

are a trifle gloomy. Though smaller, those overlooking the indoor garden are much more cheerful, and from the sixth floor, they offer a view of the Matignon gardens—and, on occasion, the prime minister's garden parties!

 ## La Tour d'Auvergne

9th arr. - 10, rue de La Tour d'Auvergne
01 48 78 61 60, fax 01 49 95 99 00
Open year-round. 24 rms 450-750. Bkfst 52. Garage pkg.
Modigliani once lived in this hotel. We wonder how he would feel about its current kitsch décor (don't miss the draped headboards). Nonetheless, a competently run, comfortable establishment.

 ## Hôtel Le Tourville

7th arr. - 16, av. de Tourville
01 47 05 62 62, fax 01 47 05 43 90
Open year-round. 2 stes 1,390-1,990. 28 rms 690-1,090. Bkfst 60. Rm ser. Air cond.
A smart, quiet hotel, the Tourville provides cozy and attractive rooms that are much appreciated by a well-bred clientele.

 ## Varenne

7th arr. - 44, rue de Bourgogne
01 45 51 45 55, fax 01 45 51 86 63
Open year-round. 24 rms 530-710. Bkfst 45.
A cheerful reception is assured at this small hotel whose provincial air is underlined by a courtyard filled with flowers and trees (where breakfast and drinks are served on sunny days). The rooms overlooking the street have double windows.

 ## Vieux Marais

4th arr. - 8, rue du Plâtre
01 42 78 47 22, fax 01 42 78 34 32
Closed Aug. 30 rms 410-560. Bkfst 38. No pets.
Bright, spacious accommodations with small but adequate bathrooms, in a friendly, quiet

hotel. Rooms on the fourth floor have streetside balconies.

 ## La Villa des Artistes

6th arr. - 9, rue de la Grande-Chaumière
01 43 26 60 86, fax 01 43 54 73 70
Open year-round. 59 rms 660-860. Air cond. No pets.
An oasis of calm amid the noise and bustle of Montparnasse. Quiet and comfort are assured in this hotel, built around a garden patio. Good value for this district.

 ## La Villa Maillot

16th arr. - 143, av. de Malakoff
01 45 01 25 22, fax 01 45 00 60 61
Open year-round. 3 stes 2,300-2,500. 39 rms 1,550-1,770. Bkfst 80-100. Rms for disabled. Restaurant. Rm ser. Air cond. Conf. Valet pkg.
Formerly an embassy, the conversion is sophisticated and modern: an exemplary establishment. The very comfortable rooms (all with queen-size beds, some with camouflaged kitchenettes) have an Art Deco feel. Pink-marble bathrooms; wonderful breakfasts served in an indoor garden.

 ## Le Zéphyr

12th arr. - 31 bis, bd Diderot
01 43 46 12 72, fax 01 43 41 68 01
Open year-round. 90 rms 530-720. Bkfst 60. Half-board 670-1,000. Rms for disabled. Restaurant. Air cond. Conf. Garage pkg.
Practically next door to the Gare de Lyon, the Zéphyr is a newly renovated hotel with good equipment. Rooms are bright and neat, the welcome is friendly, and service is reliably prompt. Quality breakfasts.

PARIS: FOOD SHOPS

Paris is paradise for food lovers, a mecca for gastro-tourists in search of the rarest, the best, the most luxurious *gourmandises*. The capital's pastry shops, chocolate shops, charcuteries, bakeries, and gourmet grocers overflow with temptations to taste on the spot or to pack up and take back home. Specialties and treats from all over France can be tracked down in Paris, where new taste sensations can be discovered around every *coin de rue*.

• BAKERIES

Boulangerie Rollet-Pradier

7th arr. - 32, rue de Bourgogne - 01 45 55 57 00
Customers' lamenting about how hard it had become to find a good, chewy baguette spurred pastry-chef Étienne Pradier to become, at age 62, a *boulanger*. We guess he doesn't hear much complaining anymore, because the breads Pradier and his apprentice produce are tasty as can be: try the flûte Rollet (a hand-molded baguette), the yeasty sourdough boule, or hearty Bourgogne loaf.

La Coulée Verte

12th arr. - 124, av. Daumesnil - 01 43 43 88 02
The secret of Monsieur Roux's fine bread is in the flour, supplied by an excellent mill in the Ile-de-France. The baguette and the multigrain bread both brim with old-fashioned flavor. Good traditional pastries, too.

Daniel Dupuy

9th arr. - 13, rue Cadet - 01 48 24 54 26
Daniel's prize-winning pain de campagne, made of natural leavening agents and stoneground flour, lives up to its vaunted reputation. Connoisseurs know that bread with this sort of authentic flavor is indeed worth seeking out. The same can be said of Dupuy's specialty, the Rochetour: he keeps the recipe a closely guarded secret.

Au Panetier

2nd arr. - 10, pl. des Petits-Pères - 01 42 60 90 23
Even if you don't want to buy one of the old-fashioned loaves of hazelnut bread, raisin bread, or the house specialty: dense, delicious pain de Saint-Fiacre (all baked in a wood-fired oven), this excellent bakery is worth a visit just for a look at the adorable etched-glass and tile décor.

Lionel Poilâne

6th arr. - 8, rue du Cherche-Midi - 01 45 48 42 59
15th arr. - 49, bd de Grenelle - 01 45 79 11 49

Lionel Poilâne is indubitably the best-known baker on the planet; he can be seen hawking his famous sourdough bread in magazines and on television screens throughout the world. And even though his products are sold all over Paris in charcuteries and cheese shops, goodly numbers of Poilâne fans think nothing of crossing town and standing in line to *personally* buy their favorite bread still warm from his ovens. Poilâne's walnut bread is, in a word, scrumptious, and we are also particularly fond of the shortbread cookies (sablés) and the rustic apple turnover (which makes a delicious and inexpensive dessert, accompanied by a bowl of thick crème fraîche).

Max Poilâne

1st arr. - 42, pl. du Marché St-Honoré
01 42 61 10 53
14th arr. - 29, rue de l'Ouest - 01 43 27 24 91
15th arr. - 87, rue Brancion - 01 48 28 45 90
Max Poilâne's bread bears a distinct resemblance to that produced by his brother, Lionel (see above). That's natural enough, since their father taught both of them the secrets of the trade. Max bakes big, hearty loaves with a sourdough tang, delicious rye bread studded with raisins, and buttery white bread that makes a first-class sandwich. For a teatime treat, try the luscious apple tarts. If you can't wait to try these goodies, just take a seat in the bakery's tea room.

Poujauran

7th arr. - 20, rue Jean-Nicot - 01 47 05 80 88
He's a real darling, that Jean-Luc Poujauran! His bakery may be in a ritzy neighborhood, but he hasn't gone high-hat; food writers regularly wax lyrical over his talent, but his head hasn't swelled an inch. And though he bakes a wonderful country loaf with organically grown flour, he's not the type to think he's the greatest thing since sliced bread. Let's just hope he never changes. And let's hope that we will never have to give up his delicious little rolls (or his olive or his poppy seed or his walnut bread), his old-fashioned pound cake (quatre-quarts), his buttery Basque cakes, or the terrific frangipane-stuffed galettes that he bakes for the Epiphany (Three Kings' Day, January 6).

• CHARCUTERIE & TAKEOUT

Butard Traiteur

6th arr. - 29, rue de Buci - 01 43 25 17 72
What better place to compose an elegant late-night supper for two than this bright and invit-

ing garden of gourmandise, which fairly overflows with delicacies both savory and sweet?

Charcuterie Lyonnaise

9th arr. - 58, rue des Martyrs - 01 48 78 96 45
Lyon's reputed specialties hold pride of place here: try the rosette, jésus, or saucisson de Lyon sausages as well as the superb terrines.

Chédeville Saint-Honoré

1st arr. - 18, pl. du Marché-St-Honoré
01 42 61 04 62
The Ritz, Crillon, Plaza Athénéé and other classy hotels buy their traditional French charcuterie here (so does the president of France, incidentally). The quality is excellent, the choice is wide. Recommended are the York ham, the old-fashioned pork knuckle (great picnic food), the elaborate ballottines, and the pigs' trotters stuffed with foie gras.

Coesnon

6th arr. - 30, rue Dauphine - 01 43 54 35 80
Because true practitioners of the charcutier's art are becoming ever harder to find, and because Bernard Marchaudon is one of its most eminent representatives, we recommend that you make a special point of visiting this wonderful pork emporium. Marchaudon's boudin blanc and boudin noir are legendary (his chestnut-studded black pudding has won slews of awards); what's more, his salt-and smoke-cured pork specialties are top-notch—especially when accompanied by the crisp yet tender sauerkraut he pickles himself. So step up to counter with confidence, knowing that you will be competently and courteously served.

Flo Prestige

1st arr. - 42, pl. du Marché-Saint-Honoré
01 42 61 45 46
7th arr. - 36, av. de La Motte-Picquet
01 45 55 71 25
10th arr. - 10 rue, St-Antoine - 01 53 01 91 91
12th arr. - 211, av. Daumesnil - 01 43 44 86 36
& 22, av. de la Porte de Vincennes - 01 43 74 54 32
15th arr. - 352, rue Lecourbe - 01 45 54 76 94
16th arr. - 61, av. de la Grande-Armée
01 45 00 12 10
& 102, av. du Président-Kennedy - 01 42 88 38 00
Early or late, every day of the year, you have a sure source of delicious bread, fine wine, yummy desserts—in short, of wonderful meals with Flo Prestige. The selection of foodstuffs is varied and choice, and covers a wide range of prices, from the excellent house sauerkraut to prestigious Petrossian caviar.

Gargantua

1st arr. - 284, rue St-Honoré - 01 42 60 52 54
The opulent window displays of this well-known charcuterie could satisfy even the gigantically robust appetite of its Rabelaisian namesake. There are cured meats, foie gras, and terrines, of course, but Gargantua also carries an abundance of prepared dishes, breads, wines,

pastries, and ice cream. It's a fine place to go to put together a picnic.

Lewkowicz

4th arr. - 12, rue des Rosiers - 01 48 87 63 17
Since 1928 "Lewko" has been serving up authentic Jewish specialties made from old-country recipes. In his expanded and renovated shop, Lewkowicz Fils proposes flavorsome corned beef, pastrami, pressed veal, and Krakow sausage, as well as kosher meats and poultry, and a selection of wines, spirits, and tinned foods.

Pou

17th arr. - 16, av. des Ternes - 01 43 80 19 24
Pou is divine, an excellent charcuterie whose sober décor and rich displays resemble nothing so much as a palace of earthly delights. A look in the window is an irresistible invitation to buy and taste: black and white boudin sausages, duck pâté en croûte, glittering galantines, cervelas sausage studded with pale-green pistachios, and sumptuous pastries too. Since everything really is as good as it looks, making a choice is quite a task. And given the prices, paying isn't so easy, either.

• CHEESE

Alléosse

17th arr. - 13, rue Poncelet - 01 46 22 50 45
Father and son Roger and Philippe Alléosse purvey some of the finest cheeses in Paris. With the obsessive zeal of perfectionists, they turn, rinse, brush, and otherwise groom their farmhouse fromages down in the ideally dank depths of their seven maturing cellars. If the shop's astounding stock leaves you at a loss, don't hesitate to seek advice from the staff: they'll introduce you to little-known cheeses from all over France. We understand why so many chefs choose to shop chez Alléosse.

Androuet

8th arr. - 41, rue d'Amsterdam - 01 48 74 26 93
New owners have infused fresh life into this institution. The cheeses are chosen with care and discernment.

Barthélémy

7th arr. - 51, rue de Grenelle - 01 45 48 56 75
Roland Barthélémy reigns over a treasure trove of cheeses that he selects from farms all over the French countryside, then coddles to perfect ripeness in his cellars. He is also the creator of several marvelous specialties that have the Who's Who of French officialdom beating a path to his door (he supplies the Élysée Palace, no less). The Boulamour (fresh cream cheese enriched with crème fraîche, currants, raisins, and Kirsch) was Barthélémy's invention, as was a delicious Camembert laced with Calvados. We also enjoy the amusing Brie Surprise. But not to worry,

tradition is never neglected here, witness the rich-tasting Alpine Beaufort, French Vacherin, and other prime mountain cheeses which are a Barthélémy specialty. The luxuriously creamy Fontainebleau is made fresh on the premises. Take one of the appetizing cheese trays sold here as your contribution to a dinner party: your hostess will love it!

Marie-Anne Cantin

7th arr. - 12, rue du Champ-de-Mars - 01 45 50 43 94
The cheeses Marie-Anne Cantin selects and matures herself benefit from unstinting doses of tender loving care. She is an ardent defender of real (read: unpasteurized) cheeses and is one of the few merchants in Paris to sell Saint-Marcellins as they are preferred on their home turf—in their creamy prime, not in their chalky youth. And so it is with the other cheeses she sells, all of which retain the authentic flavors of their rustic origins.

Alain Dubois

17th arr. - 80, rue de Tocqueville - 01 42 27 11 38
& 79, rue de Courcelles - 01 43 80 36 42
Alain Dubois's Gruyère, aged for at least two years in his cellars, is a royal treat. And there's more: Dubois offers farmhouse goat cheeses, unpasteurized Camembert, and authentic Époisses (which he rinses religiously with marc de Bourgogne). The problem is, this expert cheese merchant offers so many enticements (some 150) that we don't know which way to turn. You will not be astonished to learn that Dubois supplies premium cheeses to such noted restaurants as Guy Savoy, Michel Rostang, and more.

La Ferme Saint-Hubert

8th arr. - 21, rue Vignon - 01 47 42 79 20
Cheese seller Henry Voy is so passionate about his vocation that he has no time for anything else. Morning and night you can find him tending to his Beauforts (aged for a minimum of two years), his farmhouse chèvres, Corsican sheep cheeses, or his exclusive Délice de Saint-Hubert. He travels all over France, seeking out the most flavorful specimens. For true aficionados, Voy unearths such rarities as unpasteurized butter churned with spring water, and delicate goat's-milk butter.

Fromagerie Boursault

14th arr. - 71, av. du Général-Leclerc
01 43 27 93 30
It was here that Pierre Boursault created the triple-creme cheese that bears his name. And it is here, naturally enough, that you will find Boursault at its rich, golden best. Owner Jacques Vernier has made the shop one of the most pleasant in Paris, a showcase for the rare cheeses that he seeks out himself in the French hinterlands. Like incomparable Beauforts aged under his supervision in their native Alpine air; farmhouse goat cheeses (ah, those Picodons!); handcrafted Saint-Nectaire from Auvergne,

which has nothing in common with the industrially produced variety; and flawless Camemberts. This is one of the few places on the planet where one may buy Bleu de Termignon, a blue-veined summer cheese from Savoie.

• CHOCOLATE & CANDY

Boissier

16th arr. - 184, av. Victor-Hugo - 01 45 04 87 88
Come here for puckery hard candies sold in pretty blue boxes and for delicious caramels.

Christian Constant

6th arr. - 37, rue d'Assas - 01 45 48 45 51
7th arr. - 26, rue du Bac - 01 47 03 30 00
Christian Constant, who chooses the best cocoa beans from the West Indies, Tahiti, Ecuador and elsewhere, is a genius with chocolate. His brilliant innovations include a line of flower-scented chocolates (try the ylang-ylang, vetiver, or the jasmine varieties...), chocolates filled with delicately spiced creams, others spiked with fruit brandies or cordials, still others incorporating nuts and dried fruit (the Conquistador is loaded with hazelnuts, honey, and cinnamon). Constant recommends that we buy his wares in small amounts, for optimum freshness and flavor. Well, given the prices (480 F per kilo), for most people quantity purchases are out of the question!

A l'Étoile d'Or

9th arr. - 30, rue Fontaine - 01 48 74 59 55
Denise Acabo does not make her own chocolate; rather, she is a true connoisseur who selects the very best handcrafted chocolates made in France, and presents them, in a laudable spirit of impartiality, to her delighted customers (while explaining to interested parties the connection between chocolate and eroticism...). The famed Bernachon chocolates from Lyon are sold in this beautiful turn-of-the-century shop, as well as Dufoux's incomparable palets (in twelve flavors), and Bonnat's chocolate bars. Don't miss Bochard's mandarin de Grenoble: a glazed tangerine with a chocolate mandarin's hat—it's irresistible!

La Fontaine au Chocolat

1st arr. - 101, rue St-Honoré - 01 42 33 09 09
& 201, rue St-Honoré - 01 42 44 11 66
Pervading Michel Cluizel's shop is a scent of chocolate so intense that your nose will flash an alert to your sweet tooth, and (we guarantee!) have you salivating within seconds. Whether you try one of the five varieties of palets au chocolat or the croquamandes (caramelized almonds coated with extra-dark chocolate), the mendiants studded with nuts and dried fruit, or the bold Noir Infini (99 percent cocoa, perfumed with vanilla and spices), you're in for an unforgettable treat.

Fouquet

8th arr. - 22, rue François-Ier - 01 47 23 30 36
9th arr. - 36, rue Laffitte - 01 47 70 85 00
Caramels, fondants, chocolates, candied fruits and lots of other scrumptious specialties.

Jadis et Gourmande

4th arr. - 39, rue des Archives - 01 48 04 08 03
5th arr. - 88, bd de Port-Royal - 01 43 26 17 75
8th arr. - 49 bis, av. Franklin-Roosevelt
01 42 25 06 04
& 27, rue Boissy-d'Anglas - 01 42 65 23 23
It is delightful indeed to browse around this sugarplum palace, where one is tempted in turn by delicious bonbons, hard candies, caramels, and chocolate in myriad forms (320 F per kilo). The thick slabs of cooking chocolate make one want to rush to the kitchen and whip up a rich devil's food cake! Our favorite confection here is a thick braid of dark chocolate studded with candied orange peel and hazelnuts.

La Maison du Chocolat

6th arr. - 19, rue de Sèvres - 01 45 44 20 40
8th arr. - 52, rue François-Ier - 01 47 23 38 25
& 225, rue du Fg-St-Honoré - 01 42 27 39 44
9th arr. - 8, bd de la Madeleine - 01 47 42 86 52
16th arr. - 89, av. Raymond Poincarré
01 40 67 77 83
There's something of the alchemist about Robert Linxe: never satisfied, he is ever experimenting, innovating, transforming mere cocoa beans into something very precious. His chocolates (480 F per kilo) are among the finest in Paris, maybe even in the world. His renowned buttercream fillings—lemon, caramel, tea, raspberry, and rum—will carry you away to gourmet heaven.

A la Mère de Famille

9th arr. - 35, rue du Fg-Montmartre
01 47 70 83 69
Perhaps the oldest candy shop in Paris (it dates back to 1761), La Mère de Famille is certainly the handsomest, with a façade and interior from the nineteenth century (note the Second Empire-style cashier's booth). The shop's sweet inventory includes luscious jams, candied fruits, and bonbons from all over France. The chocolates are prepared by the current owner, Serge Neveu, and sell for 368 F per kilo. We love the Whiskadines (soft chestnut centers laced with whisky) and the Délices de la Mère with their suave almond and rum-raisin filling.

Richart

7th arr. - 258, bd Saint-Germain - 01 45 55 66 00
8th arr. - 36, av. Wagram - 01 45 74 94 00
The Richart brothers may be the most innovative *chocolatiers* around. Not only are their chocolates perfectly scrumptious (filled with single-malt ganache, for example, or wild-raspberry cream, or nutmeg praline, or prune coulis...) they are presented in imaginative packages unlike any we've seen. Just look at the Secret Pyramid, a clever box that holds fourteen ultrathin chocolates. Richart's flat Easter eggs are pretty unusual, too! And the Petits Richarts, mini-chocolates that weigh just one-sixth of an ounce, are ideal for nibbling with a clear conscience.

• COFFEE & TEA

Betjeman & Barton

8th arr. - 23, bd Malesherbes - 01 42 65 86 17
11th arr. - 24, bd des Filles-du-Calvaire
01 40 21 35 52
The name on the sign and the shop's décor are veddy, veddy British, but the firm itself is 100 percent French, directed nowadays by Didier Jumeau-Lafond. An extensive range of premium teas is on offer, comprising over 180 natural and flavored varieties. Indeed, B & B's teas are of such high quality that Harrod's of London (no less) deigns to market them. To help you choose your blend, the staff will offer you a cup of tea—a comforting and highly civilized custom. Excellent jellies and jams and a line of refreshing "fruit waters" intended to be consumed icy-cold in summer, are worth seeking out here. For nibbling with your tea, try the Duchy Originals (sponsored by Prince Charles, don't you know), cookies baked of organic, stone-ground oats and wheat. B & B now produces a line of fine hand-painted china decorated with pretty fruit and flower motifs.

Brûlerie des Ternes & Torréfaction de Passy

17th arr. - 10, rue Poncelet - 01 46 22 52 79
16th arr. - 28, rue de l'Annonciation
01 42 88 99 90
Coffees from all over the globe are roasted and ground to perfection in these commendable shops, which draws a clientele made up, in part, of the chic and famous. Featured is the fabled Blue Mountain coffee from Jamaica, a rare and costly treat. Each customer's individual blend is recorded, so the recipe need never be lost or forgotten. Flavored coffees (orange, chocolate, vanilla...) are justly popular, and there are 150 kinds of tea in stock as well.

• ETHNIC FOODS

The General Store

7th arr. - 82, rue de Grenelle - 01 45 48 63 16
16th arr. - 30, rue de Longchamp
01 47 55 41 14
Tacos, tortillas, and all the other traditional fixings for a Tex-Mex feast may be found in this spic-and-span little shop. But the inventory doesn't stop here: You'll find buttermilk-pancake mix, a selection of California wines (not just Paul Masson), familiar American packaged foods (Karo syrup, cream cheese, canned pumpkin, chocolate chips, Hellmann's mayo), and even fresh cranberries at holiday time. If you crave a sweet snack, look for the delectable pecan

squares and cookies whipped up fresh every day. As you would expect, English is spoken, and you can count on a warm welcome.

Goldenberg

17th arr. - 69, av. de Wagram - 01 42 27 34 79
Familiar deli fare, made measurably more exotic by the fact that it's served within sight of the Arc de Triomphe. There's herring, there's corned beef, there's gefilte fish (stuffed carp), there's pastrami, and that well-known Yiddish dessert, the brownie.

Marks & Spencer

4th arr. - 88, rue de Rivoli - 01 44 61 08 00
9th arr. - 35, bd Haussmann - 01 47 42 42 91
The food section of this all-British emporium provides ample evidence that English gastronomy is not, as Parisians tend to think, a joking matter. The French are genetically incapable, for example, of producing good bacon. Marks & Spencer's is wonderful: meaty, smoky, with no nasty bits of bone, no inedible rind. The cheese counter carries Stilton, Cheddar, Leicester, and other delicious English dairy products, and the grocery shelves are crowded with all sorts of piquant condiments and chutneys. Teas, biscuits, jams, and marmalades are legion, of course, and special refrigerated cases offer fresh sandwiches for a quick lunch on the run. Prices in the Paris branch are considerably higher than on Marks & Sparks' home turf.

Spécialités Antillaises

20th arr. - 14-16, bd de Belleville - 01 43 58 31 30
Here's a one-stop shop for Creole fixings and take-out foods. Among the latter, we recommend the scrumptious stuffed crabs, the crispy accras (salt-cod fritters), the Creole sausage, and a spicy avocado dish called féroce d'avocat. The grocery section offers tropical fruits flown in fresh from the West Indies, as well as a selection of exotic frozen fish (shark, gilthead...), and an intoxicating array of rums and punches.

• *FRUITS & VEGETABLES*

Le Fruitier d'Auteuil

16th arr. - 5, rue Bastien-Lepage - 01 45 27 51 08
Bernard Rapine, president of the Fruit Retailers' Union, has a personal and professional interest in displaying the best produce he can find. He claims—and we have seen it to be true—that any store posting the union label (the word *fruitier* printed over a basket of fruit) is honor-bound to provide top-quality merchandise and service. Rapine's vegetables, incidentally, are just as prime. Some are sold peeled and ready to cook. Even less prep is required for the shop's range of take-out dishes that includes delicious soups, eggplant purée, guacamole, fruit salads, and more.

Palais du Fruit

2nd arr. - 62 & 72, rue Montorgueil - 01 42 33 22 15
Superb fruits and vegetables from all over the globe, beautifully presented. Even when skies are gray in France, in Chile or the Antilles gorgeous produce ripens in the sun, then is picked and packed off to this cheerful store. Wide choice, remarkable quality.

• *GOURMET SPECIALTIES*

Faguais

8th arr. - 30, rue de la Trémoille - 01 47 20 80 91
Yes, Grandmother would feel quite at home in this charming gourmet shop. A dizzying variety of temptations is set out neatly on the shelves. Old-fashioned jams, oils, honeys, cookies, spices, vinegars, and condiments fairly cry out to be bought. As the shop's pervasive fragrance implies, fresh coffee beans are roasted on the premises daily.

Fauchon

8th arr. - 30, pl. de la Madeleine - 01 47 42 60 11
In 1886, at the age of 30, Auguste Fauchon opened his *épicerie fine* on the Place de la Madeleine, specializing in quality French foodstuffs. The rest is history. After more than a century, Fauchon is the uncontested paragon of what a luxury gourmet emporium should be. The entire staff of 360 employees is committed to the task of tasting, testing, and selling the very finest, the rarest, the most unusual foods in the world. The number of spices alone—110—is enough to make your head spin. And you'll find such delicacies as black-fig or watermelon preserves, lavender or buckwheat honey, Mim tea from India or Kee-yu tea from China, lavish displays of prime vegetables and fruits, and a world-renowned collection of vintage wines and brandies. As for the pastries, well... you try Sébastien Gaudard's creations, which are also featured in Fauchon's on-site restaurants (see Le "30" in *Restaurants*).

La Grande Épicerie de Paris

7th arr. - Le Bon Marché, 38, rue de Sèvres
01 44 39 81 00
A deluxe supermarket filled with a huge array of handsomely presented foodstuffs: a lovely place to browse.

Hédiard

7th arr. - 126, rue du Bac - 01 45 44 01 98
8th arr. - 21, pl. de la Madeleine
01 43 12 88 88
16th arr. - 70, av. Paul-Doumer - 01 45 04 51 92
17th arr. - 106, bd de Courcelles - 01 47 63 32 14
92200 Neuilly-sur-Seine - 135, rue de Longchamp
01 47 22 90 82
Only the most select foodstuffs are deemed worthy of entry into this shrine of epicureanism, founded in 1854. Distinguished smoked salmon

from the best "schools," sophisticated sugars and syrups, pedigreed Ports, vintage wines and brandies, and over 4,500 carefully chosen grocery items attract virtually every cultivated palate in town. Even the ordinary is extraordinary here: mustard spiked with Cognac; vinegar flavored with seaweed; opulent fruits and vegetables, always perfect, that hail from the ends of the earth. Many of the items are as costly as they are exotic, but the wines consistently offer excellent value for the money. Hédiard's flagship store on Place de la Madeleine was remodeled and expanded not long ago. It houses a tasting bar in the wine department. And, not to be outdone by its rival across the *place*, Hédiard, like Fauchon, has a classy restaurant above the store (see *Restaurants*).

Lafayette Gourmet

9th arr. - 48, bd Haussmann or 97, rue de Provence
01 48 74 46 06
   A huge space devoted to the pleasures of gastronomy, with fresh foods, rare condiments, teas, coffees, charcuteries, wines... And there are counters for sampling the wares, so that you can stop for a bite after shopping.

Albert Ménès

8th arr. - 41, bd Malesherbes - 01 42 66 95 63
   This pretty shop holds gourmet treats from talented producers all over France. The gift boxes are gorgeous.

Escargots

L'Escargot de la Butte

18th arr. - 48, rue Joseph-de-Maistre
01 46 27 38 27
   "It's really a shame, but there are no more escargots de Bourgogne left in Burgundy," laments Monsieur Marchal. He imports them, therefore, from the Lot and the Ardèche. But his petits-gris come straight from the Provençal countryside, and arrive still frisky at his little shop located at the foot of the Butte Montmartre. He stuffs them with a deliciously fragrant blend of pure butter, garlic, and parsley and they are a remarkable treat!

Foie Gras

Divay

17th arr. - 4, rue Bayen - 01 43 80 16 97
   Priced at 650 F per kilo, Divay sells the least expensive fattened goose liver to be found in the city. What's more, it's delicious. You'll find great traditional charcuterie here, too.

Aux Ducs de Gascogne

1st arr. - 4, rue du Marché-St-Honoré
01 42 60 45 31
4th arr. - 111, rue St-Antoine - 01 42 71 17 72
8th arr. - 112, bd Haussmann - 01 45 22 54 04

15th arr. - 221, rue de la Convention - 01 48 28 32 09
16th arr. - 54, av. Victor-Hugo - 01 45 00 34 78
20th arr. - 41, rue des Gatines - 01 43 66 99 99
   This multistore chain specializes in tinned and lightly cooked foie gras, as well as other Southwestern favorites (the thick peasant soup—garbure—sold in jars is excellent indeed). Steep prices, but the quality is dependably high.

Foie Gras Import

1st arr. - 34, rue Montmartre - 01 42 33 31 32
   Good foie gras, as well as tasty hams, sausages, and dried mushrooms. Interesting selection of gourmet foods.

Foie Gras Luxe

1st arr. - 26, rue Montmartre - 01 42 36 14 73
   This reliable, long-established shop sells raw foie gras year-round, as well as lightly cooked goose and duck livers. More luxury: Iranian caviar and savory cured hams from Parma, San Daniele, and the Ardennes are also for sale.

Honey & Jams

Le Furet-Tanrade

10th arr. - 63, rue de Chabrol - 01 47 70 48 34
   Alain Furet is a *chocolatier* first and foremost, but he also makes fabulous jams from recipes developed by Monsieur Tanrade, long the top name in French preserves. Furet took over the Tanrade plant, and now turns out succulent jams (raspberry, strawberry, apricot, blackcurrant...); he also has put the finishing touches on a recipe of his own, for *gelée au chocolat*—a landmark!

La Maison du Miel

9th arr. - 24, rue Vignon - 01 47 42 26 70
   Make a beeline to this "House of Honey" to try 28 varieties from all over France, and a few imported honeys, too. There's Corsican honey, luscious pine honey from the Vosges mountains (which comes highly recommended for bronchial irritations), Provençal lavender honey, as well as choice varieties from the Alps and Auvergne, all rigorously tested by a busy hive of honey tasters. In addition, you'll find honey "by-products," such as beeswax, candles, pollen, and royal jelly, as well as a wide range of honey-based cosmetics.

Oils

A l'Olivier

4th arr. - 23, rue de Rivoli - 01 48 04 86 59
   Connoisseurs know that this shop is an excellent source for several fine varieties of olive oil, as well as walnut oil, grilled-almond oil, pumpkin-seed oil, and hazelnut oil. The main attraction, however, is an exclusive, top-secret blend of virgin olive oils. We applaud the store policy of selling exceptionally expensive and perishable oils in quarter-liter bottles. Fine

vinegars and mustards are presented too—everything you need to mix up a world-class vinaigrette!

Truffles

Maison de la Truffe

8th arr. - 19, pl. de la Madeleine
01 42 65 53 22
Alongside extraordinary charcuterie, foie gras, smoked salmon, and take-out foods, this luxurious gourmet shop offers truffles (freshly dug or sterilized and bottled) at prices that are emphatically not of the bargain-basement variety. The season for fresh black truffles runs from October to late March; fresh white truffles are imported from Italy from October to December. Owner Guy Monier recently set aside a corner of his shop for tasting: customers may order from a brief menu featuring dishes made with the sublime fungus (truffes en salade, truffes en feuilleté, truffles with fresh pasta, in risotto...). Look too for the range of oils, vinegars, and mustards all perfumed with—you guessed it!

• ICE CREAM & SORBET

Berthillon

4th arr. - 31, rue Saint-Louis-en-l'Ile
01 43 54 31 61
Berthillon is the most famous name in French ice cream. The firm's many faithful fans think nothing of waiting in line for *hours* just to treat their taste buds to a cone or dish of chocolate-nougat or glazed-chestnut ice cream. Berthillon's sorbets are our particular weakness: pink grapefruit, fig, wild strawberry... The entire repertoire comes to some 70 flavors, including many seasonal offerings.

Glacier Vilfeu

1st arr. - 3, rue de la Cossonnerie - 01 40 26 36 40
Vilfeu's imaginative productions include surprising and sophisticated novelty flavors—tea, lavender, and foie-gras sorbets—an ice based on Beaujolais nouveau, and ice creams flavored with licorice, cinnamon, and ginger. We also strongly encourage you to sample the sumptuous frozen desserts, notably the molded cream-cheese sorbet served with a vivid raspberry coulis.

Raimo

12th arr. - 59-61, bd de Reuilly - 01 43 43 70 17
Sorbets and ice creams produced according to time-honored methods, with strictly fresh ingredients. Raimo's strong suit is concocting seductive flavor combinations; some of the most successful are piña colada, ginger-honey, and cinnamon-mandarin/orange.

• MEAT, GAME & FOWL

Au Bell Viandier

6th arr. - Marché Saint-Germain, 4, rue Lobineau
01 40 46 82 82
Serge Caillaud is a king among Parisian butchers. Rigorous selection and skillful preparation are the hallmarks of these meats, which hail from the best French producers. There's milk-fed veal and fine beef from the Limousin region, farm-bred pork, poultry from Bresse and Challans (including superb capons for the year-end holidays), and premium game in season. Caillaud's specialties include a truffled roast of beef, veal stuffed with apricots or studded with prunes and pistachios, any of which would garner applause as the centerpiece of a dinner party.

Le Coq Saint-Honoré

1st arr. - 3, rue Gomboust - 01 42 61 52 04
We might as well make it clear right away: For our money, Le Coq Saint-Honoré is one of Paris's top poulterers. It's no coincidence that among its customers are such culinary notables as Robuchon, Savoy, Senderens, and Dutournier. The refrigerated cases display choice Bresse chickens and guinea hens (fast becoming prohibitively expensive), as well as laudable Loué pullets, Challans ducks, and plump rabbits from the Gâtinais region south of Paris. In season, look for the fine selection of game, including authentic Scottish grouse—a rare and wonderful treat.

• PASTRY & COOKIES

Paul Bugat

4th arr. - 5, bd Beaumarchais - 01 48 87 89 88
Paul Bugat is a passionate esthete who orchestrates sweet pastry, chocolate, sugar, and cream into exquisite gâteaux. The specialties of the house are delicious, jewel-like petits-fours, along with the Clichy (chocolate buttercream and mocha cream on an almond-sponge base), and the Almaviva (chocolate-mousse cake). Tea room.

Noël Clément

17th arr. - 120, av. de Villiers - 01 47 63 40 90
Noël Clément is a young *pâtissier* with a bright future ahead. His pastries are nothing short of sublime: the millefeuille is a textbook example of what that often botched sweet should be; his mousses are light and full-flavored. Best of all, Clément keeps the sugar content down in all of his cakes. He bakes excellent bread as well. Prices are eminently reasonable.

Some establishments change their closing times without warning. It is always wise to check in advance.

Christian Constant

6th arr. - 37, rue d'Assas - 01 45 48 45 51
7th arr. - 26, rue du Bac - 01 47 03 30 00
After a stroll in the Luxembourg Gardens, why not indulge in a treat from Christian Constant's shop on Rue d'Assas? And one needn't feel too guilt-ridden, because these cakes are low in sugar, additive-free, all-natural, and incredibly light. Try a millefeuille, or one of Constant's deep, dark, and exotic chocolate cakes: the Feuille d'Automne, the Figaro, or the poetically named Fleur de Chine. Constant's sorbets and frozen desserts are well worth the money. Tea room.

Dalloyau

2nd arr. - 25, bd des Capucines - 01 47 03 47 00
6th arr. - 2, pl. Edmond-Rostand
01 43 29 31 10
7th arr. - 63, rue de Grenelle - 01 45 49 95 30
8th arr. - 99-101, rue du Fg-St-Honoré
01 42 99 90 00
15th arr. - 69, rue de la Convention
01 45 77 84 27
Deservedly famous, Dalloyau is a temple of *gourmandise* revered by every discerning sweet tooth in town. Among the most renowned specialties are the memorably good macaroons, the chocolate-and-mocha Opéra cake (created in 1955 and still a bestseller), and the Mogador (chocolate sponge cake and mousse napped with raspberry jam, 21 F). Christmas brings succulent glazed chestnuts and gluttonously rich Yule logs; Easter calls for chocolate hens and bunnies romping among praline eggs and bells in the adorable window displays.

Ladurée

8th arr. - 16, rue Royale - 01 42 60 21 79
Sublime macarons that are at once puffy and tender yet crisp, in an array of delicate colors and flavors.

Lenôtre

8th arr. - 15, bd de Courcelles - 01 45 63 87 63
15th arr. - 61, rue Lecourbe - 01 42 73 20 97
16th arr. - 44, rue d'Auteuil - 01 45 24 52 52
& 49, av. Victor-Hugo - 01 45 02 21 21
& 193, av. de Versailles - 01 45 25 55 88
17th arr. - 121, av. de Wagram - 01 47 63 70 30
92200 Neuilly - 3, rue des Huissiers
01 46 24 98 68
92100 Boulogne - 79 bis, route de la Reine
01 46 05 37 35
Normandy native Gaston Lenôtre opened his first shop in Paris in 1957. His pastries and elaborate desserts are now internationally recognized as classics: the Schuss, the Plaisir, the Opéra... His most memorable creation may just be the Passion des Iles—passionfruit mousse on a coconut-meringue base sprinkled with shaved chocolate—a tropical fantasy!

Gérard Mulot

6th arr. - 76, rue de Seine - 01 43 26 85 77

Mulot is an endlessly inventive personality, never happier than when he is working out a new idea to complete his line of delectable pastries. Recent creations include the Oasis (almond mousse with an apricot wafer) and the Sortilège (chocolate parfait perfumed with berry essence). In a more down-to-earth vein, Mulot also fashions wonderfully flaky, buttery croissants.

Stohrer

2nd arr. - 51, rue Montorgueil - 01 42 33 38 20
The shop is decorated with rosy, corpulent allegories of Fame painted by Paul Baudry (he also decorated the Paris Opéra) in 1860; these charming murals are pleasant to contemplate while scarfing down a few of Stohrer's butter-rich pastries: the dark-chocolate Criollo, the refreshing Royal Menthe, the Black Forest cake, and flaky croissants all come highly recommended.

• *SEAFOOD*

Le Bar à Huîtres

3rd arr. - 33, bd Beaumarchais - 01 48 87 98 92
5th arr. - 33, rue St-Jacques
or 82 bis, bd St-Germain - 01 44 07 27 37
14th arr. - 112, bd Montparnasse - 01 43 20 71 01
At the outdoor oyster bar, you can purchase dozens of succulent oysters, opened for you free of charge by the nimble-fingered *écaillers* and neatly arranged on disposable trays (no deposit, no return). Just remember to place your order in advance.

Poissonnerie du Dôme

14th arr. - 4, rue Delambre - 01 43 35 23 95
The lucky residents of Montparnasse can satisfy their urge for seafood at this marvelous fish store, perhaps the best in Paris. Manager Jean-Pierre Lopez admits only "noble" fish (sole, turbot, lotte, sea bass, and the like) to his classy emporium. The merchandise, from French (particularly Breton) and foreign waters, is snapped up by such eminent restaurants as L'Ambroisie and Laurent. Need we mention that these rare and delicate denizens of the deep command regally high prices?

• *WINE & SPIRITS*

Keep in mind that you can purchase a good bottle of wine for your dinner at many of the city's wine bars.

Les Caves Taillevent

8th arr. - 199, rue du Fg-St-Honoré - 01 45 61 14 09
Crack sommeliers—the Vrinat family and their team— select the wines presented by Taillevent. The choice is wide, and the prices are more reasonable than you might expect. Many of the producers represented use biodynamic growing

techniques: look for Château Falfas '93 for 56 F, and Nicolas Joly's superb Coulée de Serrant '92 for 190 F.

Legrand Filles et Fils

2nd arr. - 1, rue de la Banque - 01 42 60 07 12

Even if the wines were not half so interesting as they are, Legrand's wine shop would be worth a visit for its old-fashioned charm and warm atmosphere. Francine Legrand offers a fascinating selection of carefully chosen, inexpensive country wines from up-and-coming growers in the South and the Val de Loire, along with a far-ranging inventory of prestigious Alsaces, Burgundies, and Bordeaux (note the many wines from average vintage years, affordably priced). Also, a few uncommon bottlings: luscious Muscat de Beaumes-de-Venise, Vin de Paille du Jura, and some excellent vintage Ports. Legrand's impressive stock of eaux-de-vie is one of the finest in town.

Nicolas

8th arr. - 31, pl. de Madeleine - 01 42 68 00 16
250 stores in Paris.

Looking better than ever with a spruce gold-and-bordeaux décor, Nicolas's innumerable stores in the Paris area continue to present a wide, diverse, and appealing range of wines for every budget. The chain's monthly promotions are well worth following: featured are (for example) French wines from unfamiliar or underrated appellations—the Ardèche, Corbières, or Savoie—, imports (Spanish, Italian, and even Lebanese bottlings), and the occasional oenological curiosity, all offered at attractive prices. The multilevel flagship store on Place de la Madeleine has a huge inventory of more than 1,000 different wines, including rare, old Bordeaux. Nicolas is also an excellent source of fine distilled spirits (check out the selection of single-malt whiskies). The Avenue Wagram shop stays open until 10pm (01 42 27 22 07), the Ancienne-Comédie store until 9pm (01 43 26 61 22). Home delivery service available.

Vins Rares Peter Thustrup

6th arr. - 20, rue Serpente - 01 46 33 56 36

Peter Thustrup harbors an unquenchable passion for old, rare vintages. It leads him to auction rooms all over the world, in pursuit of such treasures as antique Yquem, ancient Pétrus, and Mouton-Rothschild from another age (which sell, incidentally, for about 18,000 F—just to give you an idea). Bordeaux, obviously, is well represented, but Thustrup can also show you some exceptional Vendanges Tardives from Alsace, mature Burgundies, and collectible Côtes-du-Rhônes.

For an in-depth, insider's guide to the City of Light, its restaurants and hotels, shops, nightlife, monuments, and more, consult GaultMillau's **Best of Paris.**

PARIS SUBURBS: RESTAURANTS & HOTELS

ALFORTVILLE 94140
Paris 10 - Créteil 5 - Maisons-Alfort 1 Val-de-Marne

12/20 Chinagora Restaurant
1, pl. du Confluent-France-Chine
01 45 18 33 09, fax 01 43 53 08 00
Closed Mon. Open until 11pm. No pets. Terrace dining. Garage pkg.
A bit of Beijing in Paris: Chinagora's lengthy menu holds few surprises (except when it comes to dessert—lotus-cream buns, for example), but the dim-sum, beef with saté sauce, and hot-stone grills are decent enough. C 180. M 55-75 (weekdays lunch), 260 (for 2 pers), 320 (for 4 pers), 568 (for 6 pers).

ASNIÈRES 92600
Paris 9 - Argenteuil 6 - Saint-Denis 8 Hauts-de-Seine

Le Van Gogh
2, quai Aulagnier - 01 47 91 05 10, fax 01 47 93 00 93
Closed Sat lunch, Sun, Aug 9-25. Open until 10pm. Terrace dining. Air cond. No pets. Pkg.
The dining room resembles the interior of a luxury liner, with portholes and bay windows framing views of the Seine. The cuisine looks out to sea, with dishes like brill roasted with spices and meat jus, and there are some Southwestern options, too: tender Landes pigeon or civet de canard. C 310-530. M 220 (lunch).

AULNAY-SOUS-BOIS 93600
Paris 16 - Bobigny 8 - Saint-Denis 17 Seine-St-Denis

Auberge des Saints Pères
21, av. de Nonneville
01 48 68 11 06, fax 01 48 66 25 22
Closed Sat lunch, Sun dinner, Mon, 1 wk in Jan, Aug. Open until 9:30pm. Priv rm: 12. No pets. Pkg.
Michel Liret turns premium ingredients into rich, classic dishes. Served in an elegant setting, they are accompanied by superb (and expensive) wines. Expect a smiling welcome from Emmanuelle Liret. C 350. M 200, 360, 120 (chilren).

Novotel
N 370, carrefour de l'Europe
01 48 66 22 97, fax 01 48 66 99 39
Open year-round. 139 rms 485-495. Bkfst 56. Rms for disabled. Restaurant. Rm ser. Air cond. Conf. Pool. Pkg.
Near the Villepinte exhibition grounds, this Novotel is set in a garden. The nicely equipped rooms are particularly suited to families.

BLANC-MESNIL (LE) 93150
Paris 18 - Le Bourget 3 - Aulnay-s.-Bois 3 Seine-St-Denis

Bleu Marine
219, av. Descartes - 01 48 65 52 18, fax 01 45 91 07 75
Open year-round. 130 rms 420-480. Bkfst 50. Rms for disabled. Restaurant. Rm ser. Air cond. Pkg.
Comfortable, modern rooms in a well-equipped establishment just five minutes' drive from Le Bourget and Charles-de-Gaulle airports.

Novotel Paris-Le Bourget
2, rue Jean-Perrin
01 48 67 48 88, fax 01 45 91 08 27
Open year-round. 143 rms 400-495. Bkfst 30-55. Rms for disabled. Restaurant. Rm ser. Air cond. Conf. Heated pool. Pkg.
This chain provides reliably comfortable accommodations close to the Air and Space museum.

BOULOGNE-BILLANCOURT 92100
Paris (Porte de St-Cloud) 10 - Versailles 11 Hauts-de-Seine

Acanthe
9, rond-point Rhin-et-Danube
01 46 99 10 40, fax 01 46 99 00 05
Open year-round. 1 ste 1,100. 45 rms 695. Bkfst 65. Rms for disabled. Rm ser. Air cond. Pkg.
Young sporting types will love the contemporary design of this hotel close to the French Open site of Roland-Garros. But no one likes the noise that filters through from the traffic circle.

Adagio

20-22, rue des Abondances
01 48 25 80 80, fax 01 48 25 33 13
Open year-round. 75 rms 695-795. Bkfst 65. Rms for disabled. Restaurant. Rm ser. Air cond. Pkg.
This modern, glass-and-concrete hotel has bright, spacious rooms fitted with every convenience and pleasantly furnished. The basement houses a vast complex of conference rooms. Summer terrace.

 L'Auberge

86, av. Jean-Baptiste-Clément
01 46 05 67 19, fax 01 46 05 23 16
Closed Sat lunch, Sun, Aug. Terrace dining. Air cond. Pkg.
The bright, tidy little dining room of this mellow provincial dwelling draws a public of well-heeled executive types. We share their enthusiasm for Jean-Pierre Roy's varied, deftly crafted menu. The cache of Jura wines in the cellar (which is otherwise strong on Bordeaux) is a relic of the days when the restaurant specialized in food from Franche-Comté. C 350. M 155 & 195 (wine incl).

 La Bretonnière

120, av. Jean-Baptiste-Clément
01 46 05 73 56, fax 01 46 05 73 56
Closed Sat, Sun. Open until 9:45pm.
A former head waiter, René Rossignol switched to cuisine and brought this restaurant back up to standard. In fact, Rossignol cooks as the nightingale sings: naturally and exquisitely. His single-price menu offers excellent value. Interesting cellar. M 165.

 Au Comte de Gascogne

89, av. Jean-Baptiste-Clément
01 46 03 47 27, fax 01 46 04 55 70
Closed Sat lunch, Sun, 2nd wk of Aug. Open until 10:30pm. Priv rm: 15. Garden dining. Air cond. Valet pkg.
Three palm trees, a fountain, and lots of flowers make the dining room as warm as spring all year round. And Gascon flavors warm the palate, in the half-dozen variations on foie gras, including smoked duck foie gras with cucumber and bacon. But the chef has an oddly clumsy hand with spices. Splendid cellar (with a world-class collection of Armagnacs) but too few half-bottles. C 500. M 260 (weekday lunch).

12/20 La Tonnelle de Bacchus

120, av. Jean-Baptiste-Clément - 01 46 04 43 98
Closed Sat, Sun, Christmas-beg Jan. Open until 10pm. Priv rm: 30. Terrace dining.
Here's an adorable vintage bistro with a shady summer terrace, where customers divide their interest among saucisson de Lyon, steamed salmon, and cinnamon-scented apple crumble, all washed down with delicious wines, some of which are served by the glass. C 250-350. M 90, 120, 150.

CHARENTON-LE-PONT 94220
Paris 2 - Saint-Mandé 3 - Alfortville 2   Val-de-Marne

12/20 Le Grand Bleu

21, av. du Mal-de-Lattre-de-Tassigny
01 49 77 65 65
Closed Sun dinner, Mon, Jul 28-Sep 1. Open until 10:30pm.
Here's a pleasant little seafood spot, just steps away from the Vincennes zoo. The 115 F menu brings six oysters, grilled salt-cured salmon with lentils and bacon, and tarte Tatin flambée. Good-humored atmosphere. C 250. M 115 (weekday lunch), 170.

CHAVILLE 92370
Paris 13 - Versailles 4 - Boulogne 2   Hauts-de-Seine

 La Tonnelle

29, rue Lamennais
01 47 50 42 77, fax 01 47 50 99 19
Open daily until 10pm. Air cond. Priv rm: 60. Terrace dining.
A fine spot for a Sunday lunch: a quiet terrace, a smart décor, well-dressed patrons, and a genial host create a mood conducive to enjoyment. Good food (sometimes a mite too salty) and excellent desserts; extensive cellar. C 200-250. M 155 (weekday lunch), 195, 255, 90 (children).

CHENNEVIÈRES-SUR-MARNE 94430
Paris 17 - Créteil 5 - Lagny 22   Val-de-Marne

L'Écu de France

31, rue de Champigny - 01 45 76 00 03
Closed Sun dinner, Mon, 1st wk of Sep. Open until 9:30pm. Priv rm: 60. Terrace dining. Garage pkg.
From the pink dining room you have a grand view of the River Marne, which you can savor along with Arnaud Bourguignon's classic and Provençal dishes. For dessert, don't miss the hot-chocolate and pistachio gâteau. The list of fine wines and vintage brandies will encourage you to indulge. C 250.

CHEVILLY-LARUE 94550
Paris 12 - Créteil 10 - Antony 5   Val-de-Marne

Chez Fernand

248, av. de Stalingrad - 01 46 86 11 77
Closed Sat, Sun, Aug. Open until 10pm. Pkg.
Fernand Asseline, in his neo-Norman inn by the side of the N7 highway, serves deliciously rich regional meals conclude with prize-winning Camemberts and house-made bread. Good cellar. C 250.

CLAMART 92140
Paris 10 - Versailles 13 - Boulogne-B. 6   Hauts-de-Seine

12/20 La Cosse des Petits Pois

158, av. Victor-Hugo
01 46 38 97 60, fax 01 46 38 08 75
Closed Sat lunch, Sun, Aug 9-19. Open until 10pm.
Priv rm: 20.
A soothing, provincial mood prevails in this traditional restaurant. The owner cooks and serves his classic dishes with a generous hand. Decent cellar with plenty of Bordeaux. Charming welcome. M 145 (wine incl), 195, 260.

CLICHY 92110
Paris 7 - Saint-Germain-en-Laye 17   Hauts-de-Seine

 ### La Romantica

73, bd Jean-Jaurès
01 47 37 29 71, fax 01 47 37 76 32
Closed Sat lunch, Sun. Open until 10:30pm. Terrace dining. Valet pkg.
Claudio Puglia is a self-taught cook, but his lack of diplomas is more than compensated by his passion for *la bella cucina*. You'll be dazzled by saffron-tinged spinach risotto, carpaccio like none you've ever tasted (especially those pale French copies), or lotte with raisins, pine nuts, and raspberries. Don't miss the fettuccine tossed with sage and prosciutto, then presented in a hollowed-out Parmesan cheese! In summer, these *delizie* are served on a romantic garden patio. C 350. M 195, 280 & 350 (dinner).

COURBEVOIE 92400
Paris 11 - Nanterre 6 - Argenteuil 7   Hauts-de-Seine

 ### La Safranée sur Mer

12, pl. des Reflets, La Défense 2
01 47 78 75 50, fax 01 47 76 46 20
Closed Sat, Sun, Aug. Open until 10:30pm. Terrace dining. Air cond. Valet pkg.
With its wood-paneled décor and swift service, this seafood restaurant is a favorite venue for business people with clients to impress. We'd be more impressed with the food if the flavors were more distinctly defined. Good saffron crème brûlée; pleasant summer terrace. C 400-450. M 200 (dinner, wine incl), 245.

12/20 La Valérianne

32, rue Franklin - 01 47 89 16 80
Closed Sun dinner, Aug 1-15. Open until 10pm.
The lunchtime crowd comes here for fresh, unpretentious food prepared with flair. The single-price menu is most worthwhile. Appealing cellar. C 200. M 100.

DISNEYLAND PARIS 77 → Ile-de-France

ISSY-LES-MOULINEAUX 92130
Paris (Pte de Versailles) 1 - Boulogne-B. 1 Hauts-de-Seine

12/20 Coquibus

16, av. de la République
01 46 38 75 80, fax 01 41 08 95 80
Closed Sat lunch, Sun, 3 wks in Aug. Open until 10:30pm. Priv rm: 30. Terrace dining. Garage pkg.
The sign and the winsome dining room evoke Montmartre, oddly enough, but the hearty, homestyle cooking shows a Provençal or Southwestern slant. Small but select cellar. C 200. M 125, 160.

10/20 Issy Guinguette

113 bis, av. de Verdun
01 46 62 04 27, fax 01 46 38 89 57
Closed Sat lunch, dinner Sun & Mon. Open until 10pm. Terrace dining. Pkg.
A delightful riverside *guinguette* run by wine merchant Yves Legrand. The wines, indeed, are jim-dandy...but what a pity the food lacks flair! C 180-200.

 ### Manufacture

20, esplanade de la Manufacture
01 40 93 08 98, fax 01 40 93 57 22
Closed Sat lunch, Sun, 2 wks in Aug. Open until 10:30pm. Terrace dining. Air cond.
Jean-Pierre Vigato, who runs the three-toque Apicius in Paris, has put a new chef in charge of this spacious restaurant converted from a tobacco factory. The single-price menu proposes (for example) headcheese vigorously scented with sage and served with a zesty herb salad, spiced whiting or garlicky bourride (fish stew) followed by goat cheeses and lush desserts—it's all lively, colorful, and reasonably priced. M 155-180.

LEVALLOIS-PERRET 92300
Paris (Porte de Champerret) 8 - Neuilly 4 Hauts-de-Seine

 ### Le Petit Poste

39, rue Rivay - 01 47 37 34 46
Closed Sat, Sun, 1 wk at Christmas. Open until 10:30pm. Air cond.
Fifteen tables crowded around the bar—this is the type of bistro Brassens used to write about in his songs. Now it is a favorite with the good people of Levallois, who come to enjoy the cooking of Michel Wante. Excellent single-price menu; alert service. C 230. M 170.

 ### La Rôtisserie

24, rue Anatole-France
01 47 48 13 82, fax 01 47 48 07 87
Closed Sat lunch, Sun. Open until 10pm. Air cond. Valet pkg.
A former hangar converted into a loft-brasserie with Art Deco fittings is the scene for Daniel Ballester's remarkably generous cooking. A 155 F single-price menu offers interesting appetizers followed by spit-roasted meats and

poultry, and tasty desserts. The well-chosen wines are a hair too expensive. M 155.

MEUDON   92190
Paris 12 - Versailles 10 - Boulogne-B. 3   Hauts-de-Seine

 ## Relais des Gardes

42, av. du Général-Gallieni
01 45 34 11 79, fax 01 45 34 44 32
Closed Sat lunch, Sun dinner. Open until 10pm. Terrace dining. Pkg.
A classic repertoire and style reign supreme, yet an occasional—and welcome—creative touch lends extra interest to lobster salad dressed with a subtle vinaigrette, turbot with lemongrass and excellent crisp potatoes, and a rich chocolate tart. Discreet, courteous service. C 300-420. M 190.

NANTERRE   92000
Paris 13 - Neuilly 5 - St-Germain-en-L. 8   Hauts-de-Seine

12/20 La Rôtisserie

180, av. Georges-Clemenceau
01 46 97 12 11, fax 01 46 97 12 09
Closed Sat lunch, Sun. Open until 10pm. Terrace dining. Valet pkg.
The incongruous Greek exterior leads into a bright, pleasant dining room; there, you can dig into a satisfying 155 F single-price menu of handily prepared bistro classics. M 155, 80 (children).

NEUILLY-SUR-SEINE   92200
Paris (Porte de Neuilly) 8 - Nanterre 8   Hauts-de-Seine

 ## Le Bistrot d'à Côté

4, rue Boutard
01 47 45 34 55, fax 01 47 45 15 08
Closed 2 wks in Aug. Open until 11pm. Terrace dining. Valet pkg.
See *Paris 17th arr.* M 109 (weekday lunch), 142, 189.

12/20 Bistrot Saint-James

2, rue du Gal-Henrion-Berthier - 01 46 24 21 06
Closed Sat, Sun. Open until 10pm. Terrace dining.
Genial François Pagnoux treats his patrons to old-time French favorites (blanquette, navarin d'agneau, boudin with apples and potatoes) and expertly grilled meats, washed down by fine Bordeaux wines he selects himself. C 200-250.

12/20 Brasserie des Arts

2, rue des Huissiers - 01 46 24 56 17
Closed Sun, May 1. Open until 10:30pm. No pets.
A simple and unpretentious address often filled with celebrities from this chic suburb. They come for foie gras maison, thyme-scented rack of lamb, shellfish platters, and nougat glacé. C 210-320. M 109-135 (weekday dinner, Sat).

12/20 Café de la Jatte

60, bd Vital-Bouhot
01 47 45 04 20, fax 01 47 45 19 32
Open daily until midnight. Air cond. Terrace dining. Valet pkg.
The décor revolves around the giant skeleton of a pterodactyl surrounded by a jungle of plants. The food is OK, but can we really call it cooking? The speedy young waiters zoom around serving salads, raw or steamed fish, and sorbets to tables of tanned people "in advertising." C 240-350. M 100 (weekday lunch).

 ## Coco d'Isles

31, rue Madeleine-Michelis
01 46 40 17 21, fax 01 46 40 71 21
Closed Sun, Mon, Aug. Open until 11:45pm. No pets. Pkg.
Wonderful West Indian dishes served in a tropical setting. Every one of the starters is a treat: spiced eggplant and codfish, skate salad, stuffed clams and crab... Follow them with poached or stewed fish or a fiery colombo of chicken or kid. C 250-300. M 95 & 125 (lunch), 145, 210.

 ## Les Feuilles Libres

34, rue Perronet - 01 46 24 41 41, fax 01 46 40 77 61
Closed Sat lunch, Aug 5-20. Open until 10:30pm. Terrace dining. Air cond.
Quality ingredients paired in clever ways: that's the kitchen's recipe for success. The local gentry gather here for the delicious likes of rabbit and prunes in aspic, baby mackerel in broth with fresh vegetables, and sea bream with saffron-spiced ratatouille. Guests are courteously welcomed and briskly served in this comfy, country-style dining room. C 250. M 185.

Foc Ly

"Chez Mommaton," 79, av. Charles-de-Gaulle
01 46 24 43 36, fax 01 46 24 48 46
Open daily until 11pm. Air cond. Pkg.
No dragons or pagodas in the conservative dining room, no outlandish listings on the menu. Foc Ly serves a classic repertoire of sautéed crab with crispy noodles, rice with shellfish, curried lamb, and ginger ice cream, all skillfully prepared. The salt-and-pepper scampi are exceptional. C 200-280. M 99 & 109 (weekday lunch), 75 (children).

12/20 Chez Gérard

10, rue Montrosier - 01 46 24 86 37
Closed Sat lunch, Sun. Open until 11pm. No pets.
Better than the usual bistro chow, Joël Leduc's versions of saffron-stained mussel soup, calf's liver with beans, and crème brûlée are several cuts above standard. C 180.

 ## La Guinguette de Neuilly

Ile de la Jatte, 12, bd Georges Seurat - 01 46 24 25 04
Open daily until 11pm. Garden dining. Air cond. Pkg.

An arty crowd frequents this old barge, fitted out with a handful of tables; Francois Beauvais's cooking suits the scene's holiday mood: try the pork and lentil salad, thyme-scented rack of lamb, and blancmange with fresh fruit. In fine weather, try to nab riverside seats. C 240-370.

10/20 Chez Livio

6, rue de Longchamp - 01 46 24 81 32
Closed Sat & Sun (in Aug), Dec 24, Jan 1. Open until 10:45pm. Priv rm: 24. Garden dining. Air cond.
A real Italian trattoria in the heart of Neuilly, manned by the Innocenti clan. The simple bill of fare features ravioli al magro, gnocchi with basil, risotto with wild mushrooms, osso buco, and *tutti quanti*. The roof of the dining room rolls back so that you can dine under a canopy of blue sky or stars. Reservations (sometimes hard to come by) are a must. C 200-250. M 120 (weekdays, wine incl), 75 (children).

12/20 Au New Café Russe

16, rue du Commandant-Pilot - 01 46 24 72 36
Closed Sat lunch, Sun. Open until 11pm.
Something of a surprise in this neighborhood: a Russian restaurant serving good zakuskis, beef Stroganoff, veal cutlet Pojarski, and lush, caloric desserts. Two Fridays per month, Tziganes musicians. C 200-300. M 82 (lunch), 128, 158, 75 (children).

Hôtel du Parc

4, bd du Parc - 01 46 24 32 62, fax 01 46 40 77 31
Open year-round. 67 rms 310-520. Bkfst 38. Rms for disabled. Conf. Pkg.
The rooms in this plain and simple establishment on the Ile de la Jatte have all been carefully renovated. Be sure to choose quarters on the courtyard side (the quay side can be very noisy).

Paris Neuilly

1, av. de Madrid - 01 47 47 14 67, fax 01 47 47 97 42
Open year-round. 6 stes 985-1,090. 74 rms 735-935. Bkfst 70. Rms for disabled. Rm ser. Garage pkg.
The soundproofed rooms are comfortable enough; all are identically decorated in red and beige, and look out over a befrescoed atrium.

12/20 San Valero

209 ter, av. Charles-de-Gaulle
01 46 24 07 87, fax 01 47 47 83 17
Closed Sat lunch, Sun, Dec 24-Jan 1. Open until 10:30pm. No pets.
Come for a fiesta at Valero's Spanish restaurant: the menu offers paella of course, but also more authentic dishes such as quails en escabèche, scallops in a garlicky sauce with dried tuna, and baby lamb marinated in herbs, a specialty of the Rioja region. The Spanish offerings on the wine list are worthy of your attention. C 300. M 150 (weekdays), 190.

12/20 Sébillon

"Paris-Bar," 20, av. Ch.-de-Gaulle
01 46 24 71 31, fax 01 46 24 43 50
Open daily until midnight. Priv rm: 30. Air cond.
The chefs come and go, but Sébillon's menu is immutable. Specialties of the house are delicious roast lamb and a giant éclair. Add to that a superb rib of beef and tarte Tatin "à l'ancienne," as well as sparkling fresh seafood. To drink, there's a selection of nice Loire wines at affordable prices. C 250-350. M 179 (wine & coffee incl).

La Truffe Noire

"Jenny Jacquet", 2, pl. Parmentier
01 46 24 94 14, fax 01 46 37 27 02
Closed Sat (exc dinner Jan-Mar), Sun, 3 wks in Aug. Open until 10pm. Air cond. No pets. Terrace dining.
A real stickler when it comes to choosing his ingredients, Jenny Jacquet also has the technique to turn out such first-rate traditional dishes as pike mousseline with beurre blanc, foie gras de canard en terrine, and a textbook pot-au-feu with delicious vegetables. In his provincial-style restaurant near Porte Maillot, he also proposes a different themed menu each month (truffles, mushrooms, shellfish...) which can be partnered by one of the fine growers' wines that Jacquet selects himself. Whatever you order, save room for dessert: the feuillantine au café or truffe au chocolat are the highlight of the meal! C 350. M 195.

ORLY	94310
Paris 16 - Créteil 8	Val-de-Marne

Maxim's

Aérogare d'Orly-Ouest
01 46 86 87 84, fax 01 46 87 05 39
Closed Sat, Sun, hols, Aug, 1 wk at Christmas-New Year's. Open until 10pm. Air cond. Priv rm: 25. Pkg.
In the cockpit of Maxim's Orly is Gil Jouanin, whose inspired cooking flies high. To wit, his langoustines and scallops roasted with garlic salt, turbot crusted with black pepper and paprika, and iced pear amandine. The 30,000-bottle cellar holds wines in every price range, from modest to outrageous. C 330. M 195, 46 (children).

Paris-Orly Airport-Hilton

Aérogare Orly-Sud 267
01 45 12 45 12, fax 01 45 12 45 00
Open year-round. 12 stes 1,350-1,650. 345 rms 990-1,350. Bkfst 65-90. Rms for disabled. Restaurant. Rm ser. Air cond. Conf. Heated pool. Tennis. Garage pkg.
Functional, comfortable rooms near the airport (free shuttle) with round-the-clock room service. In addition to excellent facilities for conferences or seminars, there are ten tennis courts, a pool, a fitness center, and a piano bar open from Monday to Thursday.

PANTIN 93500
Paris 3 - Bobigny 4 - Saint-Denis 7   Seine-St-Denis

 Référence Hôtel

22, av. Jean-Lolive
01 48 91 66 00, fax 01 48 44 12 17
Open year-round. 3 stes 1,000-1,450. 120 rms 590-810. Bkfst 50-75. Half-board 890-1,070. Rms for disabled. Restaurant. Rm ser. Air cond. Conf. Pkg.
This hotel has two major assets: fine, recently renovated rooms; and an energetic staff. On the downside: looks (it resembles a blockhouse) and position (near the beltway).

PERREUX (LE) 94170
Paris 15 - Créteil 11 - Vincennes 6   Val-de-Marne

 Les Magnolias

48, av. de Bry - 01 48 72 47 43, fax 01 48 72 22 28
Closed Sat, Sun. Open until 10pm. Air cond.
A brilliant and inviting room is concealed behind Les Magnolias' graceless façade. Gérard Royant presents an appetizing roster that features cool crab aspic made cooler still by a ginger-spiced cucumber granita, veal sweetbreads and kidney in a Sherried sauce, and gingerbread cake with a bright apricot coulis. Expensive wine list. C 350. M 190, 290.

PETIT-CLAMART 92140
Paris 13 - Clamart 5 - Versailles 9   Hauts-de-Seine

12/20 **Au Rendez-Vous de Chasse**

1, av. du Général-Eisenhower
01 46 31 11 95, fax 01 40 94 11 40
Closed Sun dinner. Open until 10pm. Priv rm: 90.
Settle down in the comfortable, spacious dining room and let the courteous staff serve you a pan-roast of wild mushrooms, cod brightened with a basil emulsion, and crêpes Suzette flamed with Grand Marnier. C 320. M 130 & 170 (weekdays), 170 & 230 (Sat, Sun lunch), 210 & 310 (wine incl), 95 (children).

PRÉ-SAINT-GERVAIS (LE) 93310
Paris (Pte de Pantin) 7 - Pantin 3   Seine-St-Denis

 Le Pouilly Reuilly

68, rue André-Joineau - 01 48 45 14 59
Closed Sat, Sun, hols, Aug-Sep 6. Open until 10pm. Priv rm: 30. Pkg.
The place may not look like much, but inside you'll find a warm bistro atmosphere and Jean Thibault's generous cooking, inspired by the French countryside and the market's best seasonal produce. The cellar holds a rich (and pricey) cache of premium Burgundy and Bordeaux. C 280.

PUTEAUX 92800
Paris 10 - Saint-Germain-en-Laye 11   Hauts-de-Seine

 Les Communautés

Sofitel-CNIT, Grande Arche de La Défense, in the CNIT, 2, pl. de La Défense
01 46 92 10 10, fax 01 46 92 10 50
Closed Sat, Sun, 2 wks in Aug. Open until 10:30pm. Air cond. Air cond. Valet pkg.
Pierre Miécaze offers sunny and sometimes unpredictable exotic cuisine: langoustine ravioli in satay sauce, superb red mullet enhanced with exceptional olive oil, tiramisù. Beautiful cellar with wines from everywhere. Professional service. C 290-400. M 310 (lunch), 180 (dinner).

 Sofitel-CNIT

(See restaurant above)
Closed 2 wks in Aug. 6 stes 1,700-3,000. 141 rms 1,500. Bkfst 95-120. Rms for disabled. Restaurant. Rm ser. Air cond. Conf. Valet pkg.
The hotel caters to business travelers, providing huge rooms (some boast a view of the Grande Arche), luxurious bathrooms, and 24-hour room service.

 Dauphin

Esplanade de La Défense, 45, rue Jean-Jaurès
01 47 73 71 63, fax 01 46 98 08 82
Open year-round. 30 rms 380-470. Bkfst 40. Tennis. Valet pkg.
The Dauphin stands opposite the Princesse Isabelle, and is run by the same family. Generous buffet breakfasts are set up in the sitting room; rooms are comfortable and pretty, with cable television. Some rooms are reserved for non-smokers. Free shuttle to the RER station.

Les Deux Arcs

Sofitel Paris-La Défense, 34, cours Michelet,
La Défense 10 - 01 47 76 44 43, fax 01 47 73 72 74
Closed Sat, Sun lunch. Open until 10:30pm. Terrace dining. Air cond. Priv rm: 100. Valet pkg.
The elder of the two Sofitel hotels at La Défense is home to a quiet, comfortable restaurant, where wheeler-dealers can talk business in peace while enjoying deft, delicious cuisine. Langoustines are barely seared to juicy perfection; salmon comes lightly cooked (as requested) on one side only; and lamb arrives in a perfumed crust of spices. The fine wine list provides many half-bottles; and the service is just superb. A second toque. C 350. M 290, 345 (weekday lunch).

Sofitel Paris-La Défense

(See restaurant above)
Open year-round. 1 ste 2,500. 149 rms 1,400. Rms for disabled. Restaurant. Rm ser. Air cond. Conf. Valet pkg.
A creditable chain hotel, warmly decorated with gilt mirrors and pale marble. Rooms are quiet, with lovely pink-marble bathrooms. Top-

notch service; yummy breakfasts. Good facilities for conferences.

Princesse Isabelle

Esplanade de La Défense, 72, rue Jean-Jaurès
01 47 78 80 06, fax 01 47 75 25 20
Open year-round. 1 ste 950. 30 rms 570-660. Bkfst 50. Air cond. Valet pkg.
The rooms of this hotel near La Défense are prettily decorated, and have bathtubs with Jacuzzi or multijet showers. Some rooms open onto the flowered patio. Note that there's a convenient free chauffeur service to the RER and Pont de Neuilly Métro station.

Syjac Hôtel

20, quai de Dion-Bouton
01 42 04 03 04, fax 01 45 06 78 69
Open year-round. 2 stes 980-1,500. 29 rms 570-750. Bkfst 60. Rm ser. Conf. Pkg.
This modern hotel offers a pleasant alternative to concrete high-rises. Rooms are very pleasing, large and well appointed. There are some nice two-level suites (with fireplace) overlooking the Seine, and a pretty flowered patio.

ROISSY-EN-FRANCE	95700
TGV Paris 26 - Meaux 36 - Senlis 28	Val-d'Oise

Maxim's

Aéroport Charles-de-Gaulle, Terminal 1, Level 11, beyond customs area
01 48 62 92 13, fax 01 48 62 45 96
Closed Sat, Sun, Aug. Open until 10pm. Priv rm: 70. Air cond. No pets. Pkg.
Rich rewards await intrepid gastronomes who venture in level 11 of Roissy airport number one. They'll get to savor Alain Bariteau's wonderful stuffed saddle of rabbit, juicy veal tenderloin en pot-au-feu, and wildly rich vanilla and licorice ice creams. Oh yes, and the cellar is magnificent, too. C 200-250. M 120, 180.

Sheraton Paris Airport Hotel

Aérogare 2 - 01 49 19 70 70, fax 01 49 19 71 71
Open year-round. 12 stes 2,000-3,500. 240 rms 680-880. Bkfst 90-120. Rms for disabled. Restaurants. Rm ser. Air cond. Conf. Fitness center. Pkg.
This new 4-storey structure conveniently located at the center of the airport offers guests hassle-free "hub" access to their plane, TGV and RER connections. Bold geometric marble, metal and glass architecture and impressive views of the surrounding air and rail traffic are tempered by Andrée Putman's calm, comfortably elegant interiors. Streamlined order and true European flavor prevail in this high-quality establishment, designed with cutting-edge traveler comfort in mind.

Sofitel

Aéroport Charles-de-Gaulle
01 49 19 29 29, fax 01 48 62 78 49
Open year-round. 8 stes 800-1,700. 344 rms 700-1,400. Bkfst 80. Rms for disabled. Restaurant. Rm ser. Air cond. Conf. Heated pool. Tennis. No pets. Garage pkg.
A comfortable airport hotel that provides round-the-clock room service and a free shuttle to the airport. Entertainment facilities include a disco and piano bar, and there's a coffee shop, too.

ROMAINVILLE	93230
Paris 10 - Livry-Gargan 9	Seine-St-Denis

Chez Henri

72, route de Noisy
01 48 45 26 65, fax 01 48 91 16 74
Closed Sat lunch, Sun, Mon dinner, hols, Aug. Open until 9:30pm. Priv rm: 18. Air cond. Pkg.
Chef Henri Bourgin is back on track! We could barely restrain ourselves from begging for seconds (or thirds) of his lobster millefeuille with grenadine-glazed baby onions, his winy civet of oxtail and pig's foot, or lush licorice fondant served with rose-petal jam and a poppyseed brioche. Connoisseur's cellar; convivial atmosphere in a comfortable, flower-filled dining room. C 310-420. M 160.

RUEIL-MALMAISON	92500
Paris 15 - Versailles 11 - Nanterre 13	Hauts-de-Seine

El Chiquito

126, av. Paul-Doumer
01 47 51 00 53, fax 01 47 49 19 61
Closed Sat, Sun, 2 wks in Aug. Terrace dining. Pkg.
No, not another Tex-Mex—El Chiquito is a venerable institution where quality seafood is handled with care. Best bets are the grilled scampi, flash-cooked rock lobster and turbot, and hot oysters. The friandise de merlan (whiting) and apple chaud-froid impressed us less. Terrifying prices. C 290-500. M 210 (dinner).

RUNGIS	94150
Paris 13 - Créteil 12 - Évry 19	Val-de-Marne

Holiday Inn Orly

4, av. Charles-Lindbergh
01 46 87 26 66, fax 01 45 60 91 25
Open year-round. 23 stes 1,025. 168 rms 825-925. Bkfst 70. Rms for disabled. Restaurant. Rm ser. Air cond. Conf. Pkg.
Comfortable and well-kept rooms near Orly airport (free shuttle). From your window, you'll look down on the Rungis *halles* (the Paris wholesale food market). Shops.

Pullman Paris-Orly

20, av. Charles-Lindbergh
01 46 87 36 36, fax 01 46 87 08 48
Open year-round. 2 stes 1,400. 188 rms 660-890. Bkfst 63. Restaurant. Rm ser. Air cond. Conf. Heated pool. Pkg.
A reliable, comfortable chain hotel with excellent soundproofing, air conditioning, and such

amenities as a non-stop shuttle to and from the airports, a panoramic bar, a restaurant, lounges, shops, and a swimming pool.

SAINT-CLOUD   92210
Paris 12 - Boulogne-B. 3 - Versailles 10   Hauts-de-Seine

10/20   Quai Ouest

1200, quai Marcel-Dassault
01 46 02 35 54, fax 01 46 02 33 02
Closed Dec 24 dinner, Jan 1. Open until midnight. Terrace dining. Air cond. Valet pkg.
Lots of young, perma-tanned faces at this trendy spot, a New York–style eatery with a terrace overlooking the Seine. A squadron of smiling waiters recently delivered decent chicken with baby spinach, good thyme-roasted rack of lamb—and a disastrous tarte Tatin! C 250. M 130, 70 (children).

   Villa Henri IV

43, bd de la République
01 46 02 59 30, fax 01 49 11 11 02
Closed Jul 26-Aug 26. 36 rms 460-510. Bkfst 48. Restaurant. Rm ser. Conf.
This charming establishment perched high atop Saint-Cloud features eye-pleasing period furniture. However, the dated striped carpeting and "melancholy gray" marble bathrooms could definitely use an overhaul.

SAINT-DENIS   93200
Paris 10 - Argenteuil 10 - Chantilly 30   Seine-St-Denis

   La Saumonière

1, rue Lanne - 01 48 20 25 56
Closings not available. Open until 10pm. No pets.
Traditional cooking for robust appetites: lobster bouillabaisse, parsleyed pork croquettes with morels, and old-fashioned crêpes Suzette are all worthy of your notice. It deserves a toque. C 310-510. M 140.

12/20   La Table Gourmande

32, rue de la Boulangerie - 01 48 20 25 89
Closed dinner Mon-Wed, Sun, 2nd wk of Feb, last 2 wks of Aug. Open until 9pm.
You won't go wrong with the perfectly seasoned tuna tartare, savory beef piccata, and baked-to-order apple tart. Small, well-composed cellar, with an attractive choice of half-bottles. C 200-300. M 108.

SAINT-OUEN   93400
Paris 7 - Saint-Denis 4 - Bobigny 10   Seine-St-Denis

   Le Coq de la Maison Blanche

37, bd Jean-Jaurès
01 40 11 01 23, fax 01 40 11 67 68
Closed Sun, Aug 15-18. Open until 10pm. Terrace dining. Air cond. Valet pkg.
Alain François is a genial host, who cultivates a convivial atmosphere in his cheerful, bustling

restaurant. Chef André Gamon turns out an immutable list of bistro and bourgeois dishes that satisfy the sauce-lover in us all. In season, savor his tasty asparagus hollandaise; any time of year is right for codfish and vegetables with zesty sauce aïoli. Plenty of fine wines to choose from in the wide-ranging cellar. C 300.

12/20   Chez Serge

7, bd Jean-Jaurès - 01 40 11 06 42
Closed Sun. Open until 9:30pm. Air cond. Pkg.
You won't notice the dreary décor once your waiter plunks down a generous plateful of roast rack of lamb or a huge serving of yummy chocolate cake with custard sauce. Worthwhile wine list. C 150-210.

SURESNES   92150
Paris (Pte Maillot) 11 - Boulogne-B. 6   Hauts-de-Seine

   Les Jardins de Camille

70, av. Franklin-Roosevelt
01 45 06 22 66, fax 01 47 72 42 25
Closed Sun dinner. Open until 11pm. Terrace dining. Valet pkg.
From the terrace, guests can take in a panoramic view of Paris, but the dining room is inviting, too, with its bright and cheerful look. The single-price menu is rooted in Burgundy: try the snail rissoles with fresh pasta and mushrooms, jambon persillé (the aspic is made with sprightly Aligoté wine), braised lamb, and orange-spiked crêpes Suzette. Splendid cellar, accessibly priced. M 160, 80 (children).

VANVES   92170
Paris 8 - Nanterre 12   Hauts-de-Seine

   Le Pavillon de la Tourelle

10, rue Larmeroux
01 46 42 15 59, fax 01 46 42 06 27
Closed Sun dinner, Mon, Aug. Open until 10pm. Terrace dining. Pkg.
Akio Ikeno, a chef trained by Paul Bocuse, presents a repertoire of delicate dishes like scallops enhanced with truffles or a whiff of vanilla and sole à la japonaise. Try the satisfying 195 F menu: asparagus salad, suckling pig in a mustard sauce, cheeses or desserts. Elegant dining room, with a view of leafy grounds. C 400-560. M 150, 195, 250 (wine incl), 90 (children).

VARENNE-ST-HILAIRE (LA)   94210
Paris 16 - Lagny 22 - Saint-Maur 3   Val-de-Marne

   Brasserie du Regency

96, av. du Bac - 01 48 83 15 15, fax 01 48 89 99 74
Closed Dec 24-26. Open until 1:30am. Air cond. Terrace dining. Pkg.
Michel Croisille's menu is better than ever this year, with ultrafresh ingredients heightened by even more delicate sauces. Among the updated classics on offer, we like the warm oysters,

seafood assortment, and luscious soufflé Grand Marnier. **C** 300. **M** 140, 40 (children).

 La Bretèche

171, quai de Bonneuil
01 48 83 38 73, fax 01 42 83 63 19
Closed Sun dinner, Mon, Feb school hols. Open until 10pm. Priv rm: 16. Terrace dining. Air cond.
Choose a table on the terrace or in the bright, pink-hued dining room to savor Philippe Regnault's nicely wrought lobster croustillant with smoky bacon, lotte with a zingy jus d'épice, and raspberry tartlet in a spun-sugar cage. Extensive cellar; gracious welcome. **C** 260-330. **M** 160.

VILLENEUVE-LA-GARENNE	92390
Paris 11 - Saint-Denis 2 - Pontoise 22	Hauts-de-Seine

 Les Chantereines

Avenue du 8-Mai-1945
01 47 99 31 31, fax 01 41 21 31 17

Closed Sat, Sun dinner, Aug 4-24. Open until 10:15pm. Priv rm: 30. Terrace dining. Air cond. Pkg.
You'll soon forget the restaurant's unlovely exterior once you're seated in the comfortable dining room, which looks out over the municipal park and pond. Vivid, modern, and precisely wrought, the cooking is often inspired: memorable anchoïade, toothsome tuna grilled with olive oil, and chocolate "childhood dream" for dessert. **C** 300-380. **M** 180, 90 (children).

VINCENNES	94300
Paris (Pte de Vincennes) 6 - Montreuil 2	Val-de-Marne

 Hôtel Saint-Louis

2 bis, rue Robert-Giraudineau
01 43 74 16 78, fax 01 43 74 16 49
Open year-round. 1 ste 850. 25 rms 410-850. Bkfst 45. Rms for disabled. Conf.
Large rooms, with equally spacious bathrooms, are provided in this pleasant hotel just steps from the château de Vincennes.

PLAN TO TRAVEL?

Look for GaultMillau's other *Best of* guides to Chicago, Florida, France, Germany, Hawaii, Hong Kong, Italy, London, Los Angeles, New England, New Orleans, New York, Paris, San Francisco, Thailand, Toronto, and Washington, D.C.

ILE-DE-FRANCE: RESTAURANTS & HOTELS

ANET   28260
Paris 71 - Dreux 16 - Évreux 37 - Chartres 51   Eure-et-Loir

Dousseine

Route de Sorel - 02 37 41 49 93, fax 02 37 41 90 54
Open year-round. 20 rms 250-280. Bkfst 35. Rms for disabled. Conf. Pkg.
This modern complex on a vast wooded estate offers simple, well-kept guest quarters with nice bathrooms. Friendly welcome and service.

ARPAJON   91290
Paris 33 - Étampes 19   Essonne

Le Saint-Clément

16, av. Hoche - 01 64 90 21 01, fax 01 60 83 32 67
Closed dinner Sun & Mon, 3 wks in Aug. Open until 9:30pm. Air cond.
It's too bad such a wonderful meal had to end with such ordinary desserts. Guy Courtaux's classic, interesting, inspired cuisine—with its excellent ingredients and delicate sauces—is the stuff memories are made of. Precise, nicely varied wine list with an impressive selection of Armagnacs. The elegant pastel dining room features an indoor garden extension, and diners benefit from a warm welcome and top-notch service. C 300-500. M 220.

AUVERS-SUR-OISE   95430
Paris 42 - Pontoise 7 - Chantilly 29 - Taverny 6   Val d'Oise

12/20 Auberge Ravoux

"Maison de Van Gogh," pl. de la Mairie
01 30 36 60 60, fax 01 30 36 60 61
Closed dinner Sun, Mon-Wed Jan-Mar 21. Open until 11pm. Terrace dining. Pkg.
This historic inn full of turn-of-the-century charm is where Vincent Van Gogh spent his final days. Visitors from around the world gather here to sample tasty home-cooked fare and decent wines, all affordably priced. C 190. M 140, 175.

12/20 Hostellerie du Nord

6, rue du Gal-de-Gaulle
01 30 36 70 74, fax 01 30 36 72 75
Closed Sun dinner, Mon, Aug 16-Sep 3. Open until 10pm. Terrace dining. Pkg.
The chef's classic cuisine shows a penchant for the finest ingredients and careful cooking, but he'd do well to give his flavors better definition and add a bit of lemon to his hollandaise sauce.

High-precision wine list, though short on half-bottle offerings. While the welcome is warm, the service in the country-style dining room overlooking a mini-garden could be a tad snappier. C 300-400. M 120 (exc Sun), 190 (Sun).

BARBIZON   77630
Paris 56 - Melun 11 - Fontainebleau 10   Seine-et-Marne

12/20 Auberge Les Alouettes

4, rue Antoine Barye
01 60 66 41 98, fax 01 60 66 20 69
Closed Sun dinner. Open until 9:30pm. Terrace dining. HOTEL: 22 rms 180-380. Bkfst 35. Half-board 345-545. Rm ser. Conf. Tennis. Pkg.
It's a toss-up as to whether to sit outdoors and enjoy the surrounding flora and fauna, or indoors in the cozy dining room done up with attractive coffered ceilings. But wherever you settle, you're sure to enjoy the resolutely traditional fare on hand here, prepared with panache and served up in generous portions. Smallish, high-priced cellar. C 300. M 160, 190, 70 (children).

Le Bas Bréau

22, rue Grande - 01 60 66 40 05, fax 01 60 69 22 89
Open daily until 9:30pm. Garden dining. Heated pool. Tennis. Valet pkg.
The site is still as enchanting as ever, and the service commendable indeed. We liked Alain Tavernier' cuisine we sampled on our last visit: a delicious béarnaise sauce masked the taste of the braised John Dory, and rosemary committed the same offense with the Lozère lamb. And the craquant au chocolat definitely lacked finesse. The cheese tray was splendid (don't miss the Fontainebleau!) and the suprême of bass was as *suprême* as can be! Overpriced cellar. C 520-750. M 350 (weekday lunch, wine incl), 395.

Le Bas Bréau

(See restaurant above)
Open year-round. 8 stes 1,700-3,000. 12 rms 900-1,500. Bkfst 95. Half-board 1,200. Rms for disabled. Rm ser. Air cond. Conf. Heated pool. Tennis. Valet pkg.
The rooms here are beautifully decorated, but tend to heat up when summer rolls around. The setting is splendiferous, the service charming, and the breakfasts sublime: wonderful coffee, fresh pastries, and homemade jams. Relais et Châteaux.

Hostellerie Les Pléiades

21, rue Grande - 01 60 66 40 25, fax 01 60 66 41 68
Open daily until 9:30pm. Garden dining. Pkg.
The premises once belonged to the painter Daubigny, and the spacious, nicely decorated dining room, with its cozy hearth and two charming garden extensions, provides a wonderfully relaxing mealtime setting. Owners Yolande and Roger Karampournis' personal touch sets the tone, and chef Jean-Marc Héry's resolutely classical cuisine proves fresh, light, and eminently flavorful. Spot-on cellar. C 300-350. M 145-280, 85 (children).

 ## Hostellerie Les Pléiades

(See restaurant above)
Open year-round. 1 ste 620. 24 rms 270-550. Bkfst 45. Half-board 370-490. Rm ser. Conf. No pets. Pkg.
Rooms in the elegant manor house or its extension, La Villa, can be on the smallish side, but all very cozy and prettily decorated and feature nice bathrooms. Charming welcome.

BOUGIVAL
78380
Paris 18 - Versailles 7 - Saint-Germain-en-L. 7 — Yvelines

 ## Le Camélia

7, quai Georges-Clemenceau
01 39 18 36 06, fax 01 39 18 00 25
Closed Sun dinner, Mon, 1 wk Feb school hols, 3 wks in Aug, 1 wk at Christmas. Open until 10:30pm. Priv rm: 18. Air cond. Pkg.
Once a culinary mecca under chefs Jean Delaveyne and Roland Durand, Le Camélia is now a good-value venue where reasonably priced menus buy the likes of skate terrine à la provençale, caramelized spare ribs with celery-root purée, or more exotic offerings as paella with thai rice, and almond custard. The wine list needs filling out, however, and some of the desserts (that almond custard!) lack verve. C 260.

12/20 Le Cheval Noir

14, quai Georges-Clemenceau
01 39 69 00 96, fax 01 39 18 29 30
Open daily until 10pm. Priv rm: 40. Terrace dining. Pkg.
Clever seafood-based cooking draws crowds at this cozy, rustic *auberge*. The single-price menus feature tasty tagliatelle and a fine lobster navarin, but the pastries are served in rather stingy portions (though the cherries in brandy are enjoyable). C 220-300. M 129 & 149 (wine incl), 195, 70 (children).

 ## Forest Hill

10-12, rue Yvan-Tourgueneff
01 39 18 17 16, fax 01 39 18 15 80
Open year-round. 1 ste 1,600-1,700. 171 rms 450-650. Bkfst 40. Half-board 570-770. Restaurant. Rm ser. Conf. Pool. Garage pkg.

A modern hotel complex in a leafy setting on the Seine: Forest Hill offers functional rooms with views of the pool or grounds.

CELLE-SAINT-CLOUD (LA)
78170
Paris 16 - Saint-Cloud 5 - Bougival 2 — Yvelines

12/20 Au Petit Chez Soi

Pl. de l'Église - 01 39 69 69 51, fax 01 39 18 30 42
Closed Dec 24-Jan 2. Open until 10pm (11pm in summer). Terrace dining. Pkg.
A polished brasserie with a provincial air, set on a charming little square. Lots of regulars come in for the well-crafted, traditional cooking. Though the chef gives his menu an exotic touch, we find the flavors a shade too pale. Good cellar. M 163.

CERNAY-LA-VILLE
78720
Paris 48 - Rambouillet 11 - Dampierre 4 — Yvelines

12/20 Abbaye des Vaux-de-Cernay

Route d'Auffargis - 01 34 85 23 00, fax 01 34 85 20 95
Open daily until 9:30pm. Heated pool. Tennis. No pets. Pkg.
This abbey dates back eight centuries, and is set on a vast estate with its own forests. We'd be hard pressed to find a more enchanting site, despite the debatable shade of blue used to paint the doors and window trim! The cuisine is not as delectable as the setting: scrumptious vinaigrette of asparagus with langoustines, foie gras croquette with gingerbread, rhubarb crumble with sweet orange sauce. Celestial cellar. C 300-390. M 160 (weekday lunch), 255, 300, 395 (wine incl), 395 (weekday dinner), 495 (weekday dinner, wine incl), 120 (children).

 ## Abbaye des Vaux-de-Cernay

(See restaurant above)
Open year-round. 3 stes 1,500-3,800. 55 rms 390-1,080. Bkfst 80-150. Half-board 650-890. Conf. Heated pool. Tennis. Pkg.
This twelfth-century abbey is fairly brimming with mysterious, grandiose atmosphere. The Gothic lounge and music room are true splendors with their vaults and columns. Luxurious, spacious rooms, decorated with genuine period furniture.

CHANTILLY
60500
Paris 42 - Compiègne 45 - Pontoise 36 - Senlis 10 — Oise

10/20 Capitainerie du Château

Château de Chantilly
03 44 57 15 89, fax 03 44 58 50 11
Lunch only. Closed Tue, Jan-mid Feb. Priv rm: 25. No pets. Pkg.
A convenient spot for lunch after touring the château and Musée Condé. The buffet features

fresh and inviting appetizers and decent desserts, served in two very pretty dining rooms. Friendly staff. C 150-200. M 95, 125, 50 (children).

12/20 Le Relais Condé

42, av. du Mal-Joffre - 03 44 57 05 75
Closed Mon. Open until 10pm. Garden dining.
Pascal Maillet presents a traditional repertoire: escargots fricassée with wild mushrooms, loin of lamb with herbs. Charming welcome and service. C 300-330. M 162, 87 (children).

CHAPELLE-EN-SERVAL (LA)	60520
Paris 40 - Chantilly 10 - Beauvais 71	Oise

 ### Mont Royal

On D 118, route de Plailly, Le Château
03 44 54 50 50, fax 03 44 54 50 21
Open year-round. 4 stes 1,500-1,800. 96 rms 990-1,100. Bkfst 90-150. Half-board 1,270-1,380. Restaurant. Rm ser. Air cond. Conf. Heated pool. Tennis. Pkg.
Tucked away in the green Chantilly forest, this eighteenth-century château is just 15 km from Roissy airport. You'll live like a lord or lady of the manor here, amid luxurious amenities (pool, tennis court, fitness center).

CHARTRES	28000
Paris 87 - Orléans 75 - Dreux 35 - Évreux 77	Eure-et-Loir

 ### Le Buisson Ardent

10, rue au Lait - 02 37 34 04 66, fax 02 37 91 15 82
Closed Sun dinner. Open until 9:30pm.
To judge by this restaurant's location in the shadow of the cathedral, one is likely to expect yet another tourist eatery with stratospheric prices. Not at all. The menu features nicely crafted dishes made from fresh market produce. Courteous, lively service; worthwhile cellar. C 250-350. M 98 (lunch, exc Sun), 118 (weekdays, Sat lucnh), 168, 218, 68 (children).

 ### Le Grand Monarque

22, pl. des Épars - 02 37 21 00 72, fax 02 37 36 34 18
Open daily until 10pm. Priv rm: 120. Terrace dining. Valet pkg.
On a recent visit, we found dependable and affordable offerings, with set-price menus worth their salt. And like crowns, a toque was restored. The moral of the story is that when we say "off with his head," the head gets a chance to grow back! Very good wine list, specially with Loire and Bordeaux wines. M 158, 215, 280, 80 (children).

 ### Novotel

Av. Marcel-Proust - 02 37 88 13 50, fax 02 37 30 29 56
Open year-round. 78 rms 390-470. Bkfst 52. Rms for disabled. Restaurant. Pool. Pkg.
This modern, functional hotel is located in a leafy setting and provides regularly refurbished rooms. Bar and terrace.

 ## Hôtel de la Poste

3, rue du Gal-Kœnig
02 37 21 04 27, fax 02 37 36 42 17
Open year-round. 57 rms 265-320. Bkfst 40. Half-board 265-305. Restaurant. Conf. Garage pkg.
Here's an efficiently modernized hotel close to the cathedral. The soundproofed rooms offer all the comforts one could require, and there is a bar as well as a restaurant on the premises.

La Truie qui File

Pl. de la Poissonnerie
02 37 21 53 90, fax 02 37 36 62 65
Closed Sun dinner, Mon, Aug. Open until 9:30pm. Priv rm: 22. Air cond. Terrace dining.
Gilles Chroukroun's bright blue-and-white dining room welcomes local gourmets and food-loving tourists with a menu full of bright, vivid dishes. Mackerel fondant, cod with roasted shallots, tarragon-scented chicken tartlet seasoned with fruity olive oil, and winy stewed ox jowls all combine elegant technique with robust flavors. Less costly fare is served in a newly added room downstairs, so that dining here needn't be a once-in-a-blue-moon treat. Take note of the 100 F set meal: what a bargain! C 300-500. M 180, 280, 360, 70 (children).

La Vieille Maison

5, rue au Lait - 02 37 34 10 67, fax 02 37 91 12 41
Closed Sun dinner, Mon, 1 wk in Jul & in Aug. Open until 9:30pm.
Chef Bruno Letartre, formerly of the Grand Monarque, officiates at this fourteenth-century house featuring rustico-bourgeois décor. Food lovers are sure to enjoy his classic cuisine revisited: duck pâté en croûte, tender farm-raised squab with wild mushrooms, delectable pear and chocolate tart. Somewhat costly cellar. C 380. M 160, 250, 350, 80 (chilren).

And also...

Our selection of places for inexpensive, quick, or late-night meals.
Café Serpente (02 37 21 68 81 - 2, cloître Notre-Dame. Open daily until midnight, 1:30am in summer): Located opposite the cathedral, this simpatico bistro draws quite a crowd any time of day or night, eager to tuck into its nicely done (though predictable) brasserie fare. Small, fairly priced cellar. Friendly, quick service–despite the throngs (150).
Les Épars (02 37 21 23 72 - 11, pl. des Épars. Closed Sun dinner, Mon, Aug. Open until 10pm.): Just opposite the Grand Monarque. Classic cooking, with simple, sincere set-price menus (77-158).

This symbol stands for "Les Lauriers du Terroir", an award given to chefs who prepare traditional or regional cuisine.

CHÂTEAUFORT 78117
Paris 28 - Versailles 10 - Orsay 11 Yvelines

 La Belle Époque

10, pl. de la Mairie
01 39 56 21 66, fax 01 39 56 87 96
*Closed Sun dinner, Mon, Aug 16-30. Open until
10pm. Terrace dining. Pkg.*
Alain Rayé made the transition from urban
chef to country *cuisinier* with nary a hitch. His
village inn overflows with turn-of-the-century
charm, and his menu sparkles with full-flavored
enticements. He won us over with skewers of
langoustines and zingy pickled lemons, Gâtinais
rabbit with caramelized eggplant and fabulous
olive fritters, and crunchy nougatine au sésame.
The cellar holds plenty of finds (like Marc
Angeli's white Anjou). C 400. M 215, 360.

CHATOU 78400
Paris 13 - Saint-Germain-en-L. 8 - Le Vésinet 2 Yvelines

11/20 La Maison Fournaise

Ile des Impressionnistes
01 30 71 41 91, fax 01 39 52 84 82
*Closed Sun dinner in winter. Open until 11pm.
Terrace dining. Garage pkg.*
Renoir's famed *Déjeuner des canotiers* features
the charming terrace of this establishment on the
Seine as its backdrop, and while the fairly eclectic, uncomplicated cuisine proffered here could
have a better handle on flavors, it is unfailingly
well presented. Gracious welcome. C 180. M 150,
75 (children).

CHESNAY (LE) 78150
Paris 21 - Versailles 5 - Nanterre 14 Yvelines

 L'Étoile de Mer

Pl. du Nouveau-Marché, 17, rue des Deux-Frères
01 39 54 62 70
*Closed Sat lunch, Sun dinner, Mon, Aug. Open until
9:30pm. Priv rm: 28. Terrace dining. Pkg.*
L'Étoile de Mer's intimate dining room opens
onto the town marketplace. The view features a
crowded lobster tank, and beyond it, the seafood
shop attached to the restaurant. Chef Antoine
Vieira transforms the freshest fish and shellfish
into appetizing assortments and cooked dishes.
You're sure to like his crab soup, octopus à la
portugaise, and mussels marinière. Tiny cellar.
C 140-200. M 85 & 110 (lunch).

COIGNIÈRES 78310
Paris 40 - Versailles 18 - Rambouillet 13 Yvelines

 Auberge d'Angèle

296, route Nationale 10
01 34 61 64 39, fax 01 34 61 94 30
*Closed Sat lunch, Sun dinner, Mon. Open until
9:30pm. Pkg.*
You'd never expect to find such a charming,
half-timbered inn as this one hidden between the

highway and the shopping center jungle here.
The warm interior, brightened by Delft tiles,
overlooks a verdant garden. And the classically
spirited cuisine on offer makes the most of excellent ingredients in a pertinent, exacting manner.
Precise, well-chosen wine list, high on variety. C
270-390. M 147, 180, 60 (children).

COUILLY-PONT-AUX-DAMES 77860
Paris 45 - Coulommiers 19 - Lagny 12 Seine-et-Marne

 Auberge de la Brie

14, av. Alphonse-Boulingre - 01 64 63 51 80
*Closed dinner Sun, Mon, lunch Wed, 3 wks in Aug.
Open until 9:15pm. Terrace dining. Air cond. Pkg.*
Not far from Disneyland Paris, this village has
become a food-lovers' mecca since young Alain
Pavard set up shop in this adorable inn. His
strong suits include generous set-price menus
and a seasonal menu (game, corn crêpes with
pan-roasted foie gras, fricassée of sole with langoustines, French toast brioche with fruit) where
his confirmed talents come into the spotlight. C
400. M 150 (lunch), 180, 230.

COULOMMIERS 77120
Paris 63 - Sens 77 - Meaux 28 - Melun 52 Seine-et-Marne

12/20 Le Clos du Theil

42, rue du Theil - 01 64 65 11 63, fax 01 64 03 54 66
*Closed Mon dinner, Tue, 1 wk in Feb & Aug. Open
until 9:30pm. Terrace dining. Air cond.*
What was once the village grocery store is now
a bright, comfy restaurant where the kindly
owner fills guests' plates to the brim with simple,
fresh, flavorful fare and delicious offerings from
the grill. Nice little wines are on hand to wash
everything down, with some available by the
glass or pitcher. C 180-280. M 75 (exc Sun), 150
(wine incl), 200, 60 (children).

CREIL 60100
Paris 61 - Chantilly 7 Oise

 La Ferme de Vaux

Hameau de Vaux, 11 & 19, route de Vaux
03 44 24 76 76, fax 03 44 26 81 50
*Closed Sun dinner. Open until 9:45pm. Terrace
dining. Pkg.*
This former farmhouse with its inviting stone-
walled dining room plays host to Denis Oudart's
finesse-filled cuisine. His salad of pan-roasted
red mullets brims with wonderful flavor, his
veal kidneys are tender and savory (despite their
bland jus), and the fresh fruit gratin served with
a delicate Champagne sabayon is a scrumptious
way to top off your meal. C 240-400. M 150, 200,
60 (children).

Looking for a city or a locality? Refer to the index.

La Ferme de Vaux

(See restaurant above)
Open year-round. 29 rms 295-345. Bkfst 42. Half-board 430. Rm ser. Conf. Pkg.
Comfortable, well-equipped rooms located in the former farm's outbuildings. Charming welcome.

DAMPIERRE-EN-YVELiNES	78720
Paris 44 - Versailles 18 - Rambouillet 16	Yvelines

12/20 **Auberge Saint-Pierre**

1, rue de Chevreuse
01 30 52 53 53, fax 01 30 52 58 57
Closed Sun dinner, Mon. Open until 10:30pm. Terrace dining. Pkg.
Opposite the château, this rambling, half-timbered inn plays host to a dining room replete with prettily laid, flower-bedecked tables. Chefs Ludovic Toutain and Adriano Séquirra's cooking is fairly classic, as the 140 F set-price menu attests. There are no half-bottles on the somewhat imprecise wine list, but it does mention a variety of excellent aged spirits. Friendly service. C 140, 180.

DISNEYLAND PARIS	77206
Access via A4 - Paris 28 - Meaux 28	Seine-et-Marne

Central reservation telephone number:
01 60 30 60 30.

■ **THE HOTELS
& THEIR RESTAURANTS**

 California Grill

Disneyland Hotel - 01 60 45 65 76, fax 01 60 45 65 33
Open daily until 11pm. Priv rm: 12. Air cond. No pets. Valet pkg.
The "gastronomic" restaurant of the Disneyland Hotel offers West Coast cuisine with some exotic touches based on quality ingredients. Elegant service, and nary a Disney character in sight! C 250. M 195 & 320 (dinner), 110 (children).

 Cheyenne Hotel

Desperado Road - 01 60 45 62 00, fax 01 60 45 62 33
Open year-round. 1,000 rms 450-750. Bkfst 45. Rms for disabled. Restaurant. No pets. Pkg.
Perhaps the most amusing of all the resort's hotels: fourteen separate structures recall the frontier towns of the Far West. It's not luxurious, but the rooms are tidy and spacious. Adults can enjoy tequila and country music in the saloon-restaurant, while kids have a ball on the playground.

 Davy Crockett Ranch

01 60 45 69 00, fax 01 60 45 69 33

Open year-round. 498 rms 400-815. Restaurant. Heated pool. Tennis. No pets. Pkg.
Bungalows equipped for four to six people dot a huge stretch of forest. Kids love the pony rides, and everyone loves the gorgeous pool and the relaxing, holiday atmosphere.

 Disneyland Hotel

01 60 45 65 00, fax 01 60 45 65 33
Open year-round. 18 stes 3,850-18,000. 478 rms 1,700-3,300. Rms for disabled. Restaurant. Rm ser. Air cond. Conf. Heated pool. No pets. Valet pkg.
This enormous candy-pink Victorian pastiche is the *nec plus ultra* of Disneyland Paris hotels. Sumptuous suites, first-class service; but the "pseudo" setting and formal atmosphere are surely not everyone's cup of tea. The rates are simply staggering. Restaurants: California Grill (above) and Restaurant Inventions (below).

10/20 **Hunter's Grill**

Sequoia Lodge, near Lake Buena Vista
01 60 45 53 73 (R), fax 01 60 45 51 33
Dinner only. Open daily until 10pm. Air cond. Pkg.
Delicious charcoal-grilled meats, served up swiftly in a jolly ambience. M 145.

 Newport Bay Club

01 60 45 55 00, fax 01 60 45 55 33
Open year-round. 15 stes 1,900-2,200. 1,082 rms 675-950. Rms for disabled. Restaurant. Air cond. Conf. Heated pool. No pets. Pkg.
Were it not so enormous, the Newport Bay Club would be an almost-convincing facsimile of a summer resort in New England. The rooms are decorated with pretty white wicker furniture. Good value for the money.

 New York Hotel

01 60 45 73 00, fax 01 60 45 73 33
Open year-round. 22 stes 3,000-11,000. 536 rms 1,200. Rms for disabled. Restaurants. Rm ser. Air cond. Conf. Heated pool. Tennis. No pets. Pkg.
Manhattan in the 1930s is the theme, complete with skyscrapers, Wall Street, and Rockefeller Center—there's even an ice-skating rink in winter. The Art Deco guest rooms feature mahogany furniture, king-size beds, and impeccably equipped bathrooms. Among the many amenities are a beauty salon, athletic club, conference center, and two restaurants (Parkside Diner, see above, and the Manhattan Club).

11/20 **Parkside Diner**

New York Hotel - 01 60 45 73 00, fax 01 60 45 73 33
Open daily until 11pm. Air cond. No pets. Garage pkg.
Good, simple American food. The 145 F single-price menu includes options like hamburgers, pasta, poached salmon, grilled steaks, and caloric desserts (cheesecake, banana cream pie). C 150-200. M 95, 145.

Restaurant Inventions

Disneyland Hotel - 01 60 45 65 83, fax 01 60 45 65 33
Open daily until 11pm. Priv rm: 25. Air cond. No pets. Pool. Valet pkg.
The lunch buffet is one of the finest and freshest we've seen. Here's a tip: come to Inventions for an early midday meal that takes less than an hour. Then while other folks stand in line at restaurants and cafeterias inside the park, you can enjoy the rides! M 195 (lunch), 250 (dinner).

 ## Santa Fe Hotel

Near the Pueblos Indian Village
01 60 45 78 00, fax 01 60 45 78 33
Open year-round. 1,000 rms 300-615. Half-board 455-770. Rms for disabled. Restaurant. Air cond. Conf. No pets. Garage pkg.
Forty-two "pueblos" make up an ersatz Indian village, dotted with giant cacti. Given the size of the place, the Santa Fe is inevitably a favorite with group tours. Game rooms for the children.

 ## Sequoia Lodge

Lake Buena Vista - 01 60 45 51 00, fax 01 60 45 51 33
Open year-round. 10 stes 1,800. 1,001 rms 795. Rms for disabled. Restaurant. Air cond. Pool. No pets. Pkg.
Bare stone and rough-hewn wood evoke a Rocky Mountain lodge. The sequoias have yet to reach their majestic maturity, but guests will find plenty of entertainment at the hotel's restaurants, shops, piano bar, and exercise room.

11/20 Yacht Club

Newport Bay Club
01 60 45 55 00, fax 01 60 45 55 33
Closings vary. Open daily until 10pm. Air cond. Pool. No pets. Pkg.
New England clam chowder and grilled Maine lobster are featured in this huge blue dining room, to which a pleasant terrace was recently added. C 180. M 150, 195 (dinner), 55 (children).

■ **THE PARK**

10/20 Auberge de Cendrillon

Fantasyland
01 64 74 24 02, fax 01 64 74 31 93
Open daily until 4:40pm (10pm in summer). Terrace dining. Air cond. No pets. Pkg.
Cinderella presides over this fairytale inn, decorated with portraits of handsome princes, lovely princesses, splendid carriages, and the rest. Offerings include decent foie gras and good beef, but the children's menu lacks appeal and service is interminable. C 213. M 99.

10/20 Blue Lagoon

Adventureland
01 64 74 20 47, fax 01 64 74 38 13
Closed Wed & Tue off-seas. Open until 10pm. Air cond. No pets. Pkg.
Palm trees and a tropical lagoon are the setting for agreeably spicy dishes served by young people dressed up in pirate or West Indian costumes. Nearby are the boats that ferry passengers into the *Pirates of the Caribbean*, one of the park's most popular attractions. M 99-260.

10/20 The Lucky Nugget Saloon

Frontierland - 01 64 74 24 57
Closings vary with the season.
French cancan dancers prance onto the stage several times a day at the Lucky Nugget. Too bad that the chili and chicken wings are so dull! But then, food is not really the attraction here. C 100. M 39 & 79 (lunch), 49 & 129 (dinner).

10/20 Plaza Gardens

Main Street
01 64 74 22 76, fax 01 64 74 27 23
Open daily until 10:30pm. Air cond. Terrace dining. No pets. Pkg.
For a quick, hot meal (grilled salmon, chicken) between trips to Space Mountain and the Temple of Doom. And the best cup of coffee in the park. C 140. M 99, 110, 55 (children).

10/20 Silver Spur Steakhouse

Frontierland
01 64 74 24 56, fax 01 64 74 38 13
Open until 4:30pm (until 10:30pm in summer). Air cond. No pets. Pkg.
Hearty appetites meet their match here, with huge portions of barbecued chicken wings and prime ribs of beef served in a reconstituted Wild West saloon. C 195. M 99, 49 (children).

10/20 Walt's An American Restaurant

Main Street
01 64 74 24 08, fax 01 64 74 38 13
Closed Wed, Thu. Open until 10:30pm. Terrace dining. Air cond. No pets. Pkg.
A stairway decorated with photographs of Walt Disney leads to a series of charming little dining rooms. The best seats are on the upper floor, with a view of the parade route. Cheerful staff. C 140. M 99, 45 (children).

■ **FESTIVAL DISNEY**

11/20 Buffalo Bill's Wild West Show

01 60 45 71 00, fax 01 60 45 71 51
Open daily until 9:30pm. Air cond. No pets. Garage pkg.
As cowboys and Indians perform daredevil stunts, diners chow down on chili, spareribs, and apple crumble in what must be the biggest restaurant in France. M 325 (dinner), 200 (children, dinner).

We're always happy to hear about your discoveries and receive your comments on ours. Please feel free to write to us stating clearly what you liked or disliked. Be concise but convincing, and take the time to argue your point.

12/20 Key West Seafood

01 60 45 70 60, fax 01 60 45 71 33
Open daily until 11pm (midnight). Terrace dining. No pets. Pkg.
Overlooking the (artificial) lake is a huge space decked out to resemble an unpretentious Florida fish house. Like most of the other Festival restaurants, this one is managed by the Flo group. The menu features bistro fare, with the accent on seafood. C 150. M 140 & 175 (dinner, wine incl), 49 (children).

11/20 Los Angeles Bar

01 60 45 71 14, fax 01 60 45 70 55
Open daily until midnight. Terrace dining. Air cond. No pets. Pkg.
Also lakeside is this bright, airy, and modern dining room where you can enjoy good pastas, pizzas, and tiramisù. Warm, friendly "American-style" service. C 160. M 48 (children).

12/20 Steakhouse

01 60 45 70 45, fax 01 60 45 70 55
Open daily until midnight. Air cond. Terrace dining. No pets.
Carpaccio, T-bone steaks, and other beef dishes are the specialty at this Chicago-style steakhouse. C 200. M 198 & 260 (dinner, wine incl), 69 (children).

DREUX   28100
Paris 84 - Chartres 35 - Verneuil 34   Eure-et-Loir

Le Beffroi

12, pl. Métézeau - 02 37 50 02 03, fax 02 37 42 07 69
Open year-round. 16 rms 290-320. Bkfst 27-43. No pets.
Tastefully decorated rooms overlooking the sixteenth-century belfry and the Saint-Pierre church, or the neighboring river.

ECRENNES (LES)   77820
Paris 69 - Melun 17 - Montereau 17   Seine-et-Marne

Auberge Briarde

"Jean et Monique Guichard," on A 5, exit Châtillon
01 60 69 47 32, fax 01 60 66 60 11
Closed dinner Sun & Wed, Jan 1-15, Aug. Open until 9:30pm. Priv rm: 16. Terrace dining.
In autumn gourmets come from miles around for Jean Guichard's special game menus, full of rousing, earthy flavors. But at any time of year it's a treat to settle down by the fireplace in this comfortably rustic dining room and savor Guichard's well-wrought classic cuisine. Remarkable desserts; admirable cellar. Monique Guichard greets guests warmly, but the staff is still wet behind the ears! C 350. M 135 (weekday lunch), 195, 440.

The prices in this guide reflect what establishments were charging at press time.

ENGHIEN-LES-BAINS   95880
Paris 18 - Argenteuil 16 - Chantilly 32   Val-d'Oise

Le Grand Hôtel

85, rue du Gal-de-Gaulle
01 39 34 10 00, fax 01 39 34 10 01
Open year-round. 3 stes 920. 44 rms 650-720. Bkfst 80. Half-board 450-950. Restaurant. Conf.
This lakeside luxury hotel boasts a handsome, wood-paneled lobby (and a single glass elevator). Accommodations are quiet and roomy, but the decoration lacks personality.

ÉTAMPES   91150
Paris 49 - Orléans 66 - Melun 47 - Versailles 54   Essonne

12/20 Auberge de Courpain

At Court-Pain
01 64 95 67 04, fax 01 60 80 99 02
Closed Sun dinner & Mon end Nov-beg Apr. Open until 9pm. Priv rm: 120. Terrace dining. Pkg.
This former coaching inn is just right for business lunches or dinners with its garden abloom with flowers and finely honed cuisine, which makes the best of top-of-the-mark ingredients (lobster, monkfish with morels, etc.). The wine list alone is worth the trip. C 350-450. M 180, 65 (children).

Auberge de Courpain

(See restaurant above)
Open year-round. 3 stes 450-700. 14 rms 300-350. Bkfst 40-70. Half-board 450. Rms for disabled. Restaurant. Rm ser. Conf. Pkg.
This *auberge*, a little jewel left over from the First Empire, couldn't be more charming what with its picturesque tower, pretty garden, and cobbled courtyard. The rooms are done up in rustic style, which makes the site seem all the more authentic. Unfortunately, the stone-cold welcome and noise from the neighboring road are less than entrancing.

EZY-SUR-EURE   27530
Paris 73 - Evreux 38 - Creux 19   Eure

12/20 Maître Corbeau

15, rue Maurice-Élet
02 37 64 73 29, fax 02 37 64 68 98
Closed Tue dinner, Wed, Jan. Open until 9:15pm. Terrace dining. Pkg.
This restaurant located a short distance from the château d'Anet charms guests with a pretty flower-filled garden and prettily laid tables. But the quality of dishes on Bernard Blandeau's classic menu can be inconsistent: a delicious panaché of terrines, but the ginger-vanilla sole and cranberry-studded duck were both served with too-creamy sauces. Offerings among the three desserts on the sampler plate were disappointingly uneven. Friendly welcome; impressive wine cellar. C 250. M 98 (weekdays), 140, 150 (wine incl), 180, 220, 350 (exc Sun).

FERTÉ-SOUS-JOUARRE (LA) 77260
Paris 64 - Meaux 20 - Melun 63   Seine-et-Marne

 ### Auberge de Condé

1, av. de Montmirail
01 60 22 00 07, fax 01 60 22 30 60
Closed Mon dinner, Tue. Open until 9:30pm. Terrace dining. No pets. Air cond. Pkg.
Located smack in the center of town, this pretty, flower-bedecked house with its comfortable dining room usually serves traditional cuisine. But why, on a recent visit, was the foie gras too salty, the leeks overcooked, the desserts insipid? Precise cellar with an impressive offering of Champagnes, but a bit more ordinary as other regions go. The welcome is most courteous. **C** 430-680. **M** 250 (weekdays, wine incl), 330, 450, 125 (children).

Château des Bondons

47-49, rue des Bondons
01 60 22 00 98, fax 01 60 22 97 01
Open year-round. 2 stes 500-900. 7 rms 400-550. Bkfst 60. Restaurant. Rm ser. Conf. Pkg.
A mere twenty minutes from Disneyland Paris, this rambling mansion surrounded by vast green grounds offers guests the ultimate in peace and quiet—along with recently renovated rooms.

FLEURINES 60700
Paris 52 - Senlis 7 - Beauvais 57   Oise

12/20 Le Vieux Logis

105, rue de Paris - 03 44 54 10 13, fax 03 44 54 12 47
Closed Sat lunch, Sun dinner, Mon, Aug 1-15. Open until 9:30pm. Priv rm: 40. Terrace dining. No pets. Pkg.
The Vieux Logis's pretty terrace complements a comfortable dining room brightened by floral bouquets. But Yann Nivet was having an off-night in the kitchen when last we dined here—bland marinated salmon, runny fruit gratin...we know he can do better! Nicely balanced cellar; service with a smile. **C** 330. **M** 140, 180, 250.

FONTAINEBLEAU 77300
Paris 65 - Melun 16 - Nemours 16   Seine-et-Marne

 ### Le Beauharnais

27, pl. Napoléon-Bonaparte
01 60 74 60 00, fax 01 60 74 60 01
Closed Dec 20-30. Open until 10pm. Priv rm: 80. Garden dining. Air cond. Heated pool. Valet pkg.
Rémy Bridon presents inventive, expertly crafted cuisine in a refined yet relaxed setting. We were mighty impressed by his oyster and artichoke millefeuille, lobster and foie gras molded in an aspic spiked with orange juice, turbot "larded" with eggplant strips in a spinach-coriander coulis, and sweetbreads set off by a gingery apple compote. It all adds up to

a couple of well-deserved toques. **C** 380. **M** 180, 320, 450, 80 (children).

 ### Hôtel de l'Aigle Noir

(See restaurant above)
Open year-round. 6 stes 1,050-2,000. 51 rms 790-1,050. Bkfst 90. Half-board 1,460-2,410. Rms for disabled. Rm ser. Air cond. Conf. Heated pool. Valet pkg.
Opposite the château's gardens stands a peaceful, elegant hostelry, with luxurious rooms decorated in Louis XVI, Empire, or Restoration style. Amenities include satellite TV, books in English, a gym, and a sauna; active types can ride horses or use the indoor driving range. Courteous service.

12/20 Le Caveau des Ducs

24, rue de Ferrare - 01 64 22 05 05, fax 01 64 22 05 05
Open daily until 10:30pm. Terrace dining. Air cond. Pkg.
In a series of superbly vaulted, seventeenth-century cellar dining rooms located in the center of Fontainebleau, the chef serves forth cuisine geared to classic tastes: chausson of Burgundy snails flavored with mild garlic, duck breast cooked in cider vinegar and served with caramelized apples, and a delicate warm apple tart flambéed in Calvados for dessert. **C** 280. **M** 98 (weekdays), 169, 175 (wine incl), 230, 70 (children).

Napoléon

9, rue Grande - 01 64 22 20 39, fax 01 64 22 20 87
Closed Dec 21-30. 1 ste 790-990. 56 rms 490-700. Bkfst 60. Half-board 620-780. Restaurant. Rm ser. Conf. Garage pkg.
This beautiful hotel in the town center provides good service, excellent bathrooms, and rooms with every comfort. Note that those facing the courtyard are bigger and quieter.

Victoria

112, rue de France
01 60 74 90 00, fax 01 60 74 90 10
Open year-round. 1 ste 700. 18 rms 250-335. Bkfst 35. Half-board 335-410. Rms for disabled. Restaurant. Rm ser. Garage pkg.
This hotel, currently undergoing a total restoration, features quiet rooms on the gardens. Lots of simple, homey atmosphere (this place is a favorite among anglophone guests on extended stays).

FONTENAY-TRÉSIGNY 77610
Paris 45 - Melun 26 - Coulommiers 23   Seine-et-Marne

 ### Le Manoir

Route de Coulommiers
01 64 25 91 17, fax 01 64 25 95 49
Closed Tue (exc hols). Open until 9pm. Garden dining. Tennis. Pkg.

The warm atmosphere makes guests feel right at home in this Anglo-Norman manor with its pretty veranda overlooking the grounds. And Denis Come's ultraclassic cuisine takes its cue from the finest ingredients worked in an unfailingly precise, refined, and consistent manner. Wonderfully eclectic wine list, and a tempting selection of spirits. Affable welcome. C 350. M 240 (weekdays, Sat lunch, wine incl), 350, 120 (children).

 ## Le Manoir

(See restaurant above)
Open year-round. 4 stes 990-1,190. 15 rms 790-1,060. Bkfst 70. Half-board 790-1,060. Rms for disabled. Rm ser. Conf. Heated pool. Pkg.
This charming manor house set on calm grounds replete with century-old trees offers guests a variety of spacious, inviting rooms decorated in period or contemporary styles. Charming welcome. Relais et Châteaux.

GARANCIÈRES	78890
Paris 52 - Pontchartrain 11 - Monfort-l'A. 8	Yvelines

 ## La Malvina

4, route du Boissard, La Haute-Perruche
01 34 86 45 76, fax 01 34 86 46 11
Closed Wed dinner, Thu, Jan 2-Feb 2. Open until 9:30pm. Terrace dining.
This little village near the forest seems like something straight out of the past, and the charming inn in its midst, surrounded by gardens full of flowers, features a newly decorated dining room done up with plenty of bright, cheerful atmosphere. There's no better setting for sampling Robert Borré's well-honed traditional cuisine. Borré, who spent many a year manning the stoves on ocean liners, works his repertoire with considerable skill. Nice, reasonably priced cellar. C 250. M 95 (weekday lunch), 160, 250.

GAZERAN	78120
Paris 74 - Rambouillet 4 - Versailles 40	Yvelines

12/20 Villa Marinette

20, av. du Gal-de-Gaulle
01 34 83 19 01, fax 01 34 83 19 01
Closed dinner Sun & Tue, Wed, Nov 11-Mar 1. Open until 9pm. Terrace dining. Pkg.
The Villa is a fetching old country house that opens onto a blooming garden. Madame attends to customers, while Monsieur mans the kitchen, producing simple, flavorful dishes based on quality ingredients. M 80 (weekdays, Sat lunch, wine incl), 100, 150, 180 (wine incl), 50 (children).

GOUVIEUX	60270
Paris 43 - Chantilly 9 - Beauvais 43	Oise

 ## Château de la Tour

Chemin de la Chaussée
03 44 57 07 39, fax 03 44 57 31 97

Open year-round. 41 rms 530-930. Bkfst 65. Half-board 505. Rms for disabled. Restaurant. Conf. Heated pool. Pkg.
A certain stateliness pervades this turn-of-the-century dwelling; the accommodations and public rooms are hugely comfortable in a way the French describe as "bourgeois." And there are magnificent grounds to stroll in, as well as a delightful heated pool.

GRESSY	77410
Paris 31 - Meaux 20 - Disneyland Paris 25	Seine-et-Marne

12/20 Le Cellier du Manoir

Chemin des Carosses
01 60 26 68 00, fax 01 60 26 45 46
Open daily until 10pm. Priv rm: 100. Terrace dining. Air cond. Heated pool. Valet pkg.
Guests make their way to the restaurant at the Manoir de Gressy hotel by crossing a number of abundantly decorated lounges. But the sensory overload is well worth the trip: no-nonsense rillettes served with very good bread, pan-roasted grouper fillet (not quite firm enough) with spices and melt-in-your-mouth endives, and delicious frozen nougat with candied apricot. Attractive, nicely diversified wine list. C 280-370. M 140, 160, 280.

 ## Le Manoir de Gressy

(See restaurant above)
Open year-round. 2 stes 1,150-1,250. 88 rms 850. Bkfst 70. Rms for disabled. Restaurant. Air cond. Conf. Heated pool. Tennis. Garage pkg.
Le Manoir, built on the site of a seventeenth-century farm, is an extraordinarily modern hotel complex. Guest quarters are tastefully appointed and impeccably equipped, the welcome is consistently friendly...and it's all just a hop, skip and a jump from Roissy–Charles de Gaulle airport!

HÉROUVILLE	95300
Paris 37 - Poissy 27	Val d'Oise

 ## Les Vignes Rouges

5, pl. de l'Église - 01 34 66 54 73, fax 01 34 66 20 88
Closed Sun dinner, Mon, Jan 1-15, 1 wk in May, Aug. Open until 9pm. Terrace dining.
Chef-owner Marcel Desor is uncompromising when it comes to using only the freshest ingredients, and it shows. His traditional menu is prepared with love and care, and served in bright, serene surroundings. You'll find his garden restaurant in the heart of the village, just opposite the church. C 380. M 174 (weekday lunch), 245.

Looking for a town or restaurant? A winery? A gastronomic specialty or a celebrated chef? Consult the alphabetical index to locate them quickly and easily.

HOUDAN   78550
Paris 62 - Chartres 50 - Rambouillet 29 - Dreux 21   Yvelines

 La Poularde de Houdan

24, av. de la République
01 30 59 60 50, fax 01 30 59 79 71
*Closed Tue dinner, Wed, 2 wks in Feb. Open until
10pm. Terrace dining. No pets. Garage pkg.*
The institution itself, which stands regally
before a garden, plays host to a spacious, light-
filled dining room done up in slightly austere 50s
style. Chef Sylvain Vandenameele uses picture-
perfect ingredients and treats his great bourgeois
culinary classics with the respect and precision.
The wine list is somewhat limited and lacking in
verve. Efficient welcome. C 300. M 150, 250, 100
(children).

LAMORLAYE   60260
Paris 43 - Chantilly 5 - Beauvais 64   Oise

 Hostellerie du Lys 🌲🍴

In Lys-Chantilly, 63, 7e-Avenue
03 44 21 26 19, fax 03 44 21 28 19
*Open year-round. 30 rms 250-400. Bkfst 43. Half-
board 400-560. Rms for disabled. Restaurant. Rm
ser. Conf. Pkg.*
This opulent country inn, situated in large,
lush grounds, provides comfortable rooms in a
friendly, restful atmosphere. Tennis courts, and
golf course are within easy reach.

MAISONS-LAFFITTE   78600
Paris 21 - Pontoise 18 - St-Germain-en-L. 8   Yvelines

👨‍🍳 **Le Tastevin**

9, av. d'Eglé - 01 39 62 11 67, fax 01 39 62 73 09
*Closed Mon dinner, Tue, Aug 16-Sep 9. Open until
10pm. Priv rm: 25. Garden dining. Pkg.*
Michel Blanchet's patrons are nothing if not
faithful (no, that's not quite true: they are also—
necessarily—rich). They keep piling in to enjoy
the classic yet also contemporay bill of fare:
monkfish with greens lentils, sole and langoustines with pickled vegetables in coriander.
Amélie Blanchet is a gracious hostess, the service
is admirably precise, and the wine list qualifies
as a masterwork. Did we mention that the prices
are incredibly steep? C 380-800. M 230 (weekday
lunch).

👨‍🍳 **La Rôtisserie
de la Vieille Fontaine**

8, av. Grétry - 01 39 62 01 78, fax 01 39 62 13 43
*Closed Mon, 2 wks in Aug. Open until 10:30pm.
Garden dining.*
A cordial welcome and flawless service get
things off to a promising start, and the setting (a
Second Empire villa and garden) is as lovely as
can be. Delicious food, but oddly the dishes
don't always reflect what's announced on the
menu. Never mind. Try the sardine and ricotta
fritters in curry sauce, tender pork shank in a

spicy crust, and mellow chocolate moelleux.
And don't miss the Saint-Estèphe Château de
Bez '90—it's superb! M 172.

MANTES-LA-JOLIE   78200
Paris 60 - Évreux 44 - Rouen 81 - Versailles 44   Yvelines

 La Galiote

18, quai des Cordeliers or 1, rue du Fort
01 34 77 03 02, fax 01 34 77 07 90
*Closed dinner Sun & Mon. Open until 10pm. Priv
rm: 25. Pkg.*
Located opposite the picturesque "Port au
prêtre" which dates from the fifteenth century,
this cold-looking establishment seems barren
and austere at first. But the owner quickly warms
guests' hearts and the cuisine proffered by
Michel Perron, an apostle of the sweet-and-salty
school, does the same for taste buds. The warm
foie gras (which was slightly cool by the time it
reached us) is of the melt-in-your-mouth variety,
and the spiced Challans duck came bathed in a
delicious raspberry jus. Wonderful homemade
caramel ice cream. C 370-420. M 175, 300, 365
(wine incl).

MARLY-LE-ROI   78160
Paris 25 - Versailles 9 - St-Germain-en-L. 4   Yvelines

👨‍🍳 **Le Village**

3, Grande-Rue - 01 39 16 28 14, fax 01 39 58 62 60
Closed Sat lunch, Sun dinner, 3 wks in Aug. Pkg.
The dining room of this exquisite seventeenth-
century house is decorated with charming frescoes, a splendid stage for Éric Poutet's inventive
and polished cooking. Desserts are more adventurous, and the cellar seems a mite overpriced.
You can expect a smiling welcome and swift
service. C 200. M 130 (weekday lunch, wine incl),
250, 80 (children).

MELUN   77000
Paris 55 - Meaux 57 - Sens 66 - Orléans 104   Seine-et-Marne

👨‍🍳 **La Melunoise**

5, rue du Gâtinais - 01 64 39 68 27
*Closed Sat, dinner Sun & Mon, Feb school hols, Aug.
Open until 9:15pm.*
Claude and Michel Hinaut's short repertoire
has lost its Nordic accent in favor of traditional
favorites from the Landes and Provence regions.
And we have nary a bone to pick with them on
this front, because their hand remains steady,
their cooking exact, and their flavors as clean and
clear as ever. In addition, a number of their
ingredients are homemade. The cellar is well
stocked with Bordeaux and the décor is warm in
this quaint, flower-bedecked establishment. C
220. M 139, 269, 75 (children).

*The ratings are based solely on the restaurants
cuisine. We do not take into account the atmosphere, décor, service, and so on; these are commented upon within the review.*

MESNULS (LES)	78490
Paris 44 - Versailles 24 - Rambouillet 17	Yvelines

13 La Toque Blanche

12, Grande-Rue
01 34 86 05 55, fax 01 34 86 82 18
Closed Sun dinner, Mon, Aug, 1 wk at Christmas. Open until 10pm. Garden dining. Pkg.
Jean-Pierre Philippe, a sturdy son of Brittany, favors lightened versions of French culinary classics. He imports excellent seafood from his native province but doesn't neglect dishes to please landlubbers: try his sea bream with a brightly flavored fennel garnish or the truffled paupiette of Bresse chicken. Starters and desserts, curiously, are a tone below the rest. C 400-500. M 380.

MONTGRÉSIN	60560
Paris 45 - Chantilly 5 - Beauvais 44	Oise

12/20 Relais d'Aumale

37, pl. des Fêtes - 03 44 54 61 31, fax 03 44 54 69 15
Closed Dec 21-28. Open until 10pm. Garden dining. Tennis. Pkg.
When the weather is fine, you can enjoy the sky and trees as your outdoor dining canopy at this restaurant's forest glade location. Good curried lobster ravioli, beef fillet with a meagerly peppered sauce but an out-of-this-world potato galette, and an impeccable chocolate feuillantine. Let the expert maître d' guide you through the extensive offerings in the cellar. C 280-400. M 190 (lunch, exc Sun), 220 (dinne & Sun), 100 (children).

 Relais d'Aumale

(See restaurant above)
Open year-round. 2 stes 700-950. 22 rms 480-620. Bkfst 48. Half-board 480-720. Rms for disabled. Conf. Tennis. Pkg.
The forest primeval surrounds this inviting old hunting lodge boasting sunny, cheerful rooms done up on a modern note. All rooms are exceedingly well equipped.

MONTMORENCY	95160
Paris 18 - Pontoise 20 - Enghien 3	Val-d'Oise

12/20 Au Cœur de la Forêt

Av. du Repos-de-Diane - 01 39 64 99 19
Closed Thu, dinner Sun & Mon, 10 days in Feb, Aug 16-Sep 7. Open until 9:30pm. Priv rm: 30. Terrace dining. Pkg.
Next time you go walking in the Montmorency forest, ferret around until you find this establishment hidden among the trees. You'll enjoy the family atmosphere and the nicely crafted, seasonal cuisine. Interesting selection of Bordeaux. C 280-400. M 130, 190, 80 (children).

MORET-SUR-LOING	77250
Paris 75 - Fontainebleau 10 - Nemours 17	Seine-et-Marne

12/20 Auberge de la Palette

10, av. Jean-Jaurès - 01 60 70 50 72
Closed Tue lunch, Wed, 10 days in Jan, 10 days at Easter, 2 wks mid Aug. Open until 9:15pm. Terrace dining.
Perched on the banks of the Loing River, medieval Moret was a popular site with Impressionist painters. Today, Jean-Louis Binoche's robust cuisine draws hearty appetites to this country setting. They're especially fond of the 175 F set-price menu which features a duo of fresh fish, saddle of hare, magnificent cheese tray, and choice of desserts. Splendid cellar. C 250-300. M 175 (weekday lunch, wine incl), 169, 254, 80 (children).

MORIGNY-CHAMPIGNY	91150
Paris 53 - Étampes 3 - Évry 40	Essonne

Hostellerie de Villemartin 🌲🌷

1, allée des Marronniers
01 64 94 63 54, fax 01 64 94 24 68
Closed Sun (exc hols), Mon, Aug 5-20. 14 rms 310-490. Bkfst 47. Half-board 495. Restaurant. Rm ser. Conf. Pkg.
This turn-of-the-century bourgeois house is set just behind a magnificent fortified farm dating from the sixteenth century. Rooms here are spacious and tastefully decorated for the most part. They all overlook the bucolic splendor of the vast estate surrounding the establishment.

NEMOURS	77140
Paris 79 - Orléans 87 - Fontainebleau 17	Seine-et-Marne

12/20 L'Écu de France

3, rue de Paris - 01 64 28 11 54, fax 01 64 45 03 65
Open daily until 10pm. HOTEL: 24 rms 139-259. Bkfst 28. Half-board 220-345. Rm ser. Conf. Pkg.
L'Écu de France is the kind of nice little provincial restaurant that focuses on solid, serious, traditional fare. Maître d' Camille has been watching over his guests for 38 years now! And father and son share behind-the-stove duties day in and day out, in true family spirit. C 250. M 96, 146, 180, 260.

ORSAY	91400
Paris 27 - Versailles 20 - Évry 24	Essonne

14 Le Boudin Sauvage

6, rue de Versailles - 01 69 28 42 93
Closed Sat, Sun, Wed dinner, 3 wks in Aug, at Christmas-New Year's. Open until 10:30pm. Terrace dining.
Just ten minutes from the Pont de Sèvres in the concrete suburban wilderness, this pretty nineteenth-century house with its warm, cozy interior and pink-stone terrace bordering a gar-

den is a haven of charm and tranquility. Anne-Marie de Gennes welcome guests and cultivate a friendly atmosphere, while chef Maria Mereira's womanly culinary talents work wonders in the kitchen, starting with *crème de la crème* ingredients. Very impressive choice of Loire wines. C 285-400. M 285 (lunch, wine & coffee incl), 450 (dinner).

OSNY
95520
Paris 27 - Cergy-Pontoise 1 - Poissy 19   Val-d'Oise

 Moulin de la Renardière

Rue du Grand-Moulin
01 30 30 21 13, fax 01 34 25 04 98
Closed Sun dinner, Mon. Open until 9:15pm (9:30pm in summer). Priv rm: 40. Terrace dining. Pkg.
Jean-Louis Ganier takes justifiable pride in his adorable millhouse, recently embellished with a terrace and bower. On fine days you can sit there by the river and relish Ganier's deft, traditional cooking sparked with touches of whimsy. Well-composed wine list. M 169.

POISSY
78300
Paris 26 - Pontoise 17 - Mantes-la-Jolie 29   Yvelines

12/20 Le Bon Vivant

30, av. Émile-Zola - 01 39 65 02 14
Closed Sun dinner, Mon, 1 wk in Feb, Aug. Open until 9:30m. Terrace dining. Pkg.
Generous, classic cooking is the hallmark of Le Bon Vivant's single-price menu. The John Dory with meadow mushrooms and pavé au chocolat in particular rate kudos. Prices are reasonable on the whole. Jolly welcome and service. In summer, ask for a terrace table by the Seine. M 180.

 L'Esturgeon

6, cours du 14-Juillet - 01 39 65 00 04
Closed Thu, Aug. Open until 9:30pm (10pm in summer). Pkg.
A real pro is in the kitchen of this *guinguette* where Impressionists once gathered; he turns out traditional dishes based on top-notch fixings. A lovely view of the Seine may take your mind off the dithery service. C 250-320.

PONTAULT-COMBAULT
77340
Paris 26 - Melun 29 - Coulommiers 41   Seine-et-Marne

 Saphir Hôtel

Aire des Berchères
01 64 43 45 47, fax 01 64 40 52 43
Open year-round. 20 stes 595-870. 160 rms 400-530. Bkfst 52. Half-board 485-870. Rms for disabled. Restaurant. Rm scr. Air cond. Conf. Heated pool. Tennis. Pkg.
A hotel of recent vintage close to Disneyland. Rooms are airy, pleasant, and well equipped. Facilities include conference rooms, sauna, and a superb indoor swimming pool. Grill.

PONTOISE
95300
Paris 34 - Beauvais 55 - Rouen 91 - Mantes 39   Val-d'Oise

12/20 Auberge du Chou

4, route d'Auvers - 01 30 38 03 68
Closed Tue, dinner Sun & Mon. Open until 9:30pm (10:30pm in summer). Terrace dining. No pets. Pkg.
The leafy, flower-decked terrace of this inn on the Oise is lovely indeed. The kitchen does honor to the surroundings with a traditional roster of well-crafted, handsomely presented dishes. Wide-ranging cellar; charming service. C 180-200. M 150, 175, 75 (children).

PORT-MARLY (LE)
78560
Paris 21 - Versailles 10 - Louveciennes 3   Yvelines

12/20 Auberge du Relais Breton

27, rue de Paris - 01 39 58 64 33, fax 01 39 58 35 75
Closed Sun dinner, Mon, Aug. Open until 10pm. Garden dining. Pkg.
The décor isn't up to much and the sauces are way too rich and creamy, but among the Auberge's many assets are a genuinely warm welcome and good food served in gargantuan portions. The 229 F set meal brings an appetizer of smoked duck and avocado, sole stuffed with morels, a salad topped with warm chèvre, and vanilla-scented berry gratin—your apéritif, wine, and coffee come at no extra charge! C 250-300. M 159, 229 (wine & coffee incl).

POUILLY-LE-FORT
77240
Paris 55 - Melun 4 - Meaux 52   Seine-et-Marne

 Le Pouilly

1, rue de la Fontaine - 01 64 09 56 64
Closed Sun dinner, Mon, Aug 11-31, Dec 23-30. Open until 9:45pm. Terrace dining. Pkg.
This beautifully restored farm is replete with sensory delights: a crackling fire in the monumental hearth, prettily laid tables, an excellent menu, and elaborate but unfailingly light cuisine. The fish dishes rival one another in their ingenious approaches, and the judiciously prepared sauces don't overpower the top-notch ingredients they're paired with. Our favorites: sole beurre marinière, John Dory, and the pan-roasted lamb shoulder and sweetbreads. There's a sumptuous cheese tray, variety of homebaked breads, and post-meal sweets guaranteed to send you straight to seventh heaven. Two toques for chef-in-residence Didier Cadiet. C 400. M 185 (weekdays), 225, 380, 100 (children).

PROVINS
77160
Paris 85 - Sens 47 - Fontainebleau 53   Seine-et-Marne

11/20 Le Petit Écu

9, pl. du Châtel - 01 60 67 62 22, fax 01 60 67 77 22

Closed Jan-mid Feb. Open daily until 9:30pm. Terrace dining.
Good things come in small packages! This tiny, simple restaurant is housed in a pretty medieval dwelling. Tuck into curly endive salad with savory bacon bits, confit of duck with sorrel, and a feather-light île flottante. A smiling welcome, and the check is guaranteed to make you smile back! C 120. M 65 & 74 (weekdays), 100 (exc weekdays), 115 (weekdays), 38 (children).

12/20 Quat' Saisons
44, rue du Val - 01 64 08 99 44
Closed Sun dinner, Mon, Jan 10-22. Open until 9pm. Terrace dining.
This restaurant's favorite season has to be spring, given its spacious garden-inspired décor. And the unpretentious but carefully refined cuisine on offer is crafted from the freshest ingredients available. Short list of regional wines. Attentive welcome. C 160. M 96, 32 (children).

12/20 Aux Vieux Remparts
3, rue Couverte - 01 64 08 94 00, fax 01 60 67 77 22
Open daily until 9:30pm. Terrace dining. Garage pkg.
Handsome paneled walls, tiled floors, exposed beams, and white tablecloths prevail in this oasis of quiet in the center of the old town. Apart from the Landes foie gras, other out-of-the-ordinary house specialties include freshwater pike and braised salmon trout. Don't miss the matured Bries, served with nut-studded bread and a nicely seasoned salad. C 370. M 150 (weekdays), 175 5Sat & Sun), 350, 430, 90 (children).

Aux Vieux Remparts ♨♣
(See restaurant above)
Open year-round. 25 rms 340-650. Bkfst 50-70. Half-board 420-765. Rms for disabled. Restaurant. Rm ser. Rms for disabled. Pkg.
A more modern building plays host to the hotel, with views on the town's rooftops and ramparts. The rooms are small, but they're cozy, bright, and impeccably kept. Friendly welcome and attentive service.

ROCHEFORT-EN-YVELINES   78730
Paris 50 - Chartres 42 - Étampes 26   Yvelines

L'Escu de Rohan
15, rue Guy-le-Rouge - 01 30 41 31 33
Closed Sun dinner & Mon (exc hols). Open until 9:30pm. Pkg.
It's a pity the checks are so steep, because we'd like nothing better than to settle in more often here after our walks around the charming village. This former coaching inn is done up with a bright, harmonious décor, and Jean Chevrier, the lord of the manor, is a wonderfully attentive host. His new chef, Frédric Cauchye, works the best ingredients with prowess, turning out personalized versions of traditional fare. Nice little cellar. C 350. M 120-390.

ROLLEBOISE   78270
Paris 70 - Versailles 53 - Évreux 37 - Mantes 9   Yvelines

Château de la Corniche ♨♣
5, route de la Corniche
01 30 93 21 24, fax 01 30 42 27 44
Closed Mon off-seas, Sun (exc Easter), Dec 20-Jan 7. 35 rms 300-750. Bkfst 50-60. Half-board 460-800. Restaurant. Conf. Heated pool. Tennis. Pkg.
This château once belonged to Léopold II. The rooms within are personalized, spacious, and well equipped, and a temple of love and a splendid panoramic view of the Seine await you in the garden.

SAINT-GERMAIN-EN-LAYE   78100
Paris 21 - Chartres 81 - Dreux 70   Yvelines

11/20 Brasserie du Théâtre
Pl. du Château - 01 30 61 28 00, fax 01 39 73 98 73
Closed at Christmas. Open until 1am. Air cond. Terrace dining. Garage pkg.
Conveniently sited opposite the château, this 1930s–vintage brasserie provides solid sustenance at nearly any time of the day, just about every day of the year. C 190-360.

Cazaudehore
1, av. du Président-Kennedy - 01 34 51 93 80 (R) 01 39 73 36 60 (H), fax 01 39 73 73 88
Closed Mon (exc hols). Open until 10pm. Garden dining. Pkg.
On the edge of the forest in a setting of lawns and flowers sits this charming establishment decorated with old prints and English chintzes; for summer dining, there's a huge terrace that looks out over the trees. A few Mediterranean touches now grace Philippe Pactol's menu, but for the most part it remains dedicated to pricey French classics and rich Southwestern dishes, all ably handled. Superb cellar, stylish service. C 450. M 190 & 290 (weekday lunch, wine incl), 360 (Sat, Sun, wine incl), 130.

La Forestière ♨♣
(See restaurant above)
Open year-round. 5 stes 1,350. 25 rms 750-930. Bkfst 75. Restaurant. Conf. Heated pool. Tennis. Pkg.
Rooms and suites decorated with exquisite refinement, each in an individual style. The forest is close at hand, and is even directly accessible from some of the suites. Guests can count on a warm, attentive welcome. Relais et Châteaux.

11/20 La Feuillantine
10, rue des Louviers - 01 34 51 04 24
Open until 10pm (Sat & Sun 10:30pm). Terrace dining.
You'll be charmingly received into this bright, cozy restaurant (it's a popular spot, so remember to book ahead). Save for a flavorless Barbary duck, we have no complaints about the good

salmon crêpe, choucroute garnie with seafood, or cold apple dessert laced with Calavados. Extensively annotated wine list. C 130. M 75 & 85 (weekday lunch), 130.

 Le Pavillon Henri IV

21, rue Thiers
01 39 10 15 15, fax 01 39 73 93 73
Open daily until 10:30pm. Terrace dining. Air cond. Pkg.

With its terrific view of just a bit of the Eiffel Tower, this place where the Sun King was born caters to a distinguished clientele which appreciates the first-class ingredients of this very classic cuisine: warm oysters in Champagne sauce, perfectly cooked sea scallops, generous gratin of lobster. The wine cellar could be improved. C 350-450. M 240 (weekday lunch), 265, 320, 400.

 Le Pavillon Henri IV

(See restaurant above)
Open year-round. 3 stes 1,900. 42 rms 400-1,300. Bkfst 50-100. Half-board 670-870. Rms for disabled. Restaurant. Rm ser. Conf. Golf. Pkg.

This is where Louis XIV was born, Alexandre Dumas wrote *The Three Musketeers,* and Offenbach composed a number of operettas. We don't find the somber blue-gray furnishings very inspiring, but the 45 rooms and suites are huge and airy. The public rooms are magnificent and there's a splendid view over the extensive grounds.

SAINT-LAMBERT-DES-BOIS	78470
Paris 34 - Rambouillet 22 - Versailles 16	Yvelines

 Les Hauts de Port-Royal

2, rue de Vaumurier
01 30 44 10 21, fax 01 30 64 44 10
Closed Sun dinner, Mon, Aug 15-30. Open until 9:30pm. Terrace dining. Pkg.

Located in the middle of the forest, just a stone's throw from the abbey, the charming, restful, ochre-colored dining room here provides the ideal setting for lovers of inventive cuisine. Sweet-and-sour fans will surely appreciated the honey-lacquered suprême of squab and pears with spices, and the tart and tangy Chinon sauce in the lamb dish. The decidedly unfresh red mullets and scalding soufflé were less enticing though, and the welcome, service and timing could be better. C 350. M 150 (exc Sat dinner), 250, 120 (children).

SAINT-LÉGER-EN-YVELINES	78610
Paris 50 - Monfort-l'Amaury 8 - Rambouillet 11	Yvelines

12/20 La Belle Aventure

8, rue de la Croix-Blanche
01 34 86 31 35, fax 01 34 86 36 85
Closed Feb school hols, 3 wks in Aug. Open until 10pm. Priv rm: 40. Terrace dining. HOTEL: 2 stes

500-580. 6 rms 350. Bkfst 70. Rm ser. Conf. Tennis. Garage pkg.

A pretty village and quiet garden surround this charming thatched-roof inn with a spacious, country-style dining room—just right for a romantic getaway! Tomohiro Uido serves forth a short repertoire in the contemporary vein, based on fresh ingredients, an interesting approach, and painstaking preparation. The wine list is imprecise, and not all that appealing. Gracious welcome and friendly, competent service. C 330-440. M 159.

SAINT-SYMPHORIEN-LE-CHÂTEAU	28700
Paris 69 - Rambouillet 23 - Chartres 26	Eure-et-Loir

 Château d'Esclimont

02 37 31 15 15, fax 02 37 31 57 91
Open daily until 9:30pm. Terrace dining. Priv rm: 200. No pets. Valet pkg.

"It is my pleasure" is the motto that the Duc de La Rochefoucauld had sculpted above the entrance to this ravishing Renaissance château. Our pleasure, as we sit beneath the high ceilings of these comfortable dining rooms, is to savor Éric Douvry's delectable sweetbread salad dressed with truffle vinaigrette, move on to suckling pig cooked three ways, then conclude with spiced mangoes and coconut ice cream. All this deliciousness is served with style, and can be accompanied by superb (and awfully expensive) wines. C 400-480. M 260 (lunch exc Sun, wine incl), 320, 495.

 Château d'Esclimont

(See restaurant above)
Open year-round. 6 stes 2,800. 47 rms 600-1,850. Bkfst 85-170. Half-board 730-1,330. Rm ser. Conf. Heated pool. Tennis. Valet pkg.

The 47 rooms and 6 suites of this château are classic, comfortable, and handsomely situated amid 150 acres of enclosed grounds. The site is at the bottom of a valley traversed by a river, near the road that connects Rambouillet and Chartres. Guests can play tennis, swim in the heated pool, and attend wintertime musical evenings. Perfect for a luxurious, romantic weekend, and only 45 minutes from Paris by car. There's even a helipad. Relais et Châteaux, of course.

STE-GEMME-MORONVAL	28500
Paris 72 - Dreux 6 - Chartres 41	Eure-et-Loir

 L'Escapade

02 37 43 72 05, fax 02 37 43 86 96
Closed dinner Sun & Mon, Tue, Feb 8-Mar 5, Jul 15-Aug 7. Open until 9:30pm. Air cond. Pkg.

Paul Gomes's seriously good cooking is no mere escapade! Tuck into his sublime marinated, dill-flecked salmon, veal sweetbreads with morels, sautéed lobster with morels, and the raspberry soufflé for dessert. The Figeacs and Bourgueils in the appreciable cellar make mealtime in the Empire-style dining room all the more splendid. A charming welcome from Lúcia. C 300. M 135 (weekday lunch), 170.

SAMOREAU 77210
Paris 68 - Melun 16 - Fontainebleau 7   Seine-et-Marne

 ## La Tour de Samoiselle

2, voie de la Liberté - 01 64 23 93 31
Closed Sun dinner, Mon, Feb school hols, 2 wks in Sep. Open until 9:30pm. Terrace dining. Pkg.
The freshest ingredients, evident skill with an eye for detail, and an imaginative way with fish: these are Patrice Emery's assets in his charming old mansion set in an airy garden not far from the Seine. The dining room plays host to curious tourists, weekend pilgrims from Paris, and foreigners there to visit the château at Fontainebleau. Tuck into a scrumptious saddle of hare salad, melt-in-your-mouth homemade foie gras, turbot sprinkled with almonds, and a berry sabayon for dessert. Wonderful dessert menu, and fromage blanc served by the ladle, just like at your French grandma's house! C 280. M 142, 198.

SANCY 77580
Paris 57 - Meaux 12 - Melun 52   Seine-et-Marne

 ## Demeure de la Catounière

1, pl. de l'Église - 01 60 25 71 74, fax 01 60 25 60 55
Closed 2 wks at Christmas. 22 rms 360-400. Bkfst 80. Half-board 540-590. Restaurant. Conf. Pool. Tennis. Pkg.
This seventeenth-century country estate is located in a picturesque village, and offers guests well-equipped rooms with a view on the manicured grounds.

SENLIS 60300
Paris 50 - Compiègne 35 - Soissons 60 - Lille 172   Oise

10/20 La Mitonnée

93, rue du Moulin-Saint-Tron
03 44 53 10 05, fax 03 44 53 13 99
Closed Sun dinner, Mon. Open until 9:30pm. Pkg.
This country inn has something new on the menu: the recipes for the dishes you're about to sample! Tuck into the sweetbread terrine with foie gras, fillet of sole stew, and hazelnut truffier, all served with a healthy dose of charm. C 250. M 150, 210, 65 (children).

12/20 Le Scaramouche

4, pl. Notre-Dame - 03 44 53 16 87
Closed Wed, 1 wk at Feb school hols, 1 wk in Aug. Open until 9:30pm. Terrace dining. Pkg.
Practically next door to the cathedral, Scaramouche serves honest cooking with its roots in the Picardy *terroir*: goat cheese with Belgian endive, guinea hen à la picarde, fudgy chocolate cake. C 260. M 145, 190, 320, 60 (children).

THOMERY 77810
Paris 73 - Melun 21 - Fontainebleau 12   Seine-et-Marne

 ## Le Vieux Logis

5, rue Sadi-Carnot
01 60 96 44 77, fax 01 60 70 01 42
Open daily until 9:30pm. Garden dining. Heated pool. Tennis. Garage pkg.
The success of Le Vieux Logis stems from a team effort that starts with the way guests are greeted and extends through to the way food is cooked. Madame Plouvier rules the roost here with an iron hand in a velvet glove, and the 145 F price of the short set menu is a real *tour de force*, especially in such a refined setting. Indulge in the wonderful fish and precisely prepared garden vegetables. This is one of those restaurants that's well worth the trip from Moret-sur-Loing or Fontainebleau. The desserts are inventive, and the cellar, presided over by Monsieur Plouvier, is a reasonably priced work in progress. C 300. M 145 (exc Sun), 240.

 ## Le Vieux Logis

(See restaurant above)
Open year-round. 14 rms 400. Bkfst 50. Half-board 560. Rm ser. No pets. Conf. Heated pool. Tennis. Garage pkg.
This establishment, located in a peaceful little village renowned for its twelfth-century church, offers sunny rooms, bountiful breakfasts, and great prices. If you're tired (or just in love!), you can dine by candlelight right in your room.

TREMBLAY-SUR-MAULDRE (LE) 78490
Paris (Pte de St-Cloud) 42 - Versailles 20   Yvelines

 ## L'Astrée

Pl. de l'Église - 01 34 87 92 92, fax 01 34 87 86 27
Closed Sun dinner, Mon, Jul 15-Aug 15, 1 wk at Christmas. Open until 9:30pm. Garden dining. Pkg.
Jean-Pierre Bouchereau finally took total restoration of this pretty château—a popular site for weddings, seminars, and weekend getaways—in hand. And now he's happily ensconced behind his stoves, whipping up his celebrated sauces (he's especially gifted for the fish variety). His saffron-laced lobster and sole aumônière features clear, delicate flavors, and his turbot with cabbage and mussels is cooked to perfection. Even though its offerings tend to be costly, the cellar is exceedingly rich–especially in half-bottles. The service could be a tad warmer. C 250. M 190.

Château-Hôtel Golf du Tremblay

(See restaurant above)
Closed Jul 15-Aug 15. 30 rms 550-1,300. Bkfst 50. Rm ser. Conf. Tennis. Golf. Pkg.
This Louis XIII château set on 100 acres of land features rooms of varying sizes, some with their own fireplaces, and all with period-style furni-

ture and top-notch equipment. View on the golf course or the French-style gardens.

VERSAILLES	78000
Paris 23 - Mantes 44 - Rambouillet 31	Yvelines

 Bellevue Hôtel

12, av. de Sceaux - 01 39 50 13 41, fax 01 39 02 05 67
Open year-round. 3 stes 450-550. 24 rms 270-450. No pets. Pkg.
The Bellevue's Louis XV/XVI–style rooms are soundproofed and well equipped but a trifle old-fashioned, despite a recent remodeling. Located near the château and conference center.

11/20 **Brasserie du Théâtre**

15, rue des Réservoirs - 01 39 50 03 21
Open daily until 1am. Terrace dining.
Classic brasserie food (fresh shellfish, pepper steak, cassoulet), served in a supremely Gallic décor of mirrors, glowing woodwork, and leather banquettes. C 160.

 Brasserie La Fontaine

Trianon Palace, 1, bd de la Reine
01 30 84 38 47
Open daily until 10:30pm. Air cond. Valet pkg.
This brasserie annex of the famed Trois Marches (see below) bears the visible stamp of master chef Gérard Vié. He oversees an enticing menu that features marinated mushrooms with an unctuous purée of olives and tuna, roast lobster, and a suave (but stingily served) chocolate-pistachio tart. The superb old-fashioned décor is accented with a series of amusing animal portraits. C 230. M 165, 75 (children).

12/20 **La Flotille**

Parc du Château - 01 39 51 41 58
Open daily for lunch only. Terrace dining. Pkg.
How delightful! A restaurant with a lovely terrace planted in the grounds of the château, just steps away from the boat stand. And a kitchen that acquits itself more than respectably, with assorted Southwestern appetizers, beef tenderloin au poivre, and a yummy cherry cake (all the desserts are tempting). The escargots with oyster mushrooms (served *sans* mushrooms) are skippable. Bare-bones cellar, but the monthly wine specials merit your notice. C 190. M 132 (lunch), 45 (children).

 Home Saint-Louis

28, rue St-Louis - 01 39 50 23 55, fax 01 30 21 62 45
Open year-round. 25 rms 220-320. Bkfst 30.
Quiet, pleasant rooms close to the château.

 La Marée de Versailles

22, rue au Pain - 01 30 21 73 73, fax 01 39 50 55 87
Closed Mon dinner, Sun, Dec 23-Jan 1, Aug 4-26. Open until 10:15pm. Air cond. V.
This shipshape little establishment serves sparkling fresh and handily prepared seafood. Don't

miss the generous "all-shellfish" set menu. Skilled, stylish service. C 190. M 260.

11/20 **Le Mille et Une Nuits**

5, passage Saint-Pierre - 01 30 21 91 05
Closed Mon, Aug. Open until 10:30pm (Sat & Sun 11:30pm). Priv rm: 20. Pkg.
White arches and a fountain compose a fantasy setting, where you can indulge in adroitly turned out Moroccan classics. Tiny cellar of Mediterranean wines. C 170-250. M 85 (weekday lunch, Sat).

 Le Potager du Roy

1, rue du Mal-Joffre
01 39 50 35 34, fax 01 30 21 69 30
Closed Sun dinner, Mon. Open until 10:30pm. Priv rm: 20. Air cond.
The set meal will pique your appetite, with a soup of mussels and cockles with white beans, a sparky combination of skate and potatoes dressed with capers and lemon, and a smooth guanaja-chocolate dessert (we'd have liked a bit more of that last). Choosing from the *carte* we encountered bitter oysters and a minuscule portion of scallops, as well as some splendid vegetable dishes. Expensive. The cellar spotlights wines from the Loire. C 290-420. M 165.

 Le Quai n°1

1, av. de St-Cloud - 01 39 50 42 26, fax 01 39 51 15 45
Closed Sun dinner, Mon. Open until 11pm. Priv rm: 35. Terrace dining. Air cond.
A dependable address for fresh shellfish and decent seafood dishes at reasonable prices. Among the better offerings are a spicy fish soup, a refreshing salad of whelks with mayonnaise, and plaice in a sauce enriched with meat jus. Amusing nautical décor; casual service. One toque for encouragement's sake. C 220. M 120, 160.

 Richaud

16, rue Richaud - 01 39 50 10 42, fax 01 39 53 43 36
Open year-round. 39 rms 220-360. Bkfst 30. Garage pkg.
A classic hotel in the center of Versailles, close to the antique dealers. The rooms were all recently modernized and renovated.

11/20 **Rôtisserie Ballester**

30 bis, rue des Réservoirs
01 39 50 70 02, fax 01 39 02 24 84
Open daily until 10:30pm. Terrace dining.
Brasserie fare at real brasserie prices (starters for 45 F, main dishes for 65 F and 90 F). Decent cellar. C 170-210. M 138 (exc weekday lunch), 95 (lunch).

 Sofitel

2 bis, av. Paris - 01 39 53 30 31, fax 01 39 53 87 20
Open year-round. 6 stes 1,400. 146 rms 900. Bkfst 80. Rms for disabled. Restaurant. Rm ser. Air cond. Valet pkg.

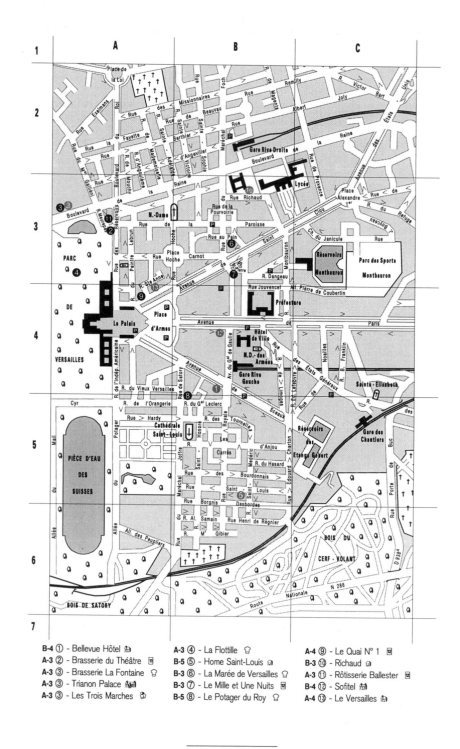

B-4 ① - Bellevue Hôtel 🏨
A-3 ② - Brasserie du Théâtre 🍽
A-3 ③ - Brasserie La Fontaine ♀
A-3 ③ - Trianon Palace 🏨
A-3 ③ - Les Trois Marches 🍽

A-3 ④ - La Flottille ♀
B-5 ⑤ - Home Saint-Louis 🏨
B-3 ⑥ - La Marée de Versailles ♀
B-3 ⑦ - Le Mille et Une Nuits 🍽
B-5 ⑧ - Le Potager du Roy ♀

A-4 ⑨ - Le Quai N° 1 🍽
B-3 ⑩ - Richaud 🏨
A-3 ⑪ - Rôtisserie Ballester 🍽
B-4 ⑫ - Sofitel 🏨
A-4 ⑬ - Le Versailles 🏨

This chain hotel is located in immediate proximity to Place d'Armes and the château. Rooms here are spacious and modern, and all of the chain's top-of-the-line services are on offer. Piano bar.

 ### Les Trois Marches

Trianon Palace, 1, bd de la Reine
01 39 50 13 21, fax 01 30 21 01 25
Closed Sun, Mon, Aug. Open until 10pm. Priv rm: 20. Terrace dining. Air cond. Valet pkg.
Gérard Vié is as happy as a king in the splendiferous kitchens of the Trianon Palace, where he and his *brigade* benefit from the state of the art equipment. Vié excels in the "sophisticated country" register that recalls his Languedoc roots: cassoulet with Couïza sausages or hearty Lacaune ham. And his updated French classics are models of the genre: morels braised in cream, asparagus with truffles, turbot with fat Tarbais beans, or a magnificent chop of milk-fed Corrèze veal. The brilliant sommelier can uncork a vintage Pauillac or Margaux to complement Vié's creations, and the maître d'hôtel will ensure that every detail of your meal is memorable. A well-earned point. C 700-900. M 270 (weekday lunch), 510, 610.

 ### Trianon Palace

(See restaurant above)
01 30 84 38 00, fax 01 39 49 00 77
Open year-round. 27 stes 2,700-7,500. 67 rms 1,300-1,800. Bkfst 110-140. Restaurant. Rm ser. Air cond. Conf. Heated pool. Tennis. Valet pkg.
Spruced up to the tune of $60 million, the Trianon Palace is a stupendously lavish hotel.

From video-conference equipment to a medically supervised spa, it is the last word in luxury. Restaurants: Les Trois Marches, Brasserie de la Fontaine, see above.

 ### Le Versailles

7, rue Ste-Anne - 01 39 50 64 65, fax 01 39 02 37 85
Open year-round. 3 stes 450-520. 42 rms 450. Bkfst 54. Rms for disabled. Conf. Garage pkg.
Some rooms are located under the rafters, and all are modern, tastefully decorated, and well equipped (satellite TV). This hotel is ideally situated at the entry to the château. Bar, flower-filled terrace where breakfast is served, patio.

VINEUIL-SAINT-FIRMIN	60500
Paris 52 - Chantilly 6 - Beauvais 56	Oise

 ### Golf-Hotel
Blue Green

Route d'Apremont, Domaine de Chantilly
03 44 58 47 77, fax 03 44 58 50 11
Open year-round. 2 stes 950-1,350. 107 rms 590-750. Bkfst 75. Half-board 565-645. Rms for disabled. Restaurant. Rm ser. Conf. Tennis. Golf. Garage pkg.
Here in the midst of the Chantilly forest is a long, low hotel with a neoclassic colonnade. Rooms are on the small side and lack air conditioning, but they are attractively decorated. Most open onto views of the hotel's eighteen-hole golf course.

André Gayot's

TASTES

THE WORLD DINING & TRAVEL CONNECTION

- New Restaurants, Hotels, Shops & Wines
- Travel Tips & Bargains
- Events in the Food World
- Special Places & Resorts

THE WORLD DINING & TRAVEL CONNECTION

Want to keep current on the best bistros in Paris? Discover that little hideaway in Singapore? Or stay away from that dreadful and dreadfully expensive restaurant in New York? André Gayot's *Tastes* newsletter gives you bi-monthly news on the best restaurants, hotels, nightlife, shopping, airline and cruiseline information around the world.

Please enter/renew my subscription to TASTES newsletter for:

☐ Six bi-monthly issues at the rate of $30 per year & $35 outside U.S./Canada.

☐ 12 bi-monthly issues at the rate of $55 for two years US & $60 outside US/Canada.

Name _____

Address _____

City _____ State _____

ZIP _____ Country _____

Phone ( ) –

☐ Enclosed is my check or money order made out to Gault Millau, Inc.

☐ $_____

☐ Charge to: _____ VISA _____AMEX _____MASTERCARD   Exp._____

Card#_____ Signature _____

323/97

FOR FASTER SERVICE CALL 1 (800) LE BEST 1

THE LOIRE VALLEY

France's valley of kings

Mention the Loire Valley and you conjure up visions of fairytale castles set against a backdrop of green fields and rows of poplars, hillside vineyards, and the swift-flowing Loire. The river, France's longest, gives the region its name; the Loire's waters nourish this land, the "garden of France," a gentle, rolling landscape that seems to breathe peace and prosperity. The magnificent châteaux that suddenly appear on the horizon take one's breath away: these manmade wonders are surely as dramatic as any natural landscape could be. Built of *pierre de Loire*, the porous local limestone, each of the region's 300-odd châteaux played a role in French history, serving first as fortresses, later as elegant residences for aristocrats and royalty, and then as barracks or even quarries after the Revolution. Now the major châteaux have been restored and transformed into museums, drawing hundreds of thousands of visitors each year from all over the world.

But the châteaux are not the whole story of the Loire Valley. This is the heartland of France, renowned for its tender light, moderate climate, and bounteous farmlands. The Renaissance poet Joachim du Bellay wrote of his longing for *"la douceur angevine"* of his native Anjou, and of how he preferred the modest house built there by his grandparents to all the palaces of Rome. Covered by the sea when the world was still young, the Loire Valley still shows its marine heritage in the rolling hills, fertile soil, and network of rivers left behind by the salty waters. This former sea bed is bordered by the Massif Central plateau to the south, Burgundy's Morvan range to the east, the green grass of Normandy and plains of Ile-de-France to the north, sea-battered Brittany to the west, and rural Poitou to the south. Within these boundaries, the pastoral landscapes of the Loire Valley display subtle but distinctive differences. The Orléanais boasts forests and fertile fields, streams and moors, and is famous for its roses: they not only enhance the beauty of the area, but also supply an export crop. From Orléans the Loire flows southwest to Touraine, with its vineyards, orchards, market and flower gardens. The Loire then meanders to Anjou, in whose most westerly reaches—known as **Black Anjou**—the countryside begins to resemble the wilder scenery of Brittany. **White Anjou**, however, remains firmly attached to the Loire Valley's pastoral tradition, with vineyards and gardens covering gentle slopes.

Turmoil, and a golden age

While the Loire Valley today may seem to be a haven of tranquility, this has not always been the case. Controlled by the Romans for the first two centuries AD, the Loire Valley fell prey to invasions by Huns, Franks, Visigoths, Vikings, and Saracens over the following centuries. Peace did not reign after the suppression of the barbarians, though, as the lords of Orléans, Blois, Touraine, Anjou, and the Maine continued to battle each other for control of the territory. In the mid-twelfth century Henri, Count of Anjou, seemed to have gained the upper hand when he was crowned Henry II of England and married Eleanor of Aquitaine, whose dowry brought him lands that reached as far as the southwest corner of France. His dominion did not endure, however, and the Loire Valley reverted to French control early in the thirteenth century. Still, the English did not relinquish the idea of owning the rich lands of France. They returned with a vengeance during the Hundred Years' War (1337-1453), inspiring Joan of Arc to take up arms to defend her king, Charles VII. The "Maid of Orleans" liberated that city, the last French fortress, in 1429. She was burned at the stake by the English in 1431, becoming a martyr who is venerated by French nationalists (and royalists) to this day.

The importation of the Italian Renaissance to France in the sixteenth century, in the relative peace after the Hundred Years' War, changed the face of the Loire Valley. Gloomy fortresses metamorphosed into graceful, light-filled castles that displayed their owners' wealth and power to best advantage. Kings Charles VIII, Louis XII, and François I brought the artistic ideals of the Italian Renaissance to the Loire Valley. To them we owe the renovation and construction of the great châteaux at Blois, Amboise, and Chambord. François I invited Leonardo da Vinci and Benvenuto Cellini from Italy to embellish his residences. Queen Catherine de Médicis, the Florentine wife of Henri II, continued the tradition of patronizing Italian artists.

The Renaissance was the golden age of the Loire Valley. When its importance as a royal seat diminished, the region reverted to its agricultural vocation. The gastronomic bounty produced by this rich land is nearly as celebrated as the châteaux. The Loire River yields shad, trout, pikeperch, eels, and (for a brief season each year) salmon. In the Orléanais and Touraine, the abundance of asparagus, leeks, strawberries, melons, pumpkins, apples, and more prove that this is indeed the garden of France. The Loire Valley is also wine country: Anjou boasts long-lived white dessert wines, aromatic reds, and tender rosés; from Touraine come tannic Chinons and Bourgueil, the best of which will improve with age. The ideal accompaniments to these wines are the region's excellent chèvres, from **Selles-sur-Cher** or **Sainte-Maure**, or the potted pork known as rillettes, a specialty of **Le Mans**.

Exploring the châteaux

Originally a feudal castle, the château de **Blois**, located in the center of the town of the same name, became a royal residence in 1498 when Louis XII ascended the throne (he's the man on horseback above the château's entrance). Louis added a brick-and-stone wing to the château. The next tenant, François I, built yet another wing in the Renaissance style with an Italianate façade and a fantastic open octagonal staircase. The classical sobriety of the Gaston d'Orléans wing, added in 1635, contrasts with the exuberance of the Renaissance portions.

The ubiquitous François I also pops up at **Chambord**, the most colossal of the Loire châteaux, with no fewer than 440 rooms. Originally a humble hunting lodge, François had Chambord enlarged to its present extravagant state in the early sixteenth century. The Italianate structure may have been influenced by Leonardo da Vinci, who had been a guest at François's court. Many perceive his genius in Chambord's celebrated double-helix staircase, which allows one person to mount and another to descend without running into each other. On Chambord's broad rooftop terraces, visitors may wander amid pinnacles, turrets, and fantasy sculptures, then pause to admire the view of the immense park that surrounds the château. Once the hunting grounds of royalty, the land is now a national wildlife reserve. Nearby, at the elegant seventeenth-century château of **Cheverny**, the hunt is still a vital tradition. After viewing the castle's richly furnished interior, one can stroll around the grounds and visit the beautiful hounds in their kennel.

Set high on a cliff, the château at **Chaumont-sur-Loire** is slightly older than Chambord but has a similar massive construction, with fat turret-tipped towers. Catherine de Médicis brought her Italian astrologer, Cosimo Ruggieri, to live at Chaumont. He beguiled his patroness by making the faces of the king and their sons appear in the moonlight, along with the number of years they had left to live (a precursor, perhaps, of today's *son et lumière* shows?).

Though the town of **Chenonceaux** is often thronged with tourists, its château is still very much worth visiting for its intrinsic beauty, interesting history, and the rare works of art it holds. Built plumb over the waters of the Cher River, Chenonceau stands on the foundations of a former mill. François I acquired the castle in 1535 as payment for debts owed the Crown. Henri II made a gift of Chenonceau to his beautiful and ambitious mistress, Diane de Poitiers, but upon his death in 1559, his widow Catherine de Médicis ousted her rival, packing her off to the less majestic château at Chaumont. Catherine had a two-storey gallery built on the bridge that links the castle to the opposite bank of the Cher. The gallery served as a hospital during World War I, and during World War II provided a precious escape route, for it spanned the line of demarcation between France's Free Zone and Occupied France.

Reflected in the tranquil waters of the Indre, **Azay-le-Rideau** is a romantic château that time has barely touched. The early Renaissance architecture shows Italian influences, and the military features—turrets, battlements, and such—serve a purely decorative purpose. Inside, period furnishings and Flemish tapestries embellish the rooms.

The château of **Amboise** is an impressive sight: set at a lordly height above the town, it affords an exceptional view of the river and the Loire Valley. François I established a brilliant court here, graced by poets and artists: Clément Marot, Pierre de Ronsard, and, Leonardo da Vinci. Just outside of Amboise, and well worth visiting, is **Clos-Lucé**, where Leonardo spent the last years of his life. Visitors can admire models of his plans for a helicopter and other amazing inventions, but the real interest is in seeing the place where the great man lived and worked. The kitchen, where he liked to sit, is especially moving.

This is just a taste of the riches of France's "valley of kings." Those interested in the region's earlier history should visit the troglodyte village of **Trôo, which features** cave dwellings dug out of limestone, grottos, a "talking well" (it has a startling echo), and Romanesque church. The château at Le Grand-Pressigny, a major prehistoric site, houses a museum with a fine collection of artifacts.

Apocalypse now... and forever

The cities of the Loire Valley hold their own share of treasures. Flower-filled **Angers**, situated on the Maine River in the western Loire Valley, is dominated by a powerful medieval fortress with seventeen striped towers. The castle houses the *Apocalypse Tapestries*, a fourteenth-century masterpiece depicting 70 scenes from the Book of Revelation. Light filters into Angers's Gothic cathedral of Saint-Maurice through magnificent stained-glass windows; those in the choir are especially fine (notice the Saint Christopher with the head of a dog).

Due east, in the heart of the Loire Valley, is **Tours**, a university town that makes a good base for both château and wine tours. Though Tours suffered bomb damage in World War II, many of its Renaissance town houses (the Hôtel Gouin is a fine example) and ancient half-timbered dwellings on Place Plumereau were spared. The cathedral of Saint-Gatien (named for Tours's first bishop) is a compendium of Gothic styles, with Renaissance towers for good measure. The glorious stained-glass windows date from the thirteenth to the fifteenth century. By all means make time to visit the Musée des Beaux-Arts in the former archbishops' palace, and admire a collection that includes works by Mantegna, Rubens, and Rembrandt in a precious setting.

Following the Loire River north and east takes the visitor to **Orléans**, a city whose main claim to fame is its association with Joan of Arc, who saved it from the English in 1429. Orléans sustained heavy bomb damage during World War II, but was meticulously reconstructed. The eclectic cathedral of Sainte-Croix (called "the ugliest in France" by one of Marcel Proust's characters), was built, destroyed, and rebuilt repeatedly over 600 years. Inside is a chapel dedicated to Joan. Those interested in the life of the warrior shepherdess will also want to visit the Maison de Jeanne d'Arc and the Centre de Jeanne d'Arc, which exhibit documents and memorabilia. Not surprisingly, Orléans hosts a Joan of Arc festival every year on May 7-8. The city's Musée des Beaux-Arts displays a *Saint Thomas* by Velázquez, and exceptional French portraits from the seventeenth and eighteenth centuries.

Completing the circle of the region's major cities is **Le Mans** in the north, between Normandy and Touraine. Its name is synonymous with car racing: the famous *24 Heures* takes place in June, at the Circuit just south of the town. Racing buffs should not miss the Musée de l'Automobile, also at the site. Le Mans's historic center, just west of the cathedral of Saint-Julien inside the ancient Gallo-Roman wall, holds a wealth of fine medieval and Renaissance houses. The cathedral itself is an architectural marvel, combining Romanesque and Gothic elements with splendid stained glass.

RESTAURANTS & HOTELS

AMBOISE   37400
Paris 206 - Vendôme 50 - Blois 35 - Tours 25   Indre/Loire

12/20 Le Blason
11, pl. de Richelieu
02 47 23 22 41, fax 02 47 57 56 18
Closed Tue, Sat lunch, Jan. Open until 9:30pm (10pm summer). Terrace dining. Air cond. HOTEL: 28 rms 270-295. Bkfst 30. Half-board 245-365. Rms for disabled. Conf. Pkg.
The menu has some surprises in store, most of them good: like the roast chicken wings, honeyed foie gras croustillant, garlic-roasted kid with ginger confit, and tea-flower mousse with prune custard sauce that figure on the 155 F set meal. Pretty surroundings; clement prices. M 75-225, 49 (children).

Château de Pray
2 km on D 751 - 02 47 57 23 67, fax 02 47 57 32 50
Closed Jan 2-Feb 3. Open until 9:30pm. Priv rm: 20. Terrace dining. No pets. Garage pkg.
Here's an enchanting Loire Valley hostelry, perfect for a romantic getaway. Chef Bruno Delagneau (who trained with Gagnaire and Boyer) is new on the scene, but he impressed us with an inventive repertoire based on premium ingredients. So long as he pays as much attention to substance as to style (watch those cooking times!), all will be well. Try the langoustine tempura with seaweed, sea bream with red cabbage, or morsels of tender spiced suckling pig. Superb desserts, and an interesting cellar to boot, with a memorable collection of Vouvrays. C 230. M 145, 160 (lunch, wine & coffee incl), 295, 70 (children).

Château de Pray
(See restaurant above)
Closed Jan 2-Feb 3. 2 stes 820-890 (4 pers). 17 rms 470-750. Bkfst 50. Half-board 550-640. Conf. Garage pkg.
Just on the edge of the royal town of Amboise sits this thirteenth-century château, flanked by

two towers and surrounded by manicured grounds. The rooms are a bit austere, but they are accented with carved pieces of solid-wood furniture.

 ## Le Choiseul

36, quai Charles-Guinot
02 47 30 45 45, fax 02 47 30 46 10
Closed Dec-Jan 20. Open until 9pm. Terrace dining. Air cond. Heated pool.
The main dining room is certainly handsome, but we prefer a table facing the Italian-style terraced garden (the room is smaller but has more charm). Pascal Bouvier puts an elegant spin on Touraine's prime ingredients, in dishes like foie gras with a caramelized balsamic-vinegar sauce, lake char in mushroom fumet with an unusual garnish of spelt and barley, or roast rack of lamb in a creamy bacon-flecked sauce with a fricassée of snow peas. For dessert, luscious babas au rhum come with tea-soaked prunes and a scoop of licorice ice cream. Connoisseur's cellar. C 270-380. M 220 (weekday lunch, wine incl), 250-440.

 ## Le Choiseul

(See restaurant above)
Closed Dec-mid Jan. 4 stes 1,400-1,700. 28 rms 600-1,300. Bkfst 85-130. Half-board 770-1,245. Rms for disabled. Conf. Heated pool. Restaurant. Garage pkg.
The hotel offers 32 well-kept, variously furnished rooms, some of which have private terraces. There is a pool in the small, very pretty garden. Relais et Châteaux.

 ## Le Lion d'Or

17, quai Charles-Guinot
02 47 57 00 23, fax 02 47 23 22 49
Closed Sun & Mon off-seas, Jan 5-Feb 10. 1 ste 394. 22 rms 185-316. Bkfst 37-49. Restaurant. Half-board 285. Garage pkg.
At the foot of the Renaissance château of Amboise stands this aging but well-equipped little hotel. The lobby and bar were renovated, and the rooms are scheduled for a facelift, too.

 ## Le Manoir Saint-Thomas

Pl. Richelieu - 02 47 57 22 52, fax 02 47 30 44 71
Closed Mon. Open until 9:30pm. Priv rm: 65. Terrace dining.
The stately décor of beamed ceilings, stained glass, antique chests, and rich table settings is as heady as the sensational cellar of Chinons and Vouvrays. Classic dishes—foie gras with wild mushrooms, pikeperch in sorrel sauce, orange craquelin—are delivered by a staff decked out in seventeenth-century costumes. Another point. C 300-350. M 175 (exc Sat dinner, Sun), 220, 300.

 ## Novotel

17, rue des Sablonnières
02 47 57 42 07, fax 02 47 30 40 76

Open year-round. 121 rms 420-570. Bkfst 50. Rms for disabled. Restaurant. Rm ser. Conf. Heated pool. Tennis. Pkg.
This chain hotel is built in typical regional style, with a slate roof and dormer windows. The quiet, comfortable rooms afford outstanding views of the Loire and the château. Bar.

ANGERS   49000

TGV Paris 305 - Rennes 126 - Tours 106   Maine/Loire

 ## Continental Hôtel

12-14, rue Louis-de-Romain
02 41 86 94 94, fax 02 41 86 96 60
Closed Sun 12:30pm-5:30pm. 25 rms 195-310. Bkfst 32-55. Rms for disabled. Rm ser.
A modern and comfortable hotel near the cathedral, with clean, smallish rooms (some are not absolutely quiet). But guests can count on a friendly reception, smiling service, and very reasonable rates.

 ## Hôtel de France

8, pl. de la Gare - 02 41 88 49 42, fax 02 41 86 76 70
Open year-round. 3 stes 550. 53 rms 330-480. Bkfst 20-50. Rms for disabled. Restaurant. Rm ser. Air cond. Conf. Garage pkg.
Double windows conceal the fact that the hotel is situated just opposite the train station. The rooms are nicely equipped, there's a brasserie on the premises, and jazz evenings are scheduled regularly. Expect a warm reception.

Le Mail

8, rue des Ursules - 02 41 88 56 22, fax 02 41 86 91 20
Open year-round. 27 rms 230-260. Conf. Pkg.
A hotel with character on a quiet street in the center of Angers, with small but prettily decorated rooms. Good amenities; charming welcome. And you can look forward to a lovely breakfast.

 ## Pavillon Paul Le Quéré

3, bd Foch - 02 41 20 00 20, fax 02 41 20 06 20
Closed Sun dinner. Open until 9:45pm. Priv rm: 55. Air cond. Pkg.
What a pleasure it is to enter this elegant town house, an ideal setting for Paul Le Quéré's limpid, luminous cuisine. His expert technique shows to advantage in the 220 F set menu, which brings grilled scallops dressed with a sparky orange vinaigrette, veal shank braised with walnuts in sweet Layon wine, escorted by potatoes dauphinois and chestnut confit, a trio of farm cheeses, and rum-spiked banana-pineapple gratin dolloped with lime sorbet. The cellar is awash in fabulous Loire wines (with an emphasis on Anjous); a knowledgeable sommelier is on hand to help you choose. C 280-420. M 220 (wine incl), 150, 450, 100 (children).

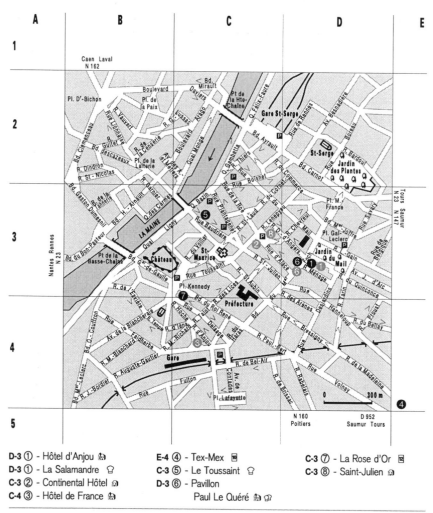

D-3 ① - Hôtel d'Anjou 🏠
D-3 ① - La Salamandre 🍴
C-3 ② - Continental Hôtel 🏠
C-4 ③ - Hôtel de France 🏠

E-4 ④ - Tex-Mex 🍴
C-3 ⑤ - Le Toussaint 🍴
D-3 ⑥ - Pavillon
Paul Le Quéré 🏠🍴

C-3 ⑦ - La Rose d'Or 🍴
C-3 ⑧ - Saint-Julien 🏠

🏠 Pavillon Paul Le Quéré

(See restaurant above)
Open year-round. 3 stes 1,200. 7 rms 450-750. Half-board 505-880. Bkfst 60. Rm ser. Conf. Pkg.

This handsome town house, vintage 1862, was renovated under the supervision of the Beaux-Arts commission. Nicely proportioned rooms, charmingly furnished with every imaginable convenience. Excellent breakfasts.

12/20 La Rose d'Or

21, rue Delaâge - 02 41 88 38 38
Closed Jul 28-Aug 18. Open until 9pm. Air cond. No pets.

Don't be put off by the look of the place (the street, the façade, the décor—ah! the décor—the dishes, and the rest), for you would miss out on some fine, fresh, uncomplicated cooking. The sauces, especially, are nicely done. Friendly prices. M 110, 180, 65 (children).

🏠 Saint-Julien

9, pl. du Ralliement
02 41 88 41 62, fax 02 41 20 95 19
Open year-round. 34 rms 160-300. Bkfst 32-50.

You'll find this modern hotel not far from the château (opposite the theater, to be precise). Rooms are on the small side.

🍴 La Salamandre

1, bd du Mal-Foch - 02 41 88 99 55 (R),
02 41 88 24 82 (H), fax 02 41 87 22 21
Closed Sun. Open until 9:45pm. Priv rm: 20. No pets. Pkg.

Sculpted woodwork and stained-glass windows impart a certain neo-Renaissance grandeur to La Salamandre's dining room. Daniel Louboutin gives a clever, personal touch to traditional recipes; his desserts are particularly tempting, and game is featured in season. The cellar holds an excellent selection of local wines. C 280-380. M 130 (lunch), 170, 210.

 ## Hôtel d'Anjou

(See restaurant above)
Open year-round. 3 stes. 53 rms 380-650. Half-board 420-550. Bkfst 62. Rm ser. Conf. Valet pkg.
Fine, spacious rooms may be had at this venerable, flawlessly renovated hotel.

10/20 Tex-Mex

9, rue de Château-Gontier - 02 41 87 96 00
Closed lunch, Aug. Open until 11pm (midnight upon reservation). Terrace dining.
The chef, who actually did learn to cook in the U. S. of A., makes laudable efforts to serve authentic Tex-Mex fare here in the French heartland. Chili, enchiladas, onion rings, gambas and the like, all washed down with Mexican beer or French wine. C 150-220. M 72, 140, 43 (children).

Le Toussaint

"Michel Bignon", 7-9, place du Pdt-Kennedy
02 41 87 46 20, fax 02 41 87 96 64
Closed Sun dinner, Mon, Feb school hols. Open until 9:30pm (10pm in summer). Priv rm: 20. Air cond.
Given its location and view of the château, this place could survive nicely on the tourist trade, even if it took no trouble with its food and service. But as it happens, the chef is not content merely to go through the motions: he takes pride in his savory shark spread (rillettes), pan-roasted andouillette sausage, and roasted pear in a zippy pepper infusion. The cellar boasts a good selection of Bordeaux and regional wines. C 200-360. M 100 (exc Sat dinner), 130-250, 65 (children).

And also...

Our selection of place for inexpensive, quick, or late-night meals.
Le Petit Mâchon (02 41 86 01 13 - 43, rue Bressigny. Closed Sat lunch, Sun, hols. Open until 9:45pm.): A former butcher's shop transformed into a bistro. Good country-style cooking at low prices (100, 69 weekdays).

ARNAGE	72230
Paris 207 - Le Mans 10	Sarthe

Auberge des Matfeux

500m beyond the village, via D 147, N 23
02 43 21 10 71, fax 02 43 21 25 23
Closed Mon, dinner Sun & hols, Feb school hols, Jul 21-Aug 11. Open until 9pm. Priv rm: 45. Pkg.
The Le Mans auto race seems worlds away from this grand old country restaurant, where Alain and Xavier Souffront take the time to select choice Loué chickens, flavorsome Pauillac lamb, and milk-fed veal; to install special ovens so that

the Auberge can bake its own bread; to grow rare herbs, fresh vegetables, tender lettuces. This commitment to quality ingredients has everything to do with the pristine flavors of their updated classic cuisine. The cellar, too, is splendid, with bargain bottles (marked in red) from every region. C 300-430. M 115, 348 55 (children).

AZAY-LE-RIDEAU	37190
Paris 254 - Tours 26 - Châtellerault 60	Indre/Loire

L'Aigle d'Or

10, rue Adélaïde-Riché
02 47 45 24 58, fax 02 47 45 90 18
Closed Sun dinner, Tue off-seas, Wed, Feb school hols, Dec 10-25. Open until 9pm. Priv rm: 40. Air cond. Terrace dining.
In a posh, pastel setting Jean-Luc Fèvre presents polished, classic cuisine made with ultrafresh ingredients. While Loire wines dominate the cellar, there's an interesting array of Bordeaux and Burgundies, too. C 250. M 92 (weekday lunch), 143-270, 50 (children).

12/20 Le Grand Monarque

3, pl. de la République
02 47 45 40 08, fax 02 47 45 46 25
Closed Mon lunch off-seas, Thu, Jan, Dec 15-31. Open until 9:30pm. Priv rm: 40. Terrace dining. Pkg.
From the look of the place, one would expect to find plates heaped high with generous portions... Well, appearances can be deceiving! Your best bet is the ably prepared 155 F menu: foie gras terrine, fillet of cod with garlicky potatoes, cheeses, and candied citrus fruits in aspic. Tasty Touraine wines fill the cellar. C 260. M 90 (lunch), 155, 275, 60 (children).

Le Grand Monarque

(See restaurant above)
Closed Jan, Dec 15-31. 1 ste 600-900. 25 rms 250-620. Half-board 360-480. Bkfst 45. Conf. Pkg.
This welcoming eighteenth-century inn offers mostly pleasant, well-kept rooms. Some are soundproofed, the majority have satellite TV.

BEAUMONT-EN-VÉRON	37420
Paris 282 - Tours 51 - Chinon 6	Indre/Loire

Château de Danzay

02 47 58 46 86, fax 02 47 58 84 35
Closed Nov 2-Mar 25. 2 stes 1,400-1,500. 8 rms 650-1,400. Half-board 695-1,120 (oblig in seas). Restaurant. Pool. Garage pkg.
This lovely fifteenth-century manor has been completely restored. Huge rooms are decorated in medieval style (solid-wood furniture, mullioned windows, canopied beds), and everywhere there reigns a warm atmosphere.

BÉZARDS (LES) 45290	**BLOIS** 41000
Paris 136 - Orléans 69 - Gien 16 Loiret	Paris 180 - Tours 60 - Orléans 56 - Le Mans 109 Loir/Cher

 ## Auberge des Templiers

N 7 - 02 38 31 80 01, fax 02 38 31 84 51
Closed Feb. Open until 9:45pm. Priv rm: 60. Terrace dining. Heated pool. Tennis. Golf. Valet pkg.
Sologne, a lovely land of mists and forest pools, is also the setting for this restaurant. An elegant French provincial ambience emanates from the oaken beams overhead, the antiques and tapestries, the tables set with candelabra and beautiful china. Owner Philippe Dépée keeps this jewel perfectly burnished, while his chef, François Rodolphe, produces the luxurious dishes that are the Templiers' hallmark. Autumn is the time to savor Rodolphe's remarkable game repertoire: terrine de gibier à l'ancienne, spit-roasted partridge swaddled in vine leaves, spiced wild duck, and venison with sauce poivrade all display rich, haunting flavors that hark back to another time. More delicate appetites can choose a saffron-tinged vegetable bouillon afloat with tiny shellfish, quick-seared scallops with barley risotto, or truffled chicken braised in a "crust" of the local blue clay—as savory as it is spectacular! The cellar's 500 wines range in price from 95 F (for a Coteaux-du-Giennois) to 14,000 F for a Romanée-Conti '29: the choice is yours! C 500-750. M 290 (lunch), 390, 690, 120 (children).

 ## Auberge des Templiers

(See restaurant above)
Closed Feb. 8 stes 1,500-3,500. 22 rms 600-1,380. Half-board 750-1,650. Rm ser. Conf. Heated pool. Tennis. Golf. Valet pkg.
The taste and attention to detail lavished on these lodgings—an opulent bungalow on the edge of the park, and a clutch of Sologne-style cottages—know no limits, nor hardly an equal anywhere. One is transported with delight by the ambience and amenities, including the regal breakfasts. Relais et Châteaux.

BLÉRÉ 37150	
Paris 230 - Blois 45 - Tours 27 - Loches 25 Indre/Loire	

 ## Le Cheval Blanc

Pl. de l'Église - 02 47 30 30 14, fax 02 47 23 52 80
Closed Sun dinner & Mon (exc Jul-Aug), Jan 2-Feb 12. Open until 9:15pm. Terrace dining. Pool.
Michel Blériot regales his patrons (lots of tourists among them) with generous, accessibly priced cuisine. You'll make a satisfying meal of his langoustines and baby vegetables swathed in beurre blanc, beef tournedos in a snappy Szechuan-pepper sauce, and peaches in apricot coulis with pistachio ice cream. Interesting cellar; plush surroundings. C 250. M 99 (weekdays), 200, 275, 60 (children).

 ## L'Espérance

189, quai Ulysse-Besnard
02 54 78 09 01, fax 02 54 56 17 86
Closed Sun dinner, Mon, Feb school hols, Aug 7-28. Open until 9:30pm. Air cond. No pets. Pkg.
Admire the view of the Loire River as you savor a clever combination of scallops with lamb's lettuce, an elegant blanquette de sole, or leek-stuffed skate surrounded by slices of grilled andouillette sausage. The cheese tray left us longing for more, but the wine list is extensively annotated and presented with flair. C 250. M 130, 175, 245, 345, 60 (children).

 ## Holiday Inn Garden Court

26, av. Maunoury - 02 54 55 44 88, fax 02 54 74 57 97
Open year-round. 78 rms 390-430. Bkfst 30-48. Half-board 383-401. Restaurant. Rm ser. Conf. Rms for disabled. Garage pkg.
High up overlooking the town of Blois, the freshly renovated Holiday Inn offers functional rooms done up in contemporary style. For entertainment, there's a piano bar where theme evenings are held. Guests can also make use of fitness and hydrotherapy facilities located nearby.

 ## L'Orangerie du Château

1, av. Jean-Laigret - 02 54 78 05 36, fax 02 54 78 22 78
Closed Sun dinner, Wed (exc hols), Feb 17-Mar 7, Aug 20-27. Open until 9:30pm. Priv rm: 50. Terrace dining.
Eager to show their good will, newcomers Karine and Jean-Marc Molveaux tend to go over the top: an avalanche of extra vegetables threatens a delicious pikeperch with pan-roasted mushrooms; terrine de foie gras with fig purée suffers from a fussy presentation. But an apple gratin with frangipane cream proves that the chef knows what he's about. Expect a pleasant welcome in this fine fifteenth-century dwelling just opposite the château. C 310. M 130 (weekday, Sat lunch), 205, 330, 70 (children).

 ## Au Rendez-Vous des Pêcheurs

27, rue de Foix - 02 54 74 67 48, fax 02 54 74 47 67
Closed Mon lunch, Sun, Feb 17-24, Aug 3-25. Open until 10pm. Priv rm: 35. Air cond.
Éric Reithler cultivates an inventive yet fresh and uncluttered culinary style. Seafood inspires him: try his langoustines en vinaigrette with bits of bacon and red beans, or sea-sweet scallops counterpointed by slightly bitter Belgian endive, the whole bound together by an earthy lentil jus. For dessert, there's a wonderful apple-walnut shortbread swirled with spiced caramel. Watch out, though: à la carte prices are steep at this

fashionable bistro. **C** 250-350. **M** 145, 90 (children).

Le Savoie

6-8, rue Ducoux - 02 54 74 32 21, fax 02 54 74 29 58
Open year-round. 26 rms 180-280. Bkfst 30. No pets.
Here's a commendable little hotel situated between the train station and the château. Rooms on the first floor have been refurbished. Cheerful personnel.

BRACIEUX	41700
Paris 198 - Blois 19 - Romorantin-Lanthenay 32	Loir/Cher

Hôtel de la Bonnheure ▲♥

02 54 46 41 57, fax 02 54 46 05 90
Closed Jan-beg Feb. 2 stes 600-800. 12 rms 250-320. Bkfst 38. Rms for disabled. Rm ser. Pkg.
A comfortable, modern hotel near the forest, enhanced by lawns and flower beds.

🍳17 Bernard Robin

"Le Relais de Bracieux,"
1, av. de Chambord
02 54 46 41 22, fax 02 54 46 03 69
Closed Tue dinner & Wed exc Jul-Aug, Dec 20-Jan 20. Open until 9pm. Terrace dining. Air cond. No pets. Pkg.
True, times are hard in the restaurant business nowadays, even out here in château land. So we must forgive the absence of a sommelier (too bad, for Bernard Robin's cellar is one of the Loire Valley's finest), and overlook the fact that Robin's repertoire may be falling into a routine. Better days will surely come. In the meantime, Robin remains a remarkable craftsman, as adept at exalting humble sardines (with fresh tomato concassée and whipped potatoes) or frogs' legs (breaded then sautéed and served with an exquisite parsley jus) or stewed rabbit (with a whiff of rosemary and a potato pâté on the side), as he is of enhancing such costly ingredients as foie gras (presented in three guises: poached with Port aspic, braised in Chinon wine, grilled with Guérande sea salt and spices). If it's game you crave, by all means book a table here in autumn, when Robin's menu highlights the bounty of Sologne's deep forests. The 180 F menu is a very good value. Relais et Châteaux. **C** 450-600. **M** 180 (lunch, exc Sun & hols), 320, 470, 590, 665.

BRIOLLAY	49125
Paris 285 - Angers 14 - Château-Gontier 41	Maine/Loire

🍳16 Château de Noirieux

26, route du Moulin
02 41 42 50 05, fax 02 41 37 91 00
Closed Sun dinner & Mon off-seas, Feb 6-Mar 15, Nov 23-Dec 4. Open until 9:30pm. Priv rm: 100. Terrace dining. Heated pool. Tennis. Valet pkg.
The famous *douceur angevine* is everywhere in evidence at this opulent château, but it hasn't (thank goodness!) sapped the energy of chef

Gérard Côme, whose delicate, delicious cuisine is sheer delight. In the bright dining room or on the tranquil terrace, guests savor scallops bathed in a meat-based jus with a crisp crab and lobster galette, rabbit with fava beans in a lush tarragon cream sauce, then finish on a high note with Côme's splendid "apple variations." Fabulous cellar; distinguished service. **C** 320-450. **M** 195 (weekday lunch), 245 (exc weekday lunch), 300, 460, 120 (children).

Château de Noirieux ▲♥

(See restaurant above)
Closed Feb 6-Mar 15, Nov 23-Dec 4. 19 rms 650-1,350. Half-board 620-1,550. Bkfst 85-135. Rm ser. Rms for disabled. Conf. Heated pool. Tennis. Pkg.
Set in lovely grounds graced with ancient chestnut trees, the eighteenth-century château and fifteenth-century manor provide nineteen individually decorated, fully equipped guest rooms. Pretty bathrooms; excellent breakfasts. Delightful welcome. Relais et Châteaux.

CANDÉ-SUR-BEUVRON	41120
Paris 194 - Blois 15 - Amboise 29	Indre/Loire

🍳14 La Caillère

36, route des Montils
02 54 44 03 08, fax 02 54 44 00 95
Closed Wed, Jan-Feb. Open until 9pm (9:30pm summer). Terrace dining. Pkg.
A quiet, leafy haven in the heart of Touraine, La Caillère stands atop a knoll overlooking the Beuvron River. Jacky Guindon possesses sure technique and a knack for bringing the best out of quality ingredients: crisp-crusted skate on a bed of lentils studded with bits of seared foie gras, rack of lamb with julienne vegetables and an aromatic jus, flaky cornucopias filled with coconut ice cream are typically delicate dishes. Fascinating, affordable cellar. **C** 300. **M** 92 (weekdays), 178 (wine incl), 60 (children).

CHAPELLE-ST-MESMIN (LA)	45380
Paris 130 - Orléans 6	Loiret

Orléans Parc Hôtel

55, route d'Orléans
02 38 43 26 26, fax 02 38 72 00 99
Open year-round. 2 stes 580. 32 rms 300-450. Bkfst 40. Rms for disabled. Restaurant. Conf. Garage pkg.
The singular charm of this hotel (the centerpiece of a vast estate) lies in its location on the banks of the Loire, and in its elegant interior decoration. The personalized rooms, done up in royal blue and old rose, are designed to include a little *salon*. The equipment is flawless, the bathrooms large and handsome. Absolute quiet guaranteed, just five minutes from central Orléans.

*Some establishments change their **closing times** without warning. It is always wise to check in advance.*

CHAUMONT-SUR-THARONNE 41600
Paris 152 - Orléans 36 - Romorantin 33 - Blois 52   Loir/Cher

La Croix Blanche de Sologne

5, pl. de l'Église - 02 54 88 55 12, fax 02 54 88 60 40
Open daily until 9:30pm. Priv rm: 40. Terrace dining. Pkg. HOTEL: 3 stes 580-780. 13 rms 250-580. Half-board 420-420 (oblig in seas). Bkfst 45. Rms for disabled. Rm ser. Conf. Tennis. Pkg.
Sologne meets Périgord in this posh little eating house. Françoise Richard coddles her patrons with rich foie gras specialties, sweetbreads with cranberries, and tarte solognote. C 300-360. M 118 (weekday lunch), 145 (weekdays), 169 (weekday, Sat dinner), 250, 350.

CHÊNEHUTTE-LES-TUFFEAUX 49350
Paris 287 - Angers 37 - Saumur 14   Maine/Loire

Le Prieuré   ❂

D 751 - 02 41 67 90 14, fax 02 41 67 92 24
Closed Jan 20-Mar 7. Open until 9:30pm. Priv rm: 40. Terrace dining. Heated pool. Tennis. Garage pkg.
Jean-Louis Lumineau presents a balanced, classic repertoire that spotlights fish and regional ingredients. Settle down in the dining room of this former convent overlooking the Loire, and tuck into the fine 230 F prix-fixe meal: it brings a fondant of rabbit and langoustines infused with tarragon, pikeperch with bacon and cabbage in a brawny Chinon sauce, cheese, and a creamy crémet with fresh berries for dessert. Admirable cellar, with a wide range of local wines, including a Chinon from Olga Raffault for 85 F the half-bottle. C 330-450. M 160 (weekdays lunch), 230, 400, 220-250 (weekdays lunch, wine incl), 525 (wine incl).

Le Prieuré

(See restaurant above)
Closed Jan 20-Mar 7. 2 stes 1,250-1,750. 33 rms 550-1,350. Half-board 695-1,170. Bkfst 85. Restaurant. Rm ser. Conf. Heated pool. Tennis. Garage pkg.
A basket of fresh fruit awaits guests in each enormous room of this medieval priory nestled in over 50 acres of verdant grounds above the Loire. Wine-tasting courses offered. Elegant breakfasts. Relais et Châteaux.

CHENONCEAUX 37150
Paris 213 - Tours 35 - Amboise 11   Indre/Loire

12/20 Le Bon Laboureur et Château

6, rue du Docteur-Bretonneau
02 47 23 90 02, fax 02 47 23 82 01
Closed Nov 15-Dec 15. Open until 9:30pm. Priv rm: 30. Terrace dining. Heated pool. Valet pkg.
A million tourists wander through Chenonceaux every year, so the Jeudi family hardly needs to make an effort to attract customers. And yet they take pride in presenting a polished repertoire of traditional dishes that includes duck-giblet salad, chicken breast in a delicate chervil sauce, and licorice parfait. C 280-400. M 180, 250, 90 (children).

Le Bon Laboureur et Château

(See restaurant above)
Closed Nov 15-Dec 15. 4 stes 800-1,000. 30 rms 300-650. Half-board 500-700. Rms for disabled. Rm ser. Conf. Pool. Valet pkg.
Here's a vine-covered *auberge* with pleasant rooms that overlook a flower-filled courtyard. Cocktail bar; herb garden; mountain bike rental.

CHEVERNY 41700
Paris 194 - Blois 15 - Romorantin-Lanthenay 30   Loir/Cher

Château du Breuil

D 52, route de Fougères-sur-Bièvre
02 54 44 20 20, fax 02 54 44 30 40
Closed Sun, Mon lunch off-seas, Jan 2-Feb 15. Open until 9:30pm. Terrace dining. No pets. Pkg.
A young chef, Patrick Léonce, has taken over the kitchens of this charming château not far from its noble peers, Chaumont, Chambord, and Cheverny. A nice place to stop, with a dining room beautifully fitted out with period furniture. As for the food, it's classic but with modern touches—sometimes we wish Léonce would keep things more simple! Good wine list, reasonably priced, and obliging service. C 380-450. M 195, 250, 120 (children).

Château du Breuil

(See restaurant above)
Closed Sun, Mon off-seas, Jan 2-Feb 15. 2 stes 1,200-1,500. 16 rms 530-890. Half-board 1,100-1,340 (oblig in seas). Bkfst 65. Conf. Pkg.
The château stands proudly in its wooded grounds, a typical Solognot edifice with fifteenth- and eighteenth-century portions, tastefully appointed and furnished. The rooms all have different, personalized décor as well as modern bathrooms and fixtures.

CHINON 37500
Paris 282 - Tours 47 - Poitiers 95 - Angers 80   Indre/Loire

Hostellerie Gargantua

73, rue Haute-St-Maurice - 02 47 93 04 71
Closed Wed & Thu lunch off-seas, Nov 11-Feb. Open until 10pm. Terrace dining. HOTEL: 8 rms 240-500. Half-board 550-850 (for 2 pers, oblig in seas). Conf. No pets. Pkg.
We give our vote of confidence to the omelette Gargamelle, cod bathed in meat juices, and duck pot-au-feu, served here in a medieval dwelling where Rabelais's father once resided. C 200. M 98, 130.

Au Plaisir Gourmand ۞

2, rue Parmentier - 02 47 93 20 48, fax 02 47 93 05 66
Closed Sun dinner, Mon, Feb. Open until 9:15pm.
Garden dining. Air cond.
Jean-Claude Rigollet is no publicity hound, and his restaurant built of tufa stone at the foot of the château de Chinon will never attract those who go out to see and be seen. Just as well. His faithful customers and tourists in the know can better appreciate the elegant surroundings and fine set meals. The 175 F menu is a paragon: it brings duck sausage in a truffled jus, pike mousseline, tangy goat cheese, and iced candied-chestnut parfait. Superb choice of Loire wines at reasonable prices; smiling welcome. C 290-380. M 175, 245.

CHISSAY-EN-TOURAINE	41400
Paris 223 - Blois 42 - Montrichard 4	Loir/Cher

La Table du Roy

02 54 32 32 01, fax 02 54 32 43 80
Open until 9:30pm. Terrace dining. Heated pool.
No pets. Valet pkg. No cards.
The vaulted Gothic dining room and massive Renaissance furniture make an elegant setting for Olivier Géraud's classic, but increasingly personalized cooking (lots of good ideas on the menu the day we swung by). Courteous welcome; competent service. But why on earth do they offer only shippers' wines here in the heart of Touraine wine country? C 350-450. M 185, 220, 295, 75 (children).

Château de Chissay ♠♣

(See restaurant above)
Closed Nov 15-Mar 15. 6 stes 920-1,600. 25 rms 390-1,000. Half-board 675-1,180. Bkfst 60. Rms for disabled. Rm scr. Conf. Heated pool. Valet pkg.
A château erected in the twelfth and fifteenth centuries (Charles VII, Louis XI, and de Gaulle stayed here), set among wooded grounds and gardens. The luxuriously decorated rooms have eighteenth-century furniture and mosaic-tile bathrooms (but no televisions). The lounges and gardens are simply magnificent, and the welcome and service are very attentive.

COMBREUX	45530
Paris 125 - Orléans 35 - Montargis 36 - Gien 49	Loiret

Domaine de Chicamour

5 km SE on N 60 - 02 38 55 85 42, fax 02 38 55 80 43
Closed Nov 15-Mar 15. Open until 9pm. Priv rm:
70. Terrace dining. No pets. Tennis. Pkg.
The kitchen has made a remarkable comeback, with fresh, contemporary takes on traditional dishes that are as lovely to look at as they are to eat. A seasonal cellar (springtime brings Loire wines to the fore) only adds to the pleasure. In fine weather, book a table on the terrace behind the château. C 280-400. M 100, 170, 230, 250 (wine incl), 350 (wine incl), 75 (children).

Domaine de Chicamour ♠♣

(See restaurant above)
Closed Nov 15-Mar 15. 12 rms 340-385. Half-board
420. Bkfst 50. Conf. Tennis. Pkg.
A peaceful stopover indeed is this Directoire château hidden in the forest of Orléans. Fresh, bright rooms open onto leafy grounds, with a riding club on the premises.

COURTENAY	45320
Paris 120 - Sens 26 - Montargis 25 - Orléans 96	Loiret

Auberge La Clé des Champs

Les Quatre-Croix
02 38 97 42 68, fax 02 38 97 38 10
Closed Tue dinner, Wed, last 3 wks of Jan, last 2 wks
of Oct. Open until 9pm. Pkg.
This elegant country restaurant, housed in a seventeenth-century farmhouse, is all the more attractive for Marc Delion's skillful cooking. His menu features classics as well as some inventive dishes, like veal sweetbreads scented with a whiff of vanilla or rabbit ballottine with escargots. Excellent but expensive cellar. C 300-460. M 120, 280 (wine incl), 450.

Auberge La Clé des Champs ♠♣

(See restaurant above)
Closed Tue, Wed, last 3 wks of Jan, last 2 wks of Oct.
1 ste 720-950. 6 rms 395-550. Bkfst 55. Pkg.
A seventeenth-century farmhouse has been converted into a luxury inn, with just a handful of rooms decorated in a chic, rustic style. Perfect for a romantic country weekend. Expensive? Of course, but can you put a price tag on true pleasure ?

FERTÉ-SAINT-AUBIN (LA)	45240
Paris 152 - Blois 54 - Salbris 35 - Orléans 21	Loiret

12/20 Auberge de l'Écu de France

6, rue du Général-Leclerc - 02 38 64 69 22
Closed Tue dinner, Wed, 2 wks in Mar, 2 wks in
Oct-Nov. Open until 9:30pm. Terrace dining. Pkg.
You'll find this handsome, half-timbered *auberge* in the center of La Ferté-Saint-Aubin, an old town of considerable character. The traditional (but not fusty) cooking is attractively presented, and the smallish cellar focuses on the wines of Touraine. C 250. M 78 (weekdays), 130, 220, 50 (children).

Ferme de la Lande

Route de Marcilly-en-Villette
02 38 76 64 37, fax 02 38 64 68 87
Closed Sun dinner, Mon, Feb school hols, Aug 18-Sep
1. Open until 9:15pm. Terrace dining. Pkg.
Set down in a bucolic landscape of ferns and pines, this seventeenth-century Sologne

farmhouse is a picturesque spot for a fine meal. From the list of regional dishes you could choose tangy céleri rémoulade with smoked chicken breast or duck breast done with cider and honey (the latter came with a disappointing garnish). There's a cool covered terrace for summer dining. Attractive cellar; hospitable welcome. C 250. M 138, 153 (weekdays & Sat lunch, wine incl), 168 (Sat dinner Sun lunch), 184, 224 (Sat dinner, Sun lunch), 80 (children).

FONTEVRAUD-L'ABBAYE	49590
Paris 306 - Chinon 23 - Saumur 16	Maine/Loire

11/20 Hôtellerie du Prieuré Saint-Lazare

Abbaye Royale de Fontevraud
02 41 51 73 16, fax 02 41 51 75 50
Closed Jan 2-Feb 28, Dec 21-26. Open until 9:30pm. Priv rm: 45. Terrace dining. No pets.
After a tour of Fontevraud's magnificent abbey church, you can set yourself up to a simple, solid meal at this unpretentious restaurant. Try the smoked-haddock carpaccio and rabbit with a fragrant thyme jus. M 98 (exc Sun), 160, 235, 75 (children).

 ## Hôtellerie du Prieuré Saint-Lazare

(See restaurant above)
Closed Jan 2-Feb 25, Dec 21-26. 52 rms 290-470. Half-board 360. Half-board 275. Bkfst 55. Conf. No pets.
The orchards, the abbey, and an austere décor magnify the impression of serenity that reigns in this hostelry's small but comfortable rooms.

 ## La Licorne

Allée Ste-Catherine
02 41 51 72 49, fax 02 41 51 70 40
Closed Sun dinner & Mon off-seas. Annual closings not available. Open until 9pm. Pkg.
Michel Lecomte does best when he sticks to the classics (his forays into creative cooking usually leave us cold). Still, his precise technique succeeds in coaxing out the flavors of choice regional ingredients. The cellar holds a full complement of Loire wines, in every price range. The lovely eighteenth-century dining room is far warmer than the welcome, but the serving staff is friendly. C 280. M 110 (weekday lunch), 168, 228.

GIEN	45500
Paris 154 - Orléans 64 - Bourges 76 - Cosne 41	Loiret

Le Rivage

1, quai de Nice - 02 38 37 79 00, fax 02 38 38 10 21
Closed beg Feb-beg Mar. Open until 9:30pm. Air cond. Pkg.
Almost too pretty to eat: the chef takes such pains over the plates he sends out that we hesitate to spoil the effect! So take a moment to admire, but then dig in... It would be a pity to

miss out on the fine, full flavors of crab and avocado tian with tomato coulis, or hake vividly spiced with paprika and saffron, or calf's liver mellowed with balsamic vinegar. Owner Christian Gaillard oversees the impeccable service; the cellar holds riches from Burgundy and Touraine. C 345. M 140, 390, 100 (children).

 ## Le Rivage

(See restaurant above)
Closed beg Feb-beg Mar. 3 stes 700. 16 rms 305-520. Bkfst 47. Air cond. Conf. Garage pkg.
On the quay by the old Anne de Beaujeu bridge. Some of the rooms are simple and well furnished, others definitely more luxurious. Very nice bathrooms, too. First-rate breakfasts; cordial reception.

GRAND-PRESSIGNY (LE)	37350
Paris 293 - Tours 58 - Châtellerault 29	Indre/Loire

 ## L'Espérance

Pl. du Carroir-des-Robins - 02 47 94 90 12
Closed Mon, Jan. Open until 9:30pm. Pkg.
Market-fresh ingredients and vegetables from his own garden are the keystones of chef Bernard Torset's menu. He updates dishes typical of Touraine with lightened sauces and a vigorous, modern touch. Try his locally produced foie gras, matelote (a winy stew) of local eels, or spiced Touraine squab. The dining room is as rosy as life becomes after a few glasses of Loire Valley wine from the well-stocked cellar. The friendly *patronne* gives excellent advice about things to see and do in the area. C 250-300. M 110 (exc Sun), 160, 200, 50 (children).

LAVAL	53000
TGV Paris 291 - Tours 140 - Angers 73	Mayenne

Le Bistro de Paris

67, rue du Val-de-Mayenne
02 43 56 98 29, fax 02 43 56 52 85
Closed Sat lunch, Sun, Aug 15-31. Open until 10:15pm. Priv rm: 25. No pets.
Envied by other restaurateurs in the region, award-winning chef Guy Lemercier creates terrific meals at unbeatable prices. His chic little establishment on the banks of the Mayenne, presided over by his smiling wife, is always booked solid. No wonder the competition wishes he would take it elsewhere! Just look at what 135 F can buy: a warm pikeperch gâteau (a *very* high-class fishcake) with shellfish coulis, duck confit with eggplant gratin, and crisp langue de chat cookies with citrus compote. From the *carte*, we recommend the calf's head given a snappy spin with hot spices, the Munster shortbread, and Kirsch-spiked raspberry gratin. The cellar is choice, and just as democratically priced as the food. But remember: reserve your table in advance! C 260-300. M 135-245 (weekdays), 85 (children).

Les Blés d'Or

83, rue Victor-Boissel
02 43 53 14 10, fax 02 43 49 02 84
*Closed Sun dinner, Mon. Open until 10pm. Priv rm:
15. Pkg.*
Gilles Arzur is the new man in the kitchen here.
His style is more forthright than that of his
predecessor, but the results are appetizing and
full of frank flavors. Among the offerings you'll
find lotte and tomatoes in a light curry sauce,
pan-roasted saddle of rabbit vigorously perfumed with rosemary, and ginger-spiced duck
confit. Pleasant desserts; fabulous Loire wines
(as well as a selection of modestly priced bottles)
overseen by owner Pierre Portier, an award-winning sommelier. M 95-120 (lunch exc Sun, 165,
55 (children).

 ## La Gerbe de Blé

(See restaurant above)
*Open year-round. 2 stes 500-550. 6 rms 340-440.
Half-board 460-520. Bkfst 60-80. Rm ser. Conf. No
pets.*
The spacious, nicely decorated rooms are well
equipped and now have double windows.
Friendly owners.

LUYNES	37230
Paris 257 - Amboise 50 - Tours 17 km	Indre/Loire

 ## Domaine de Beauvois

2 km NW on D 49 - 02 47 55 50 11, fax 02 47 55 59 62
*Closed Jan 15-Mar 15. Open until 9:30pm. Priv rm:
125. Terrace dining. Heated pool. Tennis. Garage
pkg.*
This country manor set in vast wooded
grounds ranks among the most luxurious establishments in Touraine. Stéphane Pineau cooks in
a classic style, making intelligent use of the
region's rich resources. Taste his beignets of tiny
snails with a bold sauce of violet mustard,
pikeperch with a pilaf of winter wheat, or lamb
croustillant with sweet-pepper coulis, then
polish off a lovely apple soufflé with Calvados
granita. Fine wine list at reasonable prices, with
many *grands crus* available by the glass. Irreproachable service. C 300-400. M 200-260
(lunch, exc Sun), 270, 370, 100 (children).

 ## Domaine de Beauvois

(See restaurant above)
*Closed Jan 15-Mar 15. 2 stes 1,170-1,550. 36 rms
950-1,450. Conf. Heated pool. Tennis. Pkg.*
Ideally situated for a holiday touring the Loire
Valley's châteaux, this fine hotel has huge,
delightfully furnished rooms with marble
bathrooms. Fishing, riding, and other sporting
activities are arranged, and visits to local wine
growers are organized after the autumn harvest.
Relais et Châteaux.

Looking for a celebrated chef? Refer to the **index**.

MANS (LE)	72000
TGV Paris 216 - Tours 81 - Angers 88	Sarthe

 ## Patrick Bonneville

14, rue Bourg-Belé
02 43 23 75 00, fax 02 43 23 93 10
*Closed Wed, dinner Tue & Sun, Jul 14-Aug 15.
Open until 10:30pm. Priv rm: 30. Garage pkg.*
Patrick and Chantal Bonneville's restaurant is
set in a quiet (not to say lifeless) neighborhood,
but the dining room is welcoming, with its sunny
yellow and blue walls and romantic mural. As
for the cooking, it's fresh and carefully crafted.
Good bets are the creamy watercress soup
dotted with morsels of sweetbreads, and the
thyme-roasted leg of lamb. Wide-ranging cellar.
C 290. M 135, 315.

 ## Chantecler

50, rue de la Pelouse
02 43 24 58 53, fax 02 43 77 16 28
*Open year-round. 3 stes 470-530. 32 rms 310-365.
Bkfst 47. Garage pkg.*
Centrally located near the station, this recently
redecorated hotel is thoroughly soundproofed.
Zealous service; bar and restaurant: La Feuillan-
tine, see below.

 ## La Ciboulette

14, rue de la Vieille-Porte
02 43 24 65 67, fax 02 43 87 51 18
*Closed Sat lunch, Sun, 3 wks in Aug. Open until
10pm. Air cond.*
Near Place de l'Éperon, the Ciboulette's bistro-
style dining room is a late-night favorite. Jack
Desmats's menus provide plenty of fresh, contemporary offerings, like langoustines wrapped
in pillowy crêpes with roasted bananas, cod
seasoned with a touch of vanilla, and a crispy
ginger croustillant for dessert. C 158. M 120
(weekdays).

 ## La Closerie

4 km route de Laval
02 43 28 28 44, fax 02 43 28 54 58
*Closed Sun (Oct 15-Apr 10). 29 rms 320-530. Half-
board 390-630. Bkfst 47. Rms for disabled. Restaurant. Rm ser. Air cond. Conf. Pool. Pkg.*
The outside doesn't look much, but inside
this hotel are (mostly) pretty, well-tended
rooms. Out back are a flower garden, terrace,
and pool.

La Feuillantine

Hôtel Chantecler, 19 bis, rue Foisy
02 43 28 00 38, fax 02 43 23 22 31
Closed Aug 10-18. Open until 10pm. Priv rm: 50.
Chef Jean-Claude Adam knows his way
around a kitchen. All of his dishes show a
veteran's skill and a winning personal touch,
too. Worth ordering are the escalope of
sweetbreads and foie gras, turbot with shallot
compote in a pool of crab coulis, and roasted fig
with vanilla-scented caramel. Huge mirrors,

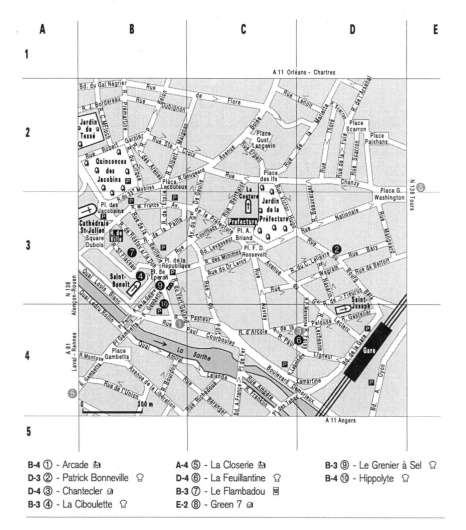

mosaics, and potted plants give the dining room a 1930s feel. **C** 225-420. **M** 75-95 (weekdays), 115-300 (weekdays, wine incl), 140 (weekdays).

12/20 Le Flambadou

14 bis, rue Saint-Flaceau - 02 43 24 88 38
Closed Sun, Easter school hols, wk of Aug 15. Open until 10:30pm. Priv rm: 30. Terrace dining.
Here's a Southwestern enclave in the middle of Le Mans: fresh foie gras with caramelized apples, duck confit with sautéed potatoes, and iced nougat with apricot sauce are washed down with a good Bordeaux from the cellar. **C** 200.

🏠 Green 7

Route de Tours, 447, av. Georges-Durand
02 43 85 05 73, fax 02 43 86 62 78

Closed Aug. 50 rms 270-330. Rms for disabled. Restaurant. Rm ser. Conf. Pkg.
A former hunting lodge, this American-style, modernized hotel is near the track of Le Mans's famous 24-hour auto race. Well-equipped rooms painted in bold colors. English breakfasts.

🍴 Le Grenier à Sel

26, pl. de l'Éperon
02 43 23 26 30, fax 02 43 77 00 80
Closed Sun dinner, Mon, Aug 1-15. Open until 10:30pm. Air cond.
Once a salt storehouse, now a handsome restaurant: Le Grenier au Sel draws an elegant crowd to its flower-filled dining room hung with contemporary paintings. Bruno Godefroy's menu shows a marked preference for fish and seafood: sample his lobster fricassée with fresh

tagliatelle. Fine wine list. C 190-260. M 130, 250, 80 (children).

 Hippolyte

12, rue Hippolyte-Lecornué
02 43 87 51 00, fax 02 43 87 51 01
Open daily until 11:30pm. Air cond.
Local competitors have envy in their hearts whenever they walk by Hippolyte's fully booked dining rooms. Franck Morillon's menu of seafood platters, grilled meats, and other brasserie dishes has a lot of fans. So does the gloriously befrescoed 1900s–style décor. Friendly welcome; professional service. C 180-250. M 79, 102, 51 (children).

MARÇAY 37500
Paris 289 - Tours 57 - Chinon 10 Indre/Loire

12/20 Château de Marçay

02 47 93 03 47, fax 02 47 93 45 33
Closed Sun dinner off-seas, Mon (exc hols), Jan 15-Mar 15. Open until 9:30pm. Terrace dining. Heated pool. Tennis. Horse riding. Garage pkg.
The setting is as majestic as ever, but the kitchen has lost its Midas touch. A recent meal brought pheasant consommé prepared "à ma façon" (we suggest the chef adopt someone else's...), a toque-worthy chicken pot-au-feu à la tourangelle, and a decent (just decent) goatcheese galette. Gorgeous cellar, but not enough half-bottles. C 380-450. M 150 (weekday lunch), 270, 385, 100 (children).

 Château de Marçay ♠♥

(See restaurant above)
Closed Jan 15-Mar 15. 4 stes 1,420-1,680. 34 rms 495-1,295. Half-board 780-1,220. Restaurant. Rm scr. Conf. Heated pool. Garage pkg. Horse riding.
Huge, bright rooms with elegant tapestry hangings adjoin spacious bathrooms, some with Jacuzzi. In these peaceful, pampering surroundings, your every need is efficiently attended to. Relais et Châteaux.

MOLINEUF 41190
Paris 189 - Blois 10 Indre/Loire

 La Poste

"Thierry Poidras", 11, av. de Blois
02 54 70 03 25, fax 02 54 70 12 46
Closed Sun dinner, Wed, Feb. Open until 9:30pm. Priv rm: 30. Air cond. Pkg.
Follow the gourmets into this blue-and-yellow dining room, adorned with a mural depicting the game-rich Sologne region. Thierry Poidras puts a fresh spin on traditional cuisine. The 90 F set menu is a real bargain: chicken-liver terrine, a juicy beef steak seasoned with fleur de sel, roasted chèvre on a bed of greens, the pastry *du jour*, and petits fours. The cellar is eclectic, and like the food, is clemently priced. C 230-300. M 90 (exc Sun), 140, 220, 50 (children).

MONTBAZON 37250
Paris 247 - Chinon 41 - Tours 12 - Loches 32 Indre/Loire

 La Chancelière

1, pl. des Marronniers
02 47 26 00 67, fax 02 47 73 14 82
Closed Sun dinner & Mon (exc hols), Aug 25-31. Open until 9:30pm. Air cond. Pkg.
In this snug and refined establishment, Michel Gangneux has simplified his flamboyant cuisine. The result is satisfying and attracts many locals. Like us, they enjoy the red mullet served osso buco style, warm oysters in Champagne sauce, or sweetbreads sparked with citrus vinegar. Magnificent Loire wines, with a wide choice of half-bottles. Le Jeu de Carte, a bistro annex, offers excellent menus at attractive prices in an elegant, postmodern garden décor. C 330-350.

 Château d'Artigny

Route d'Azay-le-Rideau
02 47 26 24 24, fax 02 47 65 92 79
Closed Jan 1-11, Nov 29-Dec 31. Open until 9:30pm. Priv rm: 120. Terrace dining. Heated pool. Tennis. Pkg.
We may as well tell you: this "eighteenth-century" château seemingly steeped in history is in fact a bit of megalomania built in 1919 by perfumer René Coty. Revived at huge expense, the interior is a spectacular—if not always harmonious—jumble of antiques, tapestries, and all the other trappings of Château Life. The menu, predictably, strikes rich, full chords but it avoids the heaviness that often marks this genre. Chef Francis Maignaut's elegant offerings include a light and pretty parsleyed fish terrine, truffled Touraine chicken with asparagus risotto, and a flawless strawberry millefeuille. The cellar is one of the finest in France (the wine list is 70 pages long!). Distinguished welcome and service. C 400. M 250 (weekday lunch, wine incl), 285 (exc weekday lunch, wine incl), 280-440, 100 (children).

 Château d'Artigny ♠♥

(See restaurant above)
Closed Jan 1-11, Nov 29-Dec 31. 2 stes 2,300-2,860. 44 rms 650-1,640. Half-board 780-1,260. Bkfst 90-130. Rm scr. Air cond. Conf. Heated pool. Tennis. Pkg.
An immense terrace overlooking the River Indre, vast landscaped grounds, and formal French gardens unrolling to the horizon: such is the magnificent setting for the Château d'Artigny's luxuriously appointed, overdecorated rooms and suites. Exercise room; golf; musical weekends. Relais et Châteaux.

 Domaine de la Tortinière

2 km N on N 10 & D 287, Les Gués-de-Veigné
02 47 34 35 00, fax 02 47 65 95 70
Closed Dec 20-Feb 28. Open until 9:15pm. Priv rm: 100. Terrace dining. Pool. Tennis. No pets. Pkg.

It looks like a Renaissance château (most tourists take it for one), but in fact this imposing structure dates only from the Second Empire. Édouard Wehrlin's proficient cooking is of a classic cast, although some dishes draw inspiration from the local *terroir*, like the beef tenderloin with Chinon marmalade. Fine selection of Loire wines. C 300-400. M 215 (lunch, wine incl), 285, 360.

Domaine de la Tortinière 🌲🍷

(See restaurant above)
Closed Dec 20-Feb 28. 7 stes 1,010-1,500. 14 rms 470-890. Half-board 570-890 (oblig in seas). Bkfst 70. Rms for disabled. Heated pool. Tennis. Conf. No pets. Pkg.
Set down in wooded grounds, here is a luxurious stopover with impeccably equipped and decorated rooms (the ones in the separate pavilions were recently renovated), a heated pool, and tennis courts. Some rooms are equipped with Jacuzzis; all have good bathrooms.

MONTLOUIS-SUR-LOIRE 37270
Paris 241 - Tours 12 - Amboise 15 Indre/Loire

Château de la Bourdaisière 🌲🍷

25, rue de la Bourdaisière
02 47 45 16 31, fax 02 47 45 09 11
Open year-round. 2 stes 750-1,050. 12 rms 550-1,100. Rms for disabled. Bkfst 50. Pool. Tennis. Pkg.
Philippe-Maurice and Louis-Albert de Broglie give château buffs a princely welcome to this Renaissance castle in the Cher Valley. Rooms are large and bright, with lots of charm. Swimming pool and tennis court on the grounds. The cellars have just been opened to the public this year, and the lovely greenhouse has been freshly refurbished.

MONTRICHARD 41400
Paris 204 - Tours 44 - Blois 32 - Loches 31 Loir/Cher

Château de la Menaudière

Route d'Amboise
02 54 71 23 45, fax 02 54 71 34 58
Closed Sun dinner & Mon off-seas, Nov 30-Mar 1. Open until 9pm (10pm in summer). Terrace dining. Tennis. Pool. Pkg.
Our waiters looked a bit awkward in their formal clothes (why do they always remind us of penguins?) but the service dispensed in this Renaissance château is never anything but obliging and amiable. The menu is never anything but sedate—warm salad of sea scallops and mushrooms, fillet of turbot with truffle sabayon, stuffed saddle of rabbit—yet every dish is admirably crafted. Don't be intimidated by the setting: go ahead and order the least expensive set meals! That's what they're there for... C 270. M

90 (lunch), 150 (wine incl), 190-300, 60 (children, free until 6).

Château de la Menaudière 🌲🍷

(See restaurant above)
Closed Sun dinner & Mon off-seas, Nov 30-Mar 1. 25 rms 360-650. Half-board 475-540. Bkfst 58. Air cond. Pool. Conf. Tennis. Pkg.
This handsome old château proposes classically decorated, well-kept, comfortable rooms with views of the surrounding countryside or a pretty inner courtyard with a fountain. Warm welcome; attentive service.

La Tête Noire

24, rue de Tours - 02 54 32 05 55, fax 02 54 32 78 37
Closed Jan. 36 rms 200-330. Restaurant. Bkfst 36. Half-board 285-435. Pkg.
A respectable level of comfort can be found at this rustic hotel in château country.

NOIZAY 37210
Paris 236 - Amboise 9 Indre/Loire

Château de Noizay

Route de Chançay
02 47 52 11 01, fax 02 47 52 04 64
Closed Jan 2-Mar 14. Open until 9:45pm. Priv rm: 21. Terrace dining. Pool. Tennis. No pets. Pkg.
In the château's serenely elegant dining room, chef Didier Frébout presents a menu of such carefully wrought classics as a salad of lightly smoked pigeon and bits of pork belly, pikeperch in a sauce of Chinon wine, and rack of lamb with a delicate white-bean velouté. Desserts are no great shakes, but the cellar harbors a superb selection of Loire wines. C 350. M 150 (lunch), 225 (weekday lunch, wine incl), 240-360, 60 (children).

Château de Noizay 🌲🍷

(See restaurant above)
Closed Jan 2-Mar 14. 14 rms 650-1,300. Half-board 755-1,080. Bkfst 80-120. Restaurant. Rm ser. Conf. Pool. Tennis. Pkg. Helipad.
This sixteenth-century château offers very comfortable, prettily decorated rooms (number five has a canopied bed) that open onto a formal French garden. Professional reception, elegant ambience. Good breakfasts with homemade pastries. Relais et Châteaux.

NOYERS-SUR-CHER 41140
Paris 220 - Romorantin-Lanthenay 32 - Valençay 22 Loir/Cher

Le Clos du Cher 🌲🍷

Route de St-Aignan
02 54 75 00 03, fax 02 54 75 03 79
Closed Wed off-seas, Jan 6-Feb 5, Nov 12-19. 10 rms 390-550. Half-board 395-460. Bkfst 60. Rms for disabled. Restaurant. No pets. Pkg.
At the heart of the château circuit, this posh hostelry occupies a vast, wooded estate. The

comfortable rooms are decorated in an understated style. Attractive packages for cycling holidays are offered.

ONZAIN 41150
Paris 198 - Blois 19 - Amboise 21   Indre/Loire

 ## Domaine des Hauts de Loire

Route d'Herbault - 02 54 20 72 57, fax 02 54 20 77 32
Closed Mon & Tue lunch off-seas, Dec-Jan. Open until 9:30pm. Priv rm: 60. Terrace dining. Heated pool. Tennis. No pets. Valet pkg.
Oak paneling, antiques, and subtle color schemes compose a setting of restrained elegance in this vine-covered former hunting pavilion. Restrained is not the word we'd use to describe the prices, however. Diners who wish to indulge in Rémy Giraud's appealing cuisine (which has taken on an exotic, Mediterranean flavor) will need to line their wallets first! Irreproachable staff; short but diversified wine list. C 350-400. M 290-360, 300 (lunch exc Sun, wine incl), 150 (children).

 ## Domaine des Hauts de Loire

(See restaurant above)
Closed Feb-Mar, Nov-Jan. 8 stes 1,600-2,200. 27 rms 550-1,400. Half-board 1,100-1,200. Bkfst 85. Rms for disabled. Rm ser. Heated pool. Tennis. No pets. Valet pkg.
The immense rooms, suites, and bathrooms of this enchanting estate have been decorated in impeccable taste. The best suites are in the Sologne-style annex. To relax, guests may fish in the lake, swim in the heated pool, or go for a ride in a hot-air balloon. Relais et Châteaux.

ORLÉANS 45000
Paris 116 - Chartres 72 - Tours 113 - Blois 56   Loiret

 ## Les Antiquaires

2-4, rue au Lin - 02 38 53 52 35, fax 02 38 62 06 95
Closed Sun, Mon, Apr 13-21, Aug 3-26, Dec 24-Jan 2. Open until 10pm. Priv rm: 15.
France's provincial bourgeoisie loves to eat well. Their favorite restaurant in Orléans is Michel Pipet's refined establishment near the Pont Royal. You'll discover the sure-handed skill of a veteran chef whose cooking simply never misfires. Try his elegantly balanced warm salad of sweetbreads and foie gras, an exceptional duo of John Dory and mussels with Belgian endive (the latter's faint bitterness points up the sweet shellfish), and a thin apple-caramel tart with cinnamon ice cream. Remember to book ahead at this, the best table in Orléans. Magnificent cellar. C 300. M 115 (weekday lunch), 200 (wine & coffee incl), 300.

The ratings are based solely on the restaurants' cuisine. We do not take into account the atmosphere, décor, service, and so on; these are commented upon within the review.

 ## L'Archange

66, rue du Faubourg-Madeleine
02 38 88 64 20, fax 02 38 43 08 81
Closed Sun dinner, Mon (exc Jul-Aug), Tue dinner, Feb school hols, Aug 3-28. Open until 10pm. Priv rm: 20. Terrace dining.
It's not for the atmosphere that we come here (the faded sea-green décor doesn't raise the spirits), but for the "nougat" of beef and foie gras, spiced sea bass in a meat-based jus, and apple-raspberry crumble. The wine list offers a diverse choice of shippers' wines. Efficient service. C 220. M 90 (exc Sun), 138, 235, 60 (children).

 ## Eugène

24, rue Ste-Anne - 02 38 53 82 64, fax 02 38 54 31 89
Closed lunch Sat & Mon, Sun, Aug. Open until 10pm. Air cond.
Ludovic keeps the crowds coming to his retro-style bistro with an affordable menu that offers the enticing likes of asparagus and foie gras salad, red mullet with vegetables à la grecque, and minted berry gazpacho. Limited cellar of inexpensive wines. And the welcome, like the service, is faultless. C 230. M 125, 180.

 ## Le Florian

70, bd Alex-Martin
02 38 53 08 15, fax 02 38 53 08 49
Closed Sun, Aug 4-25. Open until 10pm. Terrace dining.
A lively brasserie décor, a pretty garden, and Bernard Viron's good cooking bring us back time and again to Le Florian. You're sure to savor the curried leek and mussel tart, tiny red mullet cooked with puckery pickled lemons, and peach soup perfumed with fresh mint. The wine list is a perfect match for the food. C 260. M 120 (weekdays, Sat lunch), 150, 200 (exc Sun).

12/20 La Loire

6, rue Jean-Hupeau - 02 38 62 76 48
Closed Sat lunch, Sun, Aug 1-17. Open until 9:30pm.
The owner's warm welcome puts patrons at ease in this cool, uncluttered blue dining room. The menu highlights seafood, prepared in a variety of clever ways, but sauces are clearly not the chef's strong suit. Limited cellar. C 195. M 105-260, 60 (children).

Novotel-La Source

11 km S on N 20, La Source,
2, rue Honoré-de-Balzac
02 38 63 04 28, fax 02 38 69 24 04
Open year-round. 119 rms 410-470. Bkfst 49. Rms for disabled. Restaurant. Rm ser. Air cond. Conf. Pool. Tennis. Pkg.
Modern, well-maintained, and comfortable, this chain hotel has sporting facilities and a children's playground. Set in wooded grounds, with a poolside bar.

	A	B	C	D	E

(Map of Orléans, The Loire Valley)

C-4 ① - Les Antiquaires 🍴
A-3 ② - L'Archange ♀
B-4 ③ - Le Bigorneau 🏨
B-4 ④ - La Crémaillère ♀
C-3 ⑤ - Eugène ♀

C-2 ⑥ - Le Florian ♀
C-3 ⑦ - Hôtel d'Orléans 🏨
A-4 ⑧ - Holiday Inn Garden Court 🏨
C-4 ⑨ - La Loire 🏨
C-5 ⑩ - Le Restaurant des Plantes ♀

B-2 ⑪ - Saint-Aignan 🏨
A-4 ⑫ - Sanotel 🏨
C-3 ⑬ - Terminus 🏨
B-5 ⑭ - Novotel-La Source 🏨
C-5 ⑮ - La Poutrière ♀

🏨 Hôtel d'Orléans

6, rue Adolphe-Crespin
02 38 53 35 34, fax 02 38 53 68 20
Open year-round. 18 rms 260-380. Bkfst 38. Pkg.
The modern rooms of this centrally situated hotel lack charm, but they are well equipped and practical.

🍴 Le Restaurant des Plantes

44, rue Tudelle - 02 38 56 65 55, fax 02 38 51 33 27
Closed Sat lunch, Sun, Mon dinner, 1 wk at Christmas, May 1-9, 3 wks in Aug. Open until 9:30pm.
This cozy dining room has the look of a family house, and the cooking is homestyle, too, with some bright touches. Try the fricassée

d'escargots perked up with a fresh tomato fondue, savory goujonnettes of cod and red mullet in balsamic vinegar sauce, and wreath of roasted apple slices topped with cinnamon ice cream. Fine regional wines. C 250-320. M 98 (weekdays), 138, 220.

🍴 La Poutrière

8, rue de la Brèche
02 38 66 51 71, fax 02 38 51 19 38
Closed Sun dinner, Mon, Dec 24-Jan 10. Open until 10pm. Air cond. Terrace dining. Pool. Pkg.
Imposing beams, country furniture, and pretty *bibelots* make a charming setting for Simon Le Bras's good classic cooking. On fine days, the tables set out by the pool are awfully inviting! Nice wine list with a good choice of Burgundies

and Bordeaux; cheerful welcome and stylish service. C 280. M 120 (lunch, exc Sun), 240, 350.

 Saint-Aignan

3, pl. Gambetta - 02 38 53 15 35, fax 02 38 77 02 36
Open year-round. 27 rms 200-325. Bkfst 35. Conf. Garage pkg.
Under new management, this hotel has been fully renovated. Pleasant and inexpensive. A warm welcome. Simple meals are served in the evening.

 Sanotel

16, quai Saint-Laurent
02 38 54 47 65, fax 02 38 62 05 91
Open year-round. 50 rms 296-370. Rms for disabled. Air cond. Conf. Garage pkg.
Behind the eighteenth-century façade is a modern hotel with quiet, perfectly adequate rooms. Located on the western edge of town, on the banks of the Loire.

 Terminus

40, rue de la République
02 38 53 24 64, fax 02 38 53 24 18
Closed Dec 22-Jan 3. 47 rms 310-370. Bkfst 40. Restaurant. Conf.
Opposite the train station (as the name implies), this hotel's drab exterior conceals a truly comfortable place to stay. Rooms are not large, but are elegantly furnished.

PETIT-PRESSIGNY (LE)	37350
Paris 305 - Tours 64 - Loches 35	Indre/Loire

 La Promenade

02 47 94 93 52, fax 02 47 91 06 03
Closed Sun dinner, Mon, Jan 6-28, Sep 22-Oct 7. Open until 9:30pm. Air cond.
Jacky Dallais has few peers when it comes to serving up bold, generous cooking at top-value prices. Consider this: 195 F buys creamy scrambled eggs with morels, followed by sole stuffed with chive butter, roast local chicken with salsify, cheese (with homemade bread), and a dessert. The *carte* lists a host of irresistible offerings, like Dallais's famous bacon-flecked carrot bouillon with fava beans and wild thyme, a huge chop of farm-bred pork, and a cocoa feuilleté lavished with molten spiced chocolate. Come here with an appetite, but leave your watch at home: the kitchen and the staff like to take their time. C 375. M 120 (weekdays, Sat lunch, wine incl), 195, 360.

ROCHECORBON	37210
Paris 232 - Tours 5	Indre/Loire

 Les Hautes Roches

86, quai de la Loire
02 47 52 88 88, fax 02 47 52 81 30
Closed Sun dinner & Mon off-seas, mid Jan-mid Mar. Open until 9:30pm. Priv rm: 25. Terrace dining. Heated pool. Pkg.

Here's an uncommon—and uncommonly charming—restaurant built into the tufa cliffs above the Loire. The view from the riverside terrace will take your breath away! Chef Didier Édon's deft cooking sometimes tips over into excess, but that shouldn't mar your enjoyment of his squab with glazed citrus peel or mocha tart with a buttery short crust. Superb wine list. Service is straightforward and smiling. C 360. M 150 (weekday lunch), 270, 355, 100 (children).

 Les Hautes Roches 🌲🍸

(See restaurant above)
Closed mid Jan-mid Mar. 3 stes 1,350. 12 rms 600-1,250. Half-board 735-1,110. Bkfst 85. Rms for disabled. Rm ser. Heated pool. Conf. Pkg.
The stupendous size of these twelve rooms and three suites easily absorbs the opulent décor: refined appointments provide an exquisite contrast to the walls of bare, pale stone. The Loire flows below, with vineyards all around, and the spire of Tours cathedral keeps watch from a distance. Relais et Châteaux.

12/20 L'Oubliette

34, rue des Clouets - 02 47 52 50 49
Closed Sun dinner, Mon, 1 wk in Jan, 2 wks in Feb, 1 wk in Aug, 1 wk in Nov. Open until 9:30pm. Terrace dining. Pkg.
Our enthusiasm for menu at this rock-walled restaurant has waned a bit, but the site remains most attractive. The new chef is still getting his bearings, so we won't be too severe in our criticism of the bland (was it really truffled?) sauce that escorted our magret de canard. On balance, the food is simple, honest, and based on good ingredients. Decent little cellar. C 280. M 104 (weekdays, Sat lunch), 165, 298.

ROMORANTIN-LANTHENAY	41200
Paris 183 - Tours 92 - Bourges 65 - Blois 41	Loir/Cher

 Grand Hôtel du Lion d'Or

69, rue Georges-Clemenceau
02 54 94 15 15, fax 02 54 88 24 87
Closed Feb 17-Mar 20. Open until 9:30pm. Priv rm: 45. Terrace dining. Air cond. Valet pkg.
Didier and Marie-Christine Clément spend their free hours exploring the countryside, coming up with new sources for rare vegetables, herbs, and authentic wild game. Both are experts on exotic spices, and Marie-Christine seeks out forgotten recipes in her library of antique cookery books. The cuisine that evolves from this passionate quest is complex, cerebral—and very expensive. The 410 F menu is inventive, with fresh tuna set off by gooseberry chutney, oysters cooked in Muscat wine and poised in a ryebread croûte, Loire salmon with purslane and anchovies, and iced figs with date confit. But (because this is "just" the cheaper set meal?) the execution fell short somehow, was less exciting than we remembered... Didier Clément is uncompromising on the quality of his ingredients; at these prices, patrons—whatever they spend—

are bound to be uncompromising, too. C 660-1,000. M 410, 600.

Grand Hôtel du Lion d'Or

(See restaurant above)
Closed Feb 17-Mar 20. 3 stes 1,200-2,100. 13 rms 600-1,800. Bkfst 100. Rms for disabled. Rm ser. Air cond. Conf. Valet pkg.
What was formerly a dilapidated post house is now an inn with luxurious rooms and suites overlooking a Renaissance fountain. Elegant public rooms (a pianist plays on Friday evenings in the delightful lounge by the garden). Relais et Châteaux.

ROSIERS-SUR-LOIRE (LES)   49350
Paris 279 - Angers 29 - Saumur 16   Maine/Loire

Auberge Jeanne de Laval

54, rue Nationale - 02 41 51 80 17, fax 02 41 38 04 18
Closed Mon off-seas, 2 wks in winter. Open until 10pm. Terrace dining. No pets. Pkg.
Michel Augereau's sauce au beurre blanc is truly one of a kind, a culinary secret handed down from his father. Michel also picked up a few tips from Joël Robuchon, and these old and new influences combine to produce beautifully crafted classic cuisine. You must taste Michel's poached foie gras glazed with Saumur wine aspic, Loire River pikeperch with that famous beurre blanc, pigeon ballottine perfumed with truffles, and crayfish cooked in Chardonnay. Game is featured in hunting season, and the cellar is a treasure house of venerable Loire vintages. Charming welcome. C 330-450. M 170, 300, 400.

Ducs d'Anjou   ♠♥

(See restaurant above)
Closed 2 wks in winter. 10 rms 350-550. Half-board 540-620 (oblig in seas). Bkfst 50. Rms for disabled. Restaurant. Rm ser. Pkg.
Here you'll find a handful of large, freshly renovated, thoughtfully appointed rooms that look onto a garden and the village church. Marvelous breakfasts; good soundproofing; excellent service.

SAINT-OUEN-LES-VIGNES   37530
Paris 206 - Tours 39 - Amboise 11   Indre/Loire

L'Aubinière

Rue J.-Gauthier - 02 47 30 15 29, fax 02 47 30 02 44
Closed Tue dinner & Wed exc Jul-Aug, Sun dinner Nov-Easter, Feb 15-Mar 15. Open until 9:45pm. Priv rm: 18. Terrace dining. Garage pkg.
The village is tucked away in a verdant valley, but food-loving locals quickly discovered L'Aubinière. Jacques Arrayet's precise, full-flavored cooking wins more fans every day, with the likes of slow-roasted tomatoes dressed with

oxtail vinaigrette, sea bass with zucchini in a saffron-tinged shellfish fumet, and poached cherries with red-wine coulis and verbena ice cream. In fine weather, book a table on the bucolic terrace. Cordial service. C 320. M 98-160 (weekday lunch), 190, 340, 95 (children).

SAINT-PATRICE   37130
Paris 273 - Chinon 26 - Tours 33 - Langeais 9   Indre/Loire

Château de Rochecotte

02 47 96 16 16, fax 02 47 96 90 59
Closed Feb. Open until 9:30pm. Priv rm: 90. Heated pool. Pkg.
In this ravishingly beautiful Renaissance château, you can choose a table on the flower-decked Italianate terrace or in the elegant contemporary dining room: both are seductive settings for Emmanuelle Pasquier's flawless, full-flavored cooking. Taste the perfection of her basil-scented shrimp risotto, then go on to a superb turbot with asparagus and morels, or beef tenderloin spiced with pink peppercorns. Franck Joly signs the haute-couture desserts, while Christelle Pasquier guides guests through the connoisseur's cellar. Stylish, smiling service. C 350. M 195, 285, 80 (children).

Château de Rochecotte   ♠♥

(See restaurant above)
Closed Feb. 3 stes 580-1,250. 27 rms 580-1250. Half-board 505-680. Bkfst 60-90. Rms for disabled. Rm ser. Conf. Heated pool. Pkg. Helipad.
Talleyrand gave this breathtaking château to the Duchesse de Dino, his last love. French formal gardens and Italianate terraces form an exquisite setting for the hotel's magnificent contemporary rooms. The atmosphere is relaxed, the Pasquier family's welcome heartfelt. Gorgeous swimming pool.

SAINT-SYLVAIN-D'ANJOU   49480
Paris 283 - Angers 17 - La Flèche 41   Maine/Loire

Auberge d'Éventard   ۞

N 23, route de Paris
02 41 43 74 25, fax 02 41 34 89 20
Closed Sun dinner, Mon. Open until 10pm. Priv rm: 20. Terrace dining. Air cond. No pets. Pkg.
The superhighway has siphoned off the traffic that used to thunder by this pretty inn on the side of the *route nationale*. Though close to Angers, the Auberge has a decidedly country feel. So does the menu, reflecting Jean-Pierre Maussion's commitment to the authentic flavors of market-fresh, local ingredients. Choose from zesty andouillette sausage with shallots, osso buco of farm-raised chicken with fresh tomatoes, Anjou squab in a honeyed sauce, pikeperch with citrus fruit in a suave sauce based on Savennières wine... The admirable cellar of Loire wines includes magnificent finds straight from the

growers. **C** 300-500. **M** 155 (weekday lunch), 210-355, 100 (children).

SAUMUR 49400
Paris 300 - Angers 53 - Tours 65 - Nantes 127 Maine/Loire

 Anne d'Anjou

32-33, quai Mayaud
02 41 67 30 30, fax 02 41 67 51 00
Closed Dec 23-Jan 4. 50 rms 285-575. Bkfst 48. half-board 400-450. Rms for disabled. Restaurant. Rm ser. Conf. No pets. Garage pkg.
At the foot of Saumur's château and overlooking the Loire, this wonderful eighteenth-century hotel is in part a registered landmark (the façade and grand staircase). Recently remodeled, the rooms are pleasant and well equipped (the spectacular number 102 was designed by Napoléon's architects).

12/20 Les Chandelles

71, rue Saint-Nicolas
02 41 67 20 40, fax 02 41 50 64 21
Closed Wed, Thu lunch off-seas, Feb 1-20. Open until 10pm. Priv rm: 30. Terrace dining.
The freshly refurbished dining room makes Les Chandelles more welcoming than ever, adding to the enjoyment of the kitchen's updated classic cuisine. The cellar, naturally enough, majors in Loire Valley wines. **C** 270. **M** 98, 110.

11/20 Le Clos des Bénédictins

2 km SW on D 751, in St-Hilaire-St-Florent
02 41 67 28 48, fax 02 41 67 13 71
Closed Nov 15-Feb 28. Open until 9:15pm. Priv rm: 20. Terrace dining. Pool. No pets. Pkg.
Though rustic in tone, the setting is polished to a high sheen, and there is a very pretty view of the Thouet Valley. What a shame that the cooking is so uneven! But the cellar is a dream, with wines from the best local growers. **C** 280. **M** 120 (weekdays lunch, Sat), 159, 189, 75 (children).

 Le Clos des Bénédictins

(See restaurant above)
Closed Nov 17-Feb 28. 3 stes 600-800. 2 rms 300-500. Half-board 380-550 (oblig in seas). Rms for disabled. Rm ser. Conf. Pool. Pkg.
This quiet hotel affords a lovely view of Saumur and the Loire. The welcoming rooms are modern, well-equipped, spacious, and considerably more comfortable than in the past.

12/20 Les Délices du Château

Les Feuquières
02 41 67 65 60, fax 02 41 67 74 60
Closed Sun dinner, Dec. Open until 10:30pm. Priv rm: 45. Terrace dining. Pkg.
Foremost among the *délices* of this particular château are appetizing, lively dishes like duck livers and pears under a fluffy potato blanket, squab stuffed with foie gras, and chocolate-raspberry millefeuille. Fine cellar; devoted ser-

vice. **C** 330. **M** 130 (lunch, exc Sun), 200 (wine incl), 175, 285.

 Loire Hôtel

Rue du Vieux-Pont
02 41 67 22 42, fax 02 41 67 88 80
Open year-round. 1 ste 530-670. 43 rms 270-560. Bkfst 48. Half-board 380-535. Rms for disabled. Restaurant. Rm ser. Air cond. Conf. Pkg.
Precisely opposite the château, on the île d'-Offard, the Loire Hôtel offers charming views of wild ducks on the river and large, blessedly peaceful rooms decorated in a fresh, dainty style.

Les Ménestrels

11, rue Raspail - 02 41 67 71 10, fax 02 41 67 89 64
Closed Sun (exc lunch in seas). Open until 9:30pm. Priv rm: 45. Terrace dining. Pkg.
The dining room's stone walls and beamed ceiling set a mood of rustic refinement, a mood mirrored in Lucien Vion's menu. He pairs costly and countrified ingredients in (mostly successful) dishes brimming with personality. The wine list presents an appealing selection of Loire Valley vintages. **C** 230-380. **M** 120 (weekdays lunch) 160, 340, 65 (children).

TAVERS 45190
Paris 150 - Blois 31 - Orléans 25 Loiret

12/20 La Tonnellerie

12, rue des Eaux-Bleues
02 38 44 68 15, fax 02 38 44 10 01
Closed Jan-Feb. Open until 10pm. Terrace dining. Pool.
Tourists adore this pretty establishment with its soothing décor and summer terrace. The cooking has its ups and downs, though: on the downside, carelessly peeled asparagus tips and lobster presented in clumsy slices on salad greens "cooked" by a long soak in their vinaigrette. These lapses were (nearly) redeemed by a ginger-spiced pikeperch, very good blue-cheese feuilleté, and a wonderful banana Tatin with orange-flavored caramel. The service lacks polish. **C** 200. **M** 95 (lunch exc Sun), 125, 230, 65 (children).

 La Tonnellerie

(See restaurant above)
Closed Jan-Feb. 3 stes 840-1,825. 17 rms 350-1,095. Bkfst 55. Half-board 505-730 (oblig in seas). Rm ser. Conf. Pool.
Bright, fully renovated rooms and suites decorated with quiet good taste. Lovely swimming pool; hiking excursions and river cruises arranged.

This symbol stands for "Les Lauriers du Terroir", an award given to chefs who prepare traditional or regional cuisine.

TOURS   37000

TGV Paris 234 - Angers 105 - Orléans 113   Indre/Loire

 ## L'Alliance

292, av. de Grammont
02 47 28 00 80, fax 02 47 27 77 61
Open year-round. 5 stes 600-1,200. 119 rms 380-450. Bkfst 50. Restaurant. Rm ser. Conf. Pool. Tennis. Pkg.
    A large hotel (vintage 1970) with a formal French garden built close (too close, we say) to the A-10 highway. The lobby is oddly ostentatious, the rooms are decorated in period style.

 ## Jean Bardet   ✪

57, rue Groison
02 47 41 41 11, fax 02 47 51 68 72
Closed Mon lunch Avr-Oct, Sun dinner & Mon Nov-Mar. Open until 10pm. Priv rm: 40. Pool. Valet pkg.
    Jean Bardet is a real gardener, and he grows his own vegetables and herbs. He can coax delectable nuances from his better-than-prime ingredients, and we admire his fine-tuned taste and fine-honed technique. Bardet is an alchemist when it comes to sauces, like the jus that embellish his eels in aged wine vinegar or foie gras de canard au Maury; an artist who creates compositions of rare beauty, like the lobster civet perfumed with ginger, Vouvray wine, and a hint of lime. Oh, and his cellar! It's immense, with a wealth of rare bottles from all over France and some affordable Loire wines, too. C 600-900. M 420 (exc Sat dinner, wine incl), 300 (weekdays, Sat lunch, wine incl), 450 (Sun lunch, wine incl), 380-750, 150 (children).

 ## Jean Bardet   ♠♣

(See restaurant above)
Open year-round. 5 stes 500-1,900. 16 rms 500-1,900. Bkfst 120. Rm ser. Air cond. Pool. Valet pkg.
    This early-nineteenth-century villa, remodeled during the Second Empire, is surrounded by romantic, stream-fed grounds. The Bardets have taken infinite pains to restore and enlarge the premises—a beautifully refurbished greenhouse with a befrescoed ceiling is their most recent accomplishment. Just over the reception area and gift shop, several new suites and English-style guest rooms have been added. Several boast balconies and sumptuous marble baths (the latter hold all the accessories and complimentary toiletries one could wish). Fabulous breakfasts. Relais et Châteaux.

 ## Barrier

101, av. Tranchée - 02 47 54 20 39, fax 02 47 41 80 95
Closed Sun dinner. Open until 9:30pm. Priv rm: 30. Air cond. Pkg.
    Charles Barrier has sold his restaurant, but he lingers on like a persistent ghost. For the next year, he has veto rights over everything that goes on in his former establishment. The new chef, for example, is not allowed to take any of Barrier's

signature dishes off the menu; so far, only two new offerings have been added. We'll come back to rate the restaurant after Barrier is definitely out of the picture. Stay tuned! M 150 (weekdays), 230-560.

 ## Hôtel Harmonie   ♠♣

15, rue Frédéric-Joliot-Curie
02 47 66 01 48, fax 02 47 61 66 38
Closed Dec mid-Jan mid. 6 stes 550-950. 48 rms 400-500. Bkfst 55. Rms for disabled. Conf. Pkg.
    Music fills the air (even in the elevator!) at this pleasant hotel, located on a quiet street not far from the railway station. The modern rooms are beautifully appointed in a bright, Art Deco spirit. English bar.

 ## Holiday Inn

15, rue Édouard-Vaillant
02 47 31 12 12, fax 02 47 38 53 35
Open year-round. 2 stes 980. 103 rms 440-515. Half-board 410. Bkfst 60. Rms for disabled. Restaurant. Rm ser. Conf. Air cond. Pkg.
    This futuristic, mirror-clad Holiday Inn provides air conditioned, soundproofed rooms furnished with wicker pieces.

 ## Mirabeau

89 bis, bd Heurteloup
02 47 05 24 60, fax 02 47 05 31 09
Open year-round. 25 rms 250-310. Bkfst 39. Garage pkg.
    Conveniently close to the train station, the Mirabeau occupies a stately town house, whose attractive rooms are decorated with antique furniture. A terrace looks out on the pleasant garden.

 ## La Roche Le Roy

55, route de Saint-Avertin
02 47 27 22 00, fax 02 47 28 08 39
Closed Sat lunch, Sun dinner, Mon, Feb school hols, 3 wks in Aug. Open until 9:30pm. Priv rm: 40. Terrace dining. Pkg.
    Touraine's food lovers flock to this lovely Renaissance manor, so you must reserve in advance for a chance to sample Alain Couturier's polished, seasonal cuisine. The menu includes a lush combination of scallops and lobster in a butter sauce hinting of vanilla, John Dory with chanterelles enhanced by a meaty jus, roast breast of squab with bacon-flecked potatoes, and a delectable bitter-chocolate and raspberry tart. Distinguished cellar; service charmingly directed by Marilyn Couturier. C 300-400. M 160 (lunch), 200, 350.

 ## Rôtisserie Tourangelle

23, rue du Commerce
02 47 05 71 21, fax 02 47 61 60 76
Closed Sun dinner, Mon. Open until 10pm. Priv rm: 60. Terrace dining. Pkg.
    This airy eating house next to the town's archaeological museum is understandably

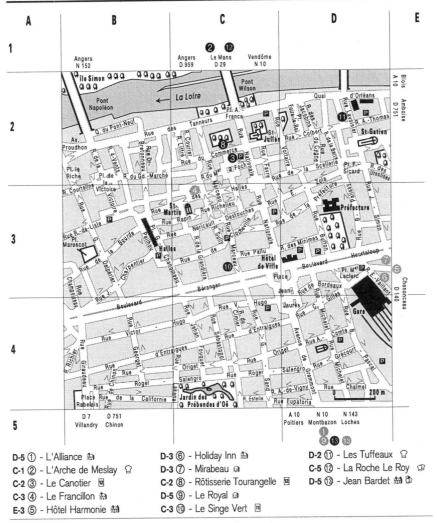

D-5 ① - L'Alliance 🏛
C-1 ② - L'Arche de Meslay ♀
C-2 ③ - Le Canotier 🎏
C-3 ④ - Le Francillon 🏛
E-3 ⑤ - Hôtel Harmonie 🏨

D-3 ⑥ - Holiday Inn 🏨
D-3 ⑦ - Mirabeau 🏠
C-2 ⑧ - Rôtisserie Tourangelle 🎏
D-5 ⑨ - Le Royal 🏠
C-3 ⑩ - Le Singe Vert 🎏

D-2 ⑪ - Les Tuffeaux ♀
C-5 ⑫ - La Roche Le Roy ♀
D-5 ⑬ - Jean Bardet 🏨 🏛

popular: diners are warmly welcomed and nicely fed. True, there are occasional lapses, but on the whole there's nothing at all wrong with sea scallops in a delicate jus, tiny red mullets spiced with cardamom (we could have done without the pistachio garnish), and tender crêpes in a bright orange-flavored jus. Lots of fine Chinons in the cellar. An extra point this year. C 230. M 95 (weekdays, Sat lunch), 145, 195.

The C (A la carte) restaurant prices given are for a complete three-course meal for one, including a half-bottle of modest wine and service. M (Menu) prices are for a complete fixed-price meal for one, excluding wine (unless otherwise noted).

🏠 Le Royal-Clarine

65, av. de Grammont
02 47 64 71 78, fax 02 47 05 84 62
Open year-round. 50 rms 295-350. Bkfst 39. Rms for disabled. Conf. Garage pkg.
A hideous modern building conceals beautiful, well-equipped rooms, most with period furnishings. Private garage. Professional reception.

🏠 Les Tuffeaux

19, rue Lavoisier - 02 47 47 19 89
Closed Sun, Mon lunch. Open until 9:30pm. Air cond.
We needled chef Gildas Marsollier last year for what looked like lethargy in the kitchen. Well, he's back on track again, we're pleased to say, cooking up the creative likes of pigeon on a bed of Belgian endive with a suave walnut sauce, veal kidney with a radish gratin, and a lush pear

stuffed with caramelized nuts. Perfectly decent cellar. C 230. M 110 (weekdays, Sat lunch), 130 (weekdays, Sat lunch, wine incl), 150 (wine incl), 200, 50 (children).

And also...

Our selection of places for inexpensive, quick, or late-night meals.
Le Singe Vert (02 47 20 02 76 - 65, rue Marceau. Closed Sun off-seas. Open until 12:30am.): Traditional Touraine specialties are featured at this old-fashioned bistro, run by a likable chap who's fond of accordion music (*musette* evenings are held here twice a month) (68-260).
Zafferano (02 47 38 90 77 - 47, rue du Grand-Marché. Closed Sun, Mon, at Christams. Open until 10:30pm.): Genuine Italian food and wine in Tours's historic center (95-150).

VENDÔME	41100
TGV Paris 170 - Tours 55 - Orléans 75 - Blois 32	Loir/Cher

🍽13 La Cloche Rouge

15, fg Chartrain - 02 54 77 02 88, fax 02 54 73 90 71
Closed Fri & Sun dinner Nov-Jan. Open until 9:30pm. Priv rm: 30. Pkg. HOTEL: "Le Vendôme," 35 rms 210-435. Half-board 260-380. Bkfst 45. Conf.
After visiting Vendôme's charming old town (don't miss the truly splendid church), relax in this posh, peach-toned dining room with the good-value 130 F menu: it brings warm pike terrine, steak with bone marrow à la bordelaise, a selection of cheeses, and a fine fruit tart. The local wines are affordably priced, too. C 225. M 75, 130, 190, 55 (children).

REGIONAL FOODS

Best known for its collection of royal and aristocratic châteaux, the Loire Valley also deserves its reputation as the Garden of France. So as you tour the châteaux, do take time to pause to take in the region's many and varied gastronomic glories: charcuterie (rillettes, rillons, terrines...), cheeses, distinctive candies and cookies, and wines (see Wine, below).

• BAKERIES

ANGERS	49100 – Maine/Loire

La Maison du Pain

4, pl. de la Visitation - 02 41 87 53 11
Breads based on a natural sourdough sponge. Don't miss the delicious whole-grain bread (pain aux céréales) and the splendid round country loaves. Good brioches and buns, too.

BLOIS	41100 – Loir/Cher

Jean-Paul Marchau

147, bis av. du Maréchal Maunoury - 02 54 78 27 78
Very good bread and delicious, buttery buns and brioches.

Jacky Sailly

7, rue du Commerce - 02 54 78 07 41
Jacky Sailly, who trained with the famed Parisian baker Jean-Luc Poujauran, creates chewy, full-flavored loaves that bear comparison with those of the master. Exceptional whole-grain bread.

CONTRES	41700 – Loir/Cher

Dubois-Coquin

6, rue Bracieux - 02 54 79 53 90
Remarkable sourdough breads, with special mention for the whole-grain loaf (pain aux céréales) and the pain bûcheron. Do try the tasty potato galette, too.

• CHARCUTERIE

AMBOISE	37400 – Indre/Loire

Michel Budts

26, pl. du Général-Leclerc - 02 47 57 23 71
Top-notch rillettes (minced pork spread), made with quality meat and expert seasoning.

ANGERS	49100 – Maine/Loire

Noël Amiot

13, rue Saint-Lazare - 02 41 73 89 83
Stop by this charcuteries for rich, delectable rillettes and excellent pâté en croûte.

CHÂTILLON-SUR-LOIRE	45360 – Loiret

Coilbeau

23, Grande-Rue - 02 38 31 45 52
Excellent charcuteries of all types, but andouillettes (AAAAA) are the house specialty.

CONNERE	72160 – Sarthe

Jean-Louis Guéret

27, rue de Paris - 02 43 89 01 05
This expert charcutier has won prizes for his rillettes (minced pork spread), but he also serves up delicious chunks of belly bacon (rillons), juicy

roast pork, and an authentic andouille (chitterling sausage).

CONTRES 41700 – Loir/Cher

Gilles Gasnier

1, rue Julien Nadau - 02 54 79 51 60
Come here for tender, tasty rillettes and rillons, as well as full-flavored andouillettes (tripe sausages).

JARGEAU 45150 – Loiret

Charcuterie Martroy

14, pl. du Martroy - 02 38 59 71 48
Come here for the andouillette de Jargeau, tasty rillons (chunks of pork belly, a local specialty), and other appetizing charcuteries.

LOCHES 37600 – Indre/Loire

Gendrot

5, pl. du Blé - 02 47 59 00 67
Rillettes (minced pork spread) that boast outstanding texture and flavor.

TOURS 37000 – Indre/Loire

Yves Lebeau

34, rue des Halles - 02 47 05 66 97
Lebeau's rillettes are not minced too fine: their chunky texture is wonderfully appetizing! A very good charcuterie.

VILLEBAROU 41000 – Loir/Cher

Gillet

8, rue de la Poste - 02 54 78 25 13
Gillet's boudins blancs (white sausage made with veal or chicken and pork) are sold in Paris at Fauchon—now, that's a recommendation! The rest of his specialties are of equally high quality.

VOUVRAY 37210 – Indre/Loire

Hardouin

L'Étang Vignon - 02 47 40 40 40
The Hardouin brothers work hard to maintain their excellent reputation for rillettes, rillons, and andouillettes.

• *CHEESE*

CHEMILLE 49120 – Maine/Loire

Cabri d'Anjou

La Chaponnière - 02 41 30 60 15

The Socteleaus raise their own goats, and from the milk produce excellent fresh and matured cheeses: particularly recommended are the Chabis, Bûchettes, Crottins, and Sainte-Maures. Visitors may tour the dairy, if they like.

PONTLEVOY 41400 – Loir/Cher

Jean-Pierre et Martine Moreau

Ferme de Bellevue,
80, route de Montrichard - 02 54 32 50 39
All the best goat cheeses made in the region are on hand: Selles-sur-Cher, Sainte-Maure, Valençay, crottins...

ROMILLY-DU-PERCHE 41270 – Loire/Cher

Ferme de la Bretonnerie

02 54 80 65 14
The Pelletier family always extend a warm welcome to visitors who come to admire their goat farm and sample their fine chèvres. Among our favorites are the Petit Perche, the Pyramide, and the Crottin.

STE-MAURE-DE-TOURAINE 37800 – Indre/Loire

La Haute Piltière

N 10 - 02 47 65 65 03
You can tour the premises and sample the wares at this dairy, where prime Sainte-Maure goat cheeses are produced.

SANCERRE 18300 – Cher

Fromagerie Dubois-Boulay

Chavignol - 02 48 54 15 69
We can't decide which we like better, the creamy fresh goat cheeses sold here, or the more pungent, matured variety. Both are absolutely delicious!

SELLES-SUR-CHER 41130 – Loir/Cher

La Fromagerie

2, rue Docteur Massacré - 02 54 88 57 60
All the local chèvres are available here, in fresh or matured versions.

VILLANDRY 37510 – Indre/Loire

Béatrice de Montferrier

Domaine de la Giraudière - 02 47 50 08 60
Goat cheeses sold fresh, direct from the producer, or as ingredients in tasty prepared dishes.

• *CHOCOLATE & CANDY*

ANGERS
45000 – Loiret...

ANGERS 49100 – Maine/Loire

La Petite Marquise

22, rue des Lices - 02 41 87 43 01
Quernons d'Ardoise (nougatine coated with slate-blue chocolate) have become something of a specialty in Angers. Unusual and quite delicious.

Le Trianon

7, rue Lenepveu - 02 41 47 44 39
Elegant, unusual chocolates: try the Bouchon d'Anjou, the Plantagenêt, the Panaché d'Anjou...or opt for a rich and yummy gâteau.

BOURGES 18000 – Cher

La Maison des Forestines

3, pl. Cujas - 02 48 24 00 24
Candy fanciers come here for the justly famous Forestines de Bourges (crunchy pralines), but the other house specialties are worth tasting, too.

CHOLET 49300 – Maine/Loire

Serge Boisliveau

48, pl. Rouge - 02 41 62 20 31
Here you'll find a wonderful collection of chocolates: do sample the Cholon de Cholet, the Galet d'Or, and the Crottin de la Jument Verte (the latter would definitely lose something in the translation...).

LANGEAIS 37130 – Indre/Loire

Maison Rabelais

4, pl. Pierre-de-Brosse - 02 47 96 82 20
This chocolate maven is famed for his delectable Muscadins and Noisetons.

MANS (LE) 72000 – Sarthe

Chocolaterie Béline

5, pl. Saint-Nicolas - 02 43 28 00 43
The specialties here are (aptly enough) called Buggatises, Pavés du Vieux Mans, or Mancelles. But all of the goodies here are worth tasting, with special mention for the chocolate "rillettes."

MONTARGIS 45200 – Loiret

Au Duc de Praslin

Pl. Mirabeau - 02 38 98 63 55
Almond and hazelnut candies, including the famous pralines that are a Montargis specialty, are sold in this pretty sweet shop.

ORLÉANS 45000 – Loiret

Chocolaterie Royale

51, rue Royale - 02 38 53 93 43
No fewer than 90 varieties of chocolates, pralines, candied fruits, sugar-coated almonds, and scores of other treats: a truly royal array!

TOURS 37000 – Indre/Loire

La Chocolatière

6, rue de la Scellerie - 02 47 05 66 75
The star attractions here are ganache- and praline-filled chocolates, but the plump and tender stuffed prunes (a local specialty) are well worth tasting.

• *FRUITS & VEGETABLES*

BLOIS 41000 – Loir/Cher

Sastre

5, rue des Trois Clefs - 02 54 74 35 09
This is the best place in town for fresh fruit and vegetables: the selection is truly superb.

CONTRES 41700 – Loir/Cher

Gillet

5, av. des Platanes - 02 54 79 53 05
Top-quality fruits and vegetables in tins and jars; look for the outstanding Sologne.

LONGUÉ 49160 – Maine/Loire

Alain Guitton

Petit Chantenay - 02 41 52 16 11
Seasonal fruits and vegetables from a reliable producer.

SAINT-SYLVAIN-D'ANJOU 49480 – Maine/Loire

Gilbert Manseau

Vergers de Séné - 02 41 43 71 57
Ripe, fresh fruit sold direct by the grower.

We're always happy to hear about your discoveries and receive your comments on ours. Please feel free to write to us stating clearly what you liked or disliked. Be concise but convincing, and take the time to argue your point.

• *GOURMET SPECIALTIES*

Boar

AUTRECHE   37110 – Indre/Loire

Élevage de Sangliers Grand Veneur

Domaine de Beaumarchais - 02 47 56 22 30
Take a tour of the farm, then browse in the shop for gourmet treats based on boar meat.

Buffalo

CHAUVIGNY-DU-PERCHE   41270 – Loir/CHer

Ferme de la Sirotière

J. et M.-C. Dufournier - 02 54 80 65 46
A buffalo farm in the Loire Valley? Well, why not? Visitors may tour the "ranch," then stop for a bite of bison-based lunch, or purchase jars of buffalo terrine, rillettes, or civet (a winy stew) in the little shop on the premises.

Escargots

ST-ANTOINE-DU-ROCHER   37360 – Indre/Loire

Ferme du Plessis

02 47 56 62 74
The little gastropods are raised, prepared, and served right on the premises.

Fish

CHAMPTOCEAUX   49270 – Maine/Loire

Le Fumoir

La Marionnière - 02 40 83 50 76
Alain Deltombe harbors an irrepressible passion for fish. Depending on the season, he smokes locally caught Loire River salmon and eels, as well as farmed salmon from Norway, Scotland, and Ireland. When he's in the mood, he even cooks for visitors: Deltombe's **table d'hôte** is famed for its fine food and friendly ambience.

SAINT-DIÉ-SUR-LOIRE   41500 – Loir/Cher

La Bourriche aux Appétits

Chemin Creux de l'Ecuelle - 02 54 81 65 25
Gilles Quesneau turns Loire River fish into delectable prepared dishes that you may pur-

chase on the premises: we're fond of his cocktail spreads made from pikeperch, or crayfish, or salmon, as well as his crayfish terrine, eel stewed in wine, fish choucroute, and chicken confit with crayfish.

Foie Gras

LION D'ANGERS (LE)   49220 – Maine/Loire

Les Treilles Gourmandes

Route de Candé - 02 41 95 82 82
Swing in here to stock up on fine foie gras and very good tinned specialties based on duck and pigeon.

Jams

CHAUVIGNY-DU-PERCHE   41270 – Loir/Cher

Les Diorières

02 54 80 35 80
Franck Johanny sells traditional jams made the old-fashioned way, as well as a range of unusual flavors: caramel, cider, and wine among them. You'll also want to try the Joudry, a wonderfully mellow orange cake.

CHENU   72500 – Sarthe

La Ferme de la Métairie

La Métairie - 02 43 46 01 01
The fruit that goes into these full-flavored jams and preserves (34 varieties) is guaranteed organically grown.

CHINON   37500 – Indre/Loire

Claude Fleurisson

18, quai Jeanne d'Arc - 02 47 93 99 82
Irresistible wine jellies, made mostly with local vintages. They are wonderful on bread or in cooking, or as an unusual condiment for rillettes and other charcuteries.

SANCERRE   18300 – Cher

Maison Joseph Mellot

Route Ménétréol, Le Pavé - 02 48 54 21 50
This well-known winery also proposes an extraordinary range of wine-based jams.

Looking for a town or restaurant? A winery? A gastronomic specialty or a celebrated chef? Consult the alphabetical index to locate them quickly and easily.

Pigeon

GENNETON   79150 – Deux Sèvres

Mireille et Pierre David

Maumusson - 05 49 96 89 12
  Delicious home-prepared specialties (rillettes, terrine, confits...) based on farm-raised pigeon and squab.

Venison

EPUISAY   41360 – Loir/Cher

Ferme de la Roussetière

J.-P. Odeau - 02 54 72 04 68
  After a tour of the farm, you can stop at the little boutique to purchase rillettes, terrines, or other prepared dishes featuring farm-raised venison.

Vinegar

FLEURY-ORLÉANS   45400 – Loiret

Martin-Poulet

236, fbg Bannier - 02 38 88 78 49
  For hundreds of years, Orléans has been known for its premium vinegars. Here you'll find a wide selection of barrel-aged vinegars made from fine wines: Chinon, Bourgueil, Bordeaux, and Muscadet.

Walnut Oil

NOYERS-SUR-CHER   41140 – Loir/Cher

Huilerie du Berry

42, rue de Tours - 02 54 75 09 09
  Delicately flavored walnut oil for your vinaigrettes, as well as extra-fresh pinenuts and pistachios.

• *PASTRY & COOKIES*

AMBOISE   37400 – Indre /Loire

Pâtisserie Bigot

Pl. du Château - 02 47 57 04 46
  By all means stop here to taste the raspberry Pavé Royal, but don't overlook the creamy almond paste and fine hand-dipped chocolates.

BLOIS   41000 – Loir/Cher

Au Goût des Saveurs

74, rue du Commerce - 02 54 78 20 73
  Éric Saguez is an award-winning chocolatier, whose cakes and candies are well worth a detour. You'll love his ethereal mousses and desserts.

CORMERY   37320 – Indre/Loire

Olivier Couléon

16, rue Montrésor - 02 47 43 40 25
  Incomparable macarons (almond cookies) made according to a recipe handed down by the monks in the neighboring monastery.

GIEN   45500 – Loiret

Au Petit Chasseur

3, rue Tlemcen - 02 38 67 01 62
  Jean-Claude Bouclet proposes a range of yummy candies and several creative specialties, such as his Giennois, Tronc Solognot, and Succès.

ORLÉANS   45000 – Loiret

Les Musardises

38, rue de la République - 02 38 53 30 98
  Sweets with a sophisticated touch: we're partial to the raspberry Val de Loire, the Manjari (chocolate and hazelnut), and Plaisir (chocolate and pear). Fine hand-dipped chocolates, too.

OUSSOY-EN-GÂTINAIS   45290 – Loiret

Biscuiterie Artisanale

Michel Paupardin,
La Petite Billardière - 02 38 96 22 59
  Premium ingredients and traditional recipes produce scrumptious Croq'noisettes (hazelnut cookies), shortbread cookies, pound cakes Gingerbread.

ROMORANTIN-LANTHENAY   41200 – Loir/Cher

Aux Délices de Sologne

Jean-Claude Léchaudé
84, rue Georges Clémenceau - 02 54 96 05 10
  Come here to taste the legendary Tarte Tatin on its home turf, but don't neglect the other exquisite sweets (the chocolate cakes are divine).

TOURS   37000 – Indre/Loire

Poirault

31, rue Nationale - 02 47 66 99 99
  We stop here for the lovely Tarte Tatin and Pithiviers (puff pastry stuffed with almond

cream), as well as for such treats as Nougat de Tours, stuffed prunes (a local specialty), barley sugar, and yummy chocolates.

VENDÔME
41100 – Loir/Cher

Pierre Bouard

9, pl. Saint-Martin - 02 54 77 32 78
Here's an inventive and highly skilled candy man, who creates all manner of delectable pastries and petits fours.

VILLENY
41220 – Loir/Cher

Lionel Girard

02 54 98 34 07
Appetizing pastries and irresistible candies to bring back home: look for the almond-flavored Malice du Loup, a specialty of the house.

OFF THE BEATEN TRACK

• MUSEUMS

After you tour the châteaux, the churches, and the rest of the region's most famous sites, why not take time to explore some out-of-the-way museums that present the local crafts and customs? You'll discover a fascinating side of the Loire Valley and its age-old traditions.

BOURGUEIL
37140 – Indre/Loire

Musée de la Cave et du Vin

02 47 97 72 01
Learn about the traditions and lore of wine-making as you wander through cool cellars carved out of limestone.

BOYNES
45300 – Loiret

Musée du Safran

21, route de Pithiviers - 02 38 33 13 05
Once upon a time the Loiret region was one of the world's major centers for processing saffron. That tradition is beginning to flower again, as you'll discover when you visit this charming museum.

CHECY
45430 – Loiret

Musée de la Tonnelerie

8, pl. du Cloître - 02 38 86 93 93
If you're in the area, stop in and visit this cooperage museum, where an array of antique barrels and tools is on display.

CHINON
37500 – Indre/Loire

Musée Animé du Vin et de la Tonnelerie

12, rue Voltaire - 02 47 93 25 63
The exhibits in this wine and cooperage museum are animated by mechanical figures. Wine-tastings are offered here, too.

CHOLET
49300 – Maine/Loire

Musée du Textile

Route de Beaupréau - 02 41 75 25 40
Cholet, for the French, is synonymous with handkerchiefs. Here in the local textile museum, the town's industrial traditions are presented in a series of exhibits and demonstrations. Samples may be purchased in the gift shop.

MORMANT-SUR-VERNISSON
45700 – Loiret

Écomusée de l'Apiculture

N 7 - 02 38 89 39 95
Everything you ever wanted to know about bees and honey can be learned at this little museum. All manner of honey and beeswax products are presented for sale.

RAIRIES (LES)
49430 – Maine/Loire

La Maison de la Terre Cuite

Route de Fougeré - 02 41 76 33 12
Fashioning and firing clay are age-old activities hereabouts. These traditional crafts are amply documented in the local museum, where terracotta tiles and other objects are on display. In the town, visitors are invited to explore the clay quarry and brickyard.

RIVARENNES
371906 – Indre/Loire

Musée de la Poire Tapée

7, chemin Buronnière - 02 47 95 47 78
Now here's a find: a museum devoted to the local tradition of preserving pears by drying and flattening them with a curious wooden instrument. Don't miss it!

STE-MAURE-DE-TOURAINE 37800 – Indre/Loire

Musée de la Ville de Sainte-Maure

Pl. du Château - 02 47 65 66 20
Local crafts, folk art, and traditions are presented here, with an emphasis on raising goats and making the goat cheese for which Sainte-Maure is famous. Cheese is also offered for sale.

SAUMUR   49400 – Maine/Loire

Musée du Champignon

Route de Gennes,
Saint Hilaire-Saint Florent - 02 41 50 31 55
See how mushrooms sprout and grow along miles of underground tunnels: there are white mushrooms (champignons de Paris), oyster mushrooms, shiitakes, and more. A well-documented exhibit presents some 200 varieties of mushrooms.

VOUVRAY   37210 – Indre/Loire

Espace de la Vigne et du Vin

30, rue Victor-Hérault - 02 47 52 66 04
After examining an array of tolls and implements used to cultivate grapes and make wine, you can sample some of the local production.

• *FAIENCE & PORCELAIN*

FOECY   18500 – Cher

Philippe Deshoulières

39, rue Grandjean - 02 48 51 04 60
Smart shoppers visit this factory outlet for lovely tableware (china, crystal, silver...) at extremely attractive prices.

GIEN   45500 – Loiret

Faïencerie de Gien

78, pl. de la Victoire - 02 38 67 00 05
This charming museum, which dates from the turn of the century, houses a unique collection of Gien's world-famous blue faïence. There is a shop on the premises.

• *ROSES*

DOUE-LA-FONTAINE   49700 –Maine/Loire

La Rose en Fête

02 41 59 20 49

Roses are grown in abundance in this small town near Saumur. Early in July, a huge rose show is staged in the town's Gallo-Roman arena. Cave dwellings are another local curiosity worth visiting.

PITHIVIERS-LE-VIEIL   45300 – Loiret

Les Roses Anciennes d'André Eve

Morailles - 02 38 30 01 30
One of the most famous nurseries in France for old-fashioned roses. Tours may be arranged by appointment.

WINE

Château-hopping in the Loire Valley can be most pleasantly combined with visits to the region's wineries. Touraine and Anjou-Saumur are the major districts we cover here; they lie along the central portion of the Loire River, from Cheverny in the heart of château country, westward to Savennières in the environs of Angers.

A large palette of grape varieties is cultivated in the region, reflecting the diversity of terrains (clay, sand, limestone, gravel—you name it). Cabernet Franc for red wines, and Chenin Blanc for whites, are the Loire Valley's two most distinctive varieties, but Gamay, Cabernet Sauvignon, Pinot Noir, Pineau d'Aunis, and Cot are also employed for red wines, Sauvignon Blanc, Chardonnay, and Romorantin for whites, with Grolleau for good measure in rosés. Consequently, the Loire Valley produces just about every type of wine you could think of (yes, even sparkling red). Chenin Blanc alone can be vinified as a dry, off-dry, sparkling, or mellow dessert wine—it all depends on the weather.

Touraine has borne vines since Roman times, and in the Renaissance the comic genius, François Rabelais, lavished praise on the wines of his native region. Touraine's top red wines—Chinon, Bourgueil, and Saint-Nicolas-de-Bourgueil—share the characteristic violet and raspberry aromas of the Cabernet Franc grape, which each wine expresses differently, in response to specific soil and growing conditions. In Vouvray and Montlouis, Chenin Blanc grapes attain a nearly ideal balance of lusciousness and acidity when long, hot summers concentrate their sweetness. In cooler years, the same variety produces dry (indeed, rather sharp) or sparkling wines.

But it is in **Anjou** that the Chenin Blanc reaches its apotheosis, with the richly perfumed (and nearly immortal) late-harvested wines of Bonnezeaux, Coteaux du Layon, and Quarts-de-Chaume. At Savennières, the Chenin Blanc grape produces one of the world's greatest dry white wines. Lots of rosé is still produced in Anjou, though it is gradually falling from favor with the wine-drinking public. In Anjou and Saumur, reds based on (mostly) Cabernet Franc and (some) Cabernet Sauvignon have appetizing, fruity bouquets. Saumur-Champigny yields some of the area's most delicious red wines, which improve with a few years in the cellar.

• *TOURAINE*

BEAUMONT-EN-VÉRON   37420 – Indre/Loire

Domaine du Colombier

16, rue du Colombier
02 47 58 43 07, fax 02 47 58 93 99
Open Mon-Sat 8:30am-7pm. V.
At this estate just six kilometers outside of Chinon, taste the Assemblage Domaine (estate blend), ready to drink now and until the year 2000 (peony nose, raspberry finish—a delightful Chinon) and the cuvée made from older vines, a wine for long keeping. New this year: some white Chinon, from Chenin Blanc vines planted a few years back.

BOURGUEIL   37140 – Indre/Loire

Yannick Amirault

La Coudraye, route du Moulin-Bleu
02 47 97 78 07, fax 02 47 97 94 78
Open daily (exc Sun).
Bourgueil and Saint-Nicolas-de-Bourgueil, both born of the Cabernet Franc grape, have seductive berry bouquets and good tannic structure. Vines grown in sandy soil produce wines for early drinking, while those from the higher slopes yield wine for longer keeping. Amirault's cuvée Les Graviers of Saint-Nicolas-de-Bourgueil is worthy of note, as is his Bourgueil from old vines, with a distinctive cherry nose.

CHENONCEAUX   37150 – Indre/Loire

Château de Chenonceau

Domaine de Chenonceau
02 47 23 90 07, fax 02 47 23 89 91
Open daily 11am-6pm. V, AE, MC.
It is said that Chenin vines were first planted here in the fifteenth century. Today, the château benefits from the most modern equipment. Try the dry white Touraine called Les Dômes de Chenonceau—rich and robust, it's quite a mouthful!

COUR-CHEVERNY   41700 – Loir/Cher

Domaine des Huards

Marcel Gendrier, Les Huards
02 54 79 97 90, fax 02 54 79 26 82
Open Mon-Sat 8am-12:30pm & 2pm-7pm (Sun by appt). V, AE, MC.
Cheverny, in the heart of château country, produces crisp, fruity wines in every color. This estate's white Cheverny AOC, a blend of Sauvignon and Chardonnay, is firm with a long finish; there's a nice, spicy red Cheverny, too. Don't miss the aromatic white Cour-Cheverny AOC made from the local Romorantin grape.

CRAVANT-LES-COTEAUX   37500 – Indre/Loire

Pierre Sourdais

Le Moulin à Tan - 02 47 93 31 13, fax 02 47 98 30 48
Open daily by appt. V, AE, MC.
The best Chinons, from vines grown on chalky plateaus, have surprising depth and can age for decades. When mature, Chinons have an incomparable bouquet of violets, blackcurrants, and a hint of spice. This estate offers Chinons for early drinking and others for long keeping (like the Réserve Stanislas Vieilles Vignes '93: a monster!). There are three furnished rentals (*gîtes*) on the property.

MONTLOUIS-SUR-LOIRE   37270 – Indre/Loire

Domaine de la Taille aux Loups

Husseau, 3, rue du Serpent-Volant
02 47 39 50 80, fax 02 47 38 45 60
Open daily 9am-7pm. V.
Less well known than Vouvray, Montlouis, on the opposite bank of the Loire, also produces a complete range of wines from the Chenin Blanc grape. Slightly sparkling Montlouis Pétillant, made in years when the weather is uncooperative, is a lovely apéritif. This estate produces excellent dry Montlouis and in warm, sunny years, glorious dessert wines (the fat, full '90 vintage is a treasure).

MAREUIL-SUR-CHER   41110 – Loir/Cher

Clos Roche Blanche

Catherine Roussel, Didier Barrouillet
02 54 75 17 03, fax 02 54 75 17 02
Open by appt only.
Organically grown vines. Very tasty Touraine Gamay, and a special cuvée of red Touraine that blends Gamay, Cabernet Franc, and Cot (a local grape).

The prices in this guide reflect what establishments were charging at press time.

ST-NICOLAS-DE-BOURGUEIL 37140 – Indre/Loire

André Delagouttière

Domaine des Bergeonnières
02 47 97 75 87, fax 02 47 97 48 47
Open daily (exc Sun pm).
A new tasting cellar is an inviting spot in which to sample the estate's red and rosé wines. The Saint-Nicolas-de-Bourgueil Cuvée Vieilles Vignes (made from older vines) is our favorite.

SOINGS-EN-SOLOGNE 41230 – Loir/Cher

Domaine de la Charmoise

Henry Marionnet - 02 54 98 70 73, fax 02 54 98 75 66
Open Mon-Fri 9am-noon & 1:30pm-5:30pm.
This well-known (and justly reputed) estate offers a complete range of Touraine AOC wines in red, white, and rosé. Do sample the fruity, floral Sauvignon de Touraine.

VOUVRAY 37210 – Indre/Loire

Noël Pinguet-Huet

Le Haut Lieu - 02 47 52 78 87, fax 02 47 52 66 51
Open daily 8:30am-noon & 2pm-6pm (exc Sun). V.
Top-quality Vouvrays in every style, from dry to sparkling to honey-sweet. Huet's deep, deep cellars harbor a stock of older vintages that collectors won't want to miss.

• *ANJOU-SAUMUR*

BLAISON-GOHIER 49320 – Maine/Loire

Château-de-Bois-Brinçon

Xavier Cailleau - 02 41 57 19 62, fax 02 41 57 10 46
Open Mon-Sat 8am-7pm (Sun by appt).
This ancient estate (it dates back to the thirteenth century) presents a lovely red Anjou from very old Cabernet Franc and Cabernet Sauvignon vines, and a gorgeously honeyed Coteaux du Layon Grains Nobles. Making late-harvested wines is an arduous, labor-intensive process: the grower must wait for the grapes to be attacked by noble rot (and not just the "vulgar" sort!), then the fruit is hand-picked, bunch by bunch (sometimes grape by grape). Low yields are the rule. So don't be surprised by the 100 F–plus price tags—a fine Coteaux du Layon is well worth the money.

PUY-NOTRE-DAME (LE) 49260 – Maine/Loire

La Paleine

9, rue de la Paleine - 02 41 52 21 24, fax 02 41 52 21 66
Open Mon-Sat 8am-7pm.
Joël Levi proposes a full range of Saumur wines: red, white, rosé, and sparkling. His pure Chenin Blanc white Saumur is rich and nutty; the sparkling Saumur Brut has plenty of character.

ST-LAMBERT-DU-LATTAY 49750 – Maine/Loire

Vincent Ogereau

44, rue de la Belle Angevine
02 41 78 30 53, fax 02 41 78 43 55
Open daily 9am-noon & 2pm-7pm (exc Sun).
Vincent and Catherine Ogereau do their utmost to produce personalized wines that express the essence of their superb vineyards. Among the offerings are a deliciously fruity red Anjou-Villages, a "plain" red Anjou for early drinking, and an elegant, silky sweet Coteaux du Layon Saint-Lambert.

ST-MELAINE-SUR-AUBANCE 49320 – Maine/Loire

Domaine de Haute Perche

Christian Papin, 9, chemin de la Godelière
02 41 57 75 65, fax 02 41 45 92 51
Open daily (exc Sun). V.
Papin's dry white Anjous get better with every vintage, but we also are partial to his sweet Coteaux de l'Aubance (the '94 displays an ideal balance of acidity, alcohol, and sugar).

SAVENNIÈRES 49170 – Maine/Loire

Nicolas Joly

Château de la Roche aux Moines
02 41 72 22 32, fax 02 41 72 28 68
Open daily (exc Sun & hols). V, AE.
The best dry wine from Chenin Blanc grapes is made at Savennières: their bouquet is as richly aromatic as a sweet wine's but on the palate they are nutty with mineral notes and lively acidity. Nicolas Joly produces stupendous wines from Savennières's two great vineyards: Coulée-de-Serrant and Roche-aux-Moines.

SOUZAY-CHAMPIGNY 49400 – Maine/Loire

Chevallier

3, rue J.-Brevet - 02 41 51 14 04, fax 02 41 50 58 24
Open Mon-Sat 9am-noon & 2pm-6pm. V, AE, MC.
Hand-picked, hand-sorted grapes are vinified here into superb Saumur-Champigny, with deep color, firm tannins, and admirable richness. The Vieilles Vignes cuvée is destined for long keeping.

THOUARCÉ 49380 – Maine/Loire

Château de Fesles

02 41 54 14 32, fax 02 41 54 06 10
Open Mon-Sat 10am-noon & 2pm-6pm (& Sun in Jul-Aug-Sep). V, MC.
Gaston Lenôtre, *pâtissier extraordinaire*, owns this venerable château. He's justly proud of his Bonnezeaux: the '88, '89, and '90 vintages of this succulent dessert wine are truly fabulous. Also available: sweet Coteaux du Layon and a dry Chardonnay Vin de Pays.

INDEX

Entries in CAPITALS are names of cities and localities.
Entries in **bold print** are regional food specialties.

"Gault Millau is provocative and frank."
—*Los Angeles Times*

"You will enjoy their prose."
—*US News & World Report*

"Gault Millau is the toque of the town."
—*San Francisco Examiner*

Please send me the "The Best of" books checked below:

❏ Chicago $18.00
❏ Florida $17.00
❏ France $20.00
❏ Germany $20.00
❏ Hawaii $18.00

❏ Italy $20.00
❏ London $20.00
❏ Los Angeles $18.00
❏ LA Restaurants . . $10.00
❏ New Orleans . . . $17.00
❏ New York $18.00

❏ NYC Restaurants . $12.00
❏ Paris $20.00
❏ San Francisco . . . $18.00
❏ SF Restaurants . . $10.00
❏ Wineries of North America $18.00

Mail to:
Gault Millau, Inc., P.O. Box 361144, Los Angeles, CA 90036

Order toll-free:
1 (800) LE BEST 1 • FAX: (213) 936-2883 • *E-mail:* gayots@aol.com
In the U.S., include $4 (shipping charge) for the first book, and $3 for each additional book. Outside the U.S., $7 and $5.

❏ Enclosed is my check or money order made out to Gault Millau, Inc. for $ _____.

❏ Please charge my credit card: ❏ VISA ❏ MC ❏ AMEX

Card # _____ Exp. ___/___

Signature_____ Telephone _____

Name _____

Address _____

City _____ State_____ ZIP_____

Country_____

323/97

RECEIVE A
FREE
SUBSCRIPTION TO

André Gayot's

TASTES

THE WORLD DINING & TRAVEL CONNECTION

- New Restaurants, Hotels, Shops & Wines
- Travel Tips & Bargains
- Events in the Food World
- Special Places & Resorts

(A $30 VALUE)

BY FILLING OUT THIS QUESTIONNAIRE, YOU'LL RECEIVE A COMPLIMENTARY ONE-YEAR SUBSCRIPTION TO **"TASTES,"** OUR INTERNATIONAL NEWSLETTER.

NAME _____

ADDRESS _____

CITY _____ STATE _____

ZIP _____ COUNTRY _____

PHONE ( ) –

The Gayot/GaultMillau series of guidebooks reflects your demand for insightful, incisive reporting on the best that the world's most exciting destinations have to offer. To help us make our books even better, please take a moment to fill out this anonymous (if you wish) questionnaire, and return it to:

GaultMillau, Inc., P.O. Box 361144, Los Angeles, CA 90036;
Fax: (213) 936-2883.

1. How did you hear about the Gayot guides? Please specify: bookstore, newspaper, magazine, radio, friends or other.

2. Please list in order of preference the cities or countries which you would like to see Gayot cover.

3. Do you refer to the AGP guides for your own city, or only when traveling?

A. (Travels) .... B. (Own city) .... C. (Both) ....

(Please

4. Please list by order of preference the three features you like best about the Gayot guides.

A. ....

B. .... C. ....

5. What are the features, if any, you dislike about the Gayot guides?

6. Please list any features that you would like to see added to the Gayot guides.

7. If you use other guides besides Gayot, please list below.

8. Please list the features you like best about your favorite guidebook series, if it is not Gayot/GaultMillau.

A. ....

B. .... C. ....

9. How many trips do you make per year, for either business or pleasure?

Business: International ....   Domestic ....

Pleasure: International ....   Domestic........................

10. Please check the category that reflects your annual household income.

$20,000–$39,000 .... $40,000–$59,000 ....
$60,000–$79,000 .... $80,000–$99,000 ....
$100,000–$120,000 ....   Other (please specify) ....

11. If you have any comments on the AGP guides in general, please list them in the space below.

12. If you would like to recommend specific establishments, please don't hesitate to list them:

Name	City	Phone

We thank you for your interest in the Gayot guides, and we welcome your remarks and ⸱⸱⸱ndations about restaurants, hotels, nightlife, shops, services and so on.